LAUGHTER, TEARS & WONDERS:

An Irish Memoir

Four-year-old Niall with his pal Spot.

LAUGHTER, TEARS & WONDERS:

An Irish Memoir

Childhood & Coming of Age
in Dublin 1942-1966

Niall John Kavanagh

LAUGHTER, TEARS & WONDERS: An Irish Memoir
Childhood & Coming of Age
in Dublin 1942-1966

Paperback ISBN-13: # 978-1541390843
Paperback ISBN-10: # 1541390849
E-Book ISBN: # 978-1520592817

First Published 12 March 2017 by
Niall John Kavanagh
niallkavanagh@nkco.net

Author's Note

L AUGHTER, TEARS & WONDERS is not a novel. The people, places, and circumstances contained in this memoir are real. The situations and dialogue presented are as best as I can remember; where memory failed me, license is taken so as to complete the essence of the event. Names have been changed wherever respect for personal privacy was considered appropriate.

This memoir is illustrated: some illustrations are from *Wikipedia Free Encyclopaedia*; some street views are from *Google Map*. The majority of the included ballads are in public domain or have been written by the author; where known, authorship is cited. Permission to include the following lyrics has been secured:
Dublin Saunter by *Leo Maguire.* Walton Music.
Dublin Street Cleaner by *Leo Maguire.* Walton Music.
Gough by *Vincent Caprani.* Gill & Macmillan.
Grace by *Frank & Seán O'Meara.* Asdee Music.
Monto by *George Hodnett.* Heathside Music.

Sincere thanks to my editor Patricia Frey, my invaluable critic Dianne Hart, and my patient, wonderful wife, Darlene. Thanks are also due to my family and friends. Particularly my children, Elisa, Susan and Graeme; my 'little' brother Conor and his wife Eileen; my still beautiful big sister, Geraldine; my big brothers, Fergus and Patrick; my lifelong friends Cecil Whitty, Tommy Greeley and Tony Cunningham; my Da, Gerry and my Ma, Peg; and my first true love, Teresa.

****

*Reviews are requested: please post your review
on the <u>Laughter, Tears & Wonders</u> page at Amazon Books.*

Dedication

To Dublin,
and my parents, Peg and Gerry Kavanagh.

My Da & Ma.

Table of Contents

Epigraph

It is right that he too should have his little chronicle,
his memories, his reason,
and be able to recognise the good in the bad,
the bad in the worst, and so grow gently old
down all the unchanging days,
and die one day like any other day, only shorter.

– Samuel Beckett

My big brothers, Fergus and Paddy,
my Ma, five-year-old Niall and my beautiful big sister Geraldine.
Conor, my new little brother is also in the picture,
but you can't see him: he's hiding in my Ma's tummy.
We're all pretending to be drinking –
Peg seems to have had too much and is sleeping it off.

Prologue

WHILE ALL MY DAYS ARE LINKED, I'VE ALWAYS thought of each new day having a life of its own. Each one with an exciting virgin beginning, pregnant with its own unique potential, and gifting me with memories – treasures that enrich all my nows and my dreams of as yet unfulfilled tomorrows.

I was born in Dublin Ireland on 27 July 1942. My life has been crammed with all sorts of surprises; next July I'll be seventy-five, and the fact that I'm still alive and writing this memoir is perhaps the biggest surprise of all. I never expected to see fifty, yet here I am; I was fourteen when my Da, Gerry Kavanagh died 1 April 1956 – and he was only forty-nine.

The distinctive character and rich history of Ireland has given me so much and is a huge part of my making. What follows is a collection of reminiscences that captures my childhood and growing up in Dublin in the 1940s, '50s and early '60s. As I wrote these yarns, I laughed a lot and cried as much. Looking back, and considering all the laughter, tears and wonders of the fifty-odd years that have flown by since, I'm astounded to discover that despite how much has changed, little of what and who I am have. My parents were right when they declared, "You'll never change."

Post-WWII Dublin may have been bleak, but for me, then and for the first thirty-three years of my life, it was utopian. Sadly, however, I was forced to leave Utopia. In 1975, when I was thirty-three, I immigrated to the United States (illegally I might add), in search of work in America. My first wife Teresa, our three children Elisa, Susan and Graeme, our dog Mandy, and would you believe, my mother-in-law Rita, immigrated with me; Elisa was five, Susan was three, and Graeme was one.

After twenty-eight years of making a new life together in another country, and following a two-year battle with lymphoma, Teresa died 21 February 2003. God works in mysterious ways; however, and just between you and me, I think He made a big mistake taking Teresa up to heaven so soon – she was fifty-nine.

In July 2005 I was blessed to find a new love and a new life in San Miguel de Allende, Guanajuato, Mexico. That's where I live today, along with my beautiful wife, Darlene and our two dogs, Hannah Banana and Max Loco.

I hope you enjoy these yarns as much as I delight in sharing them with you. There are lots more where they've come from; there are at least another fifty years of laughter, tears, and wonders to be told. Being the Dublin-born Irishman I am, sure haven't I only just begun?

Niall John Kavanagh
San Miguel de Allende
Guanajuato
México
12 March 2017

Early Bloomers

I'll Tell Me Ma when I go home,
*   the boys won't leave the girls alone.*
They pull me hair and steal me comb,
*   but that's alright 'til I go home.*
She is handsome, she is pretty,
*   she's the belle of Dublin city.*
She's a courtin' one, two, t'ree,
*   please won't ye tell me who is she.*

Albert Mooney says he loves her,
*   all the boys are fightin' for her.*
Knockin' on her door and ringin' her bell,
*   hello me true love, are ye well?*
Out she comes as white as snow,
*   rings on her fingers, bells on her toe.*
Ol' Johnny Murray says he'll die,
*   if he doesn't get the girl with the rovin' eye.*

Let the wind and the rain and the hail blow high
*   and the snow come tumblin' from the sky.*
She's as sweet as apple pie,
*   she'll get her own lad by and by.*
When she gets a lad of her own,
*   she won't tell her Ma when she gets home.*
Let them all come as they will,
*   for it's Albert Mooney she loves still.*

I'll Tell Me Ma – Traditional (19th Century)

IT'S SEPTEMBER 1949 AND I'M SEVEN YEARS OLD. We're living at 20 Erris Road Cabra in Northside Dublin. I'm not the baby anymore; for almost seven years I was, but Conor my new little brother arrived 7 June, and that put an end to that.

I'm with my Ma, Peg Kavanagh nee Kelly of Rathagan County Kildare, and we're giving Conor a bath. He's only three months

1

old, and he's loving it. For close to an hour, the three of us have been splashing around, saturated, sudsy and acting silly. Ma and I are soaked, but we don't care – we're having as much fun as Conor.

20 Erris Road, Cabra.

"Will you tell me something, love?" asks my mother. She's gently drying Conor in a big, warm bath towel: "What in the name of God are you doing with all those sugar bags?"

"W'at sugar bags, Ma?"

"Those bags I put beside the bread bin in the food press, love. There's only a few left, and I need them for your Da's lunches."

I'm caught off guard. Knowing all too well what she's talking about, I'm struggling to find a way to answer without revealing the truth. *Colleen said it was our secret and we're not to tell anybody.*

Displaying a coolness any villain would be proud of, I lie.

"I'd to cover me school bo'ks, Ma. Brother Colman gave us some new ones, and he told us to cover dem and not get dem dirty."

"Well, and aren't you a good boy, Niall. If you had asked me, wouldn't I have done that for you."

"Ah, I did it meself, Ma."

"Don't worry, love. I'll ask Mr Quigley for a few more bags when I go down to him later on."

Janey Mack! That was a near one.

Peg buys the household sugar in one pound kraft-paper bags, measured out from a big sack of the stuff by Mr Quigley at Quigley's grocery store on Imaal Road. She saves the bags and uses them for my Da's lunch sandwiches, or as my Da calls them, 'my sambos'.

"Where are my sambos, Peg?" And he always asks that as he's almost out the back door on his way to work.

2

"They're over there on the table looking at you," answers Peg, and she often adds, "If they had a mouth, they'd eat you."

I've been using the sugar bags to express my love for Colleen. She lives across the road. I write love letters to her every other day. I use the front of the bag – the other side has the glued joining and isn't as good to write on.

The truth is, Colleen's a bit of a tomboy. She's my age, but she's much smarter than I'll ever be. She can rough-it-up with the best of us; her football skills make all the boys feel inferior. She's taller than me and plays in the tough midfield position.

I play right-half. Colleen, taking control of the ball in midfield, always seems to favour me with a perfectly delivered pass. We're a pair on the pitch and are destined to become a happy couple off it. It's after one of our inter-road football games that our budding relationship starts to blossom. At seven years old, you could say we're early bloomers.

COLLEEN AND I are sitting down on the pavement kerb trying to get our breath back – our Erris Road team has just demolished a Leix Road team, six goals to two. With the help of some terrific passing from Colleen, I'd scored three of the winning goals. Our usual football pitch is a section of Erris Road with some discarded clothing used for the goalposts at both ends.

"Ye were deadly, Niall," says Colleen, giving me an admiring smile. "T'ree goals! Dem Leix Roaders didn't know w'at was happenin'. And yer last goal – it was a dinger altogether."

"Sure if I didn't have you out der with me, Colleen, I'd have scored none of dem. Ye're the bestest player in all of Cabra."

"Ah go away-out-a-dat, Niall. It's the goals dat count. I love playin' with ye. Will ye be me fella?"

"Yeah, I'll be yer fella. Will you be me mot?"

"Of course I will," Colleen replies. "Now, give me a quick kiss. Wait 'til ol' Buckley passes." Mr Buckley, an old neighbour of ours, is making his shuffling way past us, walking stick in hand. "Dis is our secret, Niall, and we'll tell no one," Colleen continues, her eyes closed and her lips puckered, ready to receive my lips on hers and the sealing of the deal. "Ol' Buckley is gone – quick, give me a kiss."

3

"OK, Colleen," says I. The first kiss is ever so brief; it's a deliciously wet, salty one. We're still sweating bricks from the massacre we'd inflicted on the Leix Roaders.

Colleen and I keep it all very quiet. With our friendship now including this new relationship, we agree to some regular clandestine rendezvous.

On Saturday afternoons we go to the pictures. Holding hands in the darkness of the Cabra Grand Cinema on Quarry Road, we sit in the back and steal innocent kisses. Only when we're safely hidden away do we hold hands, and under no circumstance do we kiss unless absolute privacy is guaranteed.

Another regular rendezvous of ours is on Wednesdays; after school, we go to Kavo's field. Kavo's is an acre of waste land behind the Cabra Grand Cinema. The Dublin/Belfast railway line is on the other side of the field's end wall. We meet there to talk, kiss and hold hands. We count kisses, and one time we count to a hundred.

"Dat's a record, Colleen. Me lips are fallin' off me," says I.

"Yeep. I bet it's a record. Ye're a smashin' kisser, Niall."

"And so are you," I respond, as I lie down on the grass for a much-needed break.

Colleen needs a break too. She lies down next to me. Holding hands, we feel the Belfast Express train thunder its way past.

"Let's show each other our t'ing," I suggest, in a matter-of-fact manner only the innocence of the moment and that of its participants could create – as if I was asking Colleen what time it was rather than the suggestion I had made.

"OK, Niall. We'll do it together. One, two, t'ree, go!"

With that, I pull down my trousers and reveal myself. Colleen pulls down her knickers and exposes herself to me.

I feel bewildered, looking at the private part for the first time.

"We're different, aren't we Colleen?"

"Yeah, we are," she responds with equal bewilderment.

"Yours is nicer dan mine," says I, admiring how spick-and-span she looks compared to me. "It's tidier, and ye don't have an'in' hangin' out of ye."

"Do ye t'ink so, Niall?" replies Colleen, looking down at herself and then looking closer at my revelation.

4

"Yours must be awful hard to carry 'round," she continues. Not to further my disappointment she adds: "I like it, Niall, but I'm glad I haven't got w'at you have. Does it hurt ye when ye're runnin'?"

"No, Colleen," I respond, feeling like I was losing out on something while at the same time being encouraged by the 'I like it' part of Colleen's response. "It hurts when I get kicked in the mickey. Other dan dat it never bothers me."

"Can I touch it, Niall?"

"Ye can if ye like, but don't grab it hard."

"OK," says Colleen. "I won't hurt ye," she adds, as she ever so gently pokes at me.

"But how d'ye pee without a Mickey, Colleen?" I ask.

"I've a little hole down der, and it comes out of dat," answers Colleen.

"Oh," says I. "Our back holes are the same, but our front ones are different."

"Yeah," Colleen responds. "It's time to go, Niall. I've got to go to the Legion of Mary with me sister. Let's get dressed."

"Yeah," I respond, thinking about my school homework waiting for me. "I've got loads of ecker to do."

We climb over Kavo's wall and head home, but not before we have one last kiss.

"I wonder why we're different, Colleen," says I, as we turn the corner off Annaly Road onto Erris.

"Me Ma told me, when we grow up we'll know everyt'in'."

"When do we grow up, Colleen?"

"Me Ma didn't tell me dat," is Colleen's resigned response.

****

WE WERE an item for almost two years – Colleen and Niall. However, Colleen kept growing taller, and that was the cause of the earth-shattering breakup. My minimally increased stature resulted in Colleen dumping me for a taller bloke from Galmoy Road. A heartbreaker if ever there was one.

"Niall, ye're too small for me," she coldly declared. "And I'm not yer mot anymore."

It was as simple and as shocking as that. After announcing the separation, Colleen turned and walked away, leaving me no doubt regarding her intent, and leaving no room for me to win her cold heart back.

Tossed to the side, and all for the sake of a couple of inches.

****

The Front-Gardens & Me Da Bein' a-Bit-Bold

If I were a blackbird, I'd whistle and sing,
I'd follow the ship that my true love sails in.
And on the top rigging, I'd build me a nest,
I'd pillow my head on his lily white breast.

If I Were a Blackbird – Unknown (1920s)

THE LAWLORS LIVE NEXT DOOR. We share a semi-detached two-house unit, the Kavanaghs on Erris and the Lawlors on Offaly.

House-proud parents run both households. The front gardens are always well kept. My Da, and Mr Lawlor, father to eight girls, have year-round unspoken rivalry regarding whose grass and privet are manicured the best. Whenever Gerry, that's my Da's name, finds Mr Lawlor's garden looking better than his own, he furtively goes out with his shears and one of my Ma's old pair of scissors to do some sneaky, competitive clipping. He often executes these clandestine proceedings after coming home from work, late in the evenings and frequently in the dark. Often I go out and help him; armed with my *Eveready* torch, I make sure to get rid of the evidence and gather up all the clippings.

IT'S AN early spring 1950 evening. I'm out helping my Da put the finishing touches to his work on the front garden. The night's fast descending darkness demands the assistance of me and my trusty flashlight.

"Shine your light on that, Nialler," instructs Gerry, as together we search out those leaves of grass and privet failing to meet my Da's high standards. Judiciously, he switches from shears to scissors depending upon the requirements of each offending piece. As we make our way around the garden, Gerry is quietly whistling.

7

"I love ye whistlin', Da."

"*If I Were a Blackbird* is a grand air. The words are great too, but I think your Da's words are even better. They're a-bit-bold, but sure they're only in jest."

"Tell me the words, Da."

"Your Ma would kill me if I did that."

"Ah Da, tell us. Go on, please Da."

"Well, all right. But you're not to repeat them. And not a word to your Ma. She'll kill me altogether if she finds out I told you."

"I won't say a word, Da. I swear on a stack of bibles."

"Right then. It's only for a laugh, mind you. Pulling the English royalty's leg is all it is."

With that, Gerry clears his throat and lilts the song's lyrics.

"And now, Niall," says he, having completed his rendition of the popular song, "here's my own, albeit a-bit-bold version."

> *If I were a blackbird, I'd whistle and sing,*
> *I'd fly o'er to England and piss on the King.*
> *And on top of his palace, I'd there build my nest,*
> *I'd shit like a seagull on his lily white breast.*

Hearing my Da say the word 'piss' surprises me, but hearing him say the word 'shit' shocks me altogether.

"There are a couple of bold words in there, Niall, and maybe I shouldn't have told you. I want you to promise me you won't repeat them to anyone. Not a word to your mammy now."

"OK, I promise, Da. I won't say an'in'," says I. His trust in my ability to keep a secret makes me feel all grown up and important.

I try to ameliorate what I feel is his guilt and discomfort.

"I love helpin' ye, Da," I continue. "Our garden is much better dan Lawlor's garden. Isn't it, Da?"

"I think you're right, Niall," Gerry responds, giving me the kindness of his smile plus that heart-warming wink of his. "But that's only because I've got you to help me."

"Dem Lawlor girls know nothin' about clippin'," says I. "All they know is knittin' and stitchin' and stuff."

"Niall, isn't it an awful pity there are only twenty-four hours in the day?" says Gerry to his adoring son. "To lengthen the day, we've got to rob from the night. My own Da told me that once, and I've never forgotten it."

****

MR LAWLOR, without the added assistance of an *Eveready*-armed son, did the same type of thing as my Da. Somehow their ships never crossed in the night; they each did their sneaky clipping knowing that if they didn't, one or the other would be the winner – and neither of them would ever let that happen.

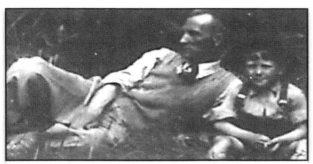

My Da and me taking a break.

Gerry was a quiet man who didn't talk a lot; however, when he did, I and anyone in earshot would want to listen. He was a good looking, slim, five-foot-nine. He often wore a sleeveless waistcoat; for the most part, all but the last waistcoat button was closed. His Brylcreemed hair was always slicked back, tight to his head, giving him a sleek look with not a single strand of hair out of place. He was always neat and clean, with himself and everything around him. He smoked *Sweet Afton* cigarettes, although there were times I saw him smoke *Woodbines* – *Woodbines* were less expensive than *Sweet Afton*. A starched, clean white shirt collar combined with everything to give him his signature. He was called the Duke by his co-workers and friends, but he was my King.

****

Mr Flynn,
Pascal the Milkman and Polly

THE ONLY REAL TRAFFIC ON ERRIS ROAD consists of Mr Flynn's old black Vauxhall, Mr Murphy's sparkling red Morris Minor, and the regular street vendors' vehicles.

Mr Flynn's car seldom if ever goes anywhere; it just sits in his driveway. Often we find him, shirt sleeves rolled up, trying to make his old rattletrap start.

"YE'RE ONLY a pile of shite!" says Mr Flynn to himself, but loud enough for us all to hear.

For some time, my friends and I have been leaning over Mr Flynn's driveway gate looking at him poke around, under and into his 'pile of shite'. As always, he has a fag stuck in his gob.

"Feck it! Ye're an awful bitch!" he asserts. We all learn our first curse words from Mr Flynn.

After some further intense poking around, plus its accompanying blasphemous language, Mr Flynn grabs hold of the Vauxhall's steel starter-handle. He vengefully inserts it through the hole in the front bumper, into the crankshaft. Twenty or thirty failed strenuous turns of that starter-handle has him sweating up a storm.

"God damn it!" he roars. "Ye're only a pile of shite!"

Bending in under the bonnet, in frustration, he lashes out with his fist. Whatever he hits, all of a sudden there's a loud bang and the car comes to life. With it sounding like a tank badly in need of service, he slams the bonnet shut, jumps in and drives it, spluttering and farting up and down the road. However, as it had suddenly started with a bang, it soon grinds to a deadly halt – with an even louder bang. Mr Flynn has to gather up a dozen kids to help him push the wreck back into his driveway. Nobody's ever likely to be mowed down by Mr Flynn's old Vauxhall.

Mr Murphy's red Morris Minor is a whole other ball of wax; Mr Murphy never stops polishing it. If you were to ask his wife, she'd tell you her husband is or is close to being 'entirely mad'.

"John! For God's sake, will you come in out-a-dat," we often hear her shout. "Ye're goin' to rub all the paint off dat damn car."

Almost every evening, he goes out to his proudest possession and polishes it. It's always sparkling. He uses his bike to get to work and only drives the car on weekends. And when he does drive it, you'd have a fair chance of passing him if you were on a smart-paced walk. The engine appears to be in perfect nick – he just drives it that slowly. Mrs Murphy lives with the man, and she should know; I think she's right – Mr Murphy is mad.

All the street vendors know the rhythm of the road. They wisely respect the rightfully or wrongfully assumed road rights of their clients' children. They're acutely aware that if, heaven forbid, they were to run over one of their customers' valued little loved ones, well let's say it would not be well received and maybe even result in the loss of a client or two.

Pascal, the Lucan Dairy milkman, comes around daily. His transportation consists of a five-foot wide by seven-foot long, four-wheeled chariot plus Polly, his old white mare.

Polly pulling Pascal's milk chariot.

Polly is one well-trained, smart horse. With incredible energy and speed, Pascal and Polly proceed up the road, stopping and starting, making left-hand and right-hand deliveries. He practically never holds the reins. He has a unique way of whistling: one whistle has Polly stop; two whistles makes her start. As they move along, Pascal goes back and forth to the chariot, restocking his two

11

milk bottle hand carriers. With circus-like precision, they're a team that brings us our milk and lots of entertainment.

My mother seems to be always waiting for Pascal. Hearing his whistles, she goes out to the front door to get the milk.

"Top of the mornin' to ye, Peggy," says Pascal. "I'm leavin' ye t'ree nice creamy ones. Look at dem standin' der, Peggy. I'd say der's more dan t'ree inches of cream on each of dem."

"And the rest of the day to yourself," answers Peg. "Thanks very much, Pascal. Now, I'm going to save that lovely cream, and we'll have it with beautiful strawberries later on. You're a good man, Pascal. Tell me now, how much do I owe you?"

"Ah sure leave it alone, Peggy. I don't have time for dat now, w'at with all the deliveries. Let me go, and I'll see ye tomorra."

"Can I go on the chariot, Pascal?" I interrupt.

"Don't mind him, Pascal," Peg responds, as she looks down at me in annoyance. "Niall, can't you see how busy Pascal is!?"

"No, Peggy," insists Pascal. "Let him come with me. Sure he can hand me down the bottles a milk – dat'll help me out."

"Tell me somethin', Niall," Pascal continues. "Polly loves an ol' carrot. Have ye err an ol' carrot for Polly?"

"All right then," Peg reluctantly agrees. "Niall, go in quick and get Polly a carrot." I'm back with the carrot in a flash.

"Now listen to me, Niall," my Ma warns. "Don't you be giving Pascal any trouble." Turning to Pascal, she continues; "You're a nice man to be bothering with him, Pascal."

With the carrot in my hand, Polly is delighted to see me. I cautiously give it to her. She chews it up, swallows it down and is looking for another one before I've climbed onto the chariot.

"Give me six of dem bottles, Niall," Pascal instructs. "Now don't you be goin' near the reins." Pascal gives one of his two-whistle edicts, and with me happily on board the chariot, off we go.

En route, Polly's long tail flips up, and much to my disgust she relieves herself of an enormous, noisome shite. No doubt, some of the garden-proud neighbours will soon be out to shovel it up. They'll use it on their flower and vegetable beds. It's all stinky shit to me, but to them, it's a godsend – free, fresh fertiliser.

****

It was More Like Findin'

Outside the world's a playground,
for idle falling snow.
All night white sheets descending,
blankets where 'er you go.
On rooves, on roads, on left out clothes,
and on a small boy's hand –
to melt.

Snow – Niall Kavanagh

T HE COALMAN COMES TO ERRIS ON THURSDAYS during cold weather and maybe once a month for the rest of the year. I'm sure it isn't his real name, but we call the coalman Mr Black. His means of transportation is a small-sized lorry with fixed metal walls at the cabin end and both sides. The back end is also metal: it's a hinged-at-top, removable bolt-at-bottom door from which all coal orders are served. Mr Black climbs into the back of the lorry and shovels the stuff through the door, into whatever receptacle his clients might have.

Mr Black's coal lorry.

"CO-AL, COAL, get yer co-al," is Mr Black's street call. He always starts at the Annaly Road end of Erris.

It's 1950, and I'm eight years old.

"I'm freezin'," says Philip, one of my Erris Road friends.

"You, me and the rest of us," says I. "Last night, didn't all me brothers and me have to sleep together to keep warm; Fergie and Paddy at one end of the bed, and me and Conor at the other end. We kept warm, but it took ages for us to go asleep."

Philip and I have exhausted ourselves sliding on the ice slide we've created. We poured water on the cold pavement in a long three-foot-wide line and nature did the rest. Sliding is fun, but after a while, we get weary and start to feel the cold again.

For the past five or six weeks, it's been freezing. Some light, fluffy snowflakes have been coming down, pleasantly painting everything white and creating that type of winter quiet only snow can. We're all running out of coal; while we get cheap subsidised turf from the Dublin Corporation's turf depot on Quarry Road, those of us who can afford to do so supplement the turf with some expensive coal. Coal is imported from England and costs a lot more than Irish turf. It lasts longer, burns better and it throws out more heat.

"More coal is w'at we need," says Philip. "Here comes Mr Black. Does yer Ma want any?"

Mr Black's lorry stops outside 20 Erris.

"Me Ma is spendin' all her money on dat stuff," I respond.

"Co-al, co-al, get yer co-al," yells Mr Black, as he climbs into the back of his lorry. He opens the lorry's back door and stands there, shovel in hand, waiting for his needy, cold clients.

And out they come. Peg is not one of them.

"Yer Ma mustn't want any," says Philip.

"Yeah." *I bet she's no money. The turf will have to do. But right der in front of me is a big pile of the stuff. I know me Ma needs some. W'at am I goin' to do?*

"Philip!" I almost scream. The thoughts of the outcome of what I'm considering is almost too much for me.

"Quick," says I, grabbing Philip by the arm. "Let's dash into me Da's shed and get shovels."

Before Philip has time to ask me what's going on, we're running back up the garden path, shovels in hand. I'm also armed with my Ma's old rusted aluminium baby's tub – the one she used to use to give Conor his bath when he was a baby.

"Niall, w'at are we goin' to do?" asks Philip.

Out of nowhere, I've been gifted with an incredible epiphany.

"When Mr Black is movin' away we'll open the back door. The coal will pour out. We'll shovel it up and bring it into me Ma."

"Great!" says Philip.

Mr Black is finishing up with his last client. He jumps down out of the coal, bolts the door shut, and gets back into the cab.

"Let's go," says I to Philip. We dash out behind the lorry. As Mr Black is turning on the ignition, I unbolt the door. His badly executed into-first-gear move helps considerably. The lorry bucks as it starts, and to my delight, out pours the coal, piles of it. And it continues to flow, all the way up the road.

"Get the tub," I yell as we pick up the shovels and go to work. It takes six tubs of warmth generating coal before we have to give up in exhaustion. Each load is carried to my Ma's backyard and dumped into the coal bin beside the turf. Our six tubs almost fill the bin.

We notice that some of the neighbours have come out. They're busy gathering up the remaining trail of coal.

"Yer Ma is goin' to be happy, Niall."

"Yeah, Phil. T'anks for helpin' me. I'm goin' in to tell her."

I run into my mother with a new, unusual kind of pride.

"Ma," I shout. "Come on out to the backyard. I've a surprise for ye." She's sitting at an unlit fireplace darning some socks that have heel and toe holes. She has a thick, long jumper on; she's saving the fire for later when my Da will be home from work.

"I'm busy darning, Niall," Peg replies. "What is it?"

"Come on out and ye'll see, Ma," I reply, a big grin on my flushed and happy face.

"God help me with you, Niall. Come on then and show me."

We both go out to the backyard. I can hear Peg; she's talking to herself while at the same time making sure I can hear her. "What's the little divil up to now? He'll be the death of me."

"I got ye a big pile of coal, Ma," I gleefully declare, as I direct her attention to the coal bin.

"Holy Mother of God," says Peg, in awe of what she's looking at. "There must be more than six weeks of coal here."

Turning to me, with her hands on her hips, she anxiously starts her enquiry into the source of the coal.

15

"And where, may I ask, did all this coal come from?"

Without hesitation and looking straight into my mother's probing eyes, I give my prepared response.

"It fell off the back of a lorry, Ma."

"What do you mean, the back of a lorry? What lorry?"

"Mr Black's, Ma," I reply, feeling so excited and happy for her. "His back door opened when he moved off. Piles of it poured out onto the road. Philip helped me shovel it up, and we brought it into ye. Are ye happy, Ma?"

"Oh my God! The gardaí will be here to arrest me any minute."

"No, they won't, Ma. Didn't all the neighbours come out with dir shovels and buckets and stuff, and didn't they do the same? Sure weren't we only cleanin' up the road?"

"Are you sure, Niall? We need the coal, but–"

"Ma!" I interrupt. "We need the coal, and now we've piles of it. It fell off the back of a lorry! I t'ink Holy God made it all happen." *Maybe I did help Him out a bit by unboltin' the door, but dat pile of coal in me Ma's coal bin is a blessin'.*

"Well, Niall . . ." Peg ponders. *She needs the coal. She's no money to buy it. And der it is, a big pile of it, right in her coal bin.*

"Well, Niall," she repeats. "I suppose you couldn't leave all that dirty stuff in the middle of the road. And didn't the neighbours come out and help you. No, I don't think it was stealing. It was more like . . . It was more like findin'."

She turns away from her pondering gaze at the coal, and with a much-welcomed smile on her face, she looks down at me.

"You're a good boy, Niall. Thinking about your mammy and gathering up all that coal for her. By the time we run out, it'll be warmer, and all this perishing cold will be gone."

"And it's all because of you, Niall," she continues.

Peg bends down and kisses me on my cold nose. Her expression of love, pride, and appreciation for what I'd done consumes me to the degree that I think that I might explode. I grab her and give her a big hug.

"T'anks, Ma," I almost cry.

"Thank you, Niall," says Peg. "I'll go back to my darning now. When your Da comes home, we'll have a blazing fire for him, and I'm going to tell him how good a boy you are."

16

****

I'VE DONE many things I feel proud of, but the pride I felt when I stole that coal and gave it to Peg has never been matched. I had meaningfully helped my mother, and she was happy and proud of me for all I'd done. It doesn't get much better than that.

****

Boo-Balla,
Mr Cullen's Spuds & Deliveries

I am an ol' Dublin Street Cleaner,
*   I work for the Dublin Corporation.*
And after a week of employment,
*   I'm sufferin' from exasperation.*
For the work, it's so diabolical,
*   ye'll not find the likes near or far.*
And after a week at the ol' job,
*   sure I'm only in form for a jar.*

One evenin' we were sweepin' up in Phibsborough,
*   the sun it was shinin' down.*
I was sweepin' the path, mindin' me business,
*   when I spied the half of a crown.*
Like a shot me mate Joxer was over,
*   claimin' half of it, one 'n' three.*
Get to hell out-a-dat says I to Joxer,
*   I found it and it belongs to me.*

Without warnin', he hits me a clobber,
*   dat changed the shape of me mush.*
And to show me disgust in retaliation,
*   I clobbered him one with me brush.*
And there we were goin' good-oh,
*   when along came the Sergeant Cantrell.*
And ye know with the temper I was in den,
*   I hit the bloody rozzer as well.*

Well here I am sweepin' up the gaol house,
*   sweepin' up me ol' prison cell.*
It's not the jingle of half-dollars I'm hearin',
*   it's the jingle of the ol' triangle.*

Ah God loves the ol' ones in Drimnagh,
*   he loves dem in Cabra I t'ink.*
Without Joxer, meself, and the brush and the shovel,
*   the country it's goin' to stink.*
But we'll not be held responsible,
*   for dis national catastrophe,*
Until the bold Minister for Justice,
*   releases me friend Joxer and me.*

Dublin Street Cleaner – Leo Maguire (1940) Copyright Waltons Music Ltd.

ALONG WITH THE COALMAN, MR BLACK, and Pascal the milkman, there are many other street vendors: the vegetable man, Mr Green; the knife grinder, Mr Sharp; the sweets man, Mr Sweet; the swill man, Mr Stink; and the list goes on. We love Mr Sweet – we can never get enough of his Bulls Eyes, Honey Bees, Nancy Balls, Gob Stoppers, Flakes, Cleeves Toffee, Crunchies, bags of broken pieces of red and white stripped rock, and Fizz Bags.

In addition to the regular vendors, the Erris Road neighbourhood has a motley crew of equally important, regular visitors. The spirit and personality of the residents, combine with those of the regular vendors and visitors and create what makes the neighbourhood what it is.

The regular visitors consist of: Mr. Swan, the insurance man; the gasman, Mr Dunne, and sometimes Mr Buckley; the Gael Linn Football Pools man who is actually a woman named Betty; Tom the newspaper man; the many different street cleaners whose names I've never known; and Garda Brown our local bobby. The not so regular visitors are: Dr Loughnan and his house calls to the sick and sometimes dying; Gardaí, often Garda Brown, with their summonses or bad news; Nurse O'Donoghue, the bicycle-propelled midwife; the Tinkers; and Canon O'Callaghan or one of the other Christ the King priests.

And then, there's old Boo-Balla; all the vendors and visitors add to the magic of the road, but Boo-Balla is a standout.

WHILE MR BLACK the coalman depends on his lorry, and Pascal the milkman has his chariot plus Polly, old Boo-Balla relies on his huge battered suitcase and his own shank's mare. He always wears a long black overcoat and a matching black fedora – even on hot,

19

sunny days. Every Wednesday, he wobbles his way from house to house dragging his enormous, heavy suitcase along with him. He must be well in his seventies.

My friends and I are very mean to Boo-Balla. We follow him around shouting, "Boo-Balla, Boo-Balla, Boo-Balla." Oddly enough, he accepts the intended ridicule in a friendly, grateful manner. Our jeering helps advertise his arrival in a way he can't – Boo-Balla has a poorly corrected cleft lip and finds it hard to talk.

Among many other things, what Boo-Balla sells is boot polish. His speech impediment makes his boot polish sound like 'boo-balla' – hence his name Boo-Balla.

In addition to two sizes of black, brown and neutral shoe polish, he sells Pickering's Blanco Whitener plus what most of us think of as being everything from a needle to an anchor. He sells all sorts of needles, from the finest silk needle all the way up to wool, darning, and regular knitting needles. Crochet hooks, pins both straight and safety, and even hat pins can be purchased. He sells sewing threads of all colours, bias binding in black and white, hook'n'eye sets in black, white and oddly red, buttons of all sizes and colours, needle threaders, measuring tapes, many types of scissors, thimbles, pencils and pens, pencil sharpeners, glue, cans of 3-in-1 oil, can openers, toothpicks, nail clippers, boxes of matches, shoe laces, and God knows what else.

Peg loves the hunt'n'find; foraging through Boo-Balla's suitcase, she always discovers something that she'd failed to realise she simply must have. No one knows Boo-Balla's real name, and my Ma would never call him by his nickname.

"And how much is this, mister?" asks Peg. Boo-Balla has come to our door; his huge suitcase is open, and my Ma is holding one of his sewing thimbles in her hand.

"Fope-ins," mumbles Boo-Balla.

"Fourpence. Is that what you said, mister?"

"Yah," Boo-Balla confirms.

"I'll take that, and give me some of your Blanco Whitener. With the way the children keep dirtying their runners, I can never have enough of that stuff."

The transaction being complete, Boo-Balla closes his suitcase and wobbles his way from our front door, on to his next sale.

20

"Hank ya berry mush," grunts Boo-Balla as he closes our garden gate behind him.

"Thank you, mister," shouts Peg. "See you next week."

MY WEEKLY pocket money allowance – sixpence – isn't cutting it. The cost of admission to the pictures in the local Cabra Grand Cinema is four pence, and that leaves me only tuppence. To supplement this trifle, I decide to get a job.

Geraldine, my big sister, is fourteen, and with every day she's becoming more beautiful. Like honey attracts bees, Geraldine attracts many young men. One of her suitors is Peter Cullen; he's the son of Mr Cullen, the owner of Cullens Grocery, one of the shops located on the stretch of stores we call the Seventeen Shops on Cabra Road.

Geraldine with my Da.

"Does yer Da need any help in the shop, Peter?" I enquire. Peter is always buzzing around 20 Erris looking for his honey.

"I don't know, Niall. But I think he could do with some extra help on Saturdays. Why don't you drop in and see him?"

"OK, Peter. T'anks. I'll tell Geraldine ye helped me."

"Thanks, Niall. Your sister is playing hard to get; a good word from you might make the difference."

That evening, I talk to Geraldine.

"Peter's a nice bloke," says I. "He's helpin' me get a job."

"That's sweet of him," says Geraldine. "He's been at me to go out on a date. Maybe I'll give him one date – just to see."

"I better get down to his Da quick," says I. "If it doesn't work out he might tell his Da not to give me the job."

The following day I'm in Cullens Grocery being interviewed.

"You can start next Saturday," declares Mr Cullen. "I'll make you my Saturday spud boy. The shop opens at eight o'clock. Eight o'clock! And I don't like my spud boy being late. Get here as early as you can. You can bring the potatoes and the weighing scales out to the front and set up the vegetables. And when needed, I'll have you do some home deliveries on the messenger boy bike."

"OK, Mr Cullen. And don't worry – I'm always early."

"Good! Every Saturday," Mr Cullen confirms. "You'll work until five. I'll give you a half-dollar for your day's work."

"Dat's great, Mr Cullen. T'anks very much for the job." *Two shillin's and sixpence plus the tanner I get from me Ma will give me three bob a week!*

I'm a quick learner, and I rapidly get to know the many tricks of the potato trade. The dirty potato trick is the first trick I learn.

"Dese potatoes are dirty, Mr Cullen," says I to the boss. "Der's loads of muck on dem. Should I clean dem off a bit?"

"You will not!" stresses Mr Cullen. "The potatoes come from the market like that, and it's the soil that keeps them fresh."

"So when I'm weighin' the spuds, I'll leave the dirt?" I confirm.

"You will!" Mr Cullen curtly replies. "The soil is part of the sale. It keeps the spuds fresh. The dirt might bring up the weight, but that's not a bad thing."

"I see, Mr Cullen," says I. *The more the dirt, the fewer the spuds. His customers are payin' money for dirt! Not altogether fair, but fair or not, Mr Cullen is the boss.*

****

I RETAINED and enjoyed that job for a year or more. With the messenger bike delivery tips I got from Mr Cullen's customers, there were many Saturdays that had me coming home with as much as five shillings or more. I learned to smile a lot: I soon realised that a happy face and a jovial manner almost always resulted in a good tip. I loved the deliveries, and not only for the tips. Riding the bike with the big basket in front was fun, and it was great meeting new people and going into homes in areas of my neighbourhood which I otherwise would never have known.

****

The Tinkers &
Me Ma's Potato Pot

I am a true born Irishman, a traveller am I,
me home's the road, no fixed abode, I'll travel 'til I die.
For few men give me campin' space and fewer call me friend,
the hard road of the travellin' man I'll travel 'til the end.

>*Hunger, hardship, and poverty are the traveller's weary load.*
>*Hunger, hardship and poverty, and the Blue Tar Road.*

To Dublin city fair we came, in the year of fifty-nine,
and we camped in Lansdowne's green valleys with others of our kind.
But Dublin Corporation, good christians to a man,
they tore down our tents, uprooted us and towed out our caravans.

And here in Cherry Orchard, where no cherry blossoms bloom,
we're forgotten and unwanted in dirt and muck and gloom.
But the man above who died for love and nailed unto a tree,
sure wasn't he a traveller, the same as you and me.

>*And some day in His own good time, he'll ease a traveller's load,*
>*and we'll bid farewell to poverty, and the Blue Tar Road.*

The Blue Tar Road – Traditional

THE TINKERS OR KNACKERS IS WHAT WE CALL the Irish Travellers. Being a half of one percent of the population, they're a small, ethnic group of itinerant, Romanic families who've been roaming the roads and highways of Ireland for over a thousand years.

By their own choice, the Tinkers have been, and continue to be, considered separate from the general population. While they speak both English and Gaelic, over the years, they've created *Shelta*, a type of cant they use amongst themselves whenever they want to exclude outsiders. They live and travel in horse-drawn, gypsy-like caravans. Not being exactly the tidiest people in the world, their unkempt encampments – usually found on unattended

23

pieces of land outside some of the bigger towns – tend to be dirty, and are eye-sores for those who live near them or for anyone who might happen to be passing by. Generally speaking, their customs and lifestyle are such that they're feared and often ostracised by the otherwise compliant, permanently housed, schooled and structured population.

The Tinkers make their living by flogging their trades to the towns' house-bound inhabitants: pot, pan and pail repair tinkering; old horse buying/slaughtering for knackeries; and knackering of abandoned or demolished buildings for saleable parts and scrap metal. Being well disposed and able to do so, they regularly supplement their income by begging – and by maybe just a tiny little bit of petty stealing. And the Tinkers have a strong penchant for the drink; they're prone to indulge in some wild, spirited fisticuffs, albeit usually amongst themselves.

They come to Erris Road about once every other month. As stressful as most of their visits turn out to be, I love it when they come. Tinkers look, talk and act differently, and it's that – their strange, foreign peculiarity – that appeals to me. They arrive in two waves: the first wave brings the women and children knocking on the doors, begging for money, food, clothes, and shoes; then the men role in, looking for any odd job or tinkering work the householders might need to be done.

"QUICK, QUICK," shouts Peg. She has just dashed into the kitchen and seems to be in a panic. "Make sure all the doors and windows are locked! Mrs Lawlor just told me the Tinkers are coming up Offaly. They'll be at our door in a few minutes!"

"OK Ma," I answer. "I'll do the doors; you do the windows."

"Good boy, Niall," says Peg. "And love, once we've got the windows and doors done you can help me take the clothes in off the clothesline," she continues. "Those Tinkers would steal the eyes out of your head if you weren't looking."

We've secured the windows and doors, and we're now taking the last of the clothes in off the clothesline; all the more canny neighbours have done the same. Parents have judiciously gathered up their children from the road; we'll be cloistered away in our homes until the waves of incoming Tinkers ebb out.

24

"But all the same, Niall," says Peg sympathetically. "God love them. Sure and aren't we all God's creatures. There but for the grace of God go I, is all I can say. We shouldn't be thinking or talking badly about the poor Tinkers."

"I've gathered up a few bits and pieces for them," Peg soulfully continues. "They're in a bag on the floor in the hotpress, love. Run up and get them for me. That's a good boy."

I'm back in a flash with a bag of discarded clothes and shoes.

"Now Niall . . . I'll throw a can of Batchelor's peas into that bag," says Peg. "Please God that will help them out a bit."

"And my potato pot has a hole in it," Peg asserts. "When the men come around I'll have them do a job on it for me."

The Tinkers may well be 'bloody', however, they are also some of 'God's creatures'. Peg has her reservations about them, but at the same time she counts her blessings; she always feels obliged to give what she can to those who she considers being needier than herself.

The first wave of Tinkers, the women and children, has arrived. It's not long before there's a bang at the front door. Opening it guardedly – open just enough to see out, but with Pegs foot firmly planted to prohibit the door from being pushed in – and having determined that all seems to be safe enough, Peg opens the door wide. One of the shawled Tinker women with two impish little girls beside her are standing outside. Peg is surprised to discover that the woman is not the Tinker who usually comes to her door.

"Good day," greets Peg. "You're not the regular woman. But you're welcome. Beannaigh Dia tú féin agus do leanaí.[1]"

"Go raibh míle mait agat,[2] me kind lady," answers the women. "And may God come down and bless you too; and may He do the same for all dat live with ye. Now tell me, me lady . . . Would ye be able to help me and me two poor little girls today?"

"There are some clothes and shoes in there for you," replies Peg, handing her the bag. "And I've put a can of peas in there too."

"And aren't you a kind lady," says the woman. Ferreting in the bag, she extracts a Fair Isle pullover that had shrunk in the wash.

"Dis lovely gansey will be grand for one of the girls," she adds. "And the peas are grand too; God knows it's seldom der's a time dat I've enough to keep the childer feed."

25

In an attempt to engage the two little girls, Peg turns to them with a warm smile: "Now . . . Aren't you two of the loveliest little girls!? Cad iad na hainmneacha?[3]"

"Alanna agus Mairead; is iad seo na hainmneacha,"[4] answers the woman on their behalf.

"I'll be movin' on now, me lady," she continues. "Say goodbye, girls. And say t'anks to the kind lady."

"Slán, agus go raibh míle maith agat,"[5] chants the girls.

"Ná habair é – is cúis mhór áthais dom,"[6] Peg replies.

Peg and I have just closed the front door when we hear some commotion outside. We go to the front parlour window, and to our horror, we see the woman engaged in vicious combat with another Tinker woman who Peg identifies as being her regular woman.

Within seconds there's blood and lumps of hair flying.

"That lady is mine!" roars the regular. "Give me dat bag, ye bitch ye." Jumping at the usurper, she grabs the bag and gives her a wallop. With blood streaming from her nose, the usurper runs at the regular; grabbing a fist-full of hair from her head, she retrieves the bag. They're rolling on the road, screaming and shouting when along comes the second wave of Tinkers – the men. The brawling women are pulled apart, and other than for some concluding shouting and screaming, the fisticuff ends.

A minute passes, and we hear another knock at the door. Once again Peg and I go to open it – with increased care this time.

"Good day, Mam," says the burly, barrel-chested Tinker. "Can I help ye out today, Mam? Is der err an odd job or some tinkerin' to be done?"

From the slightly opened door, Peg sizes things up. She does want her pot mended; recognising the man as having a somewhat familiar face, she decides to engage the enquiry. She widens the door opening to about half.

"I do have a pot you could fix for me," Peg indicates. "But with all that fighting out there on the road, I've a good mind not to give you the work. It's disgraceful seeing two women fighting like that – hair and blood flying all over the place. That's no way to behave. And two of your little girls looking on. God forgive you."

"Ye're right, Mam," says the Tinker contritely. "Agus tá brón orm.[7] But sure isn't it all over now. And I need the work somet'in'

26

fearse, Mam. Le de chead[8] – you can trust me with yer pot; I'll have it lookin' like brand new for ye in a jiffy."

Pondering for a moment, Peg accepts the man's apologies.

"All right then," says Peg. "Now . . . You do a good job on that pot of mine; it's my mother's pot, and I cook the potatoes in it – the spuds always taste better when they're cooked in that old pot. And I want you to tell those two women what I've said about them and their fighting – disgraceful, so it is, disgraceful."

"I'll do a grand job on yer pot, Mam," says the Tinker. "Ye'll see . . . It'll look like brand new. And just like ye've asked, I'll have some strong words with t'ose two women as well."

"Good," says Peg resolutely. Turning to me she says: "Niall love, run into the kitchen and bring the pot out to me. This good man here is going to do a job on it for me."

Peg has quickly dismissed the sordid fisticuff event from her mind; she's now refocused on achieving what is one of her primary goals for the day – getting her mother's pot repaired.

The Tinker quickly sets up his tools, equipment and materials outside our front garden gate.

"Can I watch the Tinker mend the pot, Ma?" I plead.

"You can," Peg answers. "But you're to stay in the front garden. I don't want you on the road until all the Tinkers are gone."

Out I go, and despite being restricted to the confines of the front garden, I'm very excited about the chance of being able to see the Tinker perform his magic.

"How'ya, mister," says I, as I go to the gate and position myself so as to be best able to observe all that would happen.

"Tá mé go maith, go raibh maith agat,[9]" answers the Tinker. "Agus conas atá tú?[10]"

"Go maith,[11] t'anks," says I.

The Tinker is sitting on what looks like a small, three-legged milking stool beside an equally low and opened folding metal-topped table. His tools and materials are neatly laded out in front of him: two sizes of ball-peen hammers; about a half-dozen different shaped metal files; a couple of stiff wire brushes; a jar of some kind of lard or thick oil; a bag of chalk dust; a number of different types of short metal rods; and a bunch of coarse sandpaper-type burnishing material.

He has Peg's pot in both hands, and he's trying to determine the best way to proceed. Holding it up to the sky, he's assessing the damage.

"Tá dhá poill beagh anseo,[12]" says the Tinker. "Beidh solder fuar a chun air.[13]"

After some further examination of the holes he decides on his choice of which file would be the most appropriate one for him to use. With the chosen file in his right hand, he sticks his left hand's centre finger into the jar, extracts a finger full of lard and liberally greases the file's surface. Having filed both the inside and outside of the pot's holes, he takes hold of one of the wire brushes and vigorously brushes away any remaining loose pieces of metal. Switching to one of his finer files, and having – much to my disgust –unhygienically dampened the damaged surfaces by spitting on them, he continues his filing. Two or three pinches of chalk dust are then applied, followed by a spate of final filing using his finest file. He finishes off his prep work by briskly burnishing both sides.

"Tá post an-maith![14]" says the Tinker, a big smile on his face as he examines the pot and expresses his pride for a job well done.

Placing the prepped pot in its upright position on the centre of the table, he selects the appropriate rod of metal filler. Grabbing one of the ball-peen hammers, he then promptly fills the holes by carefully placing the end of the rod over each hole, one at a time, and giving the rod some firm wallops with the hammer. He inspects the results of each wallop until the holes are filled to his satisfaction. He then repeats the prep filing, brushing and burnishing process – this time with the welcomed omission of the spitting part – and ends up with what looks to me as being a perfectly repaired pot. It fails to look 'like brand new', however, the Tinkers magic does not fail to impress me. Peg is going to be happy – she'll soon have her mammy's mended potato pot back in her kitchen, ready for many more years of use.

****

WITH MY overall enjoyment in observing the magic of the Tinker's tinkering skills, I somehow forgot all about the spittle part. I never told Peg about it. And it was just as well. Peg's lack of intelligence on the matter avoided her having to agonize over the decision of whether or not to throw out her much loved, but now Tinker-spittle-sullied-forever, potato pot. Peg would go to heaven on 14 October 1971 without her ever being aware of the fact that her much loved pot had been contaminated; that old pot of her's was still in her kitchen when she died.

****

Yarn #6 Footnotes
[1] God bless you and your children.
[2] May a thousand good things come to you *or* thank you very much.
[3] What are your names?
[4] Alanna and Mairead; that's their names.
[5] Goodbye, and thank you very much.
[6] Don't mention it – it's my pleasure.
[7] And I am sorry.
[8] With your permission.
[9] I'm good, thank you.
[10] And how are you?
[11] Good.
[12] There's two small holes here.
[13] A cold solder will be fine.
[14] A very good job!

Soap

DUBLIN CITY HAS A PARTICULAR SET OF road ordinance statutes: everyone has to drive on the left-hand side of the road; you have to obey all traffic signs; at a roundabout, vehicles on the roundabout have the right of way, &c. The many other street statutes include one declaring that a public road cannot be used as a football field. This particular law is pretty much ignored on Erris, by the residents and the gardaí. Garda Brown, our Dublin-born long-time local bobby, understands the circumstances and judiciously overlooks the transgression.

Playing ball on the road.

Over the years, he's established an understanding with the neighbourhood children and parents. He's determined that while Leix and Annaly have a fair amount of traffic, Erris Road has little or none. He understands the children have nowhere else to play and he wisely bends the rules to fit the circumstance.

"You can play ball on Erris," he declared. "There'll be no football on Leix or Annaly."

Garda Brown does his beat on his bicycle. He comes by almost every day. He often stops, parks his bike and becomes an ardent spectator of our games. Garda Brown knows us all by name, knows where we live and is acquainted with most of our parents.

This perfect gardaí/resident relationship is suddenly shattered – Garda Brown gets promoted to some desk job in Mountjoy. In his stead, we get a very different type of garda. Our much loved Dublin-born Garda Brown is replaced with an over-eager young culchie from County Galway.

I'M NEARLY nine, and I can't wait for me birthday. It's on T'ursday dis year. I was born on a Monday. I like me birthday on Saturdays or Sundays, but I don't care dis year, 'cause I'm gettin' a new bike. I can't wait. I hope it's a red one.

Like Garda Brown, the new garda also uses a bicycle to get around. He introduces himself to the neighbourhood by appearing at the top of Erris, jumping off his bike and apprehending myself and three of my playmates.

"Got yee, me boyos," he snarls, his eyes flashing from one to the other of his four captured outlaws. "Don't yee know it's against the law to be playin' football on the public roadway now?"

"Give me that ball," he demands as he grabs the ball out of my hands. "I'll be confiscating this ball now."

He has us pinned against one of the front-garden railings. We're mystified by what is happening. We'd been innocently playing ball like we had all our lives. The garda's strange behaviour is both confusing and frightening.

"We always play ball on the road," I assert. "Garda Brown said it was alright for us to play on Erris, now."

When Dubliners speak, we often start our sentences with a 'now.' The new garda, a Galway man, is throwing in his now at the end, using it as an ending exclamation mark rather than a soft start to what is to be stated. Subconsciously, I had added a concluding 'now' in my response.

"I'll be having no cheek from you or any of yee," he snarls. "I'll be having all of yeer names and addresses . . . now."

Tucking our confiscated ball between his knees, he extracts a black-covered notebook from his breast pocket, takes his pencil out, licks its point, and makes ready to write.

"Give them to me now," he demands.

Having written down our names and addresses, he puts his little black book back into his pocket.

31

"If any of yeer names get themselves into me book again, it'll be curtains for yee," he snarls. "No more playing football on the road now."

With that, the new garda gets back on his bike and off he goes on his miserable way, our ball along with him.

"Now w'at sort of a bolic is dat?" says Frank. Frank Frazier is one of the apprehended, and he's full of malapropos – he meant to say bollocks, not bolic.

"Bolic is right, car-feckin'-bolic soap!" I respond. "I hate dat feckin' soap. Dat's w'at we'll call the new garda – Soap!"

Lifebuoy Carbolic soap is being used by all the neighbours. Recent polio and TB epidemics are giving concern to the parents. The government's promotion of the soap's use throughout Ireland is a resounding success. It contains disinfectant and has become the public's soap of choice. It does the intended job real well. However, it also leaves a less than pleasant tar smell. A stink that always reminds me of a recently-cleaned toilet bowl.

"I t'ink Soap is mad. I'm goin' in to tell me Ma."

I run into Peg to tell her what happened.

"Ma, Soap took our ball. He said we're not allowed play on the road anymore."

"Who took your ball?"

"The new garda, Ma. We call him Soap. We were only havin' a bit of bootin' like we always do. He took our ball and our names and addresses and all."

"Did he now?" comes Peg's measured response. "Well, you just go out and play, love. Leave it to me. I'll nip down to Garda Brown and see what we can do about all this nonsense."

My resourceful mother will sort it all out. In the meantime, we spread the word: Soap is out to get us. All our football games will require recognisance. We'll need a watch-out at the Leix and Annaly ends of Erris. We'll have to recruit the younger kids and make sure our games can be curtailed before Soap's unwelcomed appearance.

While Mrs Murphy and all the neighbours have serious doubts regarding Mr Murphy's sanity and his obsessive concern for the cleanliness of his red Morris Minor, the entire neighbourhood is in no doubt regarding Soap. Everyone's convinced he's mad entirely.

"L.O.B., L.O.B., Soap!" someone roars. Two days have passed since our initial run-in with the new bobby, and we've just started a game of football. L.O.B. means 'Look Out Bobby', and when L.O.B. is followed by Soap, it means Soap is coming to get us.

We scatter, sixteen or so of us. Soap comes zooming down Erris on his trusty bike. Dashing down amongst us, he's sizing things up with the intention of improving his chances of apprehending us – get into the centre of the herd and work out.

Soap is about thirty feet away when he sees me. He jumps off his bike, and I mean he jumps off his bike as it is still moving fast. The unmanned bike bashes its way past me, jumps up onto the pavement and rams into one of the garden's railings. With Olympic-type sprinting skill, Soap directs his attention on me. I run down Offaly as fast as I can. *Where do I go to avoid bein' caught? Christ the King Church! Yeah. I'll go in the church's back gate at Galmoy and hide in the gardens.* Soap is gaining on me – his longer legs give him a distinct advantage.

As I run into the church gardens, I realise Soap is too close for any successful concealment. *I'll have to go inside the church and hide under the seats.*

I barge my way up the steps into the church. Before the swing-doors stop swinging, in walks Soap, right behind me. *So much for hidin' under the seats.* The no running in church rule, together with the presence of a few people doing the Stations of the Cross, limits me to a single hope – divine intervention.

And in such a state of affairs, what better for me to do than to go directly to the main man, Saint Jude, the patron saint of hopeless cases. His shrine is to the right of the nave.

I kneel down and make the sign of the cross. Reading from the Saint Jude prayer plaque, I start my plea for intercession. *Oh, glorious apostle Saint Jude, faithful servant and friend of Jesus, the name of the traitor who delivered yer beloved Master into the hands of His enemies has caused you to be forgotten by many, but the Church honours and invokes you universally as the patron of hopeless cases – of things despaired of. Pray for me who am so miserable; make use, I implore you, of that particular privilege, accorded you of bringing visible and speedy help where help is almost despaired of. Come to my assistance in this great need, that*

I may receive the consolations and succour of heaven in all my necessities, tribulations and sufferings, particularly Soap (the prayer plaque instructs me to insert what I want Jude to help me with, so I put in Soap), *and that I may bless God with you and all the elect throughout eternity. I promise you, Oh blessed Saint Jude, to be ever mindful of this great favour, and I'll never cease to honour you as my special and powerful patron, and to do all in my power to encourage devotion to you. Amen.*

I'm almost finished when Soap quietly kneels down beside me.

"Finish up yer prayin'," he whispers. "Saint Jude himself isn't goin' to be able to get ye out of this now."

Soap escorts me out of the church. Having checked his little black book for my recorded address, he leads me to my front door.

"We'll see what yer mother has to say about this now," barks Soap, as he grabs the door-knocker and gives it three loud thumps.

"What's the problem?" says Peg, as she opens the door; she's looking more than a little surprised and anxious.

"Garda Morrison here, Ma'am," responds Soap. "And would this lad be yer son now?"

"What's wrong?" says Peg. "Are you all right, Niall? Yes, Niall is my son. What's going on? With the way you banged the door-knocker, you nearly gave me a heart attack, so you did."

"I've warned yer son there'll be no playing ball on the road, and sure didn't he ignore me warnin'," declares Soap. "Didn't I have to run after him all the way into the church, and that's the second time I've had to put his name in me book now."

"Listen here," starts Peg. Her hands are on her hips; I know well what to expect when that happens. "Have you no better thing to be doing with your time then stopping the children playing? And what's all this about you running after Niall like as if he was a criminal?"

"And was it you who stole my son's ball?" adds Peg before Soap has time to respond. "That ball cost money, you know. I want you to give it back to Niall, so I do."

"It's against the law to play football on–," Soap tries to answer, but Peg cuts him short.

"The law be damned. Where can the children play? Here in Dublin, we don't have the fields that you and your ilk over there in the west of Ireland have. Garda Brown – and I believe he's an Inspector now, down in Mountjoy – wasn't he the one who, over the past ten-plus years declared Erris as a road the children can play on."

"I know nothing about that now, but–," Soap tries to say.

"Indeed you don't," Peg asserts. "And I'll have none of your ignorance worrying my Niall or me."

"Well, I'll be reportin' this to the station, and–," Soap tries to say, and once again he fails to take control of the situation.

"And I'll be down to Mountjoy to do the same myself," interrupts Peg. "I'm sure Inspector Brown will be able to put you in your place and make you stop upsetting the entire neighbourhood."

"Come in here to me, Niall love," Peg instructs. "We'll sort all this out with Inspector Brown."

"Yeah, Ma," I answer.

I'm in awe of and bursting with pride for my mother's innate ability to kick arse.

"Now don't forget: you give that ball back to my son," Peg barks, as she bangs the door shut in Soap's confused face.

Soap knows when to quit. Like many before him, he realises he'll never get the better of Peg. He turns, gathers up his bike, and off he goes.

****

I DON'T know what my mother did or what she might have said to Garda Brown, however, that was the last of our problems with Soap. Soap never set his foot or the wheels of his bike on Erris Road again.

I never did get my ball back.

My ninth birthday came, and so did my new bike. It had a bell, front and back breaks, mudguards, and a back seat with a saddlebag. Best of all, it was a red one!

****

The Gravediggers –
Early Birds & Pullin'-a-Pint

My THREE CHILDREN were all born in Dublin. That makes Elisa, Susan and Graeme sixth generation, Dublin-born Kavanaghs, and we're all proud of that.

My Da, Gerry Kavanagh, born 23 April 1907, was the fourth of five sons for my grandfather, John Edward Kavanagh (1879–1931) and his wife Josephine nee McKenna of Howth (1870–1943). Gerry had three older brothers; Joseph, Michael, and John. Gerry's younger brother, Fintan would complete the family.

Gerry and all of the Kavanaghs, back to my great-grandfather Joseph, who was born in 1840, were all born in a pub – the *John Kavanagh* pub, aka *The Gravediggers* – and we're equally proud of that. The pub is located at 1 Prospect Square, Glasnevin, next to the old original gate entrance to the largest graveyard in Ireland, Glasnevin Cemetery.

The John Kavanagh pub. My Granma Josie is second on the left.

It was my great-great-grandfather John (1812–78) and his wife Anna-Maria nee O'Neill (1821–95) who started the business in

1833. The pub's doors opened two years after Daniel O'Connell, the Irish hero of Catholic Emancipation, opened Glasnevin Cemetery. Anna-Maria's father, John O'Neill was an hotelier and a staunch supporter of Daniel O'Connell. As a thank you for his support, John was able to secure a permit for his daughter and son-in-law to open the pub right next door to the graveyard, a perfect spot for a pub if ever there was one.

An extraordinarily active pair, John and Anna-Maria had twenty-five children. One of their sons, my great-grandfather, Joseph (1840–1901) and his barmaid wife Margaret nee Hickey (1845–1909) were the next owners. Joseph was a member of the *Fenian Brotherhood*, an Irish republican organisation founded in the USA in 1858. He spent some years in America before coming back to Dublin and the ownership of *The Gravediggers*. Joseph and Margaret had six children, three of whom died as infants.

The next owner, my grandfather John Edward, was one of two surviving sons of Joseph and Margaret. John Edward died in 1931, and his wife Josie ran the business until she died in 1943.

My father sold his share of the pub to his two living brothers, John and Fintan. As bachelors, they would work and live together in the pub for most of their lives – they both married late in life.

Today, John Kavanagh is what you see over the pub's door, exactly as the founder identified it in 1833. It has been the *John Kavanagh* pub, aka *The Gravediggers* all these years, other than for when my great-grandfather, Joseph owned it and changed the name to read Joseph Kavanagh. Joseph's son, my grandfather, John Edward, switched it back to John when he held the reins.

That is the way John Edward's grandson, Eugene likes it – back to its original identity. My cousin, Eugene Kavanagh and his wife Kathleen are the current owners and live there. Eugene is the son of my Uncle Michael and stepson to my Uncle John: Michael died in 1948 and John was later to marry his widowed sister-in-law, Nelly, in 1954. *The Gravediggers* is the oldest family pub in Ireland.

****

"WHAT'S KEEPING YOU, NIALL," MY DA HOLLERS. "We've loads of work to do. Will ye hurry up! We're all out here waiting for you."

"I can't find me hat, Da," I shout my response. *I look great in dat hat, and I'm not goin' out without it.* I'm nine years old, and Colleen, my first love gave it to me for my eighth birthday. "Ye look massive!" Colleen declared when I first put it on my head. I don't go anywhere without it. I do everything bar sleep in it.

"It's on the hall table, ye eejit ye," Paddy yells angrily. My two-years-older brother is never one who tolerates my many shortcomings.

"Come on, Niall! We've loads of work to do," Paddy insists.

He's right. Saint Patrick's Day is coming, and as usual, on these particular occasions, we'll have loads of work to do, and barrels of fun doing it – maybe as many as three barrels this time.

It is 1951, and Guinness deliveries their product to pubs in big wooden barrels. Draught pints are served from the barrels. However, each pub is required to bottle its own Guinness on premises. Saint Patrick's Day, the All-Ireland Gaelic Football and Hurling Finals and Semi-Finals in Croke Park, plus Christmas and New Years are the pub's busiest times. My Da can always be relied upon to gather up his crew, supply free bottling labour, and get the place stocked for the crowds that would arrive.

Geraldine, my six-years-older sister; Fergus, my four-years-older brother; Paddy and my Da are at the front gate waiting for me. Conor, my little brother, is only three-and-a-half and isn't quite up to being made part of the work crew.

"I love you in that hat," says Geraldine, as I walk out the door, be-hatted and happy to join them. "And you leave him alone, Paddy," she adds. Geraldine is fifteen, the most beautiful girl in the world, and my Paddy protector. Off we go, making our way to the *John Kavanagh* pub. My Da, and Geraldine with me in hand lead the way while Fergus and Paddy follow in the rear.

"Hurry up, Da," I roar, as we make our way up the hill to the Fassaugh Avenue railway bridge. "Der's a train comin'. We can look over and see it passin'!"

"Come on, Niall," says Geraldine. The train is thundering by as she lifts me up to see it race by.

"I love the trains," says I. "Where's the train goin' to?"

"Belfast," she answers. My Da and my brothers have joined us.

"Throw him over, Geraldine," says Paddy.

"I will not! And you leave Niall alone, or I'll push you over."

"Let's get going," my Da interjects. "We don't want to be late."

We go over the railway bridge, cut into the back lanes of Shandon Park onto Leinster Street, and down to Phibsborough Road. We pass by Kilmartins, the horse-racing betting office.

"Hold a minute," my Da instructs. "Let me nip in and place a shilling. I got a tip on a horse running in Naas today. He's a winner if ever I saw one. At twenty-to-one, he's got great odds."

Now and again my Da places a bet on the horses. It's a weakness of his – horse racing and placing an odd bet.

"Now . . . We'll stop and check out how that old horse of mine does on our way home," my Da declares, as he comes out of the betting office, betting slip in hand.

We're on the homestretch to Prospect Square. We pass the Odlum Flour Mill with its tall smoke-belching chimney and go over the Royal Canal's hump-backed bridge onto Prospect Road. With its unused locks and poorly maintained flushing system, the canal always seems to be dirty, unused and sadly lifeless.

The *Brian Boru House* pub, with its painted portrait of the patron hanging over its entrance, comes next. There's a huge 'Men Only' sign painted on the pub's wall. We cross over to Harts Corner and continue down Prospect Avenue towards the Square and *The Gravediggers*. Prospect Square is a large cul-de-sac. A dead end in more ways than one; right next to the pub are the closed, large old entrance gates to Glasnevin Cemetery.

It's a little after 10:00 a.m. As usual, the pub announces the lack of a woman's presence. The pub itself is tidy enough, but as for the rest of the place – let's say it's a mess. One room in the living area over the pub, the room in which my Da was born, is filled with stacked newspapers dating back to who knows when.

Upon entering the premises, there's a small hallway with the main pub entrance door directly ahead. To the right, there's a smaller, discrete, door into the snug.

In addition to selling beer and other alcoholic drinks, the pub also sells basic groceries such as tea, sugar, salt, biscuits, Bovril, cigarettes, matches, &c. Like with most Dublin pubs, women are not allowed into the pub proper. However, they are permitted to go into the snug – to buy their groceries. Women wanting more than groceries, for instance, a drink, can then indulge themselves in the sanctuary of their snug. Groceries are also bought, and that seems to dispel any and all guilt, making it socially acceptable.

John and Fintan have two Alsatian dogs. Not being much taller than the top of the bar, I peer over, and I'm greeted by the two big dogs returning my anxious stare from the other side.

Apart from a couple of early birds, and Mrs Reilly in the snug, nothing is happening. My Uncle John is quietly pulling his early regulars a couple of pints of Guinness. It'll take three minutes for the task to produce the perfect pint. Worth every minute of the wait, each of the required three pulls has its part to play.

The first pull is drawn with the tap fully open. The dark brown liquid falls to the side of the cold, dry, pint glass held at an angle; the liquid hits the side of the glass at the halfway mark, filling it to the same level. The half-filled glass is then placed on the bar to settle for a while – for a full minute, to be exact.

Once settled, and looking dark brown in colour, the glass is then gently raised and made subject to the second pull, this time from a half-open tap. Directed to the centre of the vertically held glass, more of the precious liquid pours until the glass is three-quarters full, at a slower pour this time, without a single splash. Once again, the glass is placed on the bar to settle for another minute. When settled, the Guinness has a much darker, almost black look and a shallow, light brown head.

The third pull goes towards finishing the process. Lifting the glass and holding it vertically, the pull is made with the tap quarter-open. Moving the glass in circular motions, the liquid pours from the tap nozzle held below the top of the rising head, until the head peeps over the top of the glass. The circular motion is finished off with a final flourish into the centre of the head.

John then carefully places the pint to rest on the bar. After thirty seconds or so, he picks it up. It's as black as the ace of spades, crowned with a beautiful three-quarter-inch high, white bishops collar head. Finally, like a bishop would handle a chalice, John then places the perfect pint in front of the lucky recipient.

"Now John; and aren't you a champion thoroughbred in a stable of farm horses," says one of the regulars as he picks up his first of the day. "Der's ner-a-one can pull a pint like ye."

40

"Thank you," replies John wiping his hands on his apron. "Now . . . I'll be leaving you two. Mrs Reilly has come in for her sugar."

A perfect pint.

"It's more dan sugar, ol' Dicey Reilly will be gettin'," one of the regulars whispers to his friend. "She'll be havin' a glass or two and a couple of chasers, I'd say."

They snigger as they start their day their usual way, much like Mrs Reilly is doing, only they aren't buying sugar.

****

IN THE early-1950s, some bright Dubliner, to whom all draught Guinness drinkers should be forever grateful, discovered that the paying public was being cheated out of their drink and their hard earned money. The old certified imperial CE pint glass was made to hold a full pint of liquid. However, the Dubliner was smart enough to realise that the CE glass did not allow for the essential, three-quarter-inch-high head the Guinness pint pulling process produces. While the public was paying for an imperial pint or 20 fluid ounces, they were being served only 18 fluid ounces; for every ten pints paid for, the buyer was served nine – an absolute outrage! Guinness quickly introduced the new taller certified LCE pint glass stamped with an official pint-line mark, three-quarters of an inch from the rim. Sláinte to that Dublin genius for putting Guinness straight and ensuring that when we pay for a pint, we're served a pint.

****

The Gravediggers –
Bottlin', the Hole in the Wall &
a Darlin' Horse

Tim Finnegan lived in Walkin Street,
*   a gentle Irishman, mighty odd.*
He had a brogue both rich'n'sweet,
*   to rise in the world, he carried a hod.*
Ye see he'd a sort of a tipplin' way,
*   with a love for the liquor, he was born.*
To help him on with his work each day,
*   he'd a drop of the craytur[1] every morn'.*

*   Wack-fol-de-dah, dance with yer partner,*
*   'round the floor yer trotters[2] shake.*
*   Wasn't it the truth I told ye,*
*   lots of fun at Finnegan's Wake.*

One mornin' Tim was feelin' full,
*   his head felt heavy and it made him shake.*
He fell from the ladder and he broke his skull,
*   they carried him home, his corpse to wake.*
They rolled him up in a nice clean sheet,
*   they laid him out upon the bed,*
A gallon of whiskey at his feet,
*   and a barrel of porter at his head.*

His friends assembled at the wake,
*   and Mrs Finnegan called for lunch.*
First she brought in tea'n'cake,
*   then pipes, tobacco and whiskey punch.*
Biddy O'Brien began to cry,
*   "Such a nice clean corpse did ye ever see?*
Tim avourneeen,[3] why did ye die?"
*   "Ah hold yer gob," says Paddy McGee.*

Mary Murphy took up the job,
*   "Biddy," says she, "yer wrong, I'm sure."*
Biddy fetched her a belt in the gob,
*   and left her sprawlin' on the floor.*
Then the war did soon engage,
*   'twas woman to woman and man to man,*
Shillelagh[4] law was all the rage,
*   and a row and a ructions soon began.*

Mickey Maloney ducked his head,
*   when a bottle of whiskey flew at him.*
It missed, and landin' on the bed,
*   the whiskey scattered over Tim.*
Tim revives, see how he rises!
*   Timothy risin' from the bed!*
"Throw yer whiskey 'round like blazes,
*   be the thunderin' Jays! Do ye t'ink I'm dead?"*

Finnegan's Wake – Traditional (1850)

NOTICING OUR ARRIVAL, MY UNCLE JOHN acknowledges our appreciated presence.

"Good morning, Gerry," says John with a smile. "It's grand you're here so early. Fintan is outside, setting up. Let me look after Mrs Reilly. Go on into the back, and I'll be with you in a minute."

"Right John," my Da replies. "The crew is ready to go."

There's an established routine. We all go into the back of the bar through the dividing swing doors, sit around the old table and wait. Much like so much of the place, that table has been there since the pub opened in 1833; Daniel O'Connell was one of the first to sit at it. The pub has been the setting for many movies: David Lean's *Ryan's Daughter*; Gene Wilder's *Quackser Fortune Has a Cousin in the Bronx*; and Neil Jordan's *Michael Collins* are three that come to mind. The pub's authenticity makes it perfect.

John, having attended to Mrs Reilly's needs comes into the back to join us.

"Now, to start you four off," says John, as he looks down at his brother's brew, "how about a glass of lemonade and a Marietta? That'll get you moving. Am I right?"

"It will Uncle John," Geraldine responds. "That'll be grand."

Always the same, four bottles of Taylor Keith lemonade with accompanying glasses plus a plate of eight Jacob's Marietta biscuits are placed in front of us.

43

"And isn't that a grand looking hat you're wearing, Niall," says John, giving me a wink exactly like my Da's.

"T'anks, Uncle John. Colleen gave it to me for me birthday."

"Finish up now, and let's get bottling," encourages my Da. "Your Uncle Fintan will have everything ready for us."

Da enjoying a glass.

We finish our treats and make our way out to the back garden bottling shed.

"Hello, Fintan," my Da greets his younger brother. "The crew is raring to go. How's your leg holding up?"

Fintan has a bad limp and often uses a walking stick. He had been in a bicycle accident at Hart's Corner; one of his bike's handbreak levers stabbed him in the right calf. He doesn't look after it well, and it's infected. It's over two years since the accident, and the wound won't heal.

"Ah, sure it's not too bad, Gerry," answers Fintan. "I can see by looking at the children and yourself, you're all doing well. How's Peggy and little Conor doing?"

"All's well, Fintan," my Da responds. "It looks like you've got us all setup and ready to go."

"Yes, Gerry. I'll get out of your way, and let you get at it. I'll go into the shop now and rest my leg for a bit."

Fintan is using his walking stick today. He limps his way out of the bottling shed and up along the garden pathway towards the pub. Much to John's disappointment, Fintan drinks a bit too much – once inside, he no doubt will have a small Jameson, or two. As he would be quick to say, 'So as to ease the discomfort'.

Fintan has set up the place perfectly. Crated empty Guinness bottles are stacked up against the left end wall next to the sink/bottle washer. That is the first of five stations located on the long wall facing the shed's entrance, Geraldine's station. Next to the bottle washer is Fergus's station: a raised barrel of Guinness has been cranked up with the tap plugged in, ready for bottle filling. Beside the barrel is Paddy's station: a half-barrel of bottle caps and the bottle capper. Then comes my station: the labelling station. Oval, Guinness supplied *John Kavanagh* labels are stacked up on a shelf. A dampened sheet of thick sponge is laid out ready to dampen the pre-glued labels for mounting onto the filled and capped bottles of Guinness. At the right end wall, there are the empty crates, which will soon be filled with the completed product – that's my Da's station. Any short-filled, badly-capped or crooked-label bottles are returned down the line for a redo.

That's the work to be done, and that's the way we do it. We take breaks every hundred bottles or so. Lunch break is always looked forward to – ray'n'chips from the local Fish'n'Chipper.

During the lunch break, and while exploring the pub's big back garden, I discover a hole in the twenty-foot-high stone wall that separates the back-garden from the graveyard. The hole is about seven inches wide and ten inches tall.

"Der's a hole in the graveyard wall, Da," I declare to my Da. "Ye can see the graves and all."

"Let's go and look at what you've found," Gerry replies. "Maybe some of the dead people use it to drop into the pub for a pint," he laughs as we make our way to my discovery.

"Well, Niall," says Gerry, as he examines my find. "You've found something strange here. We'd better tell your Uncle John about it." In we go to confront John with our exciting discovery.

"I know all about that hole," is John's response to my Da's announcement.

"And I'm surprised you don't know about it, Gerry," he continues, as he goes on with his task of washing some pint glasses in the long metal sink under the bar.

"What do you mean, John?"

"I mean that hole has been there for a long time. I'm surprised, very surprised indeed, that you don't know all about it."

45

"Well as surprised as you are, John, and I might well be forgetting something, but I know nothing at all about it."

"Shouldn't you patch it up, John?" my Da continues.

"It won't be me who'll be doing that, Gerry."

"And why not, John?"

"Well, I'll tell you why," answers John, stopping his washing, and drying his hands on his apron. "Wasn't it our mother who made that hole!? The hole stays exactly as our mother left it."

"Why did she put the hole in the wall, Uncle John?" I ask.

"For the convenience of the graveyard's hard working gravediggers, Niall. That's why. During their day's work, and whenever they'd get the urge, they'd come to the hole, whistle out for Josie – that was what they called your Granma – and then wouldn't she supply them with a nice, thirst-quenching pint to help them get through their sad day's work. She made the hole so that the gravediggers could be served without them taken the risk of slipping out of work and getting themselves into trouble."

"That's a fine story you're telling us, John," my amazed Da says. "I'd forgotten all about that hole. And Niall, wasn't it a good thing for your Granma to have done – keeping the gravediggers digging and lessening their sad, heavy workload as they did it."

"Did I ever meet me Granma, Da?"

"You did, Niall. You were only one year old when she went to heaven, so you can't remember her."

"Rumour has it she often comes back here to keep an eye on us," says John. "Keep your eye out, and you might see her."

"How'll I know it's her, Uncle John?"

"You'll know her, Niall. Don't you worry about that."

WE HAVE the third barrel up and half empty, when my father calls it a day. We say our goodbyes to John and Fintan and head for home. On the way, my Da goes into Kilmartins to check out how his horse had finished the race.

Out comes my Da, a big smile on his face; he's holding a pound note in his hand, and he's waving it triumphantly above his head.

"Now that's the way to turn a shilling into a pound. A darlin' horse if ever there was one. Twenty-to-one! Let's hurry home to your mammy. She'll be as happy as Larry with this extra pound."

We are all excited with the thoughts of Gerry gifting Peg with what would be a pleasant surprise – an extra pound to spend on the often difficult task of keeping the Kavanagh food press full.

"We're home, Peg," says Gerry, as we come in through the backdoor to an aromatic kitchen. The previous evening, Peg had prepared two rabbits, my brother, Fergus had snared. All day they've been slowly cooking in a big pot on the cooker, along with Peg's delicate dumplings, some onions, carrots, Bisto, and two OXO cubes for extra taste. She has two other pots bubbling away: cabbage is in one, and she has the potatoes cooking in her mother's born-again old pot – the Tinker did a grand job on it.

We have a metered, gas-fed cooker. Once a month the 'gasman' comes around to empty the meter; it only takes florins[5], and the gas is cut off whenever there's not enough money fed into it. For a household to run out of florins is a disaster.

"Perfect timing, Gerry," says Peg. "Have you any florins, love? I've used the last I had on that bloody gas guzzler. The meter needs feeding again. All the cooking I've been doing is eating it up."

"I do," answers Gerry, taking two florins out of his pocket.

"Grand," says Peg. "Dinner is nearly ready. Geraldine darlin', keep an eye on the pots for me. I'm going to the lavatory."

Out Peg dashes. She must have been holding her toiletry needs for some time. She almost knocks me down rushing out.

I'm impatient for my Da to present his winnings to Peg. I run after her and bang on the closed toilet door.

"Hurry up, Ma. Da has a surprise for ye."

"My soul isn't my own with ye," Peg's responses. "I can't go to the toilet without you bothering me. I'll be out in a minute!"

"Leave your mammy alone, Niall," says Gerry.

"But Da, when are ye goin' to give Ma the pound?" I whisper.

"Hold your horses. Let your mammy finish the dinner. We'll give it to her at the table."

We've just finished dinner when my Da gives Peg the pound.

"There you are, Peg love," says Gerry, as he slaps the pound note on the table. "Put that in your pipe and smoke it."

"Now isn't this a nice surprise. It's grand when your horse comes home for you, Gerry. God knows we need the money. Keeping all of us fit and fed is sometimes awful hard."

47

"Ye're great, Da," says I, looking up at my Da's smiling face. Turning to me, he gives me one of his loving winks.

****

MY COUSIN Eugene, ably helped by his wife, Kathleen, their two sons, Kieran and Niall, and their daughter, Ann, have looked after *The Gravediggers* well. The old family homestead has been carefully preserved and perfectly complemented. Eugene expanded the place, effectively doubling its size. He bought the adjacent piece of property and painstakingly duplicated the original pub frontage. While the inside of the old pub, 1 Prospect Square, looks pretty much like it was when it opened in 1833, behind the perfectly matched frontage of the newer 2 Prospect Square expansion there's a spacious Victorian bar and lounge serving a fine lunch and dinner menu. You'll be missing out if you fail to make a visit to the *John Kavanagh* pub. After Anthony Bourdain's recent visit there, he listed it as being one of the five best pubs in the world.

The old and the new – Glasnevin Cemetery gate on left.

When you do visit, be sure to try the oxtail soup. A few slices of fresh Brennan's bread buttered all the way to the edges, and a bowl of that stuff, are sure to put hair on your chest. If you're up to it after the soup, have a plate of Hafner pork sausages and chips – then wash it all down with what is the best pint of Guinness in the entire world.

Being close to the graveyard, many of the pub's deceased patrons are said to frequent the place. I never ran into Josie, but every time I visit I can sense my Da's presence. Gerry and Peg are just over the wall, and sure it's no trouble for them to drop in.

****

Yarn #9 Footnotes
[1] Irish whiskey.
[2] Feet.
[3] My darling.
[4] Mallet-shaped piece of blackthorn or oak used as a weapon.
[5] Imperial Monetary System coin with a value of 24 pennies or 2 shillings. The IMS was replaced with the Decimal System in 1971.

Kick-the-Can

Der was an ol' woman, she lived in the woods, weile weile waile.
Der was an ol' woman, she lived in the woods, down by the river Saile.
She had a baby t'ree months old, weile weile waile.
She had a baby t'ree months old, down by the river Saile.

She had a penknife, long and sharp, weile weile waile.
She had a penknife, long and sharp, down by the river Saile.
She stuck the penknife in the baby's heart, weile weile waile.
She stuck the penknife in the baby's heart, down by the river Saile.

T'ree loud knocks came knockin' on the door, weile weile waile.
T'ree loud knocks came knockin' on the door, down by the river Saile.
Der was two policemen and a man, weile weile waile.
Der was two policemen and a man, down by the river Saile.

They took her away, they put her in the gaol, weile weile waile.
They took her away, they put her in the gaol, down by the river Saile.
They put a rope around her neck, weile weile waile.
They put a rope around her neck, down by the river Saile.

They pulled the rope, and she got hung, weile weile waile.
They pulled the rope, and she got hung, down by the river Saile.
Dat was the end of the woman in the woods, weile weile waile.
Dat was the end of the baby too, down by the river Saile.

Weila Weila, Waile – Traditional (19th Century)

BEING A QUIET CROSS STREET TO LEIX and Annaly roads, makes Erris the accepted safe venue for not only our football matches, but also our many other fun-filled street games: Relieve-e-Oh, Hop-Scotch, Marbles, Jackstones, Toss, Leap Frog, Blind Man's Bluff, O'Grady Says, Bicycle Racing, and Kick-the-Can, to mention a few. There's always something happening. If it isn't a football game, it's one of our many street games.

A GROUP of eight of my friends are circled around me. We're within the six-foot-diameter circle we've chalked out on the road.

50

I have my foot planted on an empty Bachelor Beans tin can. We all have our fists extended into the circle, and are in the process of executing the first of a set of rules for our game of Kick-the-Can – the critical exercise of determining who will be *it*.

"One potata, two potata, t'ree potata, four, five potata, six potata, seven potata, more." As I chant, I hit each of the extended fists with my right fist, in clockwise order. The owner of the fist I hit when I chant the word 'more' pulls the fist out and places it behind his back. The process starts off again and continues until one of the group has both fists withdrawn. We use this selection process for most of our games, securing an orderly determination of who will have the dreaded role of being *it*.

Philip Murphy is the first to have both fists withdrawn.

"Gick on it. I hate bein' *it* first," says Philip.

"I'm closin' me eyes, and I'm countin' to twenty," he screeches. "No goin' into houses. Ye have to be on the road or in the gardens. One, two, t'ree . . ." and all the way to twenty; hunkered down in the circle, Philip bangs the can with each count.

I find Mr Lawlor's big tree to hide in: I quickly squirrel my way up into its thick foliage. The others hide behind some wall, behind or under some hedge, all in their chosen hiding spots. From my vantage point up high in the tree, I can see where most of the hide-a-ways have hidden. A little away from me, one of my kind has burrowed his way underneath a big pile of hedge clippings stacked in Lawlor's driveway.

Mr Lawlor's tree is located up close to my front garden. I'm settling down in my perch when out of nowhere, and with more than a little surprise, I see my mother looking up at me. She's furtively standing in our front garden with a small bunch of flowers in her hand. Unbeknown to me, she'd been out gathering some flowers while I was busy hiding.

"You mind yourself, up there in that tree," Peg whispers. To my amazement, she's smiling. My first thought was that I was in deep trouble for being up in Mr Lawlor's tree, but no – that smile on her face is telling me otherwise.

"Philip will never find you up there," she continues, with an almost mischievous twinkle in her eyes. "You're a divil, so you are. Be careful, love. Don't hurt yourself."

And with that, Peg turns and sneaks back into the house.

"Twenty! Coming, ready or not," roars Philip, as the last of the hide-a-ways conceals himself.

The game has two primary and opposing goals. The first goal is directed exclusively to *it*. Philip's goal is to seek, find and call-out each hide-a-way, one at a time. Each of Philip's call-outs has to be called as he simultaneously bangs the tin can *within the circle*. All discovered hide-a-ways become his prisoner. With much shame and vehemence, they deliver themselves to the circle for incarceration. When and if Philip has all of the hide-a-ways imprisoned, he's then declared the winner.

"I see ye, Liam," Philip triumphantly screams, banging the can as he does so. "Ye'er in Buckley's garden behind the yella hedge."

Out comes Liam in disgust. He's wearing a red jumper.

"Knickers!" he declares. "I should've worn me yella jumper."

Much to Philip's delight, Liam slumps his way into prison. Philip is doing well; Liam is his fifth prisoner.

Kick-the-Can always goes that way. The first few easier to find hide-a-ways are imprisoned pretty quickly. However, as the prisoner count rises so does the difficulty in finding the remaining hide-a-ways. Philip had to go maybe forty feet from the circle before he was able to discover where Liam was hiding. It could have resulted in a disaster for Philip.

A real disaster, because of the game's other primary goal, which is directed to all of the hide-a-ways. Those still hiding have a choice: stay hidden from *it* and his intensified search, risking call-out and prison, or take the more daring and dangerous route – go Kick-the-Can! This is a brave and demanding task. However, as with all such tasks, not without its rewards. To kick the can out of the circle results in the kicker being declared the winner. Not only that; the kicker becomes the one to free the prisoners and start the game all over again. Only the bravest hide-a-way risks all for victory and the freedom of his imprisoned friends. He has to be smart and as swift as the best-bowed arrow. He has to be patient, waiting for the right time to strike.

"Where the hell are yees?" shouts Philip in frustration.

It is now moving closer to where my nearby compatriot and I are hiding. As Philip gets nearer to us, he is also getting farther and farther away from the circle. All of a sudden, out bursts Tom Bassett. He'd been hiding in a big empty wooden planter in the middle of one of the gardens on the other side of the road. Seeing Philip so far away from the circle, Tom had bravely decided to go Kick-the-Can. The noise of Tom's scampering towards the circle plus the encouraging cheers from the five freedom-seeking prisoners freezes Philip, for a moment. Defrosting takes only one moment more. Turning quickly, Philip sprints as fast as he can back towards the can. He knows where Tom is, but his call-out requires the simultaneous banging of the can in the circle.

Go, Tom, go! Tom is indeed going. Having jumped out of the planter, he jumps over the garden railings and sprints across the pavement. Unfortunately, he trips: down he goes, sliding on his hands and knees, off the pavement and onto the rough roadway.

Philip reaches the circle and is doing his tin can banging call-out as poor Tom struggles to get up.

"I see ye, Tom," yells Philip. "Ye're sittin' on the road with yer hands and knees all bleedin'."

"Ah, feck off out-a-dat," replies Tom as he struggles to his feet and makes his miserable way to prison.

Nursing his injuries and getting no sympathy from Philip or the prisoners, he sits down with his fellow inmates within the circle.

"Me bleedin' shoe-lace was open," groans Tom. "It tripped me. I'm bleedin'. Have any of ye a hanky?"

No one seems to have one, so Tom plonks himself down feeling the combined pain of his injuries and failure. No doubt the pain of the latter far exceeds that of the former.

Lawlor's tree and the pile of clippings are all that remains in Philip's way to victory. Like the soon-to-be-crowned king he assumes he will become, he stands over the can and glares out over his kingdom. He has to find the last two hide-a-ways. It's at times like this that patience and bravery mean a lot.

"Pssh, Charlie," I whisper. The process of elimination helps me identify who is in the pile of clippings. "Charlie, it's up to us."

"Can ye hear me, Charlie?"

"Yeah," comes Charlie's whispered response. I can't see him – being one of the smallest of my friends, it's easy for him to disappear in the mound of clippings.

"Right, Charlie. When he gets close, move 'round in yer pile. I'll be ready to hop over the railin' and go Kick-the-Can. OK?

"OK, Niall," Charlie whispers back.

Almost an hour has passed since we started the exciting game. I welcome the opportunity to get out of the tree; I've a cramp in my arse from being stuck in one of its forks. I carefully slide out of the fork and down to the ground. Mr Lawlor's railing privet protects me from Philip's view and discovery.

Philip is working his way over to where we are. I can see him through the bushes, heading to Lawlor's driveway. As planned, Charlie moves and gets Philip's attention. Philip has to identify the hide-a-way – he pauses to do so. I jump through the bushes and dash towards the can. Philip sees me go. Turning quickly, he tries to get to the circle before me. The six prisoners are screaming me on. I reach the can and give it a triumphant kick. I'm the winner! All the prisoners are free, and we can now start a new game.

Charlie crawls out of the clippings to join in the celebration. Philip is upset and chooses to exclude himself.

"Gick on it," he moans. "I nearly got yees all."

"DID PHILIP find you?" asks Peg, as I come into the kitchen and the delicious smell of dinner cooking. "I bet he didn't."

"Ye're right, Ma," I answer. "And t'anks, for not givin' away where I was hidin'."

"Sure you're only playing, love. But when you're hiding in Mr Lawlor's tree, be careful. Don't hurt yourself, and don't you be hurting the tree either."

"OK, Ma. And Ma; I kicked the can!"

****

CABRA WAS a grand place to grow up. However, it was badly planned with respect to green areas and playgrounds to play in. Their absence never bothered us, but thinking back, maybe our football and some of the games would have been even more enjoyable if we had been given access to a bit of grass. Our ability to entertain ourselves with nothing other than our imagination and an old tin can was, to say the least, extraordinary. All the games were full of fun and gave us many hours of entertainment.

Some of our games were very dangerous, and 'skate-scuttlin' was particularly so. The 12 Cabra bus terminus was located at the foot of the Fassaugh Avenue railway bridge; we hung out there for our 'skate-scuttlin'. Wearing roller skates, we'd thrill to the real dangers of scuttling behind the buses. We'd daringly wait until the bus conductor gave the signal to the driver to start off. Then we'd skate up to the back of the bus; hunkered down we'd hold on to the bumper and be pulled along Fassaugh Avenue, all the way to the bus stop at the top of Quarry Road – a distance of about a mile. Our love for scuttling was abruptly brought to an end when we learned of some unfortunate scuttler being almost killed and ending up in a wheelchair, severely paralysed.

****

Knickers, Knickers, Nothin' but Knickerses

SATURDAY IS PEG'S BIG WASH DAY. Not having a washing or drying machine, she does all the household laundry by hand. She seems to be forever at the kitchen sink. Whenever I'm looking for Peg, more often than not I find her there, a bar of Sunlight Soap in her hand, hanging over her wooden washboard and a sink full of laundry. The household washing, the hanging out of the wet clothes to dry, and the subsequent ironing takes up a lot of Peg's time.

IT'S SATURDAY, and I'm nine-and-a-half. Last night my Ma gave me my monthly haircut. Using the barber's scissors she'd bought from Boo-Balla, she does a great job cutting my hair. And I'm wearing my re-soled, favourite brown leather shoes. Within my parent's cost-cutting arsenal there's an iron shoe last, a cobbler's blade and hammer plus a can of cobbler's nails. When there's a hole in the sole of my shoes or the heels wear down, Peg gets shoe leather from Billy the cobbler on Dowth Avenue, and Gerry does his cobbler's best to repair them.

Peg has a load of washing. I help her wring out the wet bed sheets. She grabs hold of one end, and I grab a firm hold of the other end. Then, backing away from each other, we twist and twist until the last drop of water is squeezed out. Peg will end up needing some of Mrs Lawlor's clothesline before all the laundry is hanging out in the warm drying breeze.

As Peg is busy hanging out the washing, I'm climbing the tree at the end of our back garden. Conor, my four-year-old brother, is on the grass below me, admiring me as I climb higher and higher.

"Der's lovely dryin' out, Peg," says Mrs Lawlor, as she rests her large pregnant frame against the back-garden railings.

"Lovely indeed, Maggie. Gorgeous altogether and perfect for drying. Tell me, Maggie, how are you and yours this lovely day?"

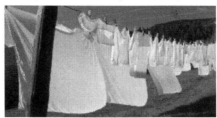

The clothesline.

"I'm grand, Peg. And Mickey and the girls are grand too, t'anks be to God. How are you and Gerry and your gang?"

Before Peg can answer, Maggie, noticing my precarious presence in the tree, turns to me and gasps. Holding both hands to her face in horror, she roars.

"Niall! Would ye look at him, Peg? Up der in harm's way in yer tree. For God's sake, Niall, don't be fallin' and hurtin' yerself. And yer little brother Conor, standin' der under ye."

"Peg, will ye look at him," she continues. "Does he put the heart crossways in ye or w'at? Now, come on down here, Niall, dat's a good boy. Mind yerself. Mind yer little brother."

"I'm alright, Mrs Lawlor," I respond. "I'm a great climber. Conor is laughin'. Look at him; he's laughin' at me."

"Don't be bothering yourself, Maggie," says Peg. "I don't even think about it anymore. That Niall of mine is a lightin' divil. With the hope that God will help me, I'm going to go down next week to Canon O'Callaghan and enrol him as an altarboy in Christ the King. I've been praying to Saint Anthony, but he doesn't seem to be listening.

"Now, behind it all, Niall's a good little boy, and we'd be lost without him. But I'm telling you Maggie, both Gerry and I are going straight to heaven when we die; we're doing all our purgatorial time down here with that little divil, so we are."

"May God and his Blessed Mother give ye strength, Peg," Mrs Lawlor responds. "And may the pair of dem come down and help Mickey and me as well. I've worn out me rosary beads beggin' dem dat Mickey and I will get it right dis time.

"Peg . . . Ye'd t'ink dat after all the girls, they'd find it in dir hearts to answer our prayers and give us a little boy, wouldn't ye?"

"Well, Maggie," is Peg's sincere response. "He and His mother are very busy, what with looking after the entire world and all the poor souls in it. Although He's told us if we knock on His door He'll open it up – so we shouldn't stop praying."

Peg discontinues hanging out her clothes and makes her way towards the garden railings.

"I love me girls, Peg," says Mrs Lawlor tearfully, "but–"

"And isn't it easy to love those girls of yours," interjects Peg. "You should be proud of each and every one of them. How many girls is it that you have anyway, Maggie? Is it seven or eight?"

"Eight, God love me," replies Maggie dejectedly.

"Mickey and meself," Mrs Lawlor continues, blowing her nose with a torn piece of bed linen she had taken from her apron pocket, "we thought the last one was goin' to be a boy when Kathleen was born. Mickey was with me as usual. When he saw it was a girl, wasn't he beside himself. He burst out cryin': 'Where's me son, Maggie?' is what he said to me, 'Where's me son?' And all I could say to the poor man was, next time Mickey, next time. Now, Kathleen was a perfect baby girl – she didn't have a penis, but she did have ten toes and ten fingers, and we welcomed her like all the rest of dem, with open arms. I'll never forget Mickey sayin', 'God's will be done. Next time it'll be a boy, wait 'til ye see, next time it'll be a boy'. And him standin' der, with little Kathleen in his arms and him googlin' at her."

"Now and isn't that a lovely thing," comes Peg's tearful response. "God's will will indeed be done."

"When are you due, Maggie," Peg asks, wiping her tears.

"Nurse O'Donoghue told me in a week. The way I've been feelin', and I don't want to jinx it, Peg, but I hope and pray it'll be a little fella dis time. As Mickey said, 'God's will be done'."

"And it will, Maggie. God's will, will be done."

"It will," says Mrs Lawlor.

"And do ye know w'at, Peg?" she continues. "It's when I'm doin' w'at you're interruptin' yerself from doin' right now, hangin' out the washin', it's den dat it hits me the worst. Knickers, knickers, nothin' but knickerses, is w'at I do be sayin' to meself. I hang dem all out, and more dan half the feckin' line is covered in dem – knickers, knickers, nothin' but knickerses."

Bursting out in laughter, their mirth dispels the solemnity that up to then dominated their conversation.

"Go on with yer hangin', Peg," says Mrs Lawlor. "I've a few t'ings to do inside. And Peg, if ye run out of room, hop over the railin' and ye can use me line," she concludes as she turns and waddles her way into her house.

A FEW days pass, when to the entire neighbourhood's delight, Mickey, Maggie and their eight girls bring home a little fella to Offaly Road. They have their boy at last. Mr Lawlor organises a big party, and everyone turns up.

Learning that the little fella is to be named after his father – Mickey, not Michael – I worry for him. Maybe his dad had managed to get through life with that label, but mickey is a name my friends and I frequently use when referring to a penis.

I decide to call the little fella, Mike and I share my decision with Peg.

"Ma, I'm goin' to call the little fella Mike," says I.

"Why do you want to do that, love?" Peg enquires.

"I don't like Mickey, Ma. And when he gets big like me, he won't like it either. On the road we call our t'ing, mickey."

"Do you now?" my Ma replies. "And isn't that a bold thing for you to be doing? Your thing is your pee-pee, not your mickey, and I don't want you to forget that. You've got to cut out that street talk. Do you hear me now, love?"

"OK, Ma, but can I call him Mike?"

"Oh, God help me with you, Niall," Peg moans. "You'll be the death of me one of these days. You can call him Mike. Now go away and play with your friends. Frank Frazier is over there. Don't forget now; it's your pee-pee, not your mickey."

****

To MRS LAWLOR'S delight, Mike Lawlor grew up and was ordained a priest. Mrs Lawlor had only one son, and bingo, he was ordained. Peg had four sons and not one of us would oblige.

****

Mr Mulligan –
A Smashin' Time

Whiskey, ye're the divil, ye're leadin' me astray,
over hills and mountains and to Americae.
Ye're sweeter, stronger, decenter, ye're spunkier na tae,
oh whiskey, ye're me darlin' drunk or sober.

Law fare ye well, with me-tidery-eye me-doodeldum me-da,
Me-tidery-eye, me-doodeldum, me da,
Me-rikes-fal-tour a laddie,
Oh, der's whiskey in the jar.

Now, brave boys, we're on the march,
off to Portugal and Spain.
Drums a-beatin', banners flyin',
the divil a home we'll see tonight.

Said the mother, "Do not wrong me,
don't take me daughter from me.
For if ye do I will torment ye,
and after death me ghost will haunt ye."

The French are fightin' boldly,
men are dyin' hot and coldly.
Give every man his flask of powder,
his firelock on his shoulder.

Whiskey Ye're the Divil – Jerry Barrington (1873)

T HE MULLIGANS LIVE ACROSS THE ROAD, two houses up from Colleen's house. Mr Mulligan, his wife Sallie and their two children, Patrick and Ronan, were at Mike Lawlor's homecoming party. Throughout the festivities, Mr Mulligan never touched a drop. Lemonade is what he had. And it had to be that way: Mr Mulligan is an alcoholic.

Sober, he's very sociable and much liked by all the neighbours. He works for one of the big law firms in Dublin city. All the neighbours go to Mr Mulligan for advice on legal matters, always given freely and with genuine interest and concern.

Typically, we see him arrive home from work before six. If we're playing ball on the road, he often comes off the pavement, out onto the roadway and joins us in our game, feinting tackles, kicking the ball and such. When his sons are playing, he calls out to them: "That's my boys; trying to take the ball from your Da, are you?" or, "Get it in the goal, Patrick! Where are you, Ronan?"

The Mulligans are perhaps the most respected family in Cabra. That is until Mr Mulligan goes on the binge. It doesn't often happen, maybe once or twice a year, but when it does, things always turn out the same – Mr Mulligan has a smashing time.

The onsets of these much-dreaded events are easily identified: Mr Mulligan is late coming home from work. Seven comes and goes and once it does, and Mr Mulligan has not yet arrived home, the red flag is raised. The Mulligan curse has struck again; like wildfire, the word goes out. Batten down your hatches – he'll be arriving soon, and we'd all better get ready for it.

It's TEN past seven, and Mr Mulligan is not home! The children know what is about to happen, just like the adults do. We all evacuate from the otherwise alive Erris roadway. With Patrick and Ronan in hand, Mrs Mulligan leaves her home and goes to one of the understanding neighbours. Sequestered in our homes, and with only the bravest of us looking out through the windows, we prepare ourselves for the entire event which usually lasts for as much as two hours. Mrs Mulligan always leaves her front door ajar and the front garden gate wide open.

The imminent appalling proceedings have a vulgar audio intro.

"Bollocks! Ye're only a bollocks!" Mr Mulligan screams as he falls around the Leix Road corner onto Erris. "Come on out! I dare ye! Ye're only a bollocks!" He has a limited vocabulary when langered drunk – and his limit is not yet reached.

"Fuck ye!" he roars, reaching his verbal limit.

Mr Mulligan makes his faltering way down Erris. Wisely, he keeps to the middle of the road rather than the pavement from which he would undoubtedly fall. Eventually, he reaches his front gate. It's then that the first of a series of smashing events occur.

Mr Mulligan grabs the gate his wife has left open, and with the ferocity of a sumo wrestler, he smashes it closed. Opening it again, he repeats the process for maybe fifty times. He renders one of his profane expletives after each bang: "Fuck ye!" The noise of his smashing is shocking. Each bang has us blink in agony, making us wish it was the last; then that set of pains would stop, and we'd move on to the next set, and nearer to the end of the entire event.

Mr Mulligan is sweating up a storm. His tie is widely loosened. To recover some of his energy, he sits or more like throws himself down on the gateway's step. Refreshed to the level where he can drag himself erect, he stands up and staggers his way to the front door. Mrs Mulligan had left the front gate open in a failed attempt to trick her beloved into forgetting about his impulsive gate smashing; she is now no doubt on her knees praying that her front door trick will work. Joining her in her hopes for success, the entire neighbourhood have their fingers firmly crossed. This time it works: after three or four failed attempts to mount the front doorstep, Mr Mulligan somehow manages to throw himself inside the house. Rather than being subjected to another set of smashes, we're treated to a short period of peace and quiet. Far too short a period – after a few minutes he re-emerges.

"Ye're only a bollocks!" Mr Mulligan roars as he stumbles out the door and wobbles his way to the back of the house. During this time we hear some low sounding shuffling; there are no expletives – just a lot of grunting and a few loud thuds.

After about ten minutes, he reappears hauling a big ladder behind him. He drags the ladder into the front garden. With guidance and agility which could only have come from the devil himself, he places the ladder up against the front wall. Moving it over, he positions the top of the ladder on the upstairs bedroom window sill. He climbs up, and with the guidance of that devil, plus the two-pound hammer he had equipped himself with, he smashes every pane of glass in the upstair's window.

"Fuck ye!" he shouts, after each smash. Each window has six panes, ending up with a rendering of six smashes and six expletives plus a heck of a lot of broken glass.

Once he's demolished the upstairs window, he somehow manages to climb down the ladder; and as if what he had accomplished wasn't enough, he then mounts the parlour window sill and smashes in those six panes as well. Six more smashes, each accompanied with its vulgar invective.

Mustering all of the remaining energy in his tired, over-pickled, bibulous body, Mr Mulligan concludes his disgraceful display by standing in the middle of the front garden and roaring.

"Fuck Ye!!" he roars. "Now . . . Ye're only a bollocks!!"

Feeling exhausted, yet very much pleased with himself, he hauls the ladder back to its place in the back-garden, puts his trusty hammer away and retires for the night. All the smashing is limited to the front of the house. Mr Mulligan sleeps in the back – he can't be bothered with all that broken glass. Into his bed he goes, and with all the drink in him, he sleeps like a baby.

How's that for the actions of our pissed-out-of-his-mind, otherwise much-respected neighbour? And aren't we lucky? It only happens once or twice a year.

"Janey Mack, Ma," says I, as I release my face from the parlour window. "Mr Mulligan is bold doin' all dat, and he curses a lot. W'at's Mrs Mulligan goin' to do with him?"

"He's very audacious, love," says Peg. "Poor Mrs Mulligan; she's doing her purgatory down here living with him. Sallie's a good woman, but I don't know how she puts up with it. If he were mine, I'd have thrown him out a long time ago. As proper as he can be all the year, and then the demon drink grabs hold of him."

"He ought to be ashamed of himself," Peg continues. "Why can't he be as good as your daddy and cut out all that drinking?"

Conor and I with our Da.

63

Gerry is sitting in his chair reading the *Evening Herald*. Lowering the paper, and with a grin on his face, he winks at me.

"I know it's only now and again he's this way," my mother goes on, "but with the trouble he's giving his poor wife and little Patrick and Ronan, he's a holy disgrace. He's lucky he's living on our road. If he were on Leix or Annaly, the neighbours there would have the gardaí with their Black Maria for him. And it wouldn't be his own bed he'd be sleeping in – it'd be in Mountjoy gaol."

"Well, he won't do it again, Ma," I respond, trying to minimise Mr Mulligan's boldness. I understand, directly from my mother, that I'm sometimes bold like Mr Mulligan is. I feel obliged to come to the defence of the accused.

"Not until the next time, darlin'," responds Peg.

With Mr Mulligan having concluded his thing and now snoring in his bed, Mrs Mulligan and her children along with Peg and one or two of the other neighbours go over to the house and start to do their thing. We all join in and clean up the mess.

We know the routine. Mrs Mulligan retrieves her stored pre-cut sheets of thick clear plastic from the backyard shed and dusts them off. Using the roll of masking tape that Mr Ryan, the local glazier had gifted her, she carefully sticks the plastic sheets up on the two windows. While she's doing this, the rest of the crew are engaged clearing up the broken glass.

"You know, Peg," Mrs Mulligan says apologetically. "Andy never lays a hand on the children or me. The drink is his weakness, and I thank the Lord that he's given me the strength to put up with him. Andy is my man, and I'll always stand by him."

"Sure and I know, Sallie," my mother replies. "And haven't we all got our cross to carry. Look at my Niall – an angel he his, just like your Andy, but there are times, Sallie; times when the divil sneaks into them. I'm telling you, we've all got our cross to carry."

As the clean-up crew does its work, Mr Mulligan can be heard snoring in his bed. Nevertheless, like magic, and as if nothing had ever happened, he'll be up early the following morning making the breakfast for his loving family. As my mother said, 'As proper as he can be all the year, and then . . .'

"How's yer Da?" I ask Patrick, as we play ball together early the following morning. "He was bold last night. Is yer Ma OK?"

64

"Yeah," Patrick responds. "He was bold, but he's grand now. Me Ma will be OK once Mr Ryan comes and fixes the windas."

****

PATRICK MULLIGAN, the eldest of Mr Mulligan's two sons, was to join the Saint Columba's Mission Society and would die in Africa doing missionary work.

****

Peg's Master Plan

FROM THE VERY BEGINNING, MY MOTHER HAS had designs for me. Drafting me into being an altarboy is stage one of her master plan; me becoming a seminarian at All Hallows Seminary is stage two, and having me ordained a priest is stage three. Maybe, if all goes right, stage four will be her Niall becoming a bishop.

PEG HAS me firmly in hand. We're impatiently lying in wait for Canon O'Callaghan to come out of Christ the King church after his ten o'clock mass. Eventually, he appears. The canon looks like a somewhat slimmer Winston Churchill; his deep voice is a perfect match to Winston's, albeit with a County Leitrim accent. Having been recently promoted from parish priest to canon, he's proudly wearing his bright purple, rabat vest. His white clerical collar is deeper than an ordinary priest's collar – this extra collar depth plus his purple vest gives him a papal presence.

"Father, if you have a minute. I'd like to talk to you about my Niall," says Peg. "It'll only take a minute, father. I can see you're running, but can you spare me a minute?"

"Well, I'm on me way to the Mater," the canon replies. "It's Mr Finley ye know: the Lord seems to be callin' him. And didn't his good wife ask me to go down and administer Extreme Unction to the poor man – to help him on his way."

"Just one minute, father. My Niall has a longing for the altar," pleads Peg. *She's lyin': she's makin' me do dis. Me only longin' is that she'll leave me alone and let me get back to me friends.*

"He's the makings of a grand altarboy, father," says Peg, quickly laying it all out for him. "You won't regret it, father. He'll never disappoint you." Looking down at me, she adds: "Sure you won't, Niall?"

Turning back to the harassed canon, Peg pushes it further.

"Tell me, father: when can he come down to the sacristy and sign up?"

The canon knows my mother. She often attends his daily ten o'clock mass, and when she does, she always receives the Eucharist. Those close-up, face-to-face encounters have a way of burning images in one's mind.

The canon is trapped, and he has a dying man, Mr Finley, waiting for him in Eccles Street's Mater Misericordiae Hospital.

"And isn't there always room on the altar for good boys, Mrs, eh–." Rapid name recall is not the canon's strongest attribute.

"Kavanagh of Erris, father," assists Peg.

"That's right now. Yes, yes, ye're Mrs Kavanagh. Have eh, have eh–." That name recall problem of his strikes again.

"Niall, father," Peg prompts.

"That's right now. Yes, yes, Niall. Have Niall drop into me after school on Monday. We'll have a chat then, won't we, Niall," says the canon, as he hits the top of my head with his thick leather-bound daily missal.

"God bless you, father," says Peg, stepping back and allowing the opportunity for him to escape.

"Say thanks to father, Niall," Peg adds, poking at me as the unfettered canon moves towards his car and his duties to the dying.

"T'anks, father," says I as the canon squashes himself into his cardinal red Volkswagen Beetle. "I'll see ye Monday."

"God bless yee both," concludes the canon.

"Niall, we're on your way!" my mother cheers. Looking down at me penetratingly closely, she continues. "You'll be ordained before you know it."

She can see the bishop's collar already.

****

PEG'S PLAN for me becoming pope was considered, yet there was never an Irish pope. The nearest the Irish got to that was way back in 1154, when an Englishman, Nicholas Breakspear was elected. Pope Adrian IV he was called. He had short innings; he died in 1159, soon after he presented his Adrian's Bull to King Henry-II of England giving Henry permission to invade Ireland, "*. . . for the correction of morals and the introduction of virtues for the* *advancement of the Christian religion."* Saint Patrick, it would appear, didn't do a good enough job. Adrian wished Henry well when he said to him, *"May the people of that land receive thee with honour, and venerate thee as their master. Provided always that the rights of the church remain inviolate and entire, and saving to Saint Peter and the holy Roman Church, the annual pension of one penny from each house."* Rome's need for money played its part in Henry's pursuit to tame the savage Irish and make us more God fearing. England's eight-hundred-year dominion over Ireland was about to start, and it would do so with the blessings of an English pope.

Pope Adrian-IV.   *King Henry-II.*

****

A Dame Squeezed a Pussy Cat...

IT'S 1952, AND THE ROMAN CATHOLIC MASS is celebrated in Latin. It takes weeks of intensive study for me to become an able altarboy. In 1969, Pope Paul VI will decree that vernacular celebration of the mass is the way to go. For the first time, the general congregation will know what's being said.

Due to the amount of time I spend studying, or as my Da calls it, 'learning the Latin', I miss out on lots of playing time. Peg is close to being in heaven, and I'm happy about that. I rule the roost during these gruelling weeks of study – being the centre of attention, staying up late and being allowed all sorts of liberties.

As an altarboy at Christ the King, a fate worse than death is when checking the mass roster in the sacristy, you find your name opposite Canon O'Callaghan's. An average mass takes thirty-five minutes. There's a Father (Flash) Kavanagh who'd have you in and out in twenty minutes, and at the other end of the spectrum there's Canon O'Callaghan – his masses last for more than an hour. Between the prep and tidying-up, more than two hours are stolen from the few the day gives. Whenever it happens to me, I check out the names of the three other altarboys who've been dealt the same disturbing hand.

I'VE BEEN dealt the dreaded hand – I have to serve at one of the canon's masses. Frank Frazier is one of the other three altarboys. *Great! Frank is on with me. I'll have a-bit-a-gas with him.* Frank is the local postman's son, and as my mother often says, 'That Frank Frazier is a bold one.' He lives on Galmoy Road, next door to the tall bloke who stole Colleen's heart and broke mine.

"How'ye doin', Frank," says I, greeting him as he comes into the sacristy. While I'm always punctual, a product of one of my

69

Da's many maxims, namely, 'The early bird catches the worm,' Frank, not unlike the mail his father delivers, is always late.

"Massive, Niall," Frank pants. He's rushing to gear himself up in his cassock and surplice. With O'Callaghan being the canon he is, we'll be using the red surplice: the white surplice is used when serving at masses celebrated by ordinary priests.

Altarboy.

"How are you?" Frank continues. "Like meself – not lookin' forward to the next couple of hours, I bet."

"Right, Frank. It's brutal bein' on with the canon."

Canon O'Callaghan has completed his dressing. Armed with his trusty daily missal, he's now rounding up Frank, me and the two other altarboys for our grand entrance to the altar.

"Late again, I see," the Canon declares as he passes by Frank, walloping him on the head with his missal.

"Yer mammy was right, Niall," says the canon. "Ye never let me down. We should never keep the Lord waiting," he adds as he turns back to Frank, giving him a second shot with his missal.

"Will yee all come along, now!? There are souls to be saved out there. Niall, you go first, and Frank-come-lately will follow ye. Then yee two good boys take the rear after me."

I don't know the good boys, and that's no surprise. I'm never one to hang around and befriend good boys. It's not that I consider myself any better than them, it's simply that they never appear as coming anyway close to my established standards for having fun. To me, being 'good' equates to being bored out of my mind.

Part of what makes the canon's mass so long has to do with the way he gets himself to the foot of the altar. He seems to be suddenly stricken with a severe bout of something ill-effecting his ability to walk. To say he takes shuffling baby steps doesn't describe it well enough. It takes us as much as five minutes to get out to the altar.

Ad Déum qui laetíficat juventútem méam is the altarboy's opening line of the Latin mass. Its translation is, *I will go to the altar of God, to God, the joy of my youth*. Pretty appropriate, don't you think; however, what Frank Frazier and I are about to do with it is most inappropriate; it will bring Canon O'Callaghan closer to a mortaler than his otherwise cloistered life has ever brought him.

Creeping our way out, Frank starts a whispered conversation. "I've an idea, Niall. Do ye know dat *'Ad Déum qui la–'* opener?"

"Yeah, Frank. W'at about it?"

"Do ye know w'at it means?"

"No, Frank. Do you?"

"No, and other dan for O'Callaghan, nobody else does either. But do ye know w'at it sounds like?" continues Frank. Before I can reply, he informs me of the answer – an answer that I would have failed to supply had he given me sufficient time to respond.

"*A dame squeezed a pussy cat walkin' down the lane! Ad Déum qui laetíficat juventútem méam*. They're the same!"

"Janey Mack, Frank!" I reply, trying my best to keep a straight face and not burst out laughing. "Let's say dat. I can see O'Callaghan when he hears us. It'll be great."

"Yeah, Niall. We'll say it together. The good boys won't join in. Let's say it loud and drown dem out."

We finally arrive at our assigned positions at the foot of the altar. The vernacular mass hasn't arrived, nor has the change of having the celebrant face the congregation on the other side of the altar. We are all facing the altar with our backs to the congregation.

One of the good boys rings the altar bell – the kick-off signal that the mass has begun.

The moment for Frank and I to do our thing has arrived.

"*A dame squeezed a pussy cat walkin' down the lane*," we chant, at an audio level that smothers the correct rendering being simultaneously rendered by the two good boys.

71

"Good God Almighty!" whispers the canon, but clearly heard by all on the front line. "When I get yee inside, it'll be meself that'll be pussy-catin' the pair of yee. Yee're a right pair of heathens. Yee're in for it. Just wait. If I don't kill yee, it'll only be by the grace of God himself."

Normally there's a formal Latin response to the altarboy's opener: the canon's irate response isn't it. It's probably the most impassioned reply he has ever made to anything, but like our embellished opener, it has no place in the rites of the mass.

The canon's enraged response borders on being a mortal sin. He's called us heathens, and he's threatened to kill us. Frank and I are delighted with the outcome of our irreverent and perfectly executed prank: we've shocked Canon O'Callaghan beyond our wildest expectations. Despite our overwhelming sense of achievement, an amount of apprehension regarding what might happen to us barges into our consciousness.

Knowing the show must go on, the canon mounts the steps and continues with the mass. Somehow, he's able to put what he wants to do aside, for now.

Seeing the canon's angry expression during the mass is an added pleasure. His face colour coordinates with his purple vest, revealing his seething rage. However, it is also a reminder to Frank and me of his impending wrath.

While we're not excommunicated, what happens in the sacristy after mass certainly comes close to it.

"Yee two heathens!" bellows the canon. "Get yerselfs out of this sacristy before I commit a grievous sin."

We don't need any encouragement. We quickly disrobe, and miraculously we avoid being beaten to death with the canon's missal.

****

As Thick as Thieves

Cᴀɴᴏɴ O'ᴄᴀʟʟᴀɢʜᴀɴ'ѕ ᴡᴀʏ ᴏꜰ ʀᴇᴀᴘɪɴɢ ʀᴇᴠᴇɴɢᴇ is a given. He rats to my mother – and that brings down the wrath of God on me altogether.

"Gᴇᴛ ᴜᴘ to your room!" Peg growls. "You wait until your father comes home. If he doesn't kill you, I will. It's your room you'll be in for the rest of your life. How dare you, you little demon!"

My distressed mother lunges at me and gives me her open right hand across my face. Its force sends me against the kitchen wall. I whack my head against the tea caddie shelf and go unconscious.

I wake up in my mother's arms on the parlour couch. She's stroking my hair and drowning me with tears pouring from her aching eyes – two or three of her salty tears fall right into my eyes. Peg's aches are from her loving, overwhelming concern for me plus her shame for having hit me the way she had. My aches are from the pain in my head and the sting on my left cheek plus the shame for having upset my mother the way I had.

"Niall," she cries. "I'm awful sorry I did that to you. Are you all right? Look at me, darlin'. How many fingers do I have up?"

"T'ree, Ma," I answer correctly, and much to my mother's joy.

"I'm alright, Ma. Me head's hurtin'," I continue, rubbing where my head had smacked into the shelf.

"Let me see it, love," she asks, moving me to examine one of the injuries she had inflicted.

"Oh, my God! Look at what I've done to you. You're going to have a bump the size of an egg. God forgive me. And Niall, love, I want you to forgive me too. I'm a bad mother."

"No ye're not, Ma," I whine. "Sure I deserve it. Frank and I were only havin' a-bit-a-gas, but we were bold, and we shouldn't have done it. The canon was right to tell on us, and we deserve what we get. I'm bold to be upsettin' ye, Ma. I won't do it again. I swear Ma, I'm goin' to be good from now on."

"Forget all about that for now, love," Peg demands, wiping away my tears with a piece of her apron. "Let me see your face." She turns my head to examine injury number two.

"Holy Mother of God. The mark of my five fingers is on your face. Sit there love; let me go and get something cold to put on it."

Taking me from her knee, she runs into the kitchen and quickly returns with a dampened cloth.

"Hold that to your face, love. It'll bring the swelling down."

There's a statue of Saint Anthony of Padua on the mantelpiece – he's holding the baby Jesus in his arms. While I'm poulticing my cheek with the cold, wet dishcloth, Peg solemnly wanders her way over to Anthony. She's starts talking to him: "Saint Anthony guide me. If ever I need you, it's now. What am I going to do with him?"

While all this is going on, Conor, my little brother is playing in the backyard with his toy soldiers. He appears at the door.

"Niall, will ye play with me," he pleads.

"Not now, Conor," my mother replies. "Niall is having a little rest, and he's talking with his mammy. Now, there's a good boy; go and play on your own for a minute. Niall will be out to you when he's rested, and we're finished talking."

"Yeah, Conor," I add. "Line up yer soldiers. We'll have a battle when I go out to ye." Satisfied with what he had heard, Conor playfully returns to the backyard, leaving Peg and me alone.

"I'm telling you, Niall, you're going to be the death of me. I know behind it all you're a good boy. What gets into you!? I'm going to have to punish you for that awful thing you did on the altar. What possessed you to do such a thing?"

"I don't expect you to answer me," she continues. "I've asked Saint Anthony to guide me. Here's what we're going to do.

"I'm ashamed of myself for hitting you the way I did, and I hope you're ashamed too, for being bold and upsetting your mother the way you have. All my plans for you becoming a priest can be thrown out like rancid butter. It'll be okay if Canon O'Callaghan doesn't end up excommunicating you for your boldness, and me along with you for being your mother.

74

"There'll be no more playing outside for you until I see fit. It's in your room or playing with your little brother in the back garden from now on. I'm not going to upset your father by telling him of your going-ons. And that's because I couldn't face him after hitting you the way I did. So . . . You and I are going to keep it to ourselves. And if I see you with that Frank Frazier fella again I'll, I'll . . . There's no telling what I'll do to you."

"OK, Ma," I reply. "We won't tell anyone."

"Right, Niall. Now, you keep that poultice on your face and lie there. Never you mind Conor. He'll play with himself. I want you to lie quiet and rest until your Da comes home. Please God, your face will be all right."

"Don't worry, Ma. If me Da notices, I'll tell him I fell out of the tree."

"Now, only if he notices it. I don't want you telling lies."

"OK, Ma," says I.

The deal is done to our mutual satisfaction. Peg and I have become as thick as thieves.

****

UNTIL NOW, I've never spoken of that bonding incident to anyone. Peg is probably screaming her head off with me telling you.

But Peg, know that by me talkin' about it, I'm expressin' how much of a great mother you were. That event made me love you more. And don't forget, for maybe five or six weeks I was the best little devil any mother could ever want to have. Do you remember Ma, do you remember?

I'm hearing my loving mother answer me.

"Do I remember? Niall love, will I ever forget?!"

What a precious life I had in my early years. And how lucky was I to have a father and mother like Peg and Gerry? All those colourful neighbours and friends – where would I be without them? In a far poorer place, that's for sure.

****

Yo-yos, the Wage-packet & Confession

THE YO-YO CRAZE HAS HIT DUBLIN. The American yo-yo
aficionado, Jack Russell has come to town to show us how to
Walk the Dog, Rock the Baby, Loop-the-Loop and Climb the
Rope. Jack uses the cinemas to stage his demonstrations. His
shows are usually held on Saturday mornings when the children
are out of school, and the otherwise empty cinemas are available.

During Jack's displays, he invites members of the audience to
go on stage, compete in competitions, and win some of his much
sought-after yo-yos. Philip Murphy and I attend as many of his
shows as we can, and we ardently participate. We never win any
of the competitions, but we usually come away with a couple of
fancy yo-yos.

PHILIP AND I are on the number 12 bus, on our way to the State
Theatre in Phibsborough. It's a little after nine in the morning; as
usual, we'll be at the head of the queue so's to make sure we'll get
good seats up close to the stage. The show is scheduled to start at
ten o'clock. Jack will be there, mesmerising us with his incredible
yo-yo tricks and inspiring us to heights of yo-yoing skills that few
if any of us will ever reach.

As early as we are, there's a mob of kids ahead of us, milling
around the cinema's entrance.

"I hope Bulldog isn't on this mornin'," says I to Philip, as we
jump off the bus at the Phibsborough Library bus stop.

"Bulldog's always on," answers Philip. "Let's get close to the
wall. He nearly bruised me with the belt in the arm he gave me the
last time we were here."

76

We call the cinema's head usher, Bulldog. As the name suggests, he has a fierce looking, jowled face with a large bulbous nose to match. His primary purpose of being is to usher, or herd is a more accurate way of describing it, the balloons of kids outside the cinema and put us into some resemblance of an orderly queue. He barks his demands for order, pushing the kids into his requisite shape as he does so. He's dressed in a military-like green uniform and cap; his outfit has more gold and brass than any of General Patton's uniforms ever had.

"Get yerselfs in line," he barks. "None of ye are gettin' in if ye don't get into a queue. And no cuttin'. Anyone found cuttin' goes to the back of the queue."

Philip and I escape being bruised by Bulldog. We're squashed a bit, but we survive. Jack Russell doesn't disappoint us, and we come away with two of his new fancy ball bearing yo-yos.

We've come out of the crowded cinema, and I notice our bus is coming around Berkeley Road.

"Run Philip, quick," I shout. "Der's a 12 comin'."

"Let's get to the bus stop before the rest of them," I continue. "They'll fill it up, and then we'll have to wait for the next bus."

We push our way on board and are half way up the stairs to the top deck when I see it. There it is, lying on one of the steps – an opened wage-packet with some of its contents sticking out of the envelope.

I bend down, pick the wage-packet up and surreptitiously shove it into my pocket. *I can't believe it! Der must be a load of mula in it. I'm not goin' to tell Phil. If I tell him, I'll have to share it. Finders, keepers. I found it, and I'm keepin' it.*

I feel no guilt. What I've purloined is someone's wages. What I should be doing is giving the wage-packet to the first garda I see, not appropriating it and assuming ownership. I don't give a moment's thought to the poor unfortunate worker who had dropped his undoubtedly hard-earned and much-needed wages.

It is in the early-fifties, and Dublin city's businesses pay their staff weekly and in cash. While some of the larger employers have the required money delivered by armoured cars, the majority have a couple of their toughest staff go down to the bank and collect it. The company's payroll department breaks up the money into each employee's due wages, inserting the cash into the employee's wage-packet.

Phil and I have alighted the bus and are walking up Erris Road when the first sign of fitting retribution for my selfish, uncaring act comes about.

"Gick on it," I exclaim. "I left me yo-yo on the bus."

"Ye can kiss it goodbye, Niall," says Phil. "I bet ye one of the lads on the bus picked it up. Ye'll never get it back."

I say goodbye to Phil, go into my house and run up the stairs to my bedroom. My right hand has a firm sweaty grip on the hidden wage-packet shoved deep in my trousers' pocket. I can't wait to find out how much is in the envelope. Having closed the door behind me, I extract the dampened wage-packet. The owner's name is on the front, beside a red stamp identifying the company's name –

JACOB BISCUITS – Patrick Boylan

Jays! I know him! He lives 'round the corner on Fertullagh Road. This is the second sign of fitting retribution for my callous act. *How much is in it anyway?* I carefully take the money out. It's a whopping six pounds, fifteen shillings and nine pence: a five-quid note, a quid, a ten-bob note, two half-crowns, a tanner and a truppenny bit. My trembling hands have never held so much cash.

But Boylan is a nice ol' fella. He sometimes gives the kids bags of broken biscuits that he brings home from his work. Only last week didn't he give me a bag of broken Mikado, those gorgeous biscuits with coconut chips all over the marshmallow and strawberry top. I'll have to give it back to him.

I sit down on the bed, undreamt-of wealth in my hands, and a colossal aching, guilt-generated tug in my heart. *Nobody'll ever know if I keep it. I can hide it away with me Holy Communion mula. I can buy sweets and go to the pictures hundreds of times. I can get a new bell for me bike. I can even give me Ma a loan of a pound when she runs out.*

I'm drowning in guilt. *If I keep it, it'll be stealin'. And that's not like boxin'-the-fox, nickin' a few apples off Buckley's apple tree. It'll be real stealin'. No, I've got to give it back. Maybe I'll take the ten-bob note or maybe the quid. But I'm goin' to give most of it back. A quid is a lot of mula. I'll only take ten bob. But how'll*

I give the mula back to Boylan? I'll drop it into his letterbox. I'll do it tonight when it's dark, and nobody will see me.

With a tolerable amount of guilt, I settle on the ten-bob-for-me arrangement.

I take my filthy lucre and stash it away with my Holy Communion money. The remaining six pounds five shillings and nine pence is returned to the wage-packet and safely shoved back into my pocket. That night, guilty as hell and gratefully undetected, I drop the lightened wage-packet into Mr Boylan's letterbox.

"What are you doing out at this time of night, Niall?" my Ma enquiries, as I come through the back door into the kitchen.

"I lost me new yo-yo, Ma," I answer. "I went up to Phil to see if he had it," I lie. "He didn't. I must have left it on the bus."

"If you like I'll check out CIE's lost and found," Peg replies. "Maybe someone will hand it in."

"I bet another kid found it and kept it. It was one of Jack Russell's new yo-yos."

"I suppose you're right, Niall. Anyway, you've a load of those yo-yos. It's time for your bed. Wash your hands and face, brush your teeth, and get a good night's sleep. That's a good boy."

I do two of the three things my Ma asked me to do – I find it tough to go asleep. *I wonder w'at Boylan will say when he sees his wage-packet on the floor at his front door. Maybe he won't notice the missin' ten bob, and maybe he'll think he dropped it when he was goin' into his house.*

I CAN'T wait to go to confession. The Sacrament of Penance and Reconciliation is celebrated on Saturday mornings in Christ the King, and it's a full week since I stole that ten bob from Mr Boylan. I've spent the entire sleep-disturbed week worrying about what I'd done. While I am not, and never have been, an angel – Peg would be the first one to validate that – this private, personal, wrongful act of stealing ten bob from Mr Boylan is, to me, by far the worst thing I have ever done.

I very much regret taking the money. I imagine that God must be real pissed off with me. I'm ashamed of stealing it. Especially from Mr Boylan, one of the nicest ol'fellas in the neighbourhood.

I'm in desperate need of reconciliation and ache to restart my life with an immaculately new clean slate.

In I go to the church. There are eight confession boxes, four on each side of the nave. The names of the priests hearing confessions are over the centre section of the confession box within which the priest sits and administers the sacrament. Each confession box has two penitent doors, one to the left of the priest and one to the right. The sinners enter, kneel down, confess their sins, receive their penance and get absolution. As soon as they've completed their assigned penance, Bob's-yer-uncle, they're given a brand-new clean slate! It's a pretty neat process and one I'm much in need of.

The Confession box.

I walk up the nave and check out the names posted on each of the Confession boxes. *No way am I goin' to the canon or Father Burke. They're tough priests.* Flash Kavanagh's box has three pews of penitents waiting to be serviced. *I'll go to Flash. He's the easiest. I'll be able to tell him without havin' me heart in me mouth worryin' about what he'll say to me.*

After more than a half-an-hour of sliding along with the three pews of sinners, I arrive at the top of the line. I go into the confession box and kneel down. The box is dark and stays that way when the priest's small sliding door opens. Through the wire mesh screen, I can make out Flash's profile.

"'Name the Father, 'Son and 'Holy Ghost 'men," flashes Flash.

"Bless me, father, for I've sinned. It's been t'ree weeks since me last confession. I accuse meself of the followin' sins:

"I told me Ma lies a few times, father. I hid me brother Paddy's pen on him, and he got mad at me, father."

"And is there anything else, child?" asks Flash.

"I had some impure thoughts, father."

"And did you entertain them, child."

"I did, father. A little bit, father."

"And is there anything else, child?"

"Yes, father. I, I, I—"

"What is it, child," he encourages. "Is it something you said or something you did? Quick now. Tell me child."

"Somethin' I did, father."

"Come now, child. Tell the Almighty God and me what it was you did. Are you sorry you did it?"

"I'm awful sorry I did it, father."

"Well, that's the important thing, child. Tell me what you did and through me his servant, God will absolve you of your sins and give you the strength to amend your ways. Now tell me, child."

"I, I found a wage-packet and I, I kept it," I mumble.

"Speak up, child. I can't hear you."

Bringing my mouth to kissing distance from the wire screen, I repeat what I had said and add, "But it was Mr Boylan's, so I gave it back to him. But I, I, kept ten bob for meself."

"You stole ten shillings from the poor man. Is that what you're telling me, child?"

"Yeah, father."

"Is that everything?"

"Yeah, father. For dese and all me sins, I ask God's pardon, penance, and absolution, father," is my sincere response.

"For your penance, say the Rosary. Now say a good Act of Contrition."

"I will, father: *Oh my God, I'm sorry for havin' offended ye, and I hate me sins above every other evil, but most of all because they offend ye, who's all good and deserves all me love. I firmly resolve, with the help of yer grace, to sin no more. Amen.*"

Flash then gives me absolution. "I absolve you of your sins in the name of the Father, the Son and of the Holy Ghost. Amen."

"Go in peace," flashes Flash as he slams the screen door shut.

Up I get off my knees, and with all that weight of guilt and shame now removed, I feel as light as a feather. *Now, all I've got to do is do me penance. I'll say the rosary and then I'll have a brand new clean slate. Great!*

81

I commit myself to thinking about the ten bob as a reward for finding the lost wage-packet. *If it were anyone else that found the bleedin' wage-packet, they'd have kept the whole bleedin' lot!*

****

PAYING WAGES in cash was enforced by the Trade Unions. A lot of workers didn't have bank accounts. That, plus the fact that there was often little if any trust between the workers and management, made the wage-by-cash practice universal. In the late fifties/early sixties, a surge of holdups by the IRA made wage-by-cheque or bankers' transfer the standard safe way for workers to receive their earnings.

****

Insolvency & Mr Cohen

What'll ye have, will ye have a pint?
Yes, I'll have a pint with you, sir.
And if one of us doesn't order soon,
we'll be thrown out of the boozer.

Says my ol' one to your ol' one,
*   "Will ye come to the Waxie's Dargle?"*
Says your ol' one to my ol' one,
*   "Sure I haven't got a farthin'.*
I've just been down to Monto town,
*   to see Uncle McArdle,*
but he wouldn't lend me a half a crown,
*   to go to the Waxie's Dargle."*

Says my ol' one to your ol' one,
*   "Will ye come to the Galway races?"*
Says your ol' one to my ol' one,
*   "With the price of me ol' lad's braces.*
I went down to Capel Street,
*   to the pawn shop money lenders,*
but they wouldn't give me a half a crown,
*   on me ol' lad's red suspenders."*

Says my ol' one to your ol' one,
*   "We've got no beef nor mutton.*
But if we go down to Monto town,
*   we might get a drink for nothin'.*
Here's a piece of good advice,
*   I got from an ol' fish-monger.*
When food is scarce and ye see the hearse,
*   ye'll know ye've died of hunger."*

The Waxie's Dargle – Peadar Kearney (1916)

WE'RE SITTING IN THE PARLOUR. PEG IS worried sick. She's looking down at her near-empty purse lying open on her lap.

Money is always a problem, but right now the lack of it is bringing Peg close to her wits' end.

"What am I going to do?" I hear her say, more to herself than to me. "Here we are, it's only Tuesday, and we've less than a pound to last us until Friday and Gerry's next wage packet."

"I've got a few bob, Ma," I offer. "I'll go up and get it for ye."

"You're a good boy, Niall. Beggars can't be choosers, so go and get it for me now, love. I'll give it back to you on Friday."

I go up to my room and bring down Mr Boylan's ten bob note – my immodest contribution to the solving of this latest edition of what to me is a constant state of household insolvency.

Mr Boylan's ten-bob.

It's seven years since the end of the Second World War, and times are hard in Ireland. The US Marshall Plan is helping to rebuild Europe, but the little amount of funding given to Ireland doesn't have much positive effect. Ireland had remained neutral during WWII and had allowed the continued presence of both the German and Japanese Legations in Dublin. When Adolf Hitler committed suicide in 1945, Ireland's President Éamon de Valera visited the German minister to express his sympathy and sign the book of condolence. Ireland's neutrality, together with this overt act of De Valera's, damaged Ireland's standing with the allies and particularly so with Britain and the USA.

"That's grand, Niall," says Peg, as I hand her the ten bob.

"Will we be goin' to Mr Cohen, Ma?" I answer, trying to dispel my deep guilt about my offering being Mr Boylan's stolen money.

"I'm afraid so, darlin'," Peg answers, taking the cash from me and putting it carefully into her purse.

"But before we do, Niall," she continues. "I want you to kneel down with me. Let's pray to the Blessed Virgin and ask her to come and help us."

"The Blessed Virgin is up there you know," stresses Peg. "If we ask her, I know she'll guide us through this rough patch. And Niall, let's say the *Hail Holy Queen* so's to make sure she hears us. I know that's your favourite."

"OK, Ma," I respond. Kneeling down beside her, we recite one decade of the rosary – one *Our Father*, ten *Hail Marys* and one *Glory be to the Father* – topping it off with the *Hail Holy Queen*:

Hail Holy Queen, Mother of mercy,
hail our life, our sweetness and our hope.
To you do we cry, poor banished children of Eve,
to you do we send up our sighs,
mourning and weeping in this valley of tears.
Turn then, most gracious advocate,
your eyes of mercy towards us and after this our exile,
show unto us the blessed fruit of your womb, Jesus.
Oh, clement, oh loving, oh sweet Virgin Mary,
pray for us sinners now and at the hour of our death. Amen.

That prayer is my favourite. The *Our Father*, the *Hail Mary,* and the *Glory be to the Father* aren't bad, but to me, the *Hail Holy Queen* always sounds sincere and meaningful. Those other prayers are, for the most part, way too pat for me. Whenever I say them, I seldom if ever listen to what I'm saying. Unbeknown to my mother, there is another reason why the *Hail Holy Queen* is my favourite. Peg often has my Da and my siblings kneel down with her, and together we say the family rosary. The full rosary starts with an *Our Father*, three *Hail Marys* and a *Glory be to the Father* followed by five decades of *Hail Marys*, each beginning with another *Our Father* and ending with a *Glory be to the Father*. After the fifth decade, the rosary concludes with the *Hail Holy Queen*. One or two decades in and I always find myself praying that the next prayer will be the last – my favourite one. By the time we reach the *Hail Holy Queen*'s Amen, a full half-hour or more of kneeling down has passed. Precious playing time is being lost – enough of the praying already – I want to be out on the road with my friends.

Having completed our prayers to the Blessed Virgin, Peg prepares herself for our visit to Mr Cohen. She goes upstairs and packs what's needed.

The Kavanaghs of Erris are going through a real rough patch in the money department. It has crept up on us: rising prices, keeping the family fed, and needing more as my siblings and I grow older, together with stagnant income, gets us there.

Mr Cohen owns the pawn shop in Parnell Street. For the past couple of years now, my mother frequently visits Mr Cohen to pawn the only item of value she possesses, her fur coat. Her sister, Maura, gave it to her. Peg seldom if ever wears it, but she certainly uses it a lot. By rendering the coat as security at the pawn shop, the often required loan of a five-pound note can be secured.

We hate and are embarrassed by having to resort to pawning the coat. Nevertheless, it's hard times, and Peg gives thanks that Maura gifted the fur coat to her. Peg has to do what she has to do so's her family can survive.

"Now, Niall," Peg says to me, as we near Mr Cohen's pawn shop. "Make sure nobody we know sees us going in."

Standing beneath the three brass balls hanging over the pawn shop doorway, we take one final glance up and down the pavement. In we furtively go with the fur coat.

Mr Cohen's three brass balls.

"Good day to you, Mrs Kavanagh," greets Mr Cohen. He knows and values my mother as a regular customer.

"Good day, Mr Cohen," responds Peg, as she takes the parcelled fur coat from me and places it on the counter.

"The usual five pounds will be fine, Mr Cohen. It's only to tide me over until Friday, and then I'll be back to pick it up."

"As usual, indeed, Mrs Kavanagh."

"Now, Mrs Kavanagh," he continues. "If you need it, I can give you as much as twenty-five pounds for this beautiful fur coat of yours. With the cold weather coming in, sure and wouldn't it be no problem for me to sell it, at the right price, of course."

"I beg your pardon!" Peg snaps back indigently. "My coat is not for sale. And if it was, let me tell you, it's a lot more than twenty-five pounds I'd be getting for it."

"Twenty-five pounds be damned," my angry mother continues. "And then you'd turn around and sell it for a hundred.

"Not on your life, Mr Cohen, not on your life. Now, give me my pawn ticket and the five pounds, and let me and my son go. It won't be my fur coat you'll be selling. I'll be back here sooner than you think, and in the meantime, you look after it for me."

"Right, Mrs Kavanagh," Mr Cohen responds. He knows when to let go. There are no flies on my mother, and if Mr Cohen didn't know that when he started, he certainly knows it now; after being blistered by my mother's crystal-clear rebuke, he has no doubt about it, no doubt whatsoever. Mr Cohen, or anybody else for that matter, will ever make a killing on Peg.

"There you are, Mrs Kavanagh," says the disappointed, put-in-his-place Mr Cohen. "No offence intended. Here's your five pounds and your ticket. I'll see you again soon."

"The cheek of that bloody fella," mutters Peg as we make our way home. 'Bloody' is as far as it goes with my Ma's list of bold words. We're minus the fur coat, but we're plus the pawn ticket and the much needed five pounds.

"Him and his bloody twenty-five pounds," my strong, brave mother continues. "The cheek of him, indeed. And do you know what, Niall? I've a good mind to change my pawn shop – him insulting me like that."

"The loan of five pounds is all we need, love," Peg declares, as she tries to change her mood from anger to contentment. "Let's go and get ourselves two 99ers in Caffolla's," says she, ruffling my hair. "Now isn't that a good idea, Niall?"

"Are ye sure, Ma," I respond. "Have we enough money?"

"We have," she replies. "And I don't want you to be fretting yourself about money. Your mammy will always sort it out."

Somehow, Peg always did.

****

Repairs, Alterations, & Shitty Pissy Trousers

Daisy, Daisy give me your answer do,
I'm half-crazy all for the love of you.
It won't be a stylish marriage,
we can't afford a carriage,
but you'll look sweet upon the seat
of my bicycle made for two.

Daisy Bell – Harry Darce (1892)

THE VERY NEXT EVENING, WHILE PEG IS SCANNING through the *Evening Herald* newspaper, her eyes are diverted to a small advertisement:

MURPHY TAILORS
17 Westmoreland Street
Ladies and Gents Repairs and Alterations.
Repair and Alteration Help Urgently Required.
Good per Piece Rates.

Peg is an excellent seamstress, and she has a Singer sewing machine. She's well equipped for the job.

"Gerry, love," says Peg. "Murphy Tailors are looking for repair and alteration help. Sure wouldn't I be able to help them out with that? We could do with a bit more money. Will I drop in and see them, Gerry? What do you think?"

"If you're sure it won't be too much for you, Peg," my Da answers. "The extra money would be grand, but I don't want you to be killing yourself. Aren't you busy enough, darlin' – what with the house cleaning, cooking and looking after us all?"

"As you say, Gerry," Peg replies. "God knows I am a busy woman. But I think I'll drop into them tomorrow – just to see."

"I don't suppose it'll do any harm, Peg," says Gerry.

"Right then: that's settled," says Peg with a big smile on her flushed, excited face. She looks over at me and gives me a wink.

"And I'll be able to help ye, Ma," says I. "I can do the house cleanin' while you do the stitchin' and stuff."

"You're right, Niall. You can be my little helper, so you can."

"I've a good feeling, Gerry," Peg continues. "Niall and I, only yesterday, said a decade of the rosary to the Blessed Virgin asking Her to help us out during this rough patch. And here we are, with what just might be Her answer to our prayers."

"I think it was the *Hail Holy Queen* that did it, Ma," says I.

"You're probably right, Niall," answers Peg, giving me a second wink.

ARRIVING HOME from school the following day, I'm anxious to find out how my Ma got on with Mr Murphy. As I open the front gate I hear her singing:

> *Daisy, Daisy give me your answer do,*
> *I'm half-crazy all for the love of you . . .*

I go into the parlour and there she is, sitting at her Singer sewing machine as happy as Larry. With a big smile on her face, she's singing her heart out.

There's a huge pile of trousers on the table next to the Singer. Reluctantly, Peg stops her singing. Looking up from the work, she greets me.

Peg's Singer.

"Here he comes, my little helper."

"How are ya, Ma. I heard ye singin' when I was comin' in."

"You did indeed, love. Your mammy is very happy. Mr Murphy is a grand man and would you look at all the work he gave me. Over twenty pieces, and each one worth more than a shilling.

"I'm telling you, Niall, our hard times are over. I'm going to get this lot finished today. And in the morning, in I'll go into Westmoreland Street, collect my money and bring back another load. Before long we'll have money to save, so we will."

Her excitement is contagious.

"This is great, Ma. Ye're smashin'. Da's goin' to be delighted."

"I know, love. I feel so thankful to God for what He's doing for us. And it's you we've to thank – you and your *Hail Holy Queen*. The Blessed Virgin was listening, love. I told you: if we ask Her, She'll guide us through this rough patch."

"Can I help ye, Ma?" I ask, all caught up in the enjoyment of the moment.

"Most of these trousers have to be shortened or let down. You can loosen the hems. Come here, and I'll show you how to do it."

Armed with one of my Da's old Gillette razor blades, I'm carefully cutting away hem bindings in no time.

"Thanks for helping me, Niall. And for each one you do, I'll give you a penny. Now, won't that be nice?"

"Great, Ma. I'll feel like I'm gettin' paid for not'in'."

"I know what you mean," says Peg. "I feel the same myself."

It's the beginning of the end of the rough patch for the Kavanaghs of Erris Road. Peg works her tail off and enjoys each minute doing so. She often stays up into the early hours of the morning repairing and altering the bundles of clothes.

One of the things the extra income brings about is our delight in not having to make our regular, disturbing visits to that 'bloody fella', Mr Cohen and his three brass balls. The fur coat stays in Peg's wardrobe – other than for the noticeably increased occasions when Peg takes it out and proudly wears it.

"I look a real swank in this coat," says she, looking at herself in the mirror. "Don't I, Niall?"

Peg works very hard; however, she's a brighter, happier woman knowing it is her labour that's making the difference. Peg's pride in improving the family's well-being is immense.

But some parts of Peg's work stink.

"Holy Mother of God," says Peg, holding her nose with one hand while pushing away the trousers she was handling with the other. "What sort of a dirty eejit owns that?"

"The bloody eejit mustn't use underpants, never mind toilet paper. It's a lot more than a shilling I should be getting for this dirty thing. I'll need a peg on my nose when I'm working on it."

"Mr Murphy shouldn't be givin' ye work like this, Ma," says I with disgust. "The eejit that owns them should get his stinkin' pants cleaned before he leaves them in for mendin'."

It doesn't happen often, but it does happen. It's a nasty part of the price we have to pay for the household's solvency. Usually, it's all pleasurable work, but these instances stink – stink to high heavens! With the help of one of her clothes pegs, Peg willingly pays that price.

Another painful part of the job is when Peg makes some error or other. Usually, the error is minor and easily corrected, but one error comes close to killing Peg.

It's LATE Friday evening, and Peg has been working all day.

"Heaven help me!" she suddenly exclaims.

It's a gent's top-coat shortening piece. Undoubtedly brought about by being tired out from working all day, she has cut the material all the way around, six inches too short. There's no way of putting the six inches back.

Peg sits at her Singer, bawling her eyes out.

"What am I going to do? I've ruined the man's coat!"

"Don't cry, Ma," I plead, as I join her in her crying.

"I'll make ye a cup of tea, Ma. Ye'll think of somethin' while ye're drinkin' it, I know ye will."

I'm back to my tortured mother with the cup of heavily sweetened tea within a few minutes.

"There's nothing other than a new coat to fix what I've done," Peg declares as she takes the cup of tea to her trembling lips. "While you were wetting the tea, I asked the Blessed Virgin to help me, and that's what She said. God alone knows what it's going to cost. The Blessed Virgin is the only one who knows if I'll be even able to find one. But 'Get a new coat' is what She said to me."

"I told ye, Ma. I knew ye'd think of somethin'."

"OK, Niall. It's up early for us tomorrow. If it takes searching the whole of Dublin, we're going to find that coat. She wouldn't have told me to buy one if there wasn't one out there."

Early the following morning, off we go to find the new coat.

"We'll go to Clerys on O'Connell Street first," says Peg. "If we don't find it there, we'll go to Arnotts on Henry Street. Guineys on Talbot Street might have it, and if all that fails, we'll go to McBirneys at O'Connell Bridge."

And we go to all of them. Exhausted, we come out of McBirneys, stricken with disappointment and still without the coat. It's Saturday, and as usual, the city centre is crowded. The weekly shopping train excursions from towns such as Waterford, Cork and Galway, sponsored by the bigger stores, seem to double the city's population. Looking up at the Ballast Office clock at the end of Westmoreland Street, never known to tell a lie, it states it's half-past-one. We've been searching for more than four hours.

Ma and I searching for the new coat.

"Todd Burns on Exchequer Street is our only hope," says Peg. "Mrs Lawlor shops there, and she told me they've lots of stuff."

"I hope the Blessed Virgin doesn't let us down, Ma," says I. "I'll say another *Hail Holy Queen*, just to remind Her."

We make our way to Trinity College. We go up Westmoreland Street, take a right at the Central Bank onto Dame Street, a left onto South Great George's Street, and another left onto Exchequer Street. Finally, we arrive at our last hope for success, Todd Burns.

And it is in Todd Burns that we find the new coat. My mother's faith may not be in need of restoration, but the finding of that coat restores mine.

"That'll be five-pounds-two, Ma'am," says the sales clerk.

"It'll take a hell of a lot of trousers and coats for me to make this up," Peg whispers to me as she takes the required cash out of her purse. "But it's got to be done. I'll have to work quicker and bring up my number of pieces."

"Ye don't have to worry anymore, Ma," says I. "Ye'll shorten the new coat and Mr Murphy will never know the difference."

"You're right, Niall," Peg responds with a smile on her face. "The relief of knowing I can put my error right is a joy, so it is. I nearly died when I saw what I'd done."

"Anyway, Niall, we're going to earn back that five-pounds-two shillings before we know we've spent it," she adamantly asserts.

"Niall, love," she continues. "Before we get the bus home let's nip over to Hafner's on George's Street beside the fish market and get some of their pork sausages. Your Da loves Hafner's, and Mr Quigley never has them."

We buy the sausages and make our way to the 12 bus stop on Westmoreland Street. We're both satisfied and content with the results of our search, not to mention the Hafners under my oxter; I can almost smell them sizzling in my Ma's frying pan.

"I'm thinking, Niall," Peg goes on. "I can make a new coat for you out of the one I ruined. It would be a terrible shame to waste that good material. Maybe I'll put a nice belt on it for you. Would you like that, Niall?"

****

MY MOTHER'S first name was Margaret. The name Margaret has many versions, Peg being one of them. The other versions are Peggy, Marge, Maggie, Rita, and Daisy. My Ma's grandmother always called her Daisy.

Daisy Bell is the only song I ever heard Peg sing. I loved to hear her sing it. She didn't sing it often enough.

"How do ye know dat song, Ma," I once asked her.

"Darlin'," she answered. "I knew the words of that old song, long before I could talk. Didn't my Granma Tracey, ever since I was a baby, sing it to me as she dandled me on her knee?"

****

Me Da &
the Brown Trout

While goin' the road to sweet Athy, hurroo, hurroo.
While goin' the road to sweet Athy, hurroo, hurroo.
While goin' the road to sweet Athy,
> *a stick in me hand and a drop in me eye,*
> *a doleful damsel I heard cry,*
> *"Johnny I Hardly Knew Ye."*

"With yer drums and guns and guns and drums, hurroo.
With yer drums and guns and guns and drums, hurroo.
With yer drums and guns and guns and drums,
> *the enemy nearly slew ye,*
> *oh darlin' dear, ye look so queer,*
> *Johnny, I Hardly Knew Ye."*

"We're happy for to see ye home, hurroo, hurroo.
We're happy for to see ye home, hurroo, hurroo.
We're happy for to see ye home,
> *all from the island of Ceylon,*
> *so low in flesh, so high in bone,*
> *Johnny, I Hardly Knew Ye."*

"Where are yer eyes that were so mild, hurroo, hurroo?
Where are yer eyes that were so mild, hurroo, hurroo?
Where are yer eyes that were so mild,
> *when me heart, ye so beguiled?*
> *Why did ye skedaddle from me and the child?*
> *Johnny, I Hardly Knew Ye."*

"Where are yer legs that used to run, hurroo, hurroo?
Where are yer legs that used to run, hurroo, hurroo?
Where are yer legs that used to run,
> *when you went off to carry a gun?*
> *Indeed, yer dancin' days are done,*
> *Johnny, I Hardly Knew Ye."*

"Ye haven't an arm, ye haven't a leg, hurroo, hurroo.
Ye haven't an arm, ye haven't a leg, hurroo, hurroo
Ye haven't an arm, ye haven't a leg,
    ye're an armless, boneless, chickenless egg,
    ye'll have to be put with a bowl to beg,
    Johnny, I Hardly Knew Ye."

They're rollin' out the guns again, hurroo, hurroo.
They're rollin' out the guns again, hurroo, hurroo.
They're rollin' out the guns again,
    but they'll never take our sons again,
    no, they'll never take our sons again,
    "Johnny, I Hardly Knew Ye."

Johnny, I Hardly Knew Ye – Joseph Geoghegan (1867)

THE STRAWBERRY BEDS IS A NARROW STRIP of land lying between the banks of the River Liffey and a section of Lower Road in Chapelizod on the outskirts of Northside Dublin City. Strawberries are grown there and sold from roadside stalls by the locals. The simple pleasures of the Strawberry Beds' river banks are complemented by the presence of one of the Liffey's imposing weirs; the sound of the hurried waters adds just the right amount of life to what is otherwise utter tranquillity. The deep water on the Liffey's up-river side of the weir makes it a popular place for swimmers, and it's often you find people picnicking there.

I'M TEN years old. It is midday on one of those perfect, late-autumn days that the Irish don't get enough of. Not a drop of rain in sight, a pleasant soft breeze, no humidity, and lots of welcomed sunshine. Scattered buds of white cotton-like clouds supply perfectly timed interruptions to the sun's warm rays. It's the kind of a day you couldn't fight – not even if it was the devil himself who was baiting you.

My Da and I – me perched on his bicycle's crossbar – have just arrived at the Strawberry Beds. A little upriver from the weir, Gerry has found a safe, shallow place for me to paddle. I'm standing in the water, shoes and socks off and my trousers rolled up, when along comes this big brown trout. My Da and I see it at the same time. To our astonishment, the fish stops right in front of me. Gerry ever so quietly tells me to stand still.

"Don't move a muscle, Niall," he whispers. "This is your chance. That fella is begging to be caught."

95

I'm mesmerised by what's happening. I'm excited by the trout's unexpected arrival, but I also feel a bit frightened by its unexpected, continued presence right in front of me. The beautiful fish is huge. It measures over a foot head-to-tail and nearly three inches side-to-side.

"Will it bite me, Da?"

"Not at all, Niall," comes my Da's whispered response. "Quiet now. Listen to me. What I want you to do is tickle him."

"But how do I tickle him, Da?" I whisper. *I know how me Da tickles me, but how the hell do ye tickle a fish?*

"Now Niall . . . Pin your ears back. We're going to catch this fella and bring him home to your mammy. Here's how you tickle him. I'm going to count to three; then you're going to stretch out your left arm, and very gently you'll put your left hand into the water. I want you to move your fingers so's the fish will see them wriggling. No splashing – the wriggling will hypnotise him. Then I'll count to six, and as quick as you can, you'll dive your right hand in at him, grab him and throw him onto the bank."

My Da is the wisest man in the world. He knows everything and can do anything. What he says is golden.

"OK, Da," I whisper, confident that the trout will soon be gutted, seasoned, soaked in butter and sizzling on my Ma's frying pan. I follow my Da's instructions to the letter; sure enough, and to my absolute amazement, the trout is flopping about on the bank within seconds. There he is on the grassy bank, struggling in his strange, waterless environment, gasping his last breaths. The trout's struggles give me a surprising few moments of real sadness and confusion. What we had done seems to be a wicked thing. It feels wrong. All the joy and excitement of our remarkable catch is replaced with sadness for the poor upset fish.

The brown trout.

"Will we throw him back, Da? He's goin' to die if we don't."

"Well, isn't that a nice way for you to be thinking," my Da replies, as he bends down and picks the fish up. "But, sure don't we all die in the end. Don't be fretting yourself, Niall. Holy God gives us the fish so's we can eat and stay well and healthy."

With that soulful, not at all convincing explanation of the ways of the world, my Da puts the beautiful creature out of its misery by clobbering it between the eyes with a rock. Using some dock leaves, he wraps the fish up and puts it into his bike's saddle bag.

"Let's go over to the *Wren's Nest* and celebrate," says Gerry, winking at me and grinning from ear to ear. "Your very first fish! A beauty if ever I saw one. I'm going to get you a nice bottle of Taylor Keith, and I'm going to get myself a pint of Guinness."

With my Da's free hand steering his bike, hand-in-hand we walk over to the *Wren's Nest Inn*. My sadness for the executed fish hasn't gone away, but it's close to doing so: my Da approved of what we had done, so it must be OK.

While I sit outside keeping an eye on the bike and the contents of the saddle bag, Gerry goes into the inn. A few minutes pass by before a lovely looking pint of Guinness, a bubbly glass of Taylor Keith orange, and my Da come out to join me.

"Sláinte mhaith agat[1]," says Gerry, as we click our glasses together. "Here's to your first fish, Niall. May it not be your last."

We sit down on the bench together. As often happens, my Da begins to tell me some treasures known only by the few.

"This inn was used by Michael Collins during the Black'n'Tan War," says Gerry, having taken the first of his pint's eight gulps. "The Big Fella is what we called him. He often used the *Wren's Nest* as a safe house. Sure and didn't himself and Harry Boland swim over there at the weir, near where you caught your trout."

When my Da is like this, wanting to tell stories, I know the drill well: sit, give him your undivided attention, and soak it up.

"They were all brave, noble men," Gerry continues, as he takes his second of eight. "Most of them are dead now, mighty men, one and all." The third of eight gulps follows this short, solemn reverie.

"Tell me, Niall," asks Gerry. "Did I ever tell you the story about that mistake for a pint – half Guinness and half beer? That's the drink your uncles John and Fintan refuse to serve at *The Gravediggers*. Each pint of that stuff is the makings of a sin for the ruination of the Guinness that's wasted in the making of it."

"No Da," I respond. "Ye never told me."

"Well, they call it an awful name," Gerry begins. "They call it a Black'n'Tan. It's named after that crowd of bowsies the English sent over to bolster the *Royal Irish Constabulary* during the *War of Independence* in 1920. Michael Collins's guerrilla war activities were proving to be too much for the RIC. It was only a little while after the end of the First World War, and the English were pretty much banjoed. Eight-hundred thousand of them had died or were maimed. Recruitment efforts were falling flat, so the English went to their gaols, offering amnesty to prisoners who'd volunteer to join up, go over to Ireland and fight the IRA."

Gerry pauses for his fourth of eight.

"The English were not only short of recruits," he continues. "They were also short of uniforms. They got all the volunteers they needed from their gaols. They solved the uniform problem by using some old discarded uniforms. They togged out the bowsies in a combination of trousers, jackets and greatcoats from both the army's and the navy's leftovers. Some of them wore navy/black trousers, and others wore army/tan trousers; some of them wore navy/black jackets, and others wore army/tan jackets. Great coats the same, some black, some tan. To give uniformity to their outfit, they wore a silly looking French-type tasselled beret.

"The roughest bunch of gowjers to come to Ireland since Cromwell's Roundheads," my Da continues as the fifth of eight goes down. "The English called them Auxiliaries. As they marched through the cities and towns of Ireland, killing many and imprisoning many more, it wasn't long before we all started calling them Black'n'Tans.

The Black'n'Tans in 1920 Ireland.

"Years afterwards, some eejit got the lame idea of making a pint with one half Guinness and the other half beer. Seeing the way the black Guinness, being lighter than the tan beer, floated to the top, didn't the eejit give it the name Black'n'Tan.

A Black'n'Tan.

"And that is the end of my story," concludes my Da, as he downs the sixth of eight.

"It's a great story, Da," says I, looking up adoringly at the man who knows it all, my Da.

We can't wait to get back home and present the trout to Peg. My Da's last two of eight are downed one after the other, resulting in him making a loud belch. While we are laughing heartedly at his surprising breach of good manners, Gerry secures the bottom of his trouser legs with his two steel bicycle clips. We mount the bike and are ready to go – all three of us – my Da on the saddle, me on the cross bar, and the trout in the bag.

"Hello, Gerry," greets Peg. "Did you have a nice time?"

"We certainly did, Peg," answers my Da. "And wait until you see what Niall has for you."

Peg is delighted with the surprise. Giving all the glory to me, she quickly prepares and begins to fry what is the most delicious piece of fish I've ever eaten. We share the special repast with my little brother, Conor.

"Now, Conor," says Peg. "You hurry up and become a fine fisherman like your big brother. He'll show you how to do it, and without a rod'n'line, bedads."

"I'm proud of you, Niall," continues Peg. I look over at my Da, and he gives me one of his magic winks. I try to wink back, but not having perfected the art, I give him a few hard blinks.

****

Yarn #19 Footnote
[1] Good health to you.

Maura Laverty, Christie Brown
& Banned Books

In Dublin's fair city, where the girls are so pretty,
I first set me eyes on sweet Molly Malone.
As she wheeled her wheelbarrow,
through streets broad and narrow,
cryin', cockles and mussels alive, alive oh.

Alive, alive oh, alive, alive oh,
cryin', cockles and mussels alive, alive oh.

She was a fishmonger, and sure 'twas no wonder,
for so were her father and mother before.
And they both wheeled their barrow,
through streets broad and narrow,
cryin', cockles and mussels alive, alive oh.

She died of a fever, and no one could save her,
and that was the end of sweet Molly Malone.
Now her ghost wheels her barrow,
through streets broad and narrow,
cryin', cockles and mussels alive, alive oh.

Molly Malone – James Yorkston (1884)

Molloy Malone.

THERE ARE LOTS OF REASONS for you to visit Dublin city, but if for no other reason you should do so to say hello to Molly Malone. Dubliners call her 'The Tart with the Cart', 'The Dish with the Fish' or 'The Flirt in the Skirt'. Molly is what you'd call a good looker – big boobs, great figure, and an attitude to die for. You'll find her outside Trinity College at the end of Grafton Street, fish in her barrow and a twinkle in her eye.

Many such statues of equally notable personage are scattered all over the Dublin City. James Joyce hangs out at the top of Earls Street, dressed up to the nines, and leaning on his fancy walking stick; Dubliners call him 'The Prick with the Stick'. Then there's Oscar Wilde in Merrion Square Park, lying back on his large lump of craggy stone; he's been labelled 'The Fag on the Crag'. Much like James and Oscar, not to mention Molly, Dubliners have a way with words.

****

MY AUNT MAURA, ONE OF PEG'S SISTERS, was a novelist and playwright. She wrote seven well-received novels: *Never No More*; *Alone We Embark*; *No More Than Human*; *Gold of Glanaree*; *The Cottage in the Bog*; *Lift up Your Gates*; and *The Green Orchard*. Her three plays, *A Tree in the Crescent*, *Liffey Lane* and *Tolka Ro*w were also very successful. *Liffey Lane* and *Tolka Row* were later used by Radio Telefís Éireann (RTE), for *Tolka Row*, Ireland's first televised soap opera. It ran for five years, 1964–68. Maura died in 1966, and that put an end to the popular televised *Tolka Row*.

My Aunt Maura.

IT'S LATE in 1952 and Maura's play, *A Tree in the Crescent* is opening at the Gaiety Theatre in Dublin. For reasons unbeknown to me, Peg has brought me to the opening performance – just the two of us, and I'm only ten years old. We're invited backstage after the performance. My ten years makes the entire event very boring.

"Can we go now, Ma?" I enquire.

Peg is Maura Laverty's proud sister. She's enjoying Maura's moment of fame, and she doesn't welcome the interruption.

101

"Ah Niall, will you leave me alone? Why don't you go over there to Christie and say hello to him? Look at him over there, stuck in his wheelchair. Be a good boy, Niall. Go over to the poor man. Tell him Maura is your auntie. We'll be going in a minute."

Christie Brown.

Christie Brown, a paraplegia, has become well known in Ireland for his painting ability using only his left foot. Maura told us about his condition and talents. She bought one of his paintings and has invited him to come to her play's opening.

Due to his illness, cerebral palsy, Christie's mannerisms are such that for a ten-year-old, it's a bit frightening to be in his company. With some apprehension, over I go to Christie.

"Hello, Christie. My name's Niall. Maura is me auntie."

"Waa de ye wann'?" grunts Christie, as he labouriously turns towards me in his wheelchair. His distressed response, contorted face and wriggling body unnerve me.

"I just came over to say hello. I like yer paintin', Christie."

"H'ank berrie mush. Now fu'k off."

I run back to Peg, bawling crying.

"Christie told me to fuck off, Ma," I cry, sticking my teary face into my mother's belly. "I want to go home."

"Never mind love. Christie must be drinking. Sure isn't he more to be pitied than disliked."

"He's not nice, Ma," I sniffle. "Let's go home."

Peg says her goodbyes, and off we go.

"Can we sit tops in the front of the bus, Ma?" I ask as we walk our way down Grafton Street.

"Of course we can, love. And before we get on the bus we'll get a couple of 99ers in Caffolla's."

"T'anks Ma," I reply, as all my Christie Brown hurt vanishes.

****

IN 1954, Christie Brown's acclaimed biography, *My Left Foot*, was published. In the same year, many of Maura's works were banned in Ireland. Éamon de Valera had recently been re-elected, Taoiseach. He was an ardent catholic and being urged on by his old Blackrock College buddy, Dublin's Archbishop Charles McQuaid, a few peculiar censorship laws were enforced.

One of them was the banning of the sale or public library possession of books from many foreign writers such as Aldous Huxley and J.D.Salinger, plus a string of Irish writers including not only Maura but also Flann O'Brien, Samuel Beckett, Enda O'Brien and many others. Since 1926, the Irish Censorship Board had been active, but in 1954 I think it got a tad over-active. Oddly enough, James Joyce's *Ulysses*, banned for indecency in the United States from 1922 through 1933, was never banned in Ireland.

Another enforced law was that if you were a catholic, and choose to attend the protestant Trinity College, you'd have to secure written permission from the Archbishop of Dublin or risk being excommunicated. This practice continued until 1970.

"Why were Auntie Maura's bo'ks banned?" I remember asking my mother.

"I don't know, love," Peg replied. "But Mrs Lawlor told me there were things in them talking about adult stuff."

Later, Maura's daughter, Finbarra, gave me the real scoop on the banning of her mother's works. Much of Maura's writings highlighted the shame of Dublin's deplorable slum life. Some of her novels did allude to abortion, body parts and sex, but it was her unmasking of Dublin's slum life that brought about the ban. De Valera didn't want the exposure of Dublin's poverty kerbing his efforts to show the new Republic of Ireland being the virtuous place he wanted it to be.

****

Christ the King –
Waitin' to be Conquered

Dublin can be heaven, with coffee at eleven,
*   and a stroll through Stephen's Green.*
There's no need to hurry, there's no need to worry,
*   ye're a king and the lady's a queen.*
Grafton Street's a wonderland, there's magic in the air,
*   there're diamonds in the lady's eyes and gold dust in her hair.*
And if ye don't believe me, come and meet me der,
*   in Dublin on a sunny summer mornin'.*

I've been North and I've been South, I've been East and West,
*   I've been just a rolling stone.*
Yet there's one place on this earth, I've always loved the best,
*   just a little town I call me own.*

I've been here, I've been there, I've sought the rainbow's end,
*   but no crock of gold I've found.*
Now I know that come what will, whatever fate may send,
*   here my roots are deep on friendly ground.*

Dublin Saunter – Leo Maguire (1940)
Copyright held by Waltons Music Limited

CHRIST THE KING CHURCH IS THE TALLEST building in Cabra. Cruciform in shape, it has an enormous statue of the patron standing outside the main entrance. The sculpture is about thirty feet tall and centrally positioned on the outside wall, which is at least eighty feet high. The church has a sloping terracotta tiled roof, crowned by a spire with a cross perched on top. Putting it all together, Christ the King is close to one-hundred feet high. With its well-kept gardens and its eight-feet high ironwork fence and gateways, any king would be proud to have it. It is a splendid giant-like edifice that demands attention.

Christ the King Church.

And attention it receives, especially from Philip Murphy and me. We see Christ the King as Edmund Hillary saw Mount Everest – a challenge as yet unconquered. Earlier in the year, Edmund reached earth's highest point, and by so doing he became our hero. Christ the King is sitting there, waiting to be conquered by two brave boys like Philip and me.

IT'S LATE October 1953, and evening's darkness is making its presence felt. The six o'clock church bells will soon be ringing. While this daily tintinnabulation serves well in letting those so inclined know it's time to say the Angelus, it lets me know I'd better move my arse home to my dinner or suffer the pain of my mother's wrath for being late.

Philip and I are standing outside the church front gates.

"Janey Mack, Niall," says Philip. "It's awful high."

"That's what I like about it," I respond. "No one else would even think about it. Dat Hillary bloke wasn't afraid. We'll be just like him: reachin' the highest point in the whole of Cabra."

"After school tomorrow!" says I to a doubting Philip. "We'll go all-around the church and find the best way up. That's what Hillary did – Bob's yer uncle, Fanny's yer aunt – he was up."

"OK, Niall," Philip responds. With that, the church bells start ringing. We say our goodbyes and run home to our dinners.

The following day we meet to do our surveillance. We've just finished a second circling of the church. Frustrated with our failure to identify anything declaring itself as being the best way up, we've paused to consider how we should proceed.

While I'm not at all sure about Phillip, for me, failure of any kind is unacceptable. Nonetheless, being right up against the tall church walls, I have to fight hard to root out the uninvited second thoughts I have regarding my commitment to conquer.

And if I'm having second thoughts, Philip is on his one hundred and second.

"Janey Mack, Niall," says Phillip. "How're we goin' to do it?"

"As Hillary said: 'There's got to be a way.'"

"It'll have to be the drainpipe," says I resignedly. "We'll climb up, get 'round the gutter and then up onto the roof. We'll need rubber sole shoes. We don't want to be slippin'."

"OK, Niall. But the gutter seems to be stickin' out a good bit. It's goin' to be awful hard to get 'round."

Looking up at how the soffit extends out from the wall, I deliberate on Phillip's expressed concern. The iron drainpipe seems ideally placed with metal stays anchoring it, all the way up. *They'll make great hand and foot holds*. However, about three or four feet down from the soffit, it looks like the pipe bends out, then bends up again, finally connecting itself to the gutter. *Phillip's right: it's goin' to be a challenge – a challenge I'm willin' to take, but what about Phil?*

"In for a wing[1], in for a quid[2]," says I. "I'll go tops, and you follow. It's goin' to be a cinch, Phil. I'll be able to get meself 'round the bend at the gutter and get up. Then I can help you up."

"And when we're up there, gettin' to the spire will be a piece of cake," I continue. "What do ye t'ink?"

"OK," replies Philip, displaying no confidence whatsoever.

"It'll be a cinch, Phil; I swear it will. And don't forget we're goin' to be doin' what nobody else has ever, ever done. We'll be like Hillary – we'll be famous!

"And when we're up there, we'll tie a ribbon on the spire," I continue. "We'll pretend it's a flag. Hillary stuck a flag on the top of Mount Everest. We'll do the same."

"That's a smashin' idea," says Philip. "That's how we'll prove to all the kids that it was us that did it. When will we do it, Niall?"

"Tomorrow. We'll meet here after school, OK?"

"Yeah," says Philip. "It's goin' to be great," he adds, and this time with a little more confidence. The die is cast. We're willing and ready to conquer Christ the King.

THE FOLLOWING day comes quickly. After school, dressed in the prescribed rubber sole shoes, and with a piece of red ribbon stuck in my pocket, we're both at the foot of the drainpipe, ready to go.

"Are ye right, Phil?"

"Yeep, Niall. I'm right behind ye."

We climb the drainpipe with the courage and confidence of combat marines. Being only three-quarters of the way up, I can clearly see Saint Peter's Church in Phibsborough. Not that I need encouragement, but the thoughts of all we'll be able to see when sitting by the Christ the King spire urges me on.

Coming up to the soffit, which extends about three feet out from the church wall, I discover that the drainpipe's gutter-connecting piece starts to elbow-out about three feet down from the soffit – it extends out, then elbows up again and connects to the gutter. With great difficulty, I manoeuvre myself so as to be able to sit on the drainpipe connecting piece. Carefully balancing, I try to grab hold of the gutter. I can't reach it. I pause for a moment. *Jays! This is harder than I thought it would be. Maybe we should go back down. No, don't be a chicken, Niall – you can do it.* I take a deep breath. Stretching out as far and as high as I can, I somehow manage to grab the gutter with both hands; at the same time, I slide off the connecting piece. Clinging to the gratefully secure gutter, legs dangling in space, it takes all in my power to pull myself up onto the roof.

Sitting on the roof, I struggle to get my breath back. *Jays! That was a near thing.* Waiting for Philip to emerge, I become extremely anxious for him. Hands first, he starts to appear.

"Give me yer hand, Phil." *One slip and Phil's dead!*

"I'm OK," grunts Philip. "Move over. I'll hunch meself up."

Up he comes. *We've made it!*

"Jays, Phil. That was bleedin' awful hard."

"It feckin' well was!" says Philip. "I thought I was a goner."

Dismissing the horror of what could have happened, we spend a minute or two sitting in awe of all we could see.

"Janey Mack, Niall," Phil almost whispers. "Look! There's your house and there's mine, and we can even see out to the sea!" he continues, pointing out his discoveries.

"We haven't seen an'in' yet. Wait 'til we're up at the spire!"

It's a little after five. We should have enough time to conquer the hundred feet, get back to the gutter and climb down the drainpipe. The bells will be ringing at six, and we'll be on our way home to our dinner. Except for that last leg of getting onto the roof – which was difficult and very scary – it's working out as planned.

Like Sir Edmund had turned towards Everest's peak, we turn towards the spire. The roof's slant is steeper than we had imagined. There's no way of achieving our goal other than by crawling. If we were to stand, we'd tumble down and fall to our death.

The rough roof tiles are firmly held together, making the thirty-foot crawl easy enough. We're glad we have our long, thick school trousers on. Our hands are being tested with the tiles; but for the trousers, our knees would be more than tested.

Reaching the spire, we straddle the roof's capping tiles.

"We've done it," I holler. "We've conquered Christ the King!"

"And will ye look at all we can see," I exclaim. "It's galactic!"

"Yeah," Phil replies. "It's the best thing we've ever done."

"But it's gettin' dark, Niall," he adds.

Phillip is right. We observe day turning to night in a way we've never witnessed. We clearly see the darkening sky creep in from the west, its shadow lengthening right before our eyes.

"We'd better start down now before we can't see what we're doin'," says I. "Let's tie our flag to the spire and go."

I take the red ribbon out of my pocket.

"Just like Hillary on the top of Mount Everest," says I, securing the ribbon with three triumphant knots.

Reluctantly, we unstraddle ourselves; sitting on our behinds, we arse our way down to the gutter.

Reaching the gutter, I turn over on my stomach and ease myself off the roof. To my horror, I find that I can't swing my legs in far enough to be able to stand on the drainpipe-bend below me.

I pull myself back up onto the roof and a panicking Philip. He's not alone in his panic.

"Gick on it, Phil!" I almost cry. "I couldn't swing me legs in."

"Jays Niall," moans Phillip. "What are we goin' to do?"

"I didn't think about this when we were comin' up," I continue. "Let's sit here for a minute."

Philip is stuck to me with fear, yet I feel very much alone.

"It's comin' up to six, and me Ma will be worried if I'm not home for dinner," says I, more to myself than to Philip.

The impossible nature of our predicament comes crashing in. *We're trapped on the feckin' roof, and we can't get down!*

"We'll have to call for help," I mumble.

"Yeah, Niall. Our Ma's are goin' to kill us." While Philip's expressed apprehension is also very much in my mind, the demands of how to get down demand precedence.

We can see people passing by on the roadway below. There'll be no problem for any one of them hearing our screams for help.

"Help, someone, help!" we scream.

Mrs Lawlor is the first to hear us. She's on her way home from Quigley's, pushing her pram with baby Mike in it. She has a bag of groceries plus Kathleen, one of her gang of eight girls with her.

"Holy Mother of God!" Mrs Lawlor yells, letting go of her pram and groceries, and looking up at us.

"Is that you, Niall Kavanagh?" she hollers. "What in the name of God are ye doin'? Wait 'til ye're poor mother sees ye. And who's that with ye? Is that you, Philip Murphy?"

Philip is dumb with fear. I have all of his fear, but somehow I manage to respond.

"Yeah. It's us. We were only playin', but we can't get down."

"Holy Mother of God," Mrs Lawlor repeats. In a few seconds, she maps out the only safe way down.

"Kathleen," she shouts. "Run quickly to Mr Quigley and tell him what's happened. He's got a phone. Tell him to call the fire brigade. their big ladder is the only thing that'll be able to get these two down. Run now, like a good girl, for yer mammy."

A crowd is gathering around Mrs Lawlor. Soon the whole neighbourhood will know about it, including my mother.

Philip and I have a bird's eye view of Kathleen scampering up Imaal Road to Mr Quigley. We sit on the roof taking it all in. Suddenly, the six o'clock Angelus bells ring out: ding-dong, ding-dong, ding-dong-ding-dong, ding-dong, ding-dong, ding-dong-ding-dong, BONG! BONG! BONG! BONG! BONG! BONG! Being close to the sound's source is deafening.

The thought of being rescued by the fire brigade is very exciting; for now, it assuages the dreadful thoughts of what Peg might say and do to me. The fire brigade will be coming from Phibsborough. We'll have front row seats when it comes racing up Cabra Road, screeching around Imaal and up to the church, all bells ringing and red lights flashing.

The Fire Brigade.

The fire brigade pulls up to the church. The captain jumps out, and after he has opened the gates, the truck bumps its way from the roadway and comes to a halt beneath us. The captain orders the extension ladder raised and made ready for rescue. It's better than the pictures – for us and the ever increasing street audience below.

Observing all that is happening is wonderful, but the sight of the fully equipped fireman coming up to save us is overwhelming.

"Well, aren't you a right pair," is the fireman's welcoming greeting. He has a big friendly smile on his face.

"Now don't either of you two move," the fireman says. "Do what I tell you to do. Not a move until I tell you. Now lads, what would your names be? The captain said one of you is Niall."

"I'm Niall, and this is Philip."

"And how old are you, Niall?"

"I'm eleven," I answer.

"I'm eleven too," adds Philip.

"Well now, are you two ready to go down?" says the fireman. "It'll be Philip I'll take first."

Philip starts to stand up.

"No!" roars the fireman, but in a whispered manner so's not to shock Phil and send him down the quick, deadly way.

"Stay where you are, son. Didn't I tell you not to move? Keep your arse where it is! I'll be moving over to you, and only when I tell you to, stand up; then put your hand on the hand-bar, grab a hold with both hands and step into the cage."

"And Niall; you sit where you are," he continues.

The cage inches its way over to us, and as instructed, Phil stands up and climbs in. As he boards, a big cheer from the spectators below fills the night's air.

"Hooray!" they scream, as they give their applause of congratulations for the saving of the first of the trapped victims.

"Niall! This is your mother." I hear Peg's holler above the cheering crowd. Her voice terrifies me far more than the ordeal I'm going through. Looking down, I see that my Da is with her.

"Your daddy and mammy are down here waiting for you, love" she continues. "The fireman will be back up to you in a minute. Sit there, darlin'. Don't move now. He won't be a minute."

The inclusion of her 'love' and 'darlin' eases my horror of her impending wrath. However, I suddenly realise that being stuck up on the roof is far less uncomfortable than I'll be when I get down. I'm in no hurry to leave my conquered Christ the King.

The fireman comes back up to me sooner than I want. Feeling more trapped than ever, into the cage I go. There's a repeat performance from the crowd – more hoorays and clapping. I've no such joy for my rescue. I'm sick with concern about what Peg will do to me. If I had my wish, I'd be staying up on the roof.

Down I come. There she is, waiting for me. My father is behind her looking as he always does, the Duke. It isn't the Duke I'm worried about. He never puts fear in me; he always ends up making me feel safe and sound. It's his Duchess I'm anxious about. She rules the roost. It's Peg's wrath I fear the most.

"Wait until I get you home," my mother whispers in my ear as she gives me what appears to be a loving hug.

Anyone seeing this observes a grateful mother embracing her rescued son. Little do they know that while Peg is happy to grab me, her real sentiments are far from loving. She wants to kill me. Well, maybe not kill me, but coming close to doing so is a thought that undoubtedly gives her considerable pleasure.

"Gerry," says Peg, as she turns to my Da. "Let's bring Niall home now. His dinner will be cold waiting for him."

My Da hadn't heard what my mother had whispered in my ear, but he knows Peg. He knows she's putting on a face for the neighbours, and he also knows what her real desire is.

"Aren't you a right little divil," Gerry whispers.

"Now, take my hand, and we'll go home."

Before we leave, Peg does the politically correct thing.

"Thanks very much, officer," says Peg to the fire brigade captain. Turning to Mrs Lawlor, she says, "Thanks, Maggie. It's you we've to thank – you and the good officer here – for saving the little div–, for saving Niall's life." Peg almost slips up, but she's quick to catch herself and correct her manner of expression.

"I'll talk to you later, Maggie," Peg adds. "Let Gerry and me get him home for his dinner."

The three of us walk hand-in-hand and head for Erris. As we make our way through the crowd, I notice Kevin Callahan with some of his friends. Kevin is a year older than me, and he's someone I look up to. He lives on Annaly Road, and he has a gang; a group of boys who are out of the same barn as I'd come from – a fun seeking and adventurous group.

As I pass Kevin, he gives me a knowing wink and a smile that tells me of his admiration for what I had accomplished. The pleasure of receiving this accolade is short-lived. My hand-in-hand situation with my parents quickly moves me away and returns my thoughts to the horrors of atonement for my most recent crime.

The crowd quickly breaks up and gets back to whatever they had intended doing before all the excitement. They've had enough exhilaration for one night, and they're all so happy that the two little lads have been rescued.

Some neighbours accompany Peg, Gerry and me to 20 Erris, resulting in a stay of execution. An all too short stay; the noose will be around my neck soon enough.

****

Yarn #21 Footnotes
[1] One penny.
[2] A pound sterling or two hundred and forty pennies.

Christic the King – You're Not a Baby Anymore & the Cheese Sandwich

"**I**T'S NOT YOUR DINNER YOU'LL BE GETTING**," Peg screams, as the front door closes behind us. "A bloody good hiding! That's what you'll be getting! Get up to your room, you brat! Once your father and I have pulled ourselves together, we'll be up to you. God and His Mother help us. Get out of my sight before I kill you.

"Gerry . . . I'm going into the kitchen to wet the tea," she continues. "And I'm going to put three spoons of sugar in it. With that bitter little brat of ours, we need something to sweeten our lives."

I've climbed the stairs and I'm sitting on my bed as Peg pauses to catch her breath.

"As far as I'm concerned you'll be up there until you're married!" she shouts.

"Take it easy, Peg," I hear my Da say. "Make that nice cuppa sweet tea and calm yourself, Peg. You and I will put manners on him. Now, let's go into the kitchen and decide on a strategy. We'll talk about it over a cup of tea, and we'll put things right."

"He hasn't had his dinner, Peg," Gerry adds.

"Gerry . . . Bread and water is what the little brat should be getting!" replies my demented mother. "Dinner be damned; a good starving might teach him a lesson."

"Well, I'll take that as a no, Peg," Gerry replies.

Thank God me Da is here. If he wasn't, she'd kill me.

After what seems like a lifetime, my father comes up the stairs to my room. Somehow or other, Peg has agreed to allow him be the one to render the terms of the sentence.

"Do you know you're not a baby anymore?" my father starts. He has a grimmer face than I've ever known him have. Knowing a response is not expected, I keep my mouth shut.

"You're going on twelve, Niall! Twelve! And you have a little brother coming up after you.

"Now listen to me. If I thought you were a bad boy – and I know you're not – right now you'd be on your way to Artane Reformatory. You're a bold, big boy, that's what you are! And it's about time you started realising there are consequences for your actions."

Grabbing me by the shoulders and shaking me firmly, he almost whispers. "From here on in, your Ma and I are going to treat you like the big boy you are. Are you listening to me, Niall? Because if you're not, I'm telling you, it's to Artane you'll be going. You're driving your mother and me mad entirely."

"I'm listenin', Da," I answer, my head hanging on my chest and strangely, my heart beating very slowly. I can see the Artane Reformatory's locked gates in front of me – and I'm looking out from the inside. His tone of address is taking my heart and smashing it. I know the difference this time. Gerry never says much, but when he does, you listen, to the words he speaks and especially to those that he whispers. Never a word wasted, you can take it to the bank. Gerry means what he says.

Artane Reformatory gates.

"So here's what we're going to do," he continues, as he sits down beside me on the bed.

"Being the big boy you are, we're going to put you to work. Didn't I start working when I was twelve, and isn't what's good for the goose, good for the gander? Am I right, Niall?" he asks, squeezing my knee gently.

"Yeah, Da," I respond. That action of his usually tickles me and makes me laugh, but this time it has no such effect. I'm absorbed in my private world, shame and apprehension pushing all other emotions out. *I don't deserve havin' a Da as good as me Da. Me Ma hates me. I'm next door to bein' sent to Artane; I'm ruinin' me own life and that of me little brother. And on top of all this, I'm goin' to be taken out of school and sent to work.*

The surge of depression engulfing me is immense.

"You're not a bad boy, Niall. And I know you're only playing. Wasn't I a bit like you when I was a lad? But Niall, our actions have consequences. The sooner you learn that, the better."

"But I love school, Da. Brother Colman said I'm good and I'm learnin' lots of stuff and–"

"What the hell are you talking about?" interrupts my father. "Don't I know that? And isn't it that that helps me see you're not a bad boy. You're grand in school. It's when you get out of school that the devil gets into you."

"But ye're sendin' me to work, Da. I won't be able to go to school anymore."

"You'll be staying in school, you eejit you. It's after your school you'll be working. You'll be working all right, and it's going to be as near to hard labour as I can make it."

My father notices the effect his clarification creates in me. My head rises from my sunken chest, and some colour of improved well-being returns to my pouty face.

"So . . . As I was saying to you, here's what we're going to do. Get a clean page of your jotter and a sharp point to your pencil. I want you to write it all down so as you won't forget."

Doing as demanded, I ready myself for his dictation.

"Number one: starting tomorrow, you're the new gardener in the house. Every day, from now until your Ma and I feel different about it, you'll get the lawn mower and clippers out and trim the grass. And when I get home from work, it had better be done right. Done the way you know I want it, showing the up and down mowing lines, and the lines had better be as straight as an arrow. After that, you'll trim the privet, and if I find a piece of it lying on the grass, you'll be in trouble. Have you got that down?"

"How do ye spell *privet*, Da?"

"*P r i v–, p r i v–*," and not being sure of how to spell the word, he says, "You can put down bushes."

"Once the gardening is finished you'll report to your Ma. If she has something for you to do, like helping her with the washing or cleaning the house, you'll do that. If she has nothing for you to do, you'll come up here to your room and do your school homework and reading. No television, no sweets.

"Number two: every weekend you'll wash and shine every pane of glass in the house, until you can see your face in them, inside and outside. I want to see my face in them when I check out your work. You know where the ladder is, and with all your bold climbing you'll have no problem getting up there and making them shine. Now, have you got that down?"

"Yeah, Da," I respond. My mind is still on the no television, no sweets part of the sentence. We've only recently got our first tele, and I love watching it. I like gardening, the helping with the washing and house cleaning isn't bad, and the window cleaning with its ladder climbing isn't bad either, but no tele or sweets hurts.

"Number three," Gerry continues, "and this is the most important part of your punishment. The only time you'll be allowed out on the road is when your Ma or I let you."

That was the nail in the coffin.

"Janey Mack," I whimper. "For how long, Da?"

"None of your janey-mackin' with me, Niall," he gruffly responds. "For as long as I think right about it, that's how long."

"Let me see what you've written," he demands, snatching the dictated text from my hand.

"It's good enough, but use your rubber and correct it. A pane of glass is spelt *p-a-n-e* not *p-a-i-n*."

He gives the jotter back to me. Opening the door, and for effect with my mother, he roars, "No dinner for you tonight! Get into your bed and think yourself lucky you're not in Artane."

After a long time, I hear my door being gently opened. I'm about to fall asleep when my Da creeps into me with a glass of cold milk and a cheese sandwich.

"Here, Niall," Gerry whispers. "Take this from me quick, and be sure to hide the glass and plate when you're finished. If your Ma finds out, she'll kill me."

The glass of milk and the cheese sandwich.

"Niall," he adds, as he's sneaking out of my room. "Be a good boy for your Ma. You're breaking her heart."

****

MY CONQUERING of Christ the King escapade brought about some changes. It was the thoughts of me locked in and looking out of those Artane Reformatory gates that did it – for a long time I dreamt of the frightening image; that and my Da telling me I was breaking my Ma's heart is what did it. I realised there would be consequences to be paid for my actions, good ones for good actions and bad ones for the other kind.

My mother's attitude towards me was spot-on. There wasn't a love or a darlin from her. She did a phenomenal job of ignoring me; in response, I did everything I could do to please her and win her love back. Eventually, the loves and darlins returned.

I cried as I was telling you about that gorgeous cheese sandwich and glass of cold milk. That night I was starving, but it wasn't the satisfying of my hunger that makes the repast so memorable. It's the way my Da cut the crusts off the sandwich: he knew I preferred them that way. It was the way he put that extra bit of butter on the bread, all the way to the edges, and that little bit of Marmite he put on top of the thick pieces of cheese giving the sandwich its sharp mouth-watering taste.

Gerry's decision to furtively bring the refection up to me, without Peg knowing, must have been a tough one. However, it was exactly the right thing for him to have done. I'd always loved my Da, but this intimate act of his bonded that love.

117

Thank you Da, for everything. You and Ma, above all else, made me as I am. As you said, I'm 'not a baby anymore', and while I'm still a bit bold, I'm 'not a bad boy' – I'm still 'only playing'.

****

All This Sex Stuff

If ye've got a wing-o, take her up to ring-o,
  where the waxies sing-o, all the day.
If ye've had yer fill of porter, and ye can't go any farther,
  give yer man the order, back to the quay.

  Take her up to Monto, Monto, Monto,
  take her up to Monto, Langer-ru, to you.

Ye've heard of the Duke of Gloucester, the dirty ol' imposter,
  he took his mot and lost her up the Furry Glen.
He first put on his bowler, den he buttoned up his trousers,
  den he whistled for his growler, and he said, my man.

Ye've heard the Dublin Fusiliers, the dirty ol' bamboozlers,
  they went and got the childer, one, two, t'ree.
Marchin' by the Linen Hall, there's one for every cannonball,
  and Vicky's goin' to send them all, o'er the sea.

Cary told on Skin'd'Goat, O'Donnell caught him on the boat,
  he wished he'd never been afloat, the dirty skit.
It wasn't very sensible, to tell on the Invincibles,
  they stood up for their principles, day and night.

When the Czar of Russia and the King of Prussia,
  landed in the Phoenix in a big balloon.
They asked the policemen to play The Wearin' of the Green,
  but the buggers in the depot didn't know the tune.

The Queen she came to call on us, she wanted to see all of us,
  I'm glad she didn't fall on us, she's eighteen stone.
Mr, me Lord Mayor, says she, is that all you've got to show to me?
  Ah no Ma'am, sure there's more to see, Póg mo thóin! [1]

Take Her Up to Monto – George Desmond Hodnett (1958)

AS IS OFTEN THE CASE IN IRELAND, IT FEELS as if it's been raining forever. We've been housebound for far too long and the sudden break in the weather is welcomed – especially by Peg.

119

"Gerry, love," pleads my mother. "It's stopped raining. These two are driving me mad, running around the house, causing chaos. Why don't you take Niall and Conor up the Navan Road for a walk? That'll do you all good, and I'll be able to tidy the place."

My Da needs no persuading – he feels as pent-in as Conor and I. Off we gladly go for our much-needed walk.

We're strolling past some grazing fields on the Navan Road when our attention is drawn to the sorrowful sounds of a cow in some sort of distress. We stop to investigate. Distress is right! Looking over the fence, we see the poor cow, standing there sorrowfully mooing and moaning out of one end, while at the same time struggling with what appears to be a third set of legs sticking out of her other end.

"W'at's wrong with the cow, Da?" I ask.

"She's having a baby," is my Da's response.

"How does the baby get in der, Da?"

"Ask your Ma, Niall. She's abler than I am to tell you all about that stuff."

"Do ye not know, Da?" Events

"Of course I know," he assertively responds. "The daddy cow and the mammy cow get together and hug each other. Then Holy God comes down from heaven and puts the baby cow in the mammy cow's stomach. That's how baby cows are born. Your Ma knows all about it. OK?"

"OK, Da," says I, feeling informed, albeit modestly so, regarding all matters concerning the reproductive process.

DURING MY conquering Christ the King detention, I start growing facial hair. I'm amazed to find out about the many changes puberty brings: genital hair; pimples all over my face; nocturnal emissions; and sudden erections for no reason. Peg and Gerry have never discussed 'the facts of life' with me. My experiences with Colleen showed me how boys and girls are physically different, and I've often seen dogs pair off on the road. These events, along with the discussion I had with my Da about the cow calving, combine with my active imagination and enables me to realise what's what. Putting one and one together, I'm totally disgusted. All that messing around seems to be over-complicated, and far from being proper. I'm completely turned off by the entire concept. And sadly, there are instances that create significant awareness of the fact that all this sex stuff includes some real improper, disconcerting stuff.

"NIALL, I want you to go to your Auntie Maura and give her this envelope," says Peg. "Take it from me love; put it safely in your pocket. I want you to get it to her as quickly as you can. She's in a desperate state. Will you do that for me, darlin'?"

The importance of prompt delivery of the envelope demands a trusted hand courier, and my Ma is honouring me with the task.

"Sure, Ma," I eagerly respond, as I shove the envelope into my pocket.

It's packed with anti-depressant tablets. Peg suffers from Addison's disease and has access to some anxiety medication. At times, writing pressures cause Maura some real angst – this appears to be one of those times. Peg regularly passes out tablets to her friends in need. It's never considered improper for her to do so – by herself, Maura or anyone else. She's always judicious about it, and she never asks for anything in return for the kindness. The tablets help her to get through rough patches, and she feels obliged to share the magic.

"That's a two-buser across town, Ma," says I. "I know the way. Give me the bus fare, and I'll get goin'."

We live in Cabra on the Northside, the part of Dublin city north of the River Liffey; Maura lives on Leinster Road in Rathmines, on the Southside.

"Here's a half-crown[2], love," says Peg. "Now, don't forget: take the 45B single-decker, not the 45A. That 45A takes you way out to the Hell Fire Club in the Dublin Mountains – it's the B that takes you to Maura's place on Leinster Road. You get the bus at the Fun Palace on Burgh Quay."

"OK, Ma," I shout back, as I run out the door. "Love ye."

Running all the way, I get the 12 bus at the Cabra/Quarry Road bus stop. That brings me to Clerys on O'Connell Street.

A quick walk to O'Connell Bridge and across to the Fun Palace gets me to where the 45B bus terminal is located. I just missed a 45B. *Gick on it: it'll be another thirty minutes before the next one comes.* I stand outside the Fun Palace wishing the minutes away.

The 45B single-decker.

He looks like a nice man. Tall and well dressed in a long tweed overcoat, his hands are in his coat pockets, and he has a big smile on his plump round face. He comes over to where I'm standing – right next to me, uncomfortably close to my left. Suddenly, I'm consumed with some weird, unfamiliar type of trepidation. *Watch out, Niall – somethin's up. I don't know what it is, but watch out!*

"Waiting for the bus, are you, son?" the tweed coat enquires, nudging me with his right hand, still deep in his coat pocket.

With all the difficulty of an innocent, apprehensive twelve year old, I respond: "Yeah. I just missed it."

"Ah well," says he. "Another one will be here in a while. Tell me, do you like toffee?"

Looking up at him, his now bothersome smile intensifies my anxiety. I love toffee, however, being asked the question in this odd way adds to my concerns. With increasing apprehension, I mumble a tortured reply: "Yeah."

"I've a bag of Yorkshire toffees," says the tweed coat. "Would you like one?"

This bloke is frightenin' me. He's right up against me, and he's actin' creepy. I wish he'd leave me alone. Lacking in any real understanding of what was going on, I muster the required bravery and respond: "Yeah mister." *The bus will be here in a minute, and I'll be able to get away from him.*

"There you go, son," says he, as he releases his right hand from his pocket and gives me two Yorkshire toffees.

I unwrap the toffees and eat them without any of the usual toffee chewing pleasure.

"Did you like those?" the tweed coat enquires. "There's more in my pocket. Put your hand in and take what you want."

The unidentified anxiety I've been suffering – right from that first moment when the tweed coat came over and stood beside me

122

– while remaining unidentified, is now terrifying me. Once again, I muster the required courage and respond: "No, mister. I've had enough."

"Don't be silly, son," says he, taking his hand out of his coat's right pocket. Firmly holding my left arm, he continues. "The best one in the bag is in there waiting for you. Slip your hand in. Go on now: do as I tell you."

I'm petrified. Looking up at him and his now cruel and demanding smile, I'm sure of it: *there is somethin' wrong goin' on. Please God, let the bus be here in a minute.*

His hold of my arm tightens to the degree that his fat figures are pinching me. Grimacing, I whimper: "Yer hurtin' me, mister."

"Go on: do as I tell you!" he demands. "Do as I tell you, now!" Confused and frightened of the unknown consequences of denying the monster's demand, I unwillingly reply: "Alright then."

I slide my hand into his pocket. It's a deep, bottomless pocket. *Please, God, the bus will come now!* I frantically grope about for the best one in the bag: "There's nothin' in there," I whine.

"Sure there is, son. Go deeper. That's a good boy."

There are no Yorkshire toffees. What I grab hold of is the tweed coat's enlarged penis!

"Ah . . ." the tweed coat moans. "Now you've found it."

"Jaysus!" I exclaim, pulling my hand out of his pocket and jumping away in utter horror. God is only a few seconds late in answering my prayer. The 45B pulls into the terminal.

"Ye dirty bastard, ye!" I yell as I push my way onboard the bus and against the flow of disembarking passengers.

By the time I'm sitting down in the back row of seats, he's gone. I look out the window. He's vanished!

I sit there feeling great disgust and even more anger. *The dirty bastard! Him and his toffees. I wish I were big enough to bash him. Him and his tweed coat. The dirty bastard!*

And I held his langer in me hand, I gasp, frantically wiping my hand on my trousers to clean myself from the horrific realisation.

My disgust and anger are quickly replaced with guilt and shame. I cry my way to Leinster Road. *I'm goin' to tell me Da. I shouldn't have put me hand in the bastard's pocket. I knew somethin' bad was goin' on. Maybe it was my fault and me Da will*

123

be mad at me! I'll have to keep it a secret and tell nobody. No, I'll tell me Da – he'll understand, and he'll know what to do.

The bus arrives at Maura's house. Finbarra, my cousin who is my sister Geraldine's age, answers the door.

"Hello, Niall," says Finbarra, greeting me as I hand her the envelope. "Come on in. I'll get you a nice, big strawberry ice cream wafer. You look tired. Are you all right, Niall?"

"Yeah, but I galloped all the way. Me Ma said yer Ma needs the message awful urgent." *I'm not goin' to tell me cousin about the tweed coat.*

The return trip to Erris Road is uneventful. I try hard to put the awful experience out of my mind. The ice cream Finbarra gave me helps, but Maura's message for my Ma, a crispy new pound note, helps even more.

****

I **WAS** turned off Yorkshire toffee, not to mention tweed overcoats and the Fun Palace, for life. Unlike with many other cases of sexual abuse of children, that horrible event never did me any lasting harm. My loving, trusting relationship with my father was the key. I told him about what had happened that night.

"You're a good boy telling me about this," says Gerry. "Now listen to me, Niall. You did nothing wrong. I want you to forget all about it. There're some sick, evil men in the world, and unluckily, you ran into one of them. I'll go down to the gardaí; they'll be able to do what's necessary to find him and put him away."

I've never forgotten it, but thanks to my wonderful father, after a while the horror of the disturbing event all but went away. I don't know whether or not the gardaí ever found the 'sick, evil man.' I hope they did. God knows it could have done me a lot of harm. I was one of the lucky ones – I had my Da.

****

Yarn #23 Footnotes
[1] Kiss my arse.
[2] A two shillings and six pence coin.

124

YARN #24
Kevin Callahan Gang –
T'ree T'ings I Had to Do

I'VE JUST TURNED THIRTEEN. CONOR RECEIVED his First Holy Communion this morning.

Conor with his big brother, Niall.

My Ma has asked me to go to Mr Quigley for 'the messages'. 'The messages' is how we refer to the list of groceries written out on a piece of paper by Peg, and given to the grocer for fulfillment. No money changes hands: it's a groceries-on-credit system used extensively by Peg and most of the neighbours. At the end of each week, and when the household's weekly wage earners are paid, tallies are made, and payment becomes due. For the most part, the bills are paid in full each Saturday. On those occasions when Peg is not able to satisfy the debt, an arrangement is made with the grocer, usually including some small interest.

"Will ye give me a backer, Amby?"

"OK, Niall," Ambrose Daly answers me. "Hop up."

Getting a lift from Amby is a godsend. Erris is playing Annaly in about twenty minutes, and I don't want to be late.

"Where are ye goin'?" asks Amby, as he slows up on his bicycle, not stopping, but going slow enough for me to jump onto his rear passenger seat.

125

"Quigley's. I'm in a massive hurry. Kevin Callahan is the Annaly captain. Can you play, Amby? Erris could use ye in goal."

Amby is the biggest boy on Erris. I've sprouted up somewhat: I'm just shy of four-foot-eight. Amby is five-foot-six. He looks as broad as he is tall, not exactly fat, but heavy – perfect as a goalkeeper in the Erris goal. He seems to be always on his bike. As his overall bulk increases, his bike appears to be getting smaller and smaller. The pair of them are becoming increasingly top heavy.

"OK, Niall. I'll play goalie," comes Amby's hailed response.

We're down and back with my Ma's messages in no time.

"Aren't you the quick one," Peg declares. "Thanks, love. You can go out now and play, but don't you be getting yourself into trouble. Remember what your Da said about Artane."

"I will, Ma and I'll never forget," I reply, meaning it fervently. "We're playin' Annaly, and I'll be right outside."

While the Annaly Road team is warming up at the Annaly end of Erris, the Erris team is doing the same at the Leix end. Kevin is captain of the Annaly team, and I'm captain of the Erris team. We play these inter-road soccer matches without the cumbersome presence of a referee. We all know the rules and play within them, even the strict offside rules.

It's time for the kick-off. As Kevin and I face each other for the kick-off on the halfway line, I take a quick glance back to the Erris goal. I'm delighted to see that Amby is our 'keeper. It looks as if he fills the goal with his massive frame.

I look back into Kevin's eyes. *Try and get the ball past Amby. Go on Kevin – try.* I take my tosser, a halfpenny coin, out of my pocket for the toss-up. The halfpenny has a fat sow plus five piglets on one side and an Irish harp on the other.

"Heads or harps, Kevin?" says I, steely-eyed and raring-to-go.

"Harps," comes Kevin's response. I flick the coin into the air. Up and then down it spins landing on the road between us, showing all six heads of my happy porcine family looking up at me.

"It's your kick-off, Niall," concedes Kevin. "I see ye've Amby as goalie. He'll help ye out. Now, let's see what the bloke who conquered Christ the King can do with a ball."

126

I had tried hard to forget about that larger-than-life event. Being unexpectedly reminded of it gives me a surge of aberrant vanity. That august evening, as I was being led away for sentencing, Kevin had shown me his admiration by winking at me. His reference to the glory of the achievement endorsed his expressed admiration, and I'm wallowing in its pleasure.

The match is hard fought and ends up with Erris winning by two goals. But for Amby, it would have been the other way around; he stopped the ball going into the Erris goal five or six times.

After the game, Kevin comes up to me.

"Good match, Niall," says he, shaking my hand. "Amby saved it for ye. He's a brilliant goalie. Tell me, would ye like to join me gang? Ye're thirteen now, and we're lookin' for one more bloke. I t'ink you'd be a great number eight. What do ye t'ink?"

I pause for a moment. *Is the pope catholic? Do cows shit in the field? What if me Ma or Da finds out?!*

"I don't know, Kevin," I respond, trying hard not to shut the door on what is a golden opportunity for adventure, entertainment, and all I look for in life. Kevin notices my hesitation.

"It's me Ma and Da. They're down heavy on me ever since Christ the King; they've even threatened me with Artane."

"None of the gang ever gets into trouble, Niall. We plan out everythin' real careful. We do lots of stuff, and we never get caught. Our Ma's and Da's know nothin' about what we're up to."

Kevin is expressing great sincerity in wanting me to join his gang. All he's saying is roaring at me to accept his invitation.

If I don't take his offer, I'll regret it for the rest of me life.

"OK, Kevin," I reply, having convinced myself that such good fortune would never come my way again. "I'll join yer gang."

"Great, Niall. We're meetin' tomorrow after school in our secret hideout. Meet me at the end of the Offaly Road lane opposite Fertullagh. Our secret hideout is in there. I'll bring ye to it, and ye can meet all the gang."

"OK, Kevin. We'll have to be careful not to let anyone know."

"Don't worry about it, Niall. Everythin' is secret in our gang. Ye'll see. And Niall, to get into the gang, ye'll have to do t'ree t'ings. With the way ye did Christ the King, ye won't have a problem. I'll tell ye all about it tomorrow. OK."

"Yeah, Kevin. And t'anks for lettin' me join yer gang. It's goin' to be great."

"See ye, Niall," says Kevin.

Kevin and his defeated team turn and head back to Annaly. Oddly enough, I notice Amby has joined them in their exit.

THROUGHOUT THE remainder of the day and my distracted hours of sleep, my racing mind is lost in the wonder of what is to be. *I can't stand it: a secret hideout; t'ree t'ings I'll have to do; Kevin so eager to recruit me. All this and beatin' Annaly by two goals.* The possibilities of my new source of adventure are overpowering. It stays that way until I meet Kevin at the Offaly Road lane after school the following day.

"How're ye, Niall," Kevin greets me. I've been waiting for him for ten long minutes.

"Great, Kevin," I reply, trying hard to play it cool.

The lane off Offaly is an odd kind of pathway. It's barely three-feet wide. It cuts into the centre of what is the back gardens of a square block of homes: homes on a section of Erris and Annaly, all of Galmoy Road, and a section of Offaly Road. It provides bike and pedestrian access to the backs of all the homes on the square.

"When we meet," says Kevin, as we both make our way up the narrow laneway, "we meet in our secret hideout. There's a waste piece of ground next to my house, and it's in there. Only the gang knows where it is." *It's gettin' better every minute. What could be more excitin'?*

The low three-foot-high railings surrounding each home's back garden are the same type as those that enclose the front gardens; the gates are the same as the one Mr Mulligan slams whenever he's on the binge. We reach the centre and turn a little down on the right branch of the laneway.

"Climb over here and follow me," instructs Kevin. "That's my house next door," he continues, as he points out the back of his house. "And here's our hideout."

"Where is it, Kevin? I can see nothin'."

There are some bushes, but I can't identify any dwelling.

"See what I mean, Niall. It's a secret hideout, and no one except the gang knows where it is." *More intensified mystery!*

"Around this bush and we're there," says Kevin.

"Now, do you see it?" Kevin gleefully asks.

"Janey Mack, Kevin! Where the hell is it?"

"Right here. Our hideout is right here."

Kevin bends down. To my great surprise, he hinges back a two-by-three-foot piece of the ground. Grassy earth and twigs have been mounted onto what is a hidden three-quarter-inch-thick timber trapdoor!

"Jays, Kevin. This is galactic! It's under the bleedin' ground."

I'm befuddled entirely. I can see that the underground hideout has lights. The trapdoor gives easy access to the hideout via a set of sturdy wooden steps.

"Go on down, Niall. Some of the gang are down there."

Five members of the gang greet me: "How're ye, Niall."

I'm dumbfounded and can't answer.

The two electric lights, one near the end of the room and the other near the trap-door, supply more than adequate light. The hideout is about six-foot wide, eight-foot long and at least seven-foot deep. Its ceiling is made up of what must be two eight-by-four sheets of three-quarter-inch thick timber, joined in the middle and supported by a six-by-six-inch pillar of wood standing in the centre of the hideout. With the entire wooden ceiling covered by grass and earth, and the trapdoor closed, the hideout is perfectly camouflaged and impossible to see from above.

The walls and floor are covered in white tarpaulin. There are four stools lined up against each of the eight-foot-long walls. A small table is positioned at the far end wall.

"Amby will be here in a minute," says Kevin. "Once he's here we'll start. Well, Niall, what do ye t'ink?"

"It's massive, Kevin. I don't know how ye did it. How did ye get the electricity in?"

"I brought a wire over from me Da's shed. It's hidden under the ground and comes in here," Kevin replies, pointing out how the connection comes in along the ceiling to each of the two lights.

The hatch is suddenly opened.

"How're ye, lads," says Amby Daly, lowering himself down the steps, and filling the hideout to capacity.

"Amby!" says I. "I didn't know ye were in Kevin's gang."

"There's lots ye don't know, Niall," Amby responds.

"That's right," says Kevin. "Let's get started." We all sit-down and Kevin starts the meeting.

"Before Niall gets into the gang, there's t'ree t'ings he's got to do," Kevin reaffirms.

For the last twenty-four hours, I've been thinking of little else. *What's Kevin goin' to throw at me?*

"The train, a bobby's baton and nettles," Kevin announces. Everybody knows their place and sits down, quietly waiting to hear the details of what Kevin has conjured up. He has thrown a little paint on the canvas, but he has some work to do before we'll be able to see the full picture. Looking directly at me, he continues.

"We'll start with the first t'ing, the Dublin-Belfast Express train. You've to lie between the tracks and let it run over ye."

I gulp, but stare right back at him, hopefully not exposing anything other than total acceptance of the task thrown at me. *How in the name of Jays am I goin' to do that?*

"We'll all go over the back wall in Kavo's field. We'll see ye while ye do it," Kevin qualifies.

"That's a great one, Kevin," says Amby, applauding Kevin's ability to pick tasks which most would consider being impossible.

"Then the bobby's baton," Kevin continues. "That's the second t'ing. You've got to get one, a real one like the bobbies have."

Another gulp, as I try to hold my much-tested composure. *Jays, that's as bad as the first t'ing.*

"And after that, the nettles," says Kevin. "That's the t'ird t'ing." He hasn't moved his eyes from mine for even a moment.

"Kavo's field has a sea of them. Ye've to crawl through the nettles. We'll all stand on one side watchin' out for ye; you'll start on the other side. And if we see ye while ye're comin' across, ye'll have to get up and start again. Ye have to keep hidden."

"They're the t'ree t'ings you've got to do. Have ye any questions? Are ye goin' to do dem? Do ye want to be in the Kevin Callahan gang?"

"No, yeah and yeah," I reply. "When do ye want me to do them?"

Kevin is still staring at me, and I'm still mesmerised by his entire persona.

"Tomorrow, do the train. The day after ye can start on gettin' the baton, and then ye can do the nettles."

"OK, Kevin. The Dublin-Belfast Express goes by at four-thirty. I'll plan it out, and I'll meet ye there after school."

"That's the way I knew ye'd take it, Niall," says Kevin, stretching out his right hand. "Let's shake on it."

"Way to go, Niall," says Amby.

The other members, all of whom I recognise, give me similar good wishes as I go the rounds shaking hands. Kevin and three of the gang members had been on the Annaly team I'd played the previous day. The remaining two I know to see, but I've never spoken to them until now.

"Me life on ye, Niall," says one of my new friends. "I'm Matt."

"Harry is my name," says the other. "I saw ye on the church roof. Massive, Niall – bleedin' massive."

"If ye're as good as ye are playin' football," says Éamon, "ye'll have no problem here." Éamon had marked me during the Erris/Annaly match; I'd no problem running rings around him.

"Ditto," Paddy says. "Do the t'ree t'ings, and ye're in."

"It's goin' to be great with you in the gang, Niall," says Cormac. "Like Paddy said, eat up the t'ree t'ings, and ye're in."

"Right, lads," says Kevin. "The meetin' is over. Let's break up. We'll meet at Kavo's field after school tomorrow."

We all climb out of the hideout; with the lights turned off and the trapdoor closed, we go our separate ways. I'll be ready for the train. I don't know how, but I'll be ready.

****

The Kevin Callahan Gang – the First T'ing, the Train

"**G**OD ALMIGHTY, NIALL. YOU'RE SHOVELLING that food into you! Masticate for God's sake, masticate!" shouts Peg.

"I've loads of ecker, Ma. I have to get at it," I reply.

We're sitting at the table having dinner. I do have some school homework, but that's not what my rushing is about; I've to work out how I'll survive letting the Dublin-Belfast Express train run over me – and I have less than twenty-four hours to figure it out.

"I keep telling you, Niall. You have to chew your food," says Peg. "Take human bites."

"But I understand, darlin'," she continues. "Don't bother with the cleaning up tonight. I'll do it. Eat up your dinner and get your homework finished. That's a good boy."

"OK, Ma. T'anks." I gulp the last of my dinner down and go up to my room. Putting my homework aside, I begin the urgent task of solving the train challenge.

I'm familiar with the railway line. Colleen and I spent many of our Wednesday afternoons hanging out there. Often, my friends and I daringly play on the tracks.

The Dublin/Belfast Express.

A favourite track game of ours is "Dare-ye." Knowing a train will be coming soon, we put our ears to the track. We thrill to the thunder of the oncoming locomotive – a whisper at first, all the way up to the powerful sound of the speeding train only a short distance from our heads. At the last moment, we pull our heads from the track and roll down the ballast to escape decapitation.

Another game we play is 'Flatten-it'. Placing farthings and halfpennies on the track, we let the train run over them. The farthings become halfpenny-size, and the halfpennies become penny-size, doubling the value of our coins. Sometimes the shopkeeper or whoever it is we're trying to trick notices the fake, but most times we get away with it.

Unlike the standard four-foot-eight-and-a-half-inch gauge tracks used throughout most of the world, the Irish tracks are five-foot-three. The rails are mounted on tar covered, two-foot-apart wooden sleepers sitting on a bed of stone ballast.

The rail-to-rail width is over five foot, and I'm five foot. There's some old sheets of tin in Kavo's field. I'll lie down between the tracks with the tin over me. No, that won't do. I'll be up over the height of the tracks. The train's stuff that dangles down will wallop me. I know what I'll do! I'll dig out the ballast between the sleepers and make a hole. That'll do it. I'll lie between the rail tracks and the sleepers. Great!

I've got to cover meself real well. I'll make sure the tin is five-foot long. A three-foot width would be perfect. I'll have to make sure I'll be able to hold it down – I don't want it flyin' off when the train is roarin' over me. How'll I be able to hold it down? I'll make two hand holds in the tin. That'll do it! Roll on, Dublin-Belfast Express – I'm ready for ye.

Feeling proud of myself, I hop down the stairs. Passing my Ma and Da in the parlour, I make my way to the lavatory.

"How are ye?" I greet them both. "I'm burstin' to do a pee."

"You haven't finished your homework yet, have you?" my mother enquires.

"No, Ma," I reply, as I unbutton my fly, making ready to pee. "I've loads to do. I'll go back up and finish it when I finish peein'."

"Ah, Gerry," I hear my mother say as I make my way to the toilet. "Will we ever put manners on him? Did you hear the way he answered me? He shouldn't be using bad words in front of his mammy, or in front of his daddy for that matter."

"He's all right, Peg," my Da answers. "Sure pee is not a bad word. He's a grand lad, and isn't he doing his ecker and all. I think you're doing a great job on him, Peg."

Me life on ye, Da! Ye're always there standin' up for me.

"After me ecker is done, I'll go to bed," I declare, as I go by them on my way back up to my bedroom.

"Goodnight, Ma; 'night, Da," says I. "See ye in the mornin'."

"That's a good boy, Niall," says Gerry, giving me one of his winks. So as to be sure I'd hear him, as I'm closing the parlour door, he adds: "Now Peg, didn't I tell you. That Niall of ours is turning out to be a grand lad."

When I grow up, I'm goin' to be just like me Da. He's the best Da in the whole wide world.

I feel grown up and in total control. I quickly complete my homework, get into bed and fall fast asleep.

NEXT MORNING, before leaving for school, I equip myself with the required tools from my Da's work shed: a hand trowel, a tape measure, a hammer, a chisel, a set of pliers and two small pieces of sacking. I hide them in the bottom of my school bag.

"You've a lot of stuff in your bag, darlin'," Peg comments. "I worry about you hurting yourself. Are you all right, love?"

"I'm OK, Ma. I'm big now, and I'm well able to carry all me b'oks. I don't want to be late. Bye Ma, love ye."

I ask Brother Colman if I can leave school a little early. With my request granted, I run all the way and reach Kavo's field at about a quarter to four. I have a lot to do before the express train comes – and I've forty-five minutes to do it.

I'll get the tin coverin' sheet done first; I've got to size it and then I'll make the two hand holds. Once that's finished, I'll pick a spot on the railway line and dig out the ballast.

I find a suitable sheet of tin without difficulty. Using the hammer and chisel, and having measured it off to five feet, I'm able to quickly bend it back, and break off the oversize portion. Making the hand holds gives me lots of trouble; after fifteen minutes of struggling, I'm finally able to knock them out. They're rough, but that's why I brought the sacking. The sacking will save my hands when I'm holding it as the train rolls over me.

I've carried the cover sheet over the railway wall, and I'm digging out the ballast when Kevin and the gang arrive.

"How're ye, Niall," says Kevin. "It's twenty-five after four. Are ye goin' to be ready?"

"Yeep, Kevin," I grunt, as I continue to aggressively dig out the ballast with my trowel. I'm sweating; I've discarded my jacket on the grassy bank along with my school bag and tools – right where Colleen and I used to sit.

"Hurry up, Niall," Amby urges. "I hear the train comin'."

Amby's right. I have my ear very near to the rail. I don't want to believe it, but I can hear the train coming in the distance. *Another bit and I'm done, just a bit more.*

I can't wait any longer. The hole will have to do as it is. I scamper up the bank. Tossing the trowel to the ground, I grab the cover sheet and sacking, and I'm back in the hole in a flash.

"Shit, Niall," I hear Kevin bellow. "Quick, get the fuck down! The train is comin' 'round the bleedin' bend!"

He doesn't have to tell me. Being where I am, and with the increased echo volume of the train's deafening noise intensified by my cover sheet, I know all about it. As the seconds pass, the noise increases. Sacking in hand, I firmly grasp the two hand holds. I wish for four hands – fingers of the second set would be stuck in my ears. The train isn't over me yet, and the increasing noise is already horrendous. *Ye eejit ye, ye should've brought some cotton-wool for yer ears.* That is my last thought as the train roars over me.

The sensation is frightened. No – that's ridiculously inadequate. Horrific! That's it. This is not the first time, nor will it be the last, when I'd find myself in a hopeless situation, but this train roaring over me is dwarfing everything. There is absolutely no way of describing the noise. The entire event is the most unreal experience of my entire life! It's simply awful. I pee in my pants.

The train has passed and is some ways away when I'm brought back to earth. I don't know where my body and soul went to during those few moments. To say I was someplace I'd never been, soulless and without a body, feels about right.

"Are ye OK?" I hear from above. It's Kevin who has made the enquiry, not God. My hands are frozen in their grip of the cover sheet. My two sets of fingers are all that can be seen from above. With great effort, I loosen my grip and push the cover off.

"I've peed in me pants. Otherwise, I'm OK." My response brings wild laughter from Kevin and the gang.

"Jaypers Niall, that was bleedin' great," says Kevin. "Ye've passed the first t'ing with flyin' colours; I can tell ye that. Didn't he, lads?"

All the gang join with Kevin and give me a warm round of applause.

"Ye put the heart crossways in us, Niall," says Amby. "We thought we were goin' to lose ye."

"That was better than the church roof," adds Harry. "Massive, Niall – bleedin' massive."

My head is still ringing from the noise and trauma I've been exposed to. Sitting down with the gang, things slowly begin to sink in. I realise what I'd achieved: I'd completed task number one!

"I made one mistake," says I. "I didn't bring cotton-wool for me ears. The noise was brutal. I can barely hear meself talk."

"You thought through everythin' smashin', Niall," says Kevin. "The cotton wool would have helped ye, but ye're here with us, and ye'll be grand once ye've rested a bit."

"Do you know how ye're goin' to get the bobby's baton, Niall?" asks Cormac.

"Give him a break, will ye?" says Kevin. "Let him get over the train first, then he can start t'inkin' about the baton."

"I have been t'inkin' about it," says I. "Those batons are hard to find. Give me time to work it out."

It's after five o'clock. I've not been home from school yet. It's time to go if I'm to avert my mother being worried about her close-to-being good boy. I pack up my tools, put on my jacket, and with my heavy school bag on my back, I head for home.

Walking out of Kavo's field is a particularly proud moment for me. I'd impressed Kevin and all the gang. I'd done 'the first t'ing'! The bobby's baton and the nettles have yet to be conquered, however, after the train, any challenge seems easy in comparison.

****

THE DUBLIN-BELFAST Enterprise Express continues to roll by. I hope there isn't another little devil like me lying under it as it roars its way along. But if there is, I hope he hasn't forgotten to bring some cotton wool for his ears; to this day, a ringing in my left ear frequently reminds me of the error I made by not having done so.

****

The Kevin Callahan Gang – the Second T'ing, the Baton

*A*BOBBY'S BATON: WHERE IN THE HELL *am I goin' to get one? There're no gardaí livin' on Erris, and there's none in me family – no uncles nor nothin'. There's always a few bobbies on Cabra Road, but I never see any of them with batons.*

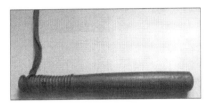

A bobby's baton.

I'm mulling over the baton challenge while sitting at the table eating my dinner; initial deliberations are drawing blanks. *I'll have to move out of Cabra. Now . . . Where could I find a load of bobbies with batons?*

"O'Connell Street!" I screech out, much to my own and my parents' surprise.

"What's wrong with you, Niall!?" exclaims Peg, coughing as she does so. Gerry is also coughing. "You nearly choked me with the fright. And didn't you nearly choke your father as well."

"I was only thinkin' Ma. It just came out."

"And what, pray tell us, were you thinking?" enquires Gerry as he extracts his handkerchief from his pocket and blows his nose.

"O'Connell Street, Da."

"And couldn't a blind man see that by the way you roared it out at us," Gerry responds. "Now . . . Can you tell us what it was about O'Connell Street you were thinking? It's that that your Ma and I are wondering about. Am I right, Peg?"

138

"You are, Gerry," confirms Peg. "Now, will you tell us, Niall?"

"O'Connell Street is awful busy, and there's always loads of gardaí all over the place," says I, hoping to satisfy their interest.

"I suppose you're right, Niall," says Gerry. "Do you remember me bringing you and Conor in there on the 12 bus? I brought you up to the top of Nelson's Pillar. We climbed all of its 168 steps. And afterwards, we sat on the bench beside Dan O'Connell's monument watching the gardaí directing the traffic."

Nelson's Pillar.

"I do, Da," I respond. "Goin' up the Pillar was smashin'. Ye had to carry Conor up – ye were nearly dyin', ye were so tired. It was great lookin' out from the top of the Pillar, seeing all over Dublin. And it was smashin' seein' the gardaí on point-duty directin' the traffic at the monument – runnin' up and down, wavin' their arms and blowin' their whistles."

Traffic at the complex set of six busy roads converging on O'Connell Street Bridge is controlled by two pairs of point-duty gardaí, one pair on each side of the bridge. Each one is as able and entertaining as the other, always on the move, each with his own unique style. One of them has a Bill Bailey moon-walk manner of moving. Another, with a whistle in his mouth, bounces around willy-nilly, his arms moving in a manner that qualifies him as being some crazy, whistle-blowing contortionist.

"Maybe you'll be joining the force when you grow up," says Gerry. "The force needs a lot more Dublin blokes. Sure these days, every garda you see is a culchie[1]." The city's population is exploding due to the increasing number of culchies moving in. My Da, being the proud Dubliner he is, appears to hold some dislike for the dilution of the purity of Dublin's bloodline.

"And being a Rathangan County Kildare girl myself," says Peg proudly, "isn't it as well we culchies come up from the countryside and take on the job. But for us, there'd be no gardaí at all."

"Yes, love," Gerry responds. "I suppose you're right."

"Now, no more shouting, Niall," continues Gerry. "Eat your dinner and help your Ma clean up when we're finished."

As I wistfully wash and dry the dishes, I'm thinking about what my Da had said, particularly the part about the gardaí on point-duty. *That's it! I remember seein' bobbies' overcoats with batons lyin' on them on the benches at the monument. Me Da has solved the problem! All I have to do is get down there and swipe one.*

Number two challenge looks like it's about to be conquered. It's not going to be easy, but it is doable. Tomorrow is Saturday; having no school, I'll have the whole day to plan it out.

THE FOLLOWING day finds me sitting tops on the 12 bus. I love travelling on the double-decker buses. Being upstairs sitting in the front makes it all the better; it allows me to see things from a different perspective.

CIE double-decker bus.

Reaching O'Connell Street, I get off the bus and make my way to the Daniel O'Connell monument.

As usual, Dan's head and shoulders are vulgarly spotted with seagull shit; despite this avian effrontery, Dan looks as proud as ever, standing up, eying south across the Liffey. His four victory angels, Patriotism, Courage, Fidelity, and Eloquence – three of them with bullet holes in their arms and boobs – are guarding him; they incurred their injuries during the 1916 Easter Rising and the 1922–3 Irish Civil War.

Daniel O'Connell Monument.

At O'Connell Bridge, right in front of Dan's monument, the gardaí are doing their usual entertaining thing, directing traffic. It's a sunny morning, and the overcoat I'm wearing – perfect for concealing a stolen baton – is making me uncomfortably warm. My discomfort vanishes when I spy the hard-to-find baton. It's on one of the monument's benches lying on top of a peeled-off garda's greatcoat.

It takes but a moment: I sit down beside the baton, and one, two, three, it's under my coat. I pause for a moment to secure a good grip; baton secured, I stand up and walk away.

I have good reason to rush, and I do. Should my brazen stealth be discovered, I'll be in more trouble than I want to think about. Scampering up O'Connell Street, I'm past the GPO and standing at the 12 bus stop outside the Capital Cinema in record time. Waiting for the bus to arrive gives me the heebie-jeebies; my unease is intensified by Mrs Mulligan, the window smasher's wife, who comes along and joins me at the bus stop.

"Is that you, Niall?" asks Mrs Mulligan. "What are you doing in town all on your own?"

"I'm doin' somethin' for me Ma," I lie.

Gratefully, the bus pulls up. Darting on board, I mount the stairs and throw myself into my usual spot, up front and tops.

I get off the bus at Quarry Road and run down Leix onto Erris. I hide the stolen baton in my Da's work shed. The sweet smell of success once again fills me. All I have to do now is show the baton to Kevin and the gang, and tell them how I got it. Then, subject to the last task's completion, the dreaded nettles, I'll be in. I'll become the proud, new member of the Kevin Callahan gang.

I don't want to waste any time in letting Kevin know about my accomplishment; I run down to where he lives on Annaly Road.

His mother answers the door.

"How're ye, Mrs Callahan? Is Kevin there?"

"Hold on a minute, and I'll get him for you."

Kevin comes to the door. He's surprised to see my smiling face. "How're ye, Niall? That was quick. Ye got the baton, right?"

"Yeep! Can I show it to ye?"

"Sure. I'll let the lads know about it. It's got to be a real baton, Niall. And ye'll have to tell us how ye got it."

"It's real, alright," says I. "And wait 'til you hear how I got it."

"OK, Niall. Let's meet in our hideout in an hour."

With the baton concealed up my jumper, and down into my pants, I'm opening the hideout hatch in no time. I turn on the lights and carefully close the hatch behind me. I place the baton on the small table and sit down to relax and wait for Kevin and the gang.

It takes about forty minutes for them to arrive. One by one, each arrival brings me more pride of my triumph. Each of the gang has his own way of expressing surprise and pleasure at seeing the baton on the table. They barely acknowledge my presence – they only have eyes for the baton.

"Ye got it," says Amby.

"Massive, Niall – bleedin' massive," says Harry.

Kevin is last to arrive. He picks the baton up with his right hand and gives it a series of slaps into the palm of his left.

"Looks real to me, Niall," says Kevin.

I slowly relay the details of how I had achieved my goal. The only interruptions are short gasps and sniggers of laughter. Once I've completed my saga, there's a round of congratulatory handshaking followed by some concluding comments from Kevin.

"Can ye do the nettles tomorrow?" asks Kevin.

"No problem," I respond. I hadn't given the nettles task much if any thought. "There's a way to do it, and I've got to find it."

"That's right, Niall," Kevin continues.

"There's always a way. So let's break up. We'll meet in Kavo's field after mass tomorrow."

We all say our goodbyes and part company. Tomorrow is Sunday, and as agreed we'll meet at Kavo's field after mass. Two t'ings down and one t'ing to go!

****

THERE WAS never a rightful place in Ireland for Nelson's Pillar. Nonetheless, it was erected by the English in 1808, right in the middle of O'Connell Street, the very heart of Dublin City. At Trafalgar in 1805, the British navy's Vice Admiral Horatio Nelson had secured a major victory for England over the combined French and Spanish navies. He was killed in the battle, along with a lot of Irishmen who had joined the British Navy as their means of living.

The Pillar would fast become the city's main architectural identity; London has Big Ben; Paris has the Eiffel Tower; and Dublin had Nelson's Pillar. For a long time, and particularly after Ireland became a Free State in 1922, Dubliners had a love/hate relationship with the Pillar. Until 1966, rightfully or wrongfully, that was the way it was. Dubliners tried very hard to find justification for the continued presence of this English warlord in the centre of the capital city of what was now a free and unencumbered Republic of Ireland. If you were to stretch it quite a bit – and I always did – you could consider that while Horatio was an Englishman of fame, more than one-third of his near 500 seamen who died with him at Trafalgar were Irishmen. However, the truth is a tough one: the moment Ireland became a Free State, if not before, is when Nelson's Pillar should have been removed. Nelson's tenancy did terminate in 1966; some IRA enthusiasts brazenly blew him up, ending his one-hundred and fifty-eight-year reign of the city.

While the task of climbing the Pillar's circling 168 steps with my brother Conor and my Da was a demanding one, it was also very exciting. The poorly lit, steep, narrow stairway could only safely accommodate one-way traffic. A group of about a dozen people at a time would go up, spend fifteen minutes enjoying the view; the next group of patrons had to wait until the preceding group came down before they could start their ascent. All this added to the excitement. It was a beautiful day, and once we were up, the view was spectacular. I remember my Da saying: "Now there's a sight for sore eyes – this is the best shilling we've ever spent." The admission fee was sixpence for my Da and truppence each for Conor and me. It was wonderful gazing down at the pedestrians, trams, buses and cars, all milling around and looking like little toys.

While we were up there, we shared the view with a small Dublin woman. She had an umbrella up. The bright day's sunshine was beautiful, but not by any means was it warm enough to require such shade. The woman's low stature and open umbrella were causing discomfort to everyone; her umbrella almost poked me in the eye a number of times. My Da politely approached her and suggested that she put her weapon down. "I'm sorry, sir, for pokin' yer child," responded the woman, "but me daughter warned me to bring me umbrella up with me when I was comin' up here. She told me that ol' Nelson fella is known to have peed on the Irish."

I've often wondered about what that poor unfortunate garda did about his stolen baton. If I was a garda and someone had stolen my baton, it's not something I'd like to have to explain. I hope he lied his way through it all and didn't get fired for gross negligence.

****

Yarn #26 Footnote
[1] Anyone born in Ireland, but not in Dublin City, is a culshie.

Kevin Callahan Gang – the T'ird T'ing, the Nettles

NETTLES STING ANYONE UNLUCKY ENOUGH TO have touched them. The slightest contact produces a raised, painful blister the size of anything from a tanner to a half-crown. Gratefully, the dock leaf grows alongside the nettles; we all know of the dock leaf's magic powers. In the absence of rubbing the leaf on the sting, immediately after being stung and before the blister has time to appear, the unfortunate victim will have to suffer that blister plus all its discomfort until getting out of bed the following day. It seems that sleep or maybe time gets rid of the affliction.

The nettle stings.   *The doc leaf cures.*

"Ma, I think I'll go to early mass tomorrow," says I.

If, as usual, I go to ten o'clock mass with Peg, I won't be able to get to Kavo's field until after eleven. I want to make sure I'll have enough time to get ready.

"Why do you want to do that, son?" Peg enquires.

"Bohs are playin' Shels in Dalyer. I don't want to miss it," I answer. Bohemians, a Northside Dublin football team are due to play Shelbourne Rovers, a Southside Dublin team in Dalymount Park, Phibsborough. I've no intention of actually going. I've the nettles to attend to.

"Who are you going with? I hope it's not that Frank Frazier."

"No, Ma, I'm goin' with Amby Daly," I lie.

145

"All right then," replies my trusting mother. "I'll get you up early and make sure you're in time for nine o'clock mass?"

"Perfect, Ma. There'll be loads goin' to the match. I don't want to risk not gettin' in."

"Have you enough money, love?" Peg asks. She's starting to make me feel uncomfortably guilty.

"I've enough, Ma," I reply, fully intent on not being paid for my lies. "I'll get in the schoolboys' gate for a tanner." *Two lies, and there she is offerin' me mula. No way am I takin' me Ma's money.*

It's time for me to work out a solution to the nettle challenge. *I'll have to wear me thickest clothes. Me hands, arms, legs and me whole head will need to be covered. Those nettles have hairs on them, and they'll sting me if me clothes aren't thick enough.*

I discover I'm not well endowed with suitable garb. Each piece, on its own, fails to come near to what is required. *I'll have to double-up. I'll wear two pairs of socks, two pairs of longers and two shirts. I'll shove me longers into me socks so's the nettles won't sting me legs. Me hands have to be covered too. Me head and face are goin' to be hard to cover. How am I goin' to do that?*

I find a thick knitted hat, which when pulled down, covers my ears. *That won't do anythin' for me face and neck.* I continue picking through my clothes. In a bottom drawer, I find a hand-me-down thick, polo neck jumper. It's been lying waiting for me to grow into it. My brother Paddy didn't like the birthday gift he'd received from our Aunt Maura; it had been bequeathed to me.

I slip the jumper over my head. It goes down and well covers my bum. The sleeves are three inches too long. While I'm putting it on, the collar unrolls, leaving a couple of inches sticking above my head. *This is smashin'. I'll be able to knot the sleeves, and that'll cover me hands. And I can knot the neck over me head, and that'll save me face.* I'm almost there.

Looking into the mirror on the back of my bedroom door, I laugh at the bizarre image. *I look like an eejit without a head, but it's goin' to do the job. I'll wear the woollen hat as well.*

I've done it. Mission accomplished!

I roll up the extra socks, trousers, shirt and hat inside the big jumper and hide them in my Da's work shed. I'm ready for tomorrow's final challenge. *I'll dress for mass and then pick up me armour on me way 'to the game'.*

THE FOLLOWING morning, with my armour tucked under my oxter, I arrive at Kavo's field at a little after ten. Kevin and the gang will be here sometime before eleven. I quickly don my protective clothing over my Sunday Mass clothes and begin the required reconnaissance.

Kevin will pick the place with the most nettles. Looking out over the field, that area is easily identified. Right across the centre of the field is a sea of tall angry-looking nettles blowing in the morning breeze. I climb onto what is the highest vantage point, the railway line wall. There's no easy way across. I notice there is a dangerous stretch of twisted scrap metal in one section. *I'll have to avoid that.*

As I'm dismounting the wall, I see Kevin plus gang-of-six, soon-to-be-seven, coming into the field. Throughout my reconnaissance I've had my armour on: I've rolled the jumper's sleeves up, and the polo-neck is as it would normally be, rolled down and around my neck.

"'Mornin', Niall," says Kevin. "Do the last t'ing and ye're in."

"Yeah," pipes in Amby. "Ye'll be crawlin' in, but ye'll be in."

"And don't forget," adds Kevin. "We'll be on the other side watchin' out for ye, and if we see ye, ye'll have to start over."

"Let's get goin'," he continues. "Ye're to start over there in the middle. We'll go to the other side and tell ye when ye're to go."

The starting point Kevin had pointed to is slab-dab on the periphery of the sea of tall nettles, now looking angrier than ever.

"Right. I'll go and get ready. Let me do me knots," says I.

"Niall, what do ye mean, 'do me knots'?" says Kevin.

A picture is worth a thousand words: I turn back to Kevin and show him what I meant.

"Massive, Niall," says Kevin.

Kevin and the gang go across to the other side of the field. They take the sensible route. I'll have to crawl my way across.

"I nearly forgot me hat," I exclaim, as I prep for the challenge. I undo the two sleeve knots plus the top knot. I get the hat out of my pocket, slam it on my head and re-knot. I'm ready to go.

147

"Right, Niall," Kevin roars from across the field. "On the count – one, two, t'ree, go!"

For the next twenty minutes, I crawl my way across. I avoid the twisted metal and all attempts from the angry nettles to sting. Kevin and the gang don't see me until I emerge in front of them on the other side. I stand up proudly, albeit exhausted, ready to claim my rightful ownership of full membership.

"Ye've done it, Niall," exclaims Kevin, applauding with all the other gang members. "Ye're in the gang!"

This declaration is given with all my knots still tied. I can see Kevin, but what he and the gang are looking at is the headless one – the proud new member of the Kevin Callahan gang.

****

KAVO'S FIELD is sadly no more. It is now covered over with a paint factory and some apartments. No more nettles or dock leaves.

****

Me Da's Goodbye

G ERRY IS IN THE PARLOUR, SITTING IN HIS CHAIR beside a blazing fireplace and reading the *Evening Herald* newspaper. Much to Peg's chagrin, he's smoking one of his cigarettes. He's been in his sick bed with a severe flu-like cold for the past few days. He's feeling a bit better today, and my Ma has coaxed him to come downstairs for his dinner. I'm in the kitchen helping her prepare the meal. Gerry suddenly starts coughing: that's not unusual, but this time it's different – it lasts longer and sounds different.

"Gerry love," shouts Peg. "Will you for God's sake cut back on those bloody cigarettes? They'll kill you, so they will."

"Do you hear me, Gerry?" says Peg. There is no response.

"Are you all right, Gerry love?" Peg anxiously enquires as she wipes her wet hands on her apron and goes into him.

"Holy Mother of God!" she screams. "What's wrong, Gerry?"

I run in to join her. To our horror, we find him slouched over in his chair. His newspaper has fallen out of his hand, onto the floor and is catching fire. Peg feverishly stamps out the burning newspaper. She looks at my Da and holding his hands she gently eases him back into his chair. Gerry's eyes are closed, and his face is ashen. Peg starts crying.

"He only fell asleep, Ma. Wake him up," says I.

"Quick! Go into the kitchen and get a glass of water, Niall."

When I return with the water, my Da is lying back, still ashen-faced, but his eyes are open.

"Take a sip of water, Gerry love," Peg begs. Bringing his head forward, she puts the glass to his lips.

"Take a sip, Gerry. It'll help you get your breath back."

"Are ye OK, Da?" I ask, confused and frightened. *Please God, make me Da better.*

"He'll be OK in a minute, Niall. Just let him get his breath back," says Peg.

"Peggy, love," my father mutters. "I'm not well. I think we'd better get me . . . get me to the hospital."

"I know, love," answers my mother. "Can you breathe, Gerry? Have you your breath back?"

"I have, but my chest feels like it's bursting. I'm awful weak, Peggy. And I'm terrible light in the head. It's nothing I've felt before. Get me to the hospital and have the doctors check me out."

While Gerry is talking, Peg's tears are flowing from her pained eyes.

"It's for the best," continues my Da. "Now Peggy, don't you be making it harder for me. Stop cryin', love. That's a good girl."

"I'm worried sick about you, but don't let my tears annoy you, Gerry. Don't you be worrying yourself about me."

"Niall, run into Mrs Lawlor and get her to ring for the ambulance. Tell her it's an emergency. Quick now! Run in!"

We don't have a telephone, but the Lawlors next door do. I dash out of the house, fault over the back-garden railings and run to Lawlor's back door.

"Mrs Lawlor!" I shout as I bang on her door. "Me Da is sick and me Ma needs ye to ring for the ambulance! Hurry, Mrs Lawlor! It's an emergency!"

Mrs Lawlor comes to the door.

"We've got to get me Da to the hospital. He's sick, and he was gettin' better, and he came down for his dinner, and he was sittin' in his chair, and he fell asleep, and the paper went on fire, and he can't breathe, and he has a pain in his chest, and me Ma is cryin', and–"

"Holy God, Niall," she responds. "Come in here and stop yer cryin'. Yer daddy will be OK. We'll call the ambulance. Is yer mammy OK?"

"She's holdin' me Da's hand, and she's makin' him have a drink of water," I sob, "and she's cryin'."

"Ambulance please, we've an emergency," Mrs Lawlor yells into the phone. "Me neighbour's husband needs an ambulance."

"Twenty Erris Road, Cabra," she continues. "On the corner of Offaly and Erris. God speed to ye, as quick as ye can."

"Now, Niall," she says to me, as she hangs up the phone, "The ambulance is on its way. Let's go into yer mammy and see w'at we can do to help."

"God love ye, Peggy," Mrs Lawlor says as we run into the parlour. "The ambulance is on its way."

"Gerry's not well, Maggie," says Peg, acknowledging our presence while keeping her eyes on my Da's face.

With his deep-set, dark eyes closed, Gerry confirms the all too obvious. "You're right, Peg. I'll be okay once the doctors get a hold of me. But you're right love – I'm not well."

"The ambulance will be here before ye know it," says Mrs Lawlor. "You lie there, Gerry. Is there an'in' I can do for ye, Peg?"

"Where's Conor, Niall?" asks my Ma.

"He's out playin' on the road."

"Good. I'll be going with your daddy to the hospital. You'll have to look after Conor for me. Geraldine, Fergie, and Paddy will be home from work in a little while, and they'll finish the dinner. The two of you will be OK until they get home."

"Sure they will, Peggy," says Mrs Lawlor. "And I'll be here to tell Geraldine and the boys w'at's happened. You look after yerself and Gerry. Don't you be worryin' about an'in' else."

"You're a good neighbour, Maggie," says Peg.

The ambulance.

The ambulance arrives. One of the EMS men runs into the house with his oxygen tank and medical bag; the other pulls a gurney from the ambulance and quickly follows his colleague. Gerry is placed on the gurney with a mask strapped to his face. They wheel him out, Peg walking beside him holding his hand.

"What's wrong, Niall," pants Conor. He and his friends had seen the ambulance, and have come to see what is happening.

"Our Da is sick. Ma's bringin' him to the hospital."

"And he'll be as right as rain once the doctors get ahold of him," Mrs Lawlor adds. "Yer big brothers and sister will be home

151

soon. Niall and I will look after ye. Yer mammy will be home once yer daddy is settled in."

As Peg is climbing into the ambulance, she turns to me in panic.

"Niall, I forgot the brown scapular! Quick! Run into the house and get it for your Da. It's hanging on a hook beside the bedroom mirror. Go now, Niall, as quick as you can."

Turning to one of the EMS men, she continues: "Mister . . . Gerry has to wear the brown scapular. He needs the protection and help of Our Lady of Mount Carmel. Niall will be back in a minute with it. Sure you won't go until he comes back? Please, mister, sure you won't?"

"Of course I won't, Ma'am," answers the EMS man. "Sure isn't me job to do all I can to help the sick. You relax in there and sit with yer husband. That scapular is all he needs to get better."

I run to my parent's bedroom, grab the scapular and I'm back to the ambulance in less than a minute.

The brown scapular.

"Here ye are, Ma," says I, climbing into the ambulance and delivering the scapular to my much-appeased mother.

"Thanks, Niall," Peg responds. Turning to my Da, she gently lifts his head and places the hallowed item around his neck.

"Now darlin', let me put the brown scapular on you. Our Lady of Mount Carmel will look after you."

This tragedy occurs on a Friday. I don't see my Da again until the following Sunday afternoon. The restricted children visiting rule, introduced because of another TB and polio scare, gives strict half-hour visits for children on Sundays only.

My Da is sitting up in his hospital bed. His oxygen mask is on, hiding his usual smile.

"How's my Nialler?" says Gerry. He sounds different. I notice he's wearing the brown scapular.

"I'm OK, Da. Are ye gettin' better?"

"Yes, son. The doctors and nurses are looking after me. We're not there yet, but we're on the way."

"Bohs are playin' Tolka Rovers today, Da. Me and the lads are goin'. It'll be a smashin' match. Bohs should beat Tolka easy."

"I bet they will," replies Gerry. Peg is sitting on a chair on the other side of the bed, holding my Da's hand.

"I can't stay long, Da. The match starts at t'ree."

"There he is," interjects Peg. "If it's not the road, it's a football game. Our little street urchin, always wanting to be out and about."

"And isn't he grand, Peg," replies Gerry. "Niall is a grand lad – out playing and enjoying himself. He's doing no harm." Turning to me, he adds, "Isn't that right, Niall? You're doing great in school, and your Da's proud of you."

"And I'll tell you something, Peg," he continues, turning to my Ma. "When I get out of here, that's what you and I are going to do. Much more than we've been doing of late. We're going to start getting out more and having some playing around."

"That'll be nice, Gerry – what with the children grown up now. Geraldine's twenty January next year, Fergie is eighteen and Paddy's sixteen. And they're all working, and Niall will be fifteen in July. There's only Conor, and he's eight in June, but the older ones will be well able to look after him."

"That's right, Peg love," my Da replies. "I'm sorry I've not been looking after you the way I should. I'll get meself better; then we'll put it right. Wait and see, Peg. Things will be different."

"Da, can I go now?" I interrupt. "I don't want to be late."

"Off you go, Niall. Let me know the results. Off you go now."

I give my Da a kiss on the cheek; turning away from him, I make my way towards the door. I turn back and wave goodbye. My Da, taking the oxygen mask from his mouth, waves his goodbye; with a smile on his face, he shouts, "Up Bohs!"

****

A Dreadful Difference is Born

IT'S THREE O'CLOCK THE FOLLOWING MORNING and my two older brothers are up. The bedroom light has been turned on.

"What's wrong?" I exclaim.

"Someone is knockin' on the front door," Fergie answers. "You stay in bed. Ma and Geraldine are seein' who it is. Paddy and I are goin' down. You stay here and look after Conor."

My brothers and I sleep in the boy's bedroom; Conor and I are together in one bed while Paddy and Fergie sleep in the other. Geraldine has her own room, and my Da and Ma use the third bedroom.

I've been awakened from a deep sleep after a busy day – going to see my Da in the hospital, seeing Bohs beat Tolka four goals to three, and playing on the road with my friends. My last thought before I'd fallen asleep was, *I can't wait to tell me Da the results of the match.*

Sitting anxiously in bed, I'm trying to determine the cause of this alarming awakening. *Who's at the door? What's wrong?* Careful not to wake Conor, I creep out of bed, open the bedroom door and go to the top of the stairs.

"I'm sorry for your loss, Ma'am," I hear some stranger say. "Bringing you this type of news is hard on me."

Everyone is crying. Worried and bewildered, I start to cry with them. "What's wrong?" I sob. "Why are ye all cryin'?"

Fergie turns to me and starts up the stairs.

"Our Da has gone to heaven. Ma is awful upset, and the garda is tellin' us all about it. I want you to stay in your bed with Conor. Come with me, and I'll tuck you in."

"We want you to be Conor's big brother," Fergie continues.

"OK, Fergie," I reply, as I get back into my bed. Fergus turns the bedroom light off and closes the door.

My Da is dead. I'll never see him again.

I've never really thought of death until this moment. I'm aware that people die, but being hit with the fact that my Da is dead, is an impossible thing for me to comprehend. I'll be fifteen in July, and here I am, lying in my bed in the dark, not able to share my thoughts with anyone. My little brother is sleeping beside me. I reach out for Conor's hand; holding it gently I cry myself to sleep.

"Waken-up, boys," Geraldine says as she sits down on our bed. She has pulled the window curtains back, and the bright early morning's sunlight is shining into my sleepy eyes.

"W'at time is it?" Conor asks. "Why are ye wakenin' us up?"

"Good mornin', Geraldine," says I, stretching myself awake. "I had an awful dream. I dreamt Fergie told me, me Da was dead."

Geraldine is wearing a black skirt and blouse; her eyes and nose look red and sore. She starts to cry.

"Da has gone to heaven," says Geraldine. "Mammy is upset."

"I want you two to be strong for our Mammy," she continues, as she pulls a hanky out of her skirt pocket and blows her nose.

"Can I go to heaven and see me Da?" asks Conor. "Is he goin' to come back to us?"

I start to cry. That terrible dream I thought I had, has been redefined as a cruel reality. *It isn't a dream. My Da is dead.*

"All the neighbours are downstairs with Mammy," says Geraldine. "I've taken out your dark clothes. We've to wear black now. When we go downstairs, I want you two to go over to your Mammy and give her a big hug. She's awful upset."

"But can I go and see me Da?" Conor asks again.

"No Conor," I answer, wiping my tears with the sleeve of my pyjamas top. "Ye can't go and see him. When yer Da is dead, ye can't see him. Ye can't see dead people."

"But if we close our eyes real tight," says Geraldine, "we'll feel as if he's here with us. And we can always talk to him. He's up in heaven, and he can hear every word we say. I bet we'll be able to hear him answer if we're quiet and listen."

"I can't see him," says Conor, his eyes tightly shut and his little face pointing to the bedroom ceiling.

"Are ye OK, Da?" Conor cries. "Do ye hear me Da?"

We sit on the bed, all three of us crying and hugging each other in a vain effort to make the pain of our Da's death go away.

"It's April Fool's Day today," I sniffle. *I wish my Da dyin' was only a joke, but it's not. My Da is dead, so he is.*

WE GO downstairs to a house full of consoling neighbours and friends. Everyone is dressed in black. In the midst of them all, is my Ma sitting in my Da's chair with Paddy and Fergus by her side. She has a small bolt of black felt cloth in her lap: she's cutting out four-by-two-inch diamond shaped pieces of cloth. Later, as a sign of mourning for the death of my Da, those black-felt diamonds will be sewn onto the left upper-arm sleeves of all our clothes. We'll still be wearing them two months after the burial.

"Here's my two little men," says Peg, putting down her scissors and felt. We both hug her and cry.

"What'll we do without Da, Ma?" I ask.

"God's will be done, Niall," answers Peg. "He'll guide us."

"Will I never see him again, Ma?" asks Conor.

"No darlin'. Holy God needs your Da up in heaven," answers Peg. "And he wants us all to be good and look after each other. And he wants you, Niall, to look after your little brother."

"I think he always loved you special, Niall," she continues. "He was always reminding me that you were a good boy, even when you climbed up onto the church roof, you little divil you."

"Der ye are," interrupts Mrs Lawlor. "I've been lookin' for you two. Niall, I want you and Conor to help me in the kitchen. What with all the neighbours droppin' in showin' dir respect and condolences, sure I can't keep up with the dish washin'."

The next week is a black blur. The house seems to be thick with people in black, all the time. Our relations, friends, and neighbours seem to be competing with my Aunt Joan in her head-to-toe black habit; Joan, my mother's sister is a Brigidine nun.

"But for your Auntie Joan, we'd have no one to put in a good word for us," said Peg to me during one of her rambling going-ons while she was washing the clothes. "Joan's the only one of us who gave themselves to the Lord, and God pays attention to nuns, so he does." Peg didn't seem to think our long-dead cousin, Edmund

Ignatius Rice, who died in 1844, had enough of God's ear. Edmund was the founder of the Irish Christian Brothers and a first cousin to Peg's Grandmother Tracey. Pope Pius XII was considering Edmund's case for beatification in Rome. "With the help of the Almighty God, the family will soon have our own family saint in heaven," Joan was to declare. "He'll become blessed first, and then he'll be made a saint. Now, aren't you the lucky little boy, Niall. You'll have a cousin a saint."

A WHITE card trimmed in black is pinned to our front door. In its cold way, it formally confirms my Da's death:

Gerald Kavanagh
Born 23 April 1907
Died 1 April 1957
R.I.P.

Not that I need any further confirmation, but my Da's wake and burial make it absolute.

That's not me Da, I ponder, as I look down at an unreal image of him laid out in his coffin. I notice the brown scapular is still around his neck. *Our Lady of Mount Carmel didn't help him.*

"Our Da looks awful different, Niall," says Conor. We had walked hand-in-hand to the open coffin with Geraldine.

"It's only his body," answers Geraldine. "Daddy has gone up to heaven. Say a few Hail Marys and ask him to help our Ma."

"But he can't hear us," Conor says.

"Yes he can," Geraldine replies.

"Ye said if I close me eyes tight I'd be able to see him, and I can't," says Conor. "I've tried millions of times, and I can't."

"You have to imagine, Conor," is Geraldine's curt and far from convincing response.

Peg picks the perfect spot in Glasnevin Cemetery for Gerry to be buried. To my surprise, standing by the crowded graveside doesn't cause me the grief I'd anticipated. I'm amazed to see so many people, including all my school classmates, attend my Da's funeral. Many people are crying, and the fact that I'm not is making me feel uncomfortable.

Looking at my Da's closed coffin beside his open, impatient grave, I drift into some strange sort of silent, comforting, one-sided banter with my Da. *I think ye'll like bein' here, Da*: his grave is positioned next to one of the graveyard walkways and is shaded by a big, pretty tree. *And ye'll be safe here too:* one of the graveyard's many guard towers is close by – they were originally built to house armed guards and reduce the many incidents of body theft by over-eager medical students. *And ye won't be lonely, Da*: his grave is a new one, and as such, he'll be on his own; but luckily, his brother Michael – my cousin Eugene's first Da – is buried only two graves to the right. Hearing the violent thumps of the first shovels of earth on the coffin brutally ends my soothing tête-à-tête. Each thump is heart-breaking, cruelly bellowing its final ratification that my Da is dead. *I'll never be able to talk, walk or laugh with him again – I'll never be able to see, hear or even touch him.* A dreadful difference is born.

****

I COPED with my Da's devastating absence by forgetting he was dead. It's something that just happened – I'd simply forget he was gone. Unfortunately, the agony of having to acknowledge the horrible reality always re-emerged.

My favourite photo of Gerry, sucking a slice of orange.

That innate succour of being able to forget did make my mourning less painful, however, those soothing periods of unreality never happened when I was at home with my Ma or siblings. I got no comfort from being with them. In fact, it's when I was out with my friends and away from my family and all that reminded me of my Da, that those comforting hiatuses came.

"You were always fond of the street," said Peg. "But ever since your Da died, I hardly see you at all."

She was right, and I wanted to explain to her why, but I just didn't know how to tell her.

****

The BBC, JJ &
Where are ye Seán?

Remember March, the ides of March remember:
did not great Julius bleed for justice sake?
What villain touched his body, that did stab,
and not for justice sake? What, shall one of us
that struck the foremost man of all this world,
but for supporting robbers, shall we now
contaminate our fingers with base bribes,
and sell the mighty space of our large honours
for so much trash as may be grasped thus?
I had rather be a dog, and bay at the moon,
than such a Roman.

Julius Caesar: The Quarrel Scene – William Shakespeare (1564-1616)

"NIALL LOVE, WHY DON'T YOU GO ON UP and see if you like it?" pleads Peg. "Garda Brown told me Mr O'Connor is a grand man. He's a barrister, and he runs the club. It's called Saint Brendan Boys Club. All the boys have great fun, playing games, and even camping. Do me a favour, Niall – go up and see if you like it?"

Peg is concerned about my changed behaviour since my Da's death, and correctly so. I hate being in the house without him. For all but meals and each day's demands for sleep, I'm out of there. My increased absence leaves my mother with well-founded worries; she thinks this boy's club idea might be her ticket to relief.

"OK, Ma," I reluctantly reply.

"Thank God!" Peg exclaims. "You're a good boy. The club will keep you busy, and you won't be hanging around the streets, getting yourself into trouble. I keep telling you, Niall: an idle mind is the devil's playmate."

160

"I'll go up on Saturday," says I. "If I don't like it, I'm not goin' to join. I'll give it a go, and we'll see. Now, stop worryin' about me, Ma. Maybe the club is goin' to be great. I hope they have soccer and stuff. And table tennis would be smashin'.""

"I'm sure they will, love. You're a good boy to do this for your mammy. Wait and see. I bet you'll love it."

Peg was right – I love the BBC. JJ O'Connor, or JJ as we call him, is a powerful generator of enthusiasm and participation. Very soon, I subconsciously make JJ my substitute father figure.

Not only does the club have soccer and table tennis, but there are also darts, rings, skittles, art classes, music, and singing. The club has a small, modestly stocked library, and there's an ongoing series of short stage presentations. This latter activity immediately interests me. On the first day of my membership, I sign up to be cast as Brutus in the *Quarrel Scene* from Shakespeare's *Julius Caesar*. Later, it was performed in the clubhouse to a small, yet enthusiastic audience of proud family members.

Niall as Brutus.

The club introduces me to a game called 'Push-Ha'penny'. I've never heard of it, and after one game, I wonder why; it's a fantastic game. With two pennies, two push-sticks, one halfpenny, the Push-Ha'penny board, and a willing competitor, you're set for hours of amusement. The smooth wooden board is the precisely reduced size of a marked-up soccer pitch. Built into a three-quarter-inch high walled type of tray, three-and-a-half-foot long by two-foot wide, it has open four-inch goals at each end of the board. One penny, hen side up, is assigned to one player and the other penny, harp side up, is assigned to the other; the halfpenny represents the ball. Using the push-stick, each competitor takes turns hitting his penny in a manner that strikes the ball and directs it into, or strategically positions it to, the opponent's goal. The objective is to score the most goals by pushing the ball into the opponent's goal. Having a right stick is a big assist in winning a game. I soon realise that the flat lollypop stick I'd started with was not the way to go; I spend hours whittling a flawless push-stick, making it the perfect size, shape, and strength for my hand. Before long I'm making a name for myself in the many fiercely competitive Push-Ha'penny tournaments the club organises.

JJ OFTEN arranges for weekend camping trips to the Dublin and Wicklow mountains. One of those weekends we find ourselves on top of Djouce Mountain. Only twenty-five miles from Dublin City, Djouce is, in fact, in County Wicklow. At one time it was part of what was then a bigger Dublin; during the sixteenth- and late seventeenth centuries, the aggressive expansion of England's colonisation of Ireland introduced a significant number of changes – Djouce becoming part of Wicklow was one of the many.

JJ arranges for a CIE single decker bus to transport us to our destination. The air is abnormally clear; more often than not, a grey smog hangs over the city – burn-off from Dublin's ubiquitous home fires would soon be identified as the source. Being blessed with the beautiful morning it is, during our bus ride through the Dublin Mountains, JJ has the driver stop so as we can view the city below. We see Dublin Bay's northern Howth peninsula stretching out into the Irish Sea, while the bay's southern point, sleepy Dalkey Village, and Dalkey Island, although failing in their efforts, try their best to compete.

Arriving in Enniskerry, a small town close to Djouce, we're met by one of the locals with an open-backed lorry. After a short, bumpy ride we arrive at the mountain's foothills.

Djouce Mountain.

At 2,379 feet, Djouce might well be called a good-sized hill. Its gradual slope makes our assent an easy and enjoyable one. We set up camp on the soft fern covering the mountain's peak. Sitting around the campfire, JJ tells us of the mountain's secrets. He explains the name Djouce, English for the Gaelic name Diogais, meaning fortified height. He tells us of the ghostly Coffin Stone, a Bronze Age portal tomb on the mountain's slopes, and of the nearby Celtic battlefield, War Hill.

We learn that local springs and streams combine with Djouce's rain run-off and become the source of the Dargle and Liffey rivers. The short 12.5 mile Dargle, moves northeast via Powerscourt Demesne, creating Powerscourt's beautiful waterfall on its way; at 398 feet, the waterfall is the second highest in Ireland. Staying within its county of source, County Wicklow, the Dargle then beelines to the town of Bray and into the Irish Sea.

County Dublin has a total of 130 rivers and streams, all of which play their part in making Dublin as it is. It would be a rare Dubliner who could name even ten of those waterways, but all Dubliners know the Liffey. From its source in the foothills of Djouce, it initially flows west for 12 miles. It then changes its mind and turns northeast, then eastwards, winding its way through County Kildare for another 50 miles. For its last 20 miles, it meanders through Dublin County, across Dublin City, into Dublin Bay and finally into the Irish Sea. The Liffey is 82 miles long.

After a satisfying camp-side meal and a lot of fun and frolic, we douse the campfire and go to our tents. JJ has called for lights-out. We're about to settle down and go to sleep when a rain storm hits us. The tents do their job; the torrential rains cause us no fears of being washed off the top of the mountain, and as quick as the storm had started, it ends. Tired out, happy as Larry, well fed and watered, we're all fast asleep in short order.

SNUGGLED DOWN and comfortably asleep in my warm sleeping bag, I'm suddenly awakened. A cold, damp night breeze gusting through the unzipped open tent-door suddenly brings me fully awake and alert.

I'm sharing the tent with three other lads. Seán, one of my new BBC friends, has his sleeping bag next to mine.

"What's wrong, Seán?" I ask. "Why's the door open?"

Getting no response and assuming that he was asleep, I stretch out and punch his sleeping bag. To my surprise, the bag's empty.

"Where are ye Seán?" says I anxiously. Again, no response. *Seán must have gone out for a pee or somethin'.*

I lie back down and wait for the return of a urinated Seán.

He doesn't return. I lie there for twenty minutes or more – there's not a sight or sound of him. JJ had stressed that if we had to pee during the night, we were to be quick about it, get back into the tent as soon as we were finished, and to keep our tent-doors zipped up. It has started to rain again, a lighter sticky rain this time, nevertheless heavy enough for me to prefer staying in the tent rather than going out to look for Seán. I'm anxious about getting him into trouble. Rather than wake the other lads in the tent, I get out of my bag, and in my underpants and vest, I go to the tent door.

"Where are ye, Seán?" I whisper, trying not to wake anyone.

Still no response, and this time its absence has me anxious. *Somethin' must be wrong. What the hell's he doin'!? Where the hell is he!?* I cautiously exit the tent into the rain.

With the cold night breeze, together with the sticky rain, my inadequate grab plus my mounting distress, I'm scared stiff. Visibility is challenging. I can just about see our circled tents with the now dead campfire in the centre. There's no sign of Seán.

"Are ye alright, Seán?" I whisper, a little louder this time, hoping not to get anyone's attention other than Seán's.

I move out nearer the campfire site. I'm about to give up when I notice something moving on the other side of the fire site.

"Is that you, Seán?" I whisper. Once again, there's no response.

Not knowing what it was that had got my attention, I'm as nervous as hell. I'm hoping it's Seán, but I'm worried sick it just might be someone else or even worse, something else – something evil and sinister – something that any second now, might jump out of the darkness and attack me!

Wanting badly to turn, run to my tent and be safe in the company of the two other lads, I pause for a second. *Maybe it is Seán and there's somethin' wrong with him. I've got to make sure – I can't leave him out here in the rain.* Moving closer to the fire site, I frantically wipe the rain from my eyes so as to get a better visual of who, or what was out there.

Jays! It is Seán! I can make him out on the other side of the dead campfire, curled up and lying on the ground.

I go over to him. He, like myself, is barefoot and wearing only a vest and underpants. He looks like he's asleep or . . . ???

"Wake up, Seán!" says I, shaking him as I start to pray that the unimaginable is not the case; for a few seconds, I'm terrified that he might be as dead as the dead campfire he was lying beside.

In response to my demand, and to my incredible relieve, a breathing Seán moves.

"What the hell are ye doin', Seán? Ye'll get yer death of cold, sleepin' out here in the rain! Get up and come back into the tent. If JJ catches us, we'll be in big trouble."

"Sometimes I sleep-walk, Niall," Seán mutters, as he struggles to stand. I have to help him up off the ground.

As we make our way back to the tent, Seán starts to cry.

"I'm fed up with this feckin' sleep-walkin'," he cries. "It's gettin' worse as I'm gettin' older. Don't say anythin' about it to the lads or JJ. Sure you won't, Niall?"

"OK, Seán," I reply. "I won't say a word. Ye should get yer Da to ask the doctor about it. I bet ye there's medicine for it."

"Yeah. It's embarrassin', and I'm fed up, so I am," says Seán. "I'm goin' to ask me Da to do somethin'."

We creep back into the tent, zip up the door, dry ourselves off and slide back into our sleeping-bags.

"Goodnight, Seán," I whisper. "Go asleep and don't be worryin' about it. It's our secret. Yer Da will get the doctor to help ye."

"OK," sniffles Seán. "And t'anks for findin' me, Niall."

Thinking about Seán and his sleep-walking problem I find it difficult to get back to sleep. I finally do, despite listening to Seán next to me, quietly crying. *He's probably afraid to go asleep – I'd be feckin' well afraid if I was him.*

When daylight comes, Seán is the first to be up and dressed, ready for the new day.

"How are ye doin'?" says I to a bright and happy Seán.

"Smashin', Niall," he replies. "Will ye help me get the fire goin' for breakfast?"

"Oh, and Niall," he continues in a whisper. "T'anks for helpin' me last night, and t'anks for keepin' it a secret – OK."

"Sure, Seán," I answer. "I'll go and get wood for the fire."

****

WITH HIS busy law practice, how JJ managed to give so much of his time to the BBC is beyond me. I wonder did that good man realise how big a part he played in guiding the early teens of so many boys who otherwise might have gone the wrong way. He played a huge part in how my post-having-my-Da behaviour was to be positively influenced. It was JJ's work, undoubtedly coupled with Peg's prayers, which directed me along the right road, as distinct from that wrong road for which I had a strong propensity.

Sean's sleep-walking problem gave me a new realisation of what some silly illnesses can do to one's otherwise normal way of life. I was very grateful that I didn't have the affliction. I don't know if Seán's da got the doctor to help him. I sure hope he did. If I had the problem, I'd be scared ever to close my eyes.

****

The Weir

GEORGIE IS ANOTHER ONE OF MY MANY NEW BBC friends. He and I have just finished a series of Push-Ha'penny games, and we've topped it all off with a few games of table tennis.

"I'm sweatin'," says Georgie. "How about goin' up to the Strawberry Beds' for a dip in the Liffey – do ye want to come?"

We're both more than ready to cool off. The suggested trip to the weir's cool waters fits the bill.

"Me Da used to bring me up there when I was a nipper," says I. "I love that place – I haven't been there for donkey's years."

"Let's go then," says Georgie. "We'll go up on me bike. I'll give ye a backer." I need that lift: I've been without a bike for the past few weeks; it's broken – the chain is missing some links.

"That'll be great," says I. "We'll go by our houses and pick up our togs. I can't wait to dive in."

Georgie and I are at the weir in record time. The fast bike ride makes us all the more in need of a cool dip. The Strawberry Beds is the right place to be. The perfect swimming hole the weir creates, its easy access, plus my wonderful brown trout memories, makes the place very special.

The *V*-shaped weir was built to control flooding in the river's lower-lying city areas during times of heavy rain; in Ireland, such times are not infrequent. Its presence gives the Liffey a ten-to-twelve-foot depth on the up-river side and an attractive fifteen foot, gradually sloping falls on the down-river side. The weir's control gate is located at the top of the weir's *V* in the centre of the river.

"Last one in is a sissy!" shouts Georgie as he parks his bike and runs towards the river. "I bet ye I'll be in first."

"Not if I can help it," I holler.

George is ahead of me. I start to disrobe while running. My efforts are hampered by me falling while trying to take my trousers off while still running.

"Shite!" I exclaim, as I sit on my arse and complete the task. I get up, and to my infuriation, I see Georgie by the river bank putting on his togs. As I run towards him, he jumps in. *I hate bein' the sissy. But what the hell. Georgie won fair. Feck it. Let's get me togs on. I'll get in and dunk him!*

"Na-na, na-na-na," shouts Georgie as he swims over to the weir wall. "Niall is the sis-sy! Na-na, na-na-na."

Jumping in and swimming under water, I go to where Georgie is sitting with his legs dangling over the side. I grab his legs and pull him in. To avoid retaliation, I swim out along the weir's wall towards the middle of the river and the top of the weir's V.

Due to an abnormally long spell without rain, and unbeknown to either of us, the river is lower than usual. As a result, the weir's control gate had been opened to near maximum. I'm about six feet away from the gate when the strong force of the released up-river water viciously sucks me into and down the weir gate's chute.

The Strawberry Beds weir.

Head over heels, I'm tossed about like as if I was a rag doll. The descent extends for fifteen feet, pouring its contents into the lower fast-moving, rocky river bed. On the way down, I bang my head; the blow causes me to blank out for an instant and gets me to the end of the chute with no other injuries apart from swallowing a lot of water. Exiting the chute, the force of the water sucks me down and slams me into the river's bed. All the little air I have is knocked out of my aching body. While being forcibly pushed along under water, I struggle towards the surface and desperately needed air. A gasp or two, and down I go again. I think that I'm about to die. The fear of being so unprepared frightens me. *There's no time to say an Act of Contrition, and it's more than a month since me last confession. I'm on me way to purgatory, if not hell.*

I'm in serious trouble, and it'll take all in my power to survive. I somehow decide that if I stop fighting and try to relax and float with the river, rather than against it, I'll be more likely to do so. After a half-dozen or more fright-filled visits under water, that's what I manage to do. Two hundred feet down river, and after what seems like a long time, I'm able to direct myself nearer to the river bank and crawl my way out onto dry land.

This horrible weir-gate-to-dry-land experience takes three or four minutes. But to me it feels like a heck of a lot more time than that. Georgie had observed the spectacle from beginning to end. From the river bank, he'd been with me all the way, shouting encouragement and doing his frustrated best to direct me to safety. I had heard him roaring out to me as I was being pushed and tossed about in the fast flowing river: "Keep yer head up, Niall! Mind the rocks, Niall! Over to the bank, Niall! Jays Niall, stop kickin', float for feck's sake."

"Are ye alright?" George anxiously enquires, as he comes up to where I'm lying on the river bank. "Are ye hurt?"

"I hit me head. But I don't think I'm bleedin'."

"Give us a look, Niall."

"Ye've a bump, but ye're not bleedin'," Georgie reports.

"I hit my back. Is it cut?" I ask, rolling over on my belly.

"It's a bit scraped. I think ye're OK, Niall. And I don't know how ye are. That was an awful goin' over ye got, so it was."

"I'm ready to head home, Georgie," says I, as I struggle to stand up. "I think I've had enough of the Liffey. How about you?"

Georgie agrees with me. We dress and head for home. It takes us the best part of three-quarters of an hour. Georgie has to peddle all the way. I sit on his back carrier feeling sore all over, but ever so grateful for being able to feel the pain. I'd been very close to not being able to feel anything. I'd almost drowned!

****

Gough & Wellington

There are strange things done, from twelve to one,
*   in the Hollow in the Phoenix Park,*
Where maidens are mobbed, and gentlemen robbed,
*   in the bushes after dark.*
But the strangest of all, within human recall,
*   concerns the statue of Gough.*
'Twas a terrible fact, and a most wicked act,
*   for his bollocks they tried to blow off!*

'Neath the horse's big prick, a dynamite stick,
*   some gallant hero did place.*
For the cause of our land, with a match in his hand,
*   bravely the foe he did face.*
Then without showin' fear, and standin' well clear,
*   he expected to blow up the pair,*
But he nearly went crackers, all he got was the knackers,
*   and he made the poor stallion a mare!*

For his tactics were wrong, and the prick was too long,
*   the horse being more than a foal.*
It would answer him better, this dynamite setter,
*   the stick to shove up his own hole.*
For this is the way our heroes today
*   are challengin' England's might,*
With a stab in the back, and a midnight attack,
*   on a statue that can't even shit!*

The Destruction of the Gough Monument – Vincent Caprani (1957)
Copyright held by Gill & Macmillan

IT'S TUESDAY, 23 JULY 1957, AND GEORGIE and I are in the Phoenix Park. Ever since my near drowning episode at the Strawberry Beds Weir, we've become great mates – we do everything together. We enjoy exploring the park's many treasures; we've been to the Magazine Fort, the Furry Glen, and the Hollow, and

170

were lucky enough to have had a good, close-up look at the park's herd of wild fallow deer in the Fifteen Acres. Now we're on our way to the nearby Gough and Wellington monuments.

The Gough equestrian monument.

For me, the striking thing about the Gough statue is the horse's massive penis and set of balls. Gough himself looks fine, however, it's the stallion's enormous genitalia that always gets my attention. We're particularly eager to go and see Gough today – he's plastered all over the news. And this time it looks serious: very early that morning, the IRA had finally managed to blast the bronze equestrian statue off its base.

"Look 'it, Georgie," says I, as we gaze at the dismounted rider and his horse, off their granite base, smashed and scattered all over the place. "They've blown the poor horse's bollocks off."

"Gough looks all fucked up as well," says Georgie. "And I'll tell ye somethin', Niall. That's the end of the horse's sex life. They didn't only get his balls; they got his Mickser Reid as well."

The Viscount Field Marshall Hugh Gough monument was unveiled in 1880. Winston Churchill cited its grand début as being one of his earliest childhood memories; he was only six at the time and attended the event with his father who was then the Lord Lieutenant of Ireland. Gough is forever getting himself into trouble. Not being at all popular with the post-1922 Irish citizenry, over the years there's been a fair few gallons of emerald-green paint thrown at him. Late on Christmas Eve 1944, his head was

171

sawed off! A very bewildered Dublin fisherman discovered it in the bottom of the River Liffey at Islandbridge, less than a mile from the scene of the crime. It was given back to the Phoenix Park authorities, and they resoldered it back onto Gough's trunk. Only last year the IRA had another go at him. They ended up giving one of the stallion's back legs a big gash, leaving rider and horse still standing up in the middle of the Phoenix Park's Chesterfield Avenue, still looking as if they owned the place.

For a long while, the Gough Monument held pride of place on the IRA's monuments-to-be-demolished list – a long list of monuments erected by the pre-1922 English Government of Ireland. Memorials that continued to defiantly glorify England's power over the once occupied, but now independent Republic of Ireland.

From a wealthy and privileged Anglo-Irish family, Gough was born in Woodstown, Waterford in 1779. Just like his father before him, he would join the English Army. He gained a reputation for savagery and brutality towards what he claimed to be the 'inferior populations of the world.' In 1849, after his victorious return from India, and having acquired the appropriate nickname 'Hammer of the Sikhs,' Gough became a viscount. His nickname was given because of the brutality he employed conquering the Punjab.

The monument's base-plate identifies Gough as being, 'An Illustrious Irishman.' However, and like so many others of his ilk, he was more English than the English themselves. He was often heard expressing dislike of his heritage, 'damn Irish' being one of his disparaging remarks. Gough died in his bed in 1869 at the age of 90. Oddly enough, he's buried in Stillorgan, Dublin.

"The sooner they take all this English shit down, the better," says I to Georgie. "It should be Tom Clarke, Pádraic Pearse, James Connolly, Robert Emmett or Wolftone, we're lookin' up at, and not all these Anglo-Irish blokes who had nothin' but hatred for Ireland and the Irish."

"I suppose your right, Niall," says Georgie.

We say our goodbyes to the unseated, very disturbed Gough and his cisgender horse, and head over to Wellington.

The Wellington Monument is a 215-foot-high obelisk and is the highest obelisk in Europe. Its foundation was laid in 1817 praising, among other things, Wellington's defeat of Napoleon in 1815 at the Battle of Waterloo.

Wellington was born in Dublin in 1769. Just like Gough, he was another privileged, protestant Anglo-Irishman. He was not only an expert soldier for England, but he was also an accomplished politician. He was Prime Minister of England twice during his lifetime. His original name was Arthur Wesley, but he changed it to the more English-sounding name, Arthur Wellesley when running for Prime Minister. He disavowed his Irish heritage, declaring, 'Being born in a barn does not make one a horse.'

The Wellington Monument.

Unlike the Gough Monument, the Wellington is still standing. The IRA never had it on their to-be-demolished-list, although there is a rumour that they were thinking hard about it. There's a little-known railway tunnel running directly under the monument – few people are aware of its existence. It's mostly used for shunting carriages to and from Connolly Station. The rumour is that the IRA once planted a lot of explosives in the tunnel with the intention of bringing the monument down. They were discovered doing the dirty, and the explosives were safely removed. It was a near thing, but other than for the disappointed IRA bombardiers, who allegedly escaped, all ended well.

While this rumour gives us a tale to be told, I think the reality is that the IRA never had the Wellington Monument on their list – and for good reasons. That Dublin bloke, Wellington, played a vital role in securing Catholic Emancipation, for not only the catholic English but also the catholic Irish.

In 1829, Wellington was Prime Minister of England. Working with Robert Peel and Daniel O'Connell in the House of Commons, he pushed for the passing of the much opposed *Roman Catholic Relief Act* through the House of Lords. England's population was eighty percent protestant. To overcome the vehement opposition of the majority, including the House of Lords and King George IV, Wellington worked hard to ensure passage and threatened to resign if the King did not agree. He was successful in his efforts; Robert and Daniel pushed the Act through the House of Commons, and the *Roman Catholic Relief Act* became law. Among many other just improvements, members of the Catholic Church were, for the first time, permitted to sit in England's Parliament.

Wellington would later pay the price for his firm insistence on trying to regulate religious prejudice. He was voted out of office. Full emancipation for all religions in Ireland was not achieved until the setting up of the Irish Free State in December 1922.

If nothing else, the IRA knows Irish history. I'm sure they see the enormous significance of Wellington's contribution and give the man a break. His *Roman Catholic Relief Act*, plus the fact that the man was a born Dubliner – and let's not forget his gift of Wellington boots to the entire world – gives him absolution for any and all other sins he may or may not have committed.

****

THE OFTEN unappreciated Phoenix Park is a Dublin treasure. It is a large public park of 1,747 acres. That's more than twice the size of Central Park in New York City and five times the size of London's Hyde Park. Whenever you find yourself in Dublin, you've got to go there. Among many other things, it includes the Irish President's residence and a well-stocked zoo. The park's herd of wild fallow deer – at times the herd rises to as high as 1,000 – while being carefully monitored and judiciously culled, is truly wild.

****

An Unusual Find

AFTER EXPLORING THE WELLINGTON MONUMENT'S large brass sculptures depicting some of the Duke of Wellington's many battles, Georgie and I have come down the monument's grand sloping steps onto the surrounding grassy park area. We notice that two other boys have arrived. They're playing kickball with each other. A poor kick from one of the boys sends the ball flying past his friend and over our heads. It goes directly towards a man who is sitting on the grass, leaning against a fence. The ball rolls its way to his feet; hitting them, it bounces over and comes to rest beside him. Georgie and I are nearer to the ball than either of the two boys, so we run over to retrieve it.

Coming closer to the man, I sense something unusual. Even though the ball had hit his feet and is now resting beside him, he hasn't moved.

"Can we have the ball back, Mister?" Georgie asks.

Getting no response, we inch closer.

"Jays, Georgie," I exclaim. "I think this ol' fella's dead."

"Jays, Niall," responds Georgie. "I think ye're right."

"I saw me Da dead," I comment. "He didn't look, ye know, himself, but he didn't look like this. This bloke looks awful. His eyes are wide open, and he's all grey and blotchy, and there's all dewy stuff on his face. I bet ye he's been sittin' here all night."

"We'd better get someone to look after him," says Georgie. "We can't just leave him sittin' here dead, all on his own. Let's get the ball and give it back to the boys," he continues, as he bravely bends over and retrieves the ball.

With the ball in hand, we run back to the boys and share the nature of our unusual find. All four of us are in disbelief, Georgie and me as much as the two boys. We run back to the corpse to

175

verify that what we had found is indeed real, and sure enough, it is – Georgie and I found a real dead ol' fella in the park!

We run to the road and wildly wave down passing cars. We have to jump in front of the fourth or fifth car before we succeed in getting one of them to stop.

"What the hell are you kids doin'?" the angry driver hollers, as he gets out of his car. "I nearly ran ye over, so I did. What the hell's wrong with ye?"

"There's a dead man over there, mister," says I. "He's just sittin' there, and the ball went over to him, and we got the ball, and we need a man or somethin' to look after him. He's a real dead man, mister. He's on his own, and he's dead, mister!"

"A real dead man!?" questions the driver. "If ye're pullin' me leg, it'll be the toe of me boot in yer arse ye'll be gettin'. Now, are you pullin' me leg, or is there a real dead man over there?"

"We swear mister," Georgie endorses. "The ol' fella is as dead as a doornail. He's not movin' nor nothin'."

"Holy God," responds the driver. "Let me lock me car, and we'll go over and see what's happened."

We all run over to the corpse. This is the third visit for Georgie and me, and oddly, I feel strangely familiar with the ol' fella.

"Will we say a prayer for him, mister?" I ask, sad for the poor man dying all alone, without kith or kin to mourn him.

"Jays, he's dead alright," the driver answers. "Prayers will do nothin' to help this poor man's mortal body, but it just might help his immortal soul."

For a minute or so we all stand around the corpse in meaningful silent prayer. There isn't a dry eye amongst us when the driver interrupts our sincere sorrow.

"I'll look after everything," the driver announces, as he makes the sign of the cross, takes out his handkerchief, and blows his dampened nose. "Sure isn't the Garda Headquarters only across the road. I'll have them here to look after him in a few minutes."

"All you boys should go on home now," he concludes. "Leave this to me. Ye've done well by the poor man. Just say a few more prayers for him. Off ye go now."

We leave the committed driver to attend to the needs of the deceased. We say our goodbyes to the two boys and head home.

We're exhausted, and the thoughts of having to walk home from the Phoenix Park is hard for us to bear. That thought, plus the ordeal Georgie and I had just been through, is more than any average day demands.

"I'm bleedin' well jacked, Georgie," says I as I plonk down on the grass.

"So am I," Georgie declares, sitting down beside me. "I couldn't believe me eyes," Georgie continues. "I saw the ol' fella sittin' on the grass when we were explorin' the Wellie. He looked like he was just sittin' down havin' a rest."

"I saw him too," says I. "Little did we know; he was takin' one feckin' long rest, so he was."

"And now, we have that long bleedin' walk ahead of us," moans Georgie.

As we had declared to each other, we're well and truly jacked and might I say, not without cause. For God's sake – we'd just found a real dead ol' fella in the Phoenix Park!

****

The Feckin' Motorbike

Oh thunder and lightnin' is no lark,
when Dublin city is in the dark.
If ye have any money go up to the park,
and view the zoological gardens

We went up der to see the zoo,
we saw the lion and the kangaroo.
Der was he-males and she-males of every hue,
up in the zoological gardens.

We went up der by Castleknock,
says she to me "Sure we'll court on the lock."
Den I knew she was one of the rare old stock,
from outside the zoological gardens.

We went up der on our honeymoon,
says she to me "If you don't come soon.
I'll have to get in with the hairy baboon,
up in the zoological gardens."

Says she to me "It's seven o'clock,
and it's time for me to be changin' me frock.
For I'd love to see dat old cockatoo
up in the zoological gardens."

Says she to me "Me lovely Jack,
sure I'd love a ride on the elephant's back.
If you don't come out I'll give you such a smack,
up in the zoological gardens."

The Zoological Gardens – Traditional

GEORGIE AND I ARE SITTING ON THE GRASS, and the thoughts of the hour or more walk ahead of us is hurting.

"I can't wait to be able to drive a motorbike," says I to Georgie. "I'll be fifteen on Saturday, but you have to be sixteen to get a licence. Me brother, Paddy, has one. I wish I was him. If we had a motorbike, we'd be home in a flash."

"Do you know how to drive, Niall?" says Georgie.

"Sure," I lie. My brother Paddy has shown me the rudiments, but I've no motorbike driving experience.

"Me brother told me how to. Ye just turn the petrol on, kick start it and rev it up. The throttle, the thing dat makes the engine go faster, is on the right handlebar along with the front brake. Ye just twist the throttle, and the engine runs faster. The important thing is to clutch before ye shift gears. The clutch is on the left handlebar. The gear shift is the foot pedal on the right side. Once the engine's goin', ye pull the clutch and press the gear shift with yer foot to get into first gear; then ye slowly release the clutch, and ye're off. Dependin' on the speed ye want to go at, ye pull the clutch, click the gear shift down or up and adjust the throttle. The foot pedal on the left is the rear wheel brake."

"It sounds simple enough," says Georgie. "If only we had one; even if we could get a loan of one."

Where we are sitting is near the entrance to the Phoenix Park Zoo. There's a parking area to the left of the entrance. With the help of the devil himself, we spot not one, but a dozen or so motorbikes neatly parked side by side, tantalisingly sparkling in the mid-afternoon sunshine.

"Any of those babies would do the job," comments Georgie. "Maybe we should take a loan of one."

"Jays, Georgie. That'll be stealin'. If we're caught, we'll get into terrible trouble."

"It won't be stealin', Niall," he replies. "It'll be only a loan."

"I suppose ye're right. But how'll we give the bike back?"

"We could park it at the seventeen shops and leave a note on it," Georgie suggests. A string of seventeen shops is located on the busy Cabra Road, only a short walk from our homes.

"In the note, we could say we took a loan of it," continues Georgie. "Someone will find it, they'll tell the gardaí, and they'll give it back to the fella that owns it."

"I don't know, Georgie," says I pensively. "If we're caught, we'll get into fierce trouble."

"We're jacked, Niall," Georgie vehemently reaffirms. "We should go for it. Let's take a loan and not shank's mare it all the way home. I'm barely able to put one foot in front of the other."

Pains of the thoughts of the long walk home plus the pains of our unusual find at the Wellington Monument are fast being challenged by a flood of other discomforts. *I've never driven a bleedin' motorbike, and if this turns out as it might, I'll end up havin' to drive one.* This demanding task would be executed under Georgie's close observation while he'd be sitting right behind me. Or maybe even worse – I could end up having to admit my deceit and suffer that humiliation.

"Some bikes have keys to turn the petrol on," says I in desperation. "If ye don't have a key, ye can't drive it." I'm grasping at straws in a frantic effort to reduce the building pressure coming from Georgie's belief in my false claim to motorbike driving expertise.

"There's bound to be one or two of them without a key," Georgie answers. "Let's go over and check them out."

With considerable trepidation regarding what the fruits of the suggested investigation might bring, I silently agree. We get up and walk over to the parking area.

They'll all have locks, I pray, as we survey the scene of what's becoming my only conscious pain – the thought of me having to take a loan of and drive some feckin' motorbike. I've removed the alternative of owning up to my untruth; the mortification of doing so is way beyond anything I could bear.

The devil who'd brought our attention to the motorbikes is working overtime. Having checked out six bikes, all of which have answered my prayers, and with the help of that devil, we find the seventh one, a shiny red one, is regrettably keyless.

The keyless feckin' motorbike.

"Great," exclaims Georgie. "I was startin' to get worried. This red one will do the job. We're away in a hack!"

While Georgie is overwhelmed with joy, I'm overwhelmed with apprehension. *The feckin' bike is keyless – there's no way out.*

I stoically resign myself to what devilish fate had bestowed.

"OK, Georgie," says I. "Let's get this bitch off its stand and get goin'."

From who knows where a surge of calm confidence envelops me. I carefully push the motorbike off its stand, turn on the petrol, and just like I had seen Paddy do many times, I kick start and throttle it into a perfect purr on the first try. I immediately mount and instruct Georgie to get on behind me.

"Keep your feet on the footrests and hold on Georgie," says I as I clutch and put the bike into first gear.

"Way to go, Niall," says Georgie. "Me life on ye! Let's get out of here before the owner comes back."

Anyone observing this novice, first-time motorbike driving display would not identify it as being such. I'm amazing myself with what appears to be my incredible innate abilities. I feel absolutely in control, clutching and shifting gear like a real pro, breaking smoothly, and even indicating correctly by hand signals when turning. I rapidly realise the importance of staying in my lane and positioning the bike on the road as if I was driving a car. For the first time, I'm moving as fast as any car, and I'm in control. It's exhilarating.

Exiting the Phoenix Park at the top of Infirmary and North Circular roads, we continue on the NCR up to Gavin's Cattle Market. We turn onto Annamoe Road at Hanlon's Corner and soon find ourselves at the seventeen shops.

"This beats the shite out of shank's mare, Niall," exclaims Georgie, smiling from ear to ear.

"It does," I reply. "And it's a hell of a lot more fun. "Will we do some more drivin' or will we park it?" I continue.

"You're drivin' brilliant, Niall. Let's go for a bit of a spin first."

"OK, Georgie," says I, as we turn onto Cabra Road at Boland's Corner and head towards Phibsborough.

At Doyle's Corner, we turn left, and it's an awful pity we didn't continue on straight. I have to break hard to avoid mowing down a garda, standing in the middle of the road with his hand held high, demanding oncoming traffic to stop.

How the hell does he know we're stealin' the bike? I have no licence, and even if I did have one, we've just stolen, or as Georgie would insist on saying, we've just taken a loan of the feckin' motorbike. *We're in real deep shit.*

Stop!

"All traffic comin' this way has to stop!" the garda shouts. He's all of six-foot-two with a tough-looking body to match. There's a minimum height of five-foot-ten for anyone wanting to join the force, and this big fella more than meets that requirement.

"There's a woman lyin' on the road outside the Bohemian Cinema," the garda continues. "She fell off her bike and hit her head on the ground. Her bike and messages are thrown pell-mell. An ambulance is on its way, so yee'll all have to stay where yee are 'til we get the poor woman up and off to the Mater."

"Jays," whispers Georgie. "I thought we were fucked."

"You and the rest of us," I whisper back, as we dismount, turn off the engine and put the motorbike on its stand.

Georgie and I are the first in a long and growing line of delayed traffic. In the distance, we can hear the ambulance siren making its way to the scene, and it is accompanied by the distinctive sound of a police car siren. We stand beside the motorbike with ever increasing anxiety, wishing we could move on and far away from the painful, soon to be increased presence of the law.

The injured woman has regained her ability to speak.

"Where's me bike?" she cries out to the gathering crowd. "Look after me bike, will ye? Is it damaged?"

"Never mind yer bleedin' bike, Missus," one of the crowd answers. "The ambulance is comin' to look after ye. We'll look after yer bike. You just lie der and don't be movin'. Ye might have broken somethin'. And look at ye, yer heads bleedin'!"

182

"Me messages," the woman cries. "Where's me messages?"

"Never mind yer bleedin' messages, Missus," the one of the crowd answers back. The woman appears to be more concerned for her bike and messages than she is for her head injury.

"We'll look after yer bike, and we'll gather up yer messages," the one of the crowd continues. "They're scattered all over the road. We'll look after t'ings for ye. You just lie der and rest yerself, Missus. The ambulance will be here in a couple of minutes."

The ambulance, accompanied by the garda squad car plus its contents arrives. Three gardaí peel out of the car. They're all equal in height to the one that had stopped the traffic.

A fourth garda, the driver, stays in the car talking on the car radio. As the other three move towards the scene of the accident, I notice their colleague in the car giving Georgie, myself and the motorbike some quick, furtive glances. Each glance is only for a second or two, but long enough for me to notice. The garda gets out of the car and nonchalantly goes over to join the other three who are busily accessing the accident scene.

"Georgie," I whisper, "that bobby in the car gave us a few sneaky looks when he was talkin' on the car radio."

"Ye're only imaginin' it, Niall," Georgie replies.

"Maybe ye're right, but I'm tellin' ye, that bugger was glancin' at us." I badly want to believe Georgie, but failing miserably, I shut my mouth and worry all the more.

The injured woman is quickly placed on a gurney and loaded into the ambulance.

"Now, won't ye look after me bike and me messages?" comes the injured woman's parting plea.

While the task of loading the injured women is efficiently discharged, I'm keeping an anxious eye on the source of my current did-he or did-he-not glance at us worry. My anxiety heightens when I see him go over to the traffic-control garda. Standing together, they get into a conversation. This produces some clearly observed glances, and this time there's no doubt about it. They're glancing at us – all three of us – Georgie, me and the feckin' motorbike.

****

Mountjoy

THOSE GLANCES THAT GEORGIE AND I ARE subjected to are of the blistering kind – burning, got-ye glances – each one producing its effervescence of increased anxiety. Before I have time to share my observations with Georgie, the two gardaí turn and start walking towards us. Arriving at the top of the line of traffic they stand directly in front of us: their towering persona is unnerving. Some of the delayed motorists start blowing their car horns to speed things up – the woman is out of the middle of the road now – everyone wants to be on their way.

"Hold yer whisht!" the traffic garda shouts. "Hold yer whisht, or I'll be issuin' all of yee fines for disturbin' the peace." His bellowing admonishment puts an end to the horn blowing.

"And tell me," says the now established he-did-feckin'-well-glance-at-us garda. "Which one of you two lads is the driver of this good looking red motorbike?"

"I am sir," I answer, struggling with all the difficulty a dry-from-fear mouth bestows.

"And tell me now; what would your name be, and perchance, would you happen to have your driving licence on your person?"

"Me name is Niall Kavanagh and me brother Paddy has a licence. I'm only learnin'," I mutter in response. "I'll be gettin' one soon, sir."

The traffic-control garda interrupts the inquisitor's pursuits by reminding him that the delayed and now increasingly aggravated stream of motorists are in urgent need of being released.

"You're right, Martin," the inquisitor responds. "Now . . . Why don't you two lads take this bike off its stand and we'll all move out of the way. Over there to the kerb now; we'll resolve this matter while the traffic is being released."

184

The abject horror of our situation engulfs us. We've been caught! And just like that brown trout knew when my Da and I entrapped it at the Strawberry Beds, we know it; just like the trout, Georgie and I feel as if we're taking our last gasping breaths.

With the notable exception of our scary circumstance, things quickly get back to normal. The injured woman is on her way to the Mater, her bike and her messages are being carefully looked after, and the traffic is once again moving.

"Before we go any further," the garda starts. "This motorbike you two buckos have been driving has been reported stolen from outside the Zoological Gardens within the last hour. That and the fact that you don't have a licence puts the pair of you in a serious situation, a very serious situation indeed."

"But we only took a loan of it, sir," Georgie pleads. "We didn't steal it. We were goin' to give it back."

"You took a loan of it, me arse," the garda gruffly responds. "You had no permission to take the bike. That's stealing."

"I'm going to impound this motorbike," he continues. "It's into the patrol car you two will be going – down to Mountjoy to be charged with stealing the bike and driving without a licence."

He's laid it out for us, very clearly: we are going to be arrested and sent to gaol.

As the garda takes a tight hold of us, one of our arms in each of his strong hands, Georgie and I start to wail. He stuffs us into the back of the car, climbs in beside us and firmly locks the doors.

"Give me your ages, names, and addresses," the garda demands. "I'll take the driver first; age, name, and address, now!"

"Niall Kavanagh. I'm fifteen on Saturday," I slobber, salty tears flowing and snot streaming from my nose.

"Your bladder is near your eyes, so it is!" he scolds. "And it's only right that you're crying; you're a pair of brats to go and steal that bike. You deserve what's coming to you. Give me your address, now."

Georgie and I sob the demanded information, and the garda writes it down in his little black book. Putting the book back into his outside breast pocket, he ever so deliberately buttons the flap. He then gets out of the car, slams the door shut and calls over to his buddies.

"That red motorbike parked outside the Bohemian needs to be brought down to the station," we hear him say. "I'll radio in for the lorry. 'Twas those two young fellas who pinched it. Like the bike, they'll be going down to Mountjoy as well."

"I need one of you to sit in the back with them," the garda continues. "They're in a state with their whingin'."

The garda is wisely setting up a good cop/bad cop scenario. He needs two snot-nosed bowsies like a hole in the head; getting Georgie and I calmed down will make it go easier at the station. The bad-cop gets into the driver's seat, one of his colleagues sits beside him, and the good cop gets in beside Georgie and me.

Our new back-seat buddy starts to play his good-cop role.

"Niall and Georgie," he starts. "Now, have I got that right?" He has a comparatively pleasant face and a smile that helps us relax somewhat from our torment-filled anxieties.

"I'm Niall, and he's Georgie, sir," I answer.

"Honest, sir," Georgie pleads. "We weren't stealin' the bike. I swear, sir. We were only taken a loan of it, sir."

"I hear what you're saying, son," the good-cop replies. "We'll sort it all out at the station. We'll get your mammies and daddies down, and they'll be able to help you."

"My Da died last April," I mutter. "Georgie has a Ma and Da."

Suddenly, I realise that dreadful aspect of what's happening: Peg will soon find out about this shit I've landed in. I've stolen a motorbike, I've been arrested, and now I'm going to Mountjoy Gaol. My guilt of upsetting Peg and having her disappointed with me become the most critical parts of a mountain of worries.

The trip to Mountjoy takes five minutes. En route, the good-cop outlines what will happen to us when we'd arrive at the station.

"When we go into the station, the charging garda – that's Garda Doyle up front – will bring you to the desk for the record."

"Once that's done." he continues, "you'll be detained in the holding cell until your parents come to bail you out."

The 'detained in the holding cell' part of what he said screams at me. *It's happenin'. I'm goin' to gaol!*

"Tell me now, have you a phone in your house," the good-cop asks. "If you have, we'll give them a call. If you haven't, we'll send someone to them and let them know what's going on."

186

Peg will once again have a garda knocking at her door. The last time it was to let her know my Da was dead. This time it'll be to let her know her Niall is in gaol. I ache with pain for my mother. I've often given her cause for worry, but now I'm pushing it. *Da, if you can hear me, please, please ask God to help Ma through this.*

Mountjoy Gaol.

The patrol car pulls up to Mountjoy Gaol. A strange, apathetic acceptance of my situation has taken over. *Maybe Garda Brown will be able to help me.* A friend in need is a friend indeed, and right now I'm in tremendous need.

"Will Garda Brown be here?" I ask the good-cop. "Garda Brown knows me and me Ma."

"Inspector Brown is off duty today," replies the good-cop. "I'll be sure to let him know you were asking for him."

"Now, out you get, boys," he instructs. The car doors open and we all get out. "Garda Doyle will look after things from here."

The bad-cop, Garda Doyle resumes his all too familiar firm-hold-of-arm mode and marches us into the station. The recording formality takes about ten minutes to execute; upon completion, we're brought to the holding cell.

"Now . . . You two can cool yourselves off in here," the bad-cop growls, as we arrive at the dirty grey, steel cell door. He unlocks it, opens it wide and gruffly ushers us in.

"You'll be in here for as long as it takes to get your parents down to the station. It's unfortunate they are having the likes of you two for children. God give them strength, that's all I can say."

With that, the bad-cop slams the cell door shut, locks it and leaves Georgie and me alone, so very alone.

The cell is eight-by-ten feet. The four, twelve-foot-high walls are painted in the same dirty grey as the door. There's a small

187

barred window high up on the end wall. A weak, naked bulb covered by wire mesh is centred on a once white and now yellowing ceiling. The only furniture in the cell is a screwed-to-floor wooden bench against one wall and a dirty single-bed hair mattress on the floor next to the opposite wall. A single-tap, steel sink is in one of the window wall's corners, and a toilet reeking of disinfectant is in the other.

We spend three hours in that cell. Every half hour or so, someone comes to the door and opens the eye-level small window. Once our presence is checked out, the window is slammed shut.

Following those three horrific hours, Peg and my brother, Fergus, plus Georgie's parents, arrive at the station courtesy of the garda police car. By the time they arrive, Peg has already spoken with both Garda Brown and JJ. Garda Brown had made a commitment to do what he could to ease Peg's stress and get involved in the case. Somehow, she's getting through the shock. Not surprisingly, JJ arrives only minutes after Peg and Fergus.

The following week is filled with drama. There's a Juvenile Court appearance at which JJ, dressed in his barrister's white powdered wig and his long black gown, speaks on our behalf. Giving the judge his pledge that we're worth saving, he offers apologies for our behaviour and assures the judge that he, along with our parents, would take responsibility for our future conduct. He further assures the judge it'll be the last time we'd be brought before the court. During the proceedings, the parts Georgie and I play are those of two pieces of stage setting where the drama is played out. We do what we're told to do – nothing other than to sit and look contrite. JJ stresses that if the judge did speak to us, we were to address him as, 'your Honour.' At the end of the proceedings, his Honour addresses me directly.

"And what have you, Niall Kavanagh, to say for yourself?" the judge asks, looking at me over his spectacles perched on the end of his nose. Not realising that the judge was addressing me, JJ has to poke me to stand up and answer.

"I'm sorry for takin' the motorbike, your Honour," I answer, as I quickly stand up, knocking my chair over as I do so. "I promise not to do anythin' like that again, your Honour. And I'm sorry for knockin' me chair over, your Honour."

The court room.

"Well, let me tell you," the judge responds. "But for Barrister O'Connor, who has spoken on your behalf, and a note from Inspector Brown from Mountjoy, I would be coming to a very different conclusion regarding what to do with you two."

"Do not disappoint this court, your parents, and those who have interceded on your behalf," he continues. "This is your first time appearing before me. Let it be the last."

"I won't disappoint ye, your Honour," I reply. "And ye'll never see me again, your Honour."

"Good!" is the judge's brief, stern response. "Next case."

****

BEING LOCKED away in that holding cell was horrific. I'd been given a glimpse of this type of horror when, some years earlier, I climbed onto the roof of Christ the King church, and my Da threatened me with Artane Reformatory. Imagining looking through the reformatory gates, from the inside and not being able to get out, haunted me for a long time. Since that three-hour incarceration in one of Mountjoy Gaol's holding cell, my biggest dread in life is the violence of losing my liberty. To me, the thought of having my freedom taken away is more dreadful than going blind or maybe even death itself.

The Bohemian Cinema, outside of which I was arrested, was a family owned theatre. Admission was a comparatively modest truppence. The Cabra Grand admission was four-pence, and the State Cinema charged a whooping tanner. The peculiar thing about

'The Boh' was that not only did they charge the lowest admission, they also accepted empty jam-jars instead of legal tender for admission to children's afternoon matinees. Four one-pound jam-jars could get you in whenever cash was low. The jars had to be clean and void of any cracks. One of earliest big tragedies in my life occurred when, after queueing up to see Johnny Weissmuller in one of his Tarzan pictures, someone bumped into me and knocked one of my four jam-jars out of my hand. Tragically, it went smashing to the ground. A firm rejection of my pitiful pleas for some form of a three-jam-jar clemency admission from the cashier was cruelly denied. With my three jam-jars in hand plus great dejection in my broken heart, my friends went into the cinema without me, leaving me to make my way home all alone and feeling very miserable.

****

The Move, a Workin' Man, Cess & Jackie

I'm a rovin' sportin' blade, they call me Jack of all Trades,
I always place me chief delight in courtin' pretty fair maids.
So when in Dublin I arrived – to try for a situation,
I always heard dem shout and say 'twas the pride of all the Nation.

I'm a rovin' jack of all trades, of every trade of all trades,
and if ye wish to know me name, they call me Jack of All Trades.

On George's Quay I first began, and der became a porter,
my master we did soon fall-out dat cut our friendship shorter.
In Sackville Street a pastry cook – in James Street, a baker;
in Cook Street I did coffins make; in Eustace Street a preacher.

In Baggot Street I drove a cab, and der was well requited,
in Francis Street had lodgin' beds, to entertain all strangers.
For Dublin is of high renown – or I am much mistaken,
in Kevin Street I do declare, sold butter, eggs and bacon.

In Golden Lane I sold ol' shoes; in Meath Street a grinder;
in Barrack Street I lost my wife, I'm glad I never found her.
In Mary's Lane I dyed ol' clothes – of which I've often boasted;
in dat noted place Exchequer Street sold mutton ready roasted.

In Temple Bar I dressed ol' hats; in Thomas Street a sawyer;
in Pill Lane I did sell the plate; in Green Street an honest lawyer.
In Plunkett Street I sold cast clothes – in Bride's Alley a broker;
in Charles Street I had a shop, sold shovels, tongs and poker.

In College Green a banker was; in Smithfield a drover;
in Britain Street a waiter; and in George's Street a glover.
On Ormond Quay I sold ol' books – in King Street a nailer;
in Townsend Street a carpenter; and in Ringsend a sailor.

191

In Peter Street I was a quack; in Greek Street a grainer;
on Harbour I did carry sacks; in Werburgh Street a glazier.
In Mud Island, a dairy boy – where I became a scooper;
in Capel Street, a barber's clerk; in Abbey Street a cooper.

In Liffey Street had furniture with fleas and bugs I sold it,
and at the Bank a big placard I often stood to hold it.
In New Street I sold hay'n'straw – in Smithfield bacon;,
In Fishamble Street was at the grand ol' trade of basket makin'.

In Summerhill a coach maker; in Denville Street a gilder;
in Cork Street was a tanner; in Brunswick Street a builder.
In High Street, I sold hosiery – in Patrick Street sold blades,
and if ye wish to know me name, they call me Jack of All Trades.

Jack of All Trades – Traditional (1860)

NINETEEN-FIFTY-SEVEN BROUGHT DRAMATIC CHANGE. I was fourteen when my Da died on 1 April 1957 – his sudden absence violently altered my world. And on top of the trauma of losing my Da, I also just happened to find a dead man in the Phoenix Park, I almost drowned, I'm arrested for stealing a motorbike, and I spend time in gaol. Also, the Kavanaghs would move from Cabra to Drumcondra, and I'd leave school to become a working man.

IT'S SIX months since Gerry died. Peg is doing all she can to cope with her new life devoid of my Da. Much to my dislike, she has just announced that her coping strategies include plans to leave 20 Erris and move to 1 Mannix Road, Glasnevin. Mannix is actually in Drumcondra, right on the Glasnevin border; however, my mother always wanted to live in Glasnevin, so right or wrong, she was planning to make a new home for herself in Glasnevin.

1 Mannix Road.

"It's a grand house, Niall," says Peg. "It's at the top of Mannix Road overlooking the Tolka Park. You'll love living there."

192

"But I know nothin' about Mannix Road, Ma," I respond. "All my friends are here in Cabra. I'll know no one."

"I know, love. But that mightn't be a bad thing," says Peg. "And darlin', I just can't live in this house without your Da. I'll go mad entirely if I do."

I hear and feel my mother's pain. The heavy guilt I'm carrying, ever since the feckin' motorbike debacle, makes me all the more aware of the pain she's enduring.

"OK, Ma," I reply. "I'll get used to it. It'll be OK."

"Anyway," Peg continues, "won't you be starting work soon. Mick Smith told me he had a spot for you in the caseroom where your daddy worked. And isn't Thoms only a short walk away from Mannix."

Alexander Thom Limited.

I'm taken out of school, and in October 1957 I start working at Alexander Thom Limited, the printing and publishing company my Da had worked in; my two older brothers are also employed there. The company is on Botanic Road beside Players sweet-smelling cigarette factory, close to the Irish Christian Brothers Iona School I had just left. Suddenly, I'm a working man.

IT'S SEVEN-FORTY-FIVE in the morning, and I'm in Thom's reception area reporting for my first day of work.

"Sit down with Cecil," the receptionist instructs. "Mick – and that's Mr Smith to you two – knows you're here. He'll be out to the pair of you in a few minutes."

"My name is Niall Kavanagh," says I, as I sit down beside Cecil.

"Cess Whitty is my name. Are you startin' work like me?"

"Yeah. Where do you live, Cess?"

"Kevin Street on the Southside. Where are you from?"

193

"Erris Road in Cabra. It's on the Northside. I'm livin' on Mannix now. What school did you go to, Cess?"

"Saint Patrick's Cathedral. Where did you go?"

"The Irish Christian Brothers, Iona. It's just up the Finglas Road past Hart's Corner."

"My Da used to work here, but he died last April," I continue. "Does your Da work here?"

"He works for *The Independent*," Cess replies. The printing and publishing trades are 'closed trades' where nepotism rules.

Mick Smith is the composing room manager where Cess and I, along with Mick's son, Jackie, would spend our first years as working men.

"There you are," says Jackie, as he enters the reception area. "Which of you is Niall Kavanagh?"

"I am," I respond.

"I knew yer da, Niall. The Duke – that's what we called him. I worked my first year under him on the *Goff Catalogue*."

"My Da is up to his arse in union shit," Jackie continues as the three of us make our way to the caseroom. "He told me to bring you to Jerry Pollock. Jerry is ready for you. He'll get you started."

Looking at us with some disdain, Jerry Pollock's first words to us are, "Sister Eucharia will take care of the pair of ye." As we'd soon learn, Jerry is full of word-plays.

"It's all about points and picas," begins Jerry. "And then there's the ems, ens, thicks and thins. But for now, to get you started, we'll stay with the points and picas."

"Sit, listen and learn lads," he authoritatively instructs.

Looking intensely at us, and despite the distraction of his black horn-rimmed glasses slowly sliding down his long nose as he spoke, Jerry captures our full attention.

"Twelve points make a pica, and six picas almost make an inch. That gives you a good idea of what a point measures – it's real thin – it takes seventy-two-and-a-bit points to make an inch.

"It's called the pica system. Everything is measured in points and picas. Twenty-seven picas is a regular text line width."

"And now, could either of you two smart young men tell me how wide 27 picas is in inches?" Jerry quizzes.

"Eh-h-h," I splutter. "Four and a half inches."

"And is Niall right, Cess?" asks Jerry.

"Eh-h-h," answers Cess. "Four and a half, less, less a bit."

"Aren't you a right pair," exclaims Jerry. "You've been listenin' to me. Cess is more right, but I'm happy with you both."

BACK IN 1450, Johann Gutenberg had developed the process of casting reusable type characters in lead. While the Chinese invented ceramic movable type in 1020, it wasn't until Gutenberg came along that the world was gifted with quick, relatively cheap, mass production of the printed word. Moveable type together with some improved printing press design made it possible. Like wildfire, news, knowledge, and information would soon become accessible by everyone – not only the privileged rich and powerful.

Although some important automated hot-metal typesetting advances had been introduced by the Linotype and Monotype corporations in the late-nineteen-century, in the 1950s the way the printed word was secured for printing was the same as it was during Gutenberg's time, that is, using lead type. However it's 1957, and after more than five hundred years, the new radically changed world of phototypesetting was on the horizon, and it was rising fast. Cess and I would turn out to be the last two hot-metal typesetting compositors hired by Alex Thom.

Albeit lacking the romance and rich history of hot-metal typesetting, phototypesetting, or filmsetting as it was then called, was rapidly proven to be the better way of getting the job done. It was quicker, cost less, and offered equal or better typographic quality. Early versions of computerised digital typesetting were also emerging, albeit on a more distant horizon. Soon all that expensive material, equipment, and space required in the hot-metal caseroom would be thrown out – and a lot of equally expensive workforce along with it.

Most significantly, phototypesetting was ideally suited to the rapidly expanding lithographic printing process, as distinct from the classical world of letterpress printing. Lithography became the undisputed better way to print the ever increasing demand for four-colour printing. The print buyer's growing demand for colour played a big part in what brought about letterpress's almost overnight retraction within the industry.

Understandably, there were many Luddites about. There were lots of worried compositors and letterpress printers – troubled men fearing the dying of their trade as they knew it. They dreaded the indignity of not being equipped to learn and execute the required new skills. Many would cope by taking early retirement. And while youth enabled Cess and me to comfortably float and survive in the tides of rapid change, there were some wonderfully skilled men who would sadly drown.

****

To OTHER than the European community, the annual Eurovision Song Contest is pretty much a non-event. However, throughout Europe, it has the biggest television draws of the year. Each country has its own national song contest. The winners from each country then compete in the Eurovision Song Contest.

The contest has been televised since its inauguration in 1956, and it is one of the longest-running television programs in the world. It is the most watched non-sporting event, with audience figures as high as 600 million internationally.

Jackie, Dana and Derry.

In 1970, Jackie Smith and another Dublin man, Derry Lindsey, co-authored Ireland's Eurovision Song Contest entry. Their *All Kinds of Everything*, sung by Dana, a Northern Ireland singer, won the contest. For the first time, the Republic of Ireland was the winner. That was Jackie's crowning glory – he brought much prestige to the country with his *All Kinds of Everything*.

****

Impositions & the Long Stand

JIMMY SMITHERS IS THE DUBLIN TYPOGRAPHICAL Provident Society's (DTPS) union representative in Alex Thom. Being such, he holds the unique title, 'Father of the Chapel.' Jimmy is a muscular man. As a stoneman, he needs those muscles; the job entails a lot of heavy lifting. He does his work on a large, flat iron table, the imposition stone. Jimmy's job is to impose or position type-pages into chases, generating formes ready for printing. Jerry Pollock has asked Jimmy to let me assist with some 16-page forme impositions and to introduce me to the subject.

Hot-metal stonework.

When the pages on one side of the sheet of paper to be printed have been run, its backing set of pages when printed must register perfectly. And when the printed sheet is folded down to page size and trimmed in the bindery, each page must appear in the correct position, right side up and in the right numerical order. In other words, the pages must be properly imposed using the correct chase and imposition plan. Jimmy places the type-pages to be imposed on the imposition stone. Following the chosen imposition plan, each type-page, securely held together with page-cord, is then positioned and placed into the chase. He then inserts the required

197

below-type-height furniture, pieces of wood and metal, so as to make up the correct blank margins between the type-pages – the inside gutters, outside foredges, the heads and tails. Quions, forme-locking devices, are added, usually two quoins per side and one quoin per foot of all outside pages.

The locking of the forme is executed with great care. All those thousands of individual pieces of type and furniture must be converted to a single movable unit ready for printing – a single forme. Page-cords are carefully removed; using a quoin key to tighten the quions, the type-pages and furniture are then locked up. The quoins are gradually tightened so as to keep all the contents of the forme perfectly upright and straight. After a couple of rounds of tightening, a perfect tight fit is secured. Using a pig-skin mallet and a hard rubber-faced wooden plainer, Jimmy then plains the forme making sure that all the type-pages are level to the smooth steel imposition stone. He's careful to remove any small pieces of offending lead or chips of wood from underneath the pages before his final plaining and lock up. Once the forme has been securely locked and plained, Jimmy lifts the forme down, places it on the two-wheeled forme stand, and delivers it to the machine room for printing.

Checking the forme.

"Niall, I need a long stand," says Jimmy, a big smile on his flushed face. He has just finished lifting a completed forme down off the stone. "Go over to the bindery and ask Patricia Cowley to give you one," he continues. "A long stand is what's needed. Go on over to Patricia, and tell her I sent you."

"OK, Jimmy," says I, anxiously thinking about what the assigned task would entail. I'm a somewhat shy, self-conscious sixteen-year-old, and I've been working for a little more than a year. The bindery department occupies a long, forty-foot wide stretch of the plant, and is full of women and girls. It has a five-foot passageway all the way through, with workers and equipment on both sides. The last time I was over there it was an awful experience – all the girls started taunting me. I was nervously making my way through the department to get to the paper warehouse for some sample sheets when the attack occurred. "How'ye good lookin'? Are ye doin' an'in' tonight, love?" one of them yelled. "W'at's yer name darlin'? Can I shake yer hand, love?" shouts another. Brightly blushing, I had to walk that taunting gauntlet, feeling very embarrassed.

Patricia Cowley is the bindery overseer. Self-conscious and filled with apprehension, I go up to her.

"Jimmy Smithers asked me to come over and ask you for a long stand," says I.

"He did, did he?" she replies. "And how long of a stand did he say he wanted ye to get?"

"He just said a long stand," I answer.

"Right den," says she. "Stay there, and I'll get ye a long one."

I stand waiting for more than thirty minutes. The girls are given more than ample time to do their taunting thing. "Did ye come all the way over here just to see me, love?" "Come on over here and give me a hand, will ye?" "Yer mammy turned ye out well, so she did. Isn't he gorgeous Sally? I'd like to bring him home with me, so I would." On it went for thirty long, excruciating minutes.

Finally, Patricia Cowley returns.

"Now, Niall," says she. "Der's a long stand for ye."

"Ye can go back to Jimmy and ye can tell I gave it to ye," she continues, a big smile on her face as she laughs out loud. All the girls join in with their taunting laughter.

I'm perplexed for just a moment. The next moment is filled with the realisation that this long stand thing is a big prank. I scamper out of the bindery and back to the caseroom, where much to my further embarrassment, Jimmy, along with some other workers are splitting their sides laughing.

"Long stand, me arse," says I to Jimmy, as he leans over the stone trying to recover from the laughter his perfect prank had generated. "I feel like an eejit, so I do."

I find myself joining in with the laughter. "I'll never go back to that bleedin' bindery again," I laugh.

Jimmy has just about recovered to a state that allows him to speak. "It's all part of growing up, Niall. We all had to go through it, and you'll be a better man for it."

****

A Disastrous Success

I am a merry ploughboy, and I plough the fields all day,
'til a sudden thought came to me head dat I should roam away.
I've been sick and tired of slavery, since the day dat I was born,
so I'm off to join the IRA, and I'm off tomorrow morn.

We're all off to Dublin in the green, in the green,
where the helmets glisten in the sun.
Where the bayonets flash and the rifles crash,
to the rattle of a Thompson gun.

I'll leave aside me pick and spade, and I'll leave aside me plough,
I'll leave aside me old grey mare for no more I'll need dem now.
And I'll leave aside me Mary, she's the girl dat I adore,
I wonder if she'll t'ink of me when she'll hear the rifles roar.

And when the war is over, and dear old Ireland's free,
I'll take her to the church to wed, and a rebel's wife she'll be.
Well, some men fight for silver, and some men fight for gold,
but the IRA are fightin' for the land dat the saxons stole.

Off to Dublin in the Green – Traditional

IT IS DUE IN LARGE PART to Willy O'Brien, a proofreader in Alexander Thom, that I acquired an ardent interest in Irish history, and most particularly in the many stories surrounding the 1916 Easter Rising. My Da wet my whistle about that stuff, but it was Willy who brought it all to life. I'll be telling you about Willy and the *Irish Proclamation* later on, but before I do, I need to share with you the essential tales of the Easter Rising itself.

****

IN 1916 IRELAND, THERE WERE THREE, ARMED political organisations whose primary goals coincided: namely, after eight hundred years of British dominion, to make Ireland a free and independent nation. The three organisations were: the secret society, the *Irish Republican Brotherhood* (IRB); the *Irish Volunteers Force* (IVF); and the *Irish Citizens Army* (ICA).

There was also one particular non-political society; the *Gaelic League*. Since its founding in 1893, the *League* had re-ignited the population's love of Ireland's Gaelic language, literature, music, and song. Its membership was made up of a broad range of all levels of Irish society, both catholic and protestant, including many passionate republican nationalists.

There were some real differences between the three political organisations' overall philosophies. Their different answers to the questions of how and when to strike for freedom, and what exact type of state Ireland would become, were, to say the least, contentious. And there were strongly held dissimilarities within the organisations themselves, particularly within the IRB.

Nonetheless, in 1916 – the middle of the First World War – membership of all three political organisations and the *Gaelic League* would come together and strike for Ireland's freedom.

In 1858, James Stephens started the IRB. In the same year, on the Isle of Wight, a County Leitrim protestant Irishman, James Clarke,

James Stephens.

and his catholic wife Mary, a Tipperary woman, gave birth to their first child; they named him Thomas. Thomas's father was a soldier in the British Army. In 1865, he was redeployed to Dungannon County Tyrone, and the family moved back to Ireland.

Thomas Clarke was raised as a catholic. Despite being encouraged by his father to ready himself for becoming a British soldier, the nationalism spoken by Tom's teachers and friends in school swayed him away from a pro-British Ireland and towards the ideals of a free, independent Ireland. In 1878, he attended an IRB rally at which John Daly, a prominent IRB member spoke: the passion of Daly's speech was such that Tom immediately joined the IRB and became an ardent, active member soon afterwards. He would become very close to John Daly: he'd marry John's niece Kathleen in 1898, and would later die with John's son, Ned Daly.

In 1880, Tom Clarke immigrated to the USA to escape imprisonment. A warrant had been issued for his arrest.

A young Tom Clarke.   *John Daly.*   *John Devoy.*

Upon his arrival in the USA, Thomas joined with John Devoy and the IRB's New York branch. Three years later, he was sent to London to assist in the IRB's Dynamite Campaign. The plans included the blowing up of London Bridge. Thomas failed to blast the bridge: he was arrested with explosives in his possession and sentenced to life in prison. In 1898, he was released. After fifteen years of incarceration, Thomas looked like a man in his sixties. The terms of his release included travel restrictions. Despite this, with the help of his IRB colleagues, he was able to return to the USA.

In 1905 Thomas became a naturalised US citizen. In 1907, he was sent back to Ireland with a tough new task given to him by the IRB Supreme Council in the US. His task was to revitalise the IRB in Ireland; leadership in Ireland had become ineffective in pursuing the organisation's goals.

Thomas returned to Ireland, and as instructed by John Devoy, he joined up with IRB members, Bulmer Hobson, Denis McCullough and Seán MacDiarmada. By 1911, these four men would become the leaders of Ireland's IRB Supreme Council. New, active membership was developed and made ready to pursue the IRB's goals of an independent Irish Republic.

Clarke: 49yrs old.   *MacDiarmada.*   *Bulmer Hobson.*   *McCullough.*

IN APRIL 1912, the British House of Lords and Commons passed the *Irish Home Rule Bill*; it was declared that the Bill would be enacted in September 1914. While the vast majority of the population of Ireland's three southern provinces, Leinster, Munster, and Connacht, were catholic and welcomed *Home Rule*, Ireland's northern province, Ulster, was vehemently opposed to it. The thoughts of *Home Rule* created real fears throughout most parts of Ulster, especially so within the ardent membership of the protestant *Ulster Unionist Party* (UUP). They feared Ireland's overall papist majority; they dreaded being stripped of their local, protestant supremacy, pro-British identity and way of life. Like the majority of all the protestant Irish, those in predominately protestant Ulster passionately coveted staying part of Britain.

EDWARD CARSON, the Dublin-born Anglican leader of the UUP, was adamant when speaking against *Home Rule*; he postulated that not only Ulster but all of Ireland, was and should remain part of Great Britain. Blatantly, he put an illegal militia where his mouth was. In January 1913, he founded the *Ulster Volunteer Force* (UVF), a one-hundred-thousand strong, illegally armed military force committed to resisting any attempts by the British Government to impose Irish *Home Rule* in Ulster.

Although based upon opposed objectives, just like the UVF, the IRB also had little or no interest in *Home Rule*. Nor did they have any interest in what they considered to be Britain's puppet government of Ireland, John Redmond's *Parliamentary Party* (IPP). It was John's good work that had finally secured *Home Rule*. While its enactment would improve Ireland's ability in governing itself, and as such was popular with the majority of the population, still, with *Home Rule* the Irish government would remain controlled from Westminister. The IRB's interests went much further than that; they wanted the thirty-two counties of Ireland to be a free, unencumbered Irish Republic.

Urged on by Thomas Clarke and other members of the IRB, and ostensibly in response to Carson and his UVF's threat against the planned enactment of the *Home Rule Bill*, the *Irish Volunteer Force* (IVF) was founded in Dublin on 25 November 1913. From the start, the IVF was infiltrated with IRB members who'd soon become its designers. Nevertheless, while having this strong influence, the IRB, being the secret society it was, wasn't able to gain broad public backing. That changed when the respected *Gaelic League* leader and founder, Éoin MacNeill, gave his support to the IVF. Éoin accepted the appointment of Chief-of-Staff. With Éoin as a figurehead, the IVF soon became acceptable to the public. It became a resounding success, reaching a signed membership of over two-hundred-thousand in less than one year.

Rather than for the perceived support and defence of the soon to be enacted *Home Rule Bill*, the IRB had orchestrated this surge of popular armed nationalism as a means of gaining the population's acceptance of Ireland's right to military opposition to British rule. The IVF's growing membership would bear well for the IRB when it was ready to instigate its own rebellion.

Being the head of the installed IPP Irish Government, and observing the broad and much evident success of the IVF, John Redmond was quick to realise the necessity of being part of, if not in control of the organisation. In June of 1914, having discussed the matter with Éoin MacNeill, Redmond issued an ultimatum: he insisted that members of his party be placed on the IVF's committee. This was not well received by the majority of the committee, especially Tom Clarke and the other IRB members.

Being guided by the Machiavellian adage 'keep your friends close and your enemies closer', one of the IVF committee, Bulmer Hobson, (who was also the part of the IRB Supreme Council), gave into Redmond's demands. Bulmer knew that behind the scenes, the IRB was getting close to initiating its own rebellion; he considered that this apparent pandering to Redmond's ultimatum was well worth its expected results. With Redmond's country-wide popularity, membership of the already growing IVF would expand even further.

The horrors of the First World War started in August 1914. Given the resulting suspension of the planned September 1914 enactment of the *Home Rule Bill*, and in an effort to retain goodwill with Britain in the interim, Redmond proposed that the IVF join Irish regiments of the British army to assist in fighting the Germans. His proposal was rejected at IVF committee level. However, the majority of IVF members, just like the majority of the population, supported the war effort against the Germans. Under Redmond's leadership, 180,000 left the IVF to form the *National Volunteers* and fight for Britain. This exodus reduced the IVF membership to 20,000 men, including its Chief of Staff, Éoin MacNeill. However, with Redmond no longer having a presence on the IVF committee, the IRB were able to gain better control of its reduced and now hard-core republican membership.

JIM LARKIN, born in Liverpool in 1876, came to Dublin in 1908. There was growing unrest amongst the working class. Extreme poverty was widespread; unfair draconian wages, working hours, and hiring/firing practises by unchecked employers was rampant. Jim organised the workers and started the *Irish Transport & General Workers Union* (ITGWU). James Connelly, a Scot, born in Edinburgh in 1868, joined Jim as his right-hand man in 1910.

In reaction to the employers' and government's stance against the growing power of the ITGWU, and in particular, the employers' Labour Lock-out of August 1913 through January 1914, the *Irish Citizens Army* (ICA) was founded. The ICA's initial purpose was to create an armed military wing of the ITGWU for the protection of the workers' rights regarding wages, working hours and the rights to strike. The ICA was a small, armed socialistic group with no more than four-hundred members.

After the First World War had been declared, Jim Larkin went to the USA. The passionate, bellicose James Connelly became the sole leader of the ITGWU and the ICA. As the British got more engrossed in fighting the Germans, James increased his independent call for an armed Irish rebellion. However, James knew the ICA's numbers were far less than would be needed: any successful rebellion would require a much bigger force.

IN MAY 1915, a secret Military Committee within the IRB was set up by Thomas Clarke and Seán MacDiarmada. They did so because of the evident lack of commitment from the other IRB Supreme Council leaders. The IRB's Military Committee's goal was to bring about an immediate rebellion. Tom and Seán saw the First World War as the ideal opportunity to strike, and they considered it imperative that they do so before the war ended.

Joining Thomas and Seán, the very willing and able Pádraic Pearse, Éamonn Ceannt and Joseph Plunkett, all members of the IRB and the *Gaelic League*, became the committee's first recruits.

By the end of 1915, this secret group of five were well ahead with their rebellion strategies. They were anxious about James Connelly and his loud, militant ICA doing anything that might upset their plans. To eliminate such an eventuality, in January 1916, they invited James to one of their meetings and asked him to become the sixth member of the Military Committee.

James accepted the invitation: he considered that with the British out of the way he would be well able to push his socialistic agenda as the new Irish state was being established. Despite recognised differences regarding what type of state the newly independent Ireland might become, the Military Committee did value, James. His military intelligence and experience would be a big assist in implementing their rebellion – James had spent seven years in active service with the British army. His strong anti-British sentiments would also help, but more than anything else, it was his armed and well trained ICA that the IRB cherished the most. Soon after James's recruitment, Thomas MacDonagh, another passionate IRB man, would become the seventh and final member of the committee. Together, these seven men agreed to start the Rising on Easter Sunday, 23 April 1916.

Seán MacDiarmada. Thomas Clarke. Pádraic Pearse. Éamonn Ceannt.

James Connelly. Tom MacDonagh. Joseph Plunkett.

They initially chose Friday, 21 April. However, Pádraic Pearse was successful in getting the committee to see the symbolic value of switching it from Good Friday to Easter Sunday – just like Jesus Christ would rise, so too would the new Republic of Ireland.

Without anyone other than themselves and a small group of eleven other high ranking ICA and IRB leaders knowing of the imminent Rising, the seven committee members continued with their preparations. They choose to do so on behalf of all Irish men and women, both past and present, including the IRB's other Supreme Council members and general membership, Éoin MacNeill the Chief-of-Staff of the IVF and its hard-core republican membership, and the equally committed ICA members.

On Monday, 17 April the committee met and finalised their plans for the following Sunday. They also agreed on the wording of the *Irish Proclamation* declaring Ireland as the Irish Republic.

On Thursday, 20 April a mobilisation order for country-wide 'manoeuvres' was passed out to all members of the IRB, the IVF, and the ICA. This was done without Éoin MacNeill knowing anything about the planned rebellion. The other members of the IRB Supreme Council, Bulmer Hobson, and Denis McCullough, while being more aware that something was going on, had also been kept in the dark.

Éoin, Bulmer, and Denis learned of the mobilisation order on Thursday evening. They met and spoke with the Military Committee. While Éoin and Bulmer were furious about what had transpired without their authorisation, Denis was more receptive. Bulmer sided with Éoin in condemning what the secret Military Committee had done. They both insisted on the immediate cancellation of the plans. They met again on Friday, but in the absence of Bulmer. The Military Committee was as furious with Bulmer, a fellow IRB man, as he was with them – Bulmer had sided with Éoin, who was not an IRB member. Overnight the Military Committee secretly arrested Bulmer and confirmed Denis McCullough as being the head of the Supreme Council. Bulmer was put under house arrest with the intention of muzzling him until he would be of no further harm to their plans.

The following day's meeting had Éoin as the only remaining objector. For some time, the leaders of the Rising had been in secret negotiations with Germany. An essential part of the anticipated successful rebellion was Germany's agreement to supply arms to the IRB. The committee shared this intelligence with Éoin. Upon hearing that the weapons were about to be delivered, he was coaxed to ever so reluctantly agree to the plans. But later that day, rumours of Roger Casement's arrest gave great concern; Roger had been assigned to arrange for the delivery of the arms.

On Saturday morning, the day before the planned Rising, the rumours that Roger had been arrested were confirmed. But of even more significance was the news that the arms shipment had been scuttled after a German ship, disguised as the Norwegian *Aud*, was intercepted by the British navy.

The Aud.

Éoin immediately retracted his agreement to proceed with the Rising: without the arms, it would be an absolute failure. He sent his men across the country with a reversing order cancelling the 'manoeuvres'. He placed an announcement in the nationally distributed *Sunday Independent* newspaper instructing his Volunteers to ignore the mobilisation order.

> April 22, 1916.
>
> Owing to the very critical position, all orders given to Irish Volunteers for to-morrow, Easter Sunday, are hereby rescinded, and no parades, marches, or other movements of Irish Volunteers will take place. Each individual Volunteer will obey this order strictly in every particular.
>
> EOIN MACNEILL,

Éoin's newspaper announcement.

The Military Committee summoned an emergency meeting. Despite Éoin's revoking order, the meeting resulted in the decision to go ahead, but to move the Rising back one day to Monday, 24 April. They hoped to persuade Éoin to rescind his cancellation.

Éoin never did cancel the order. The plans for the Rising had been hit with two damaging blows: the German arms had not been delivered, and without the expected number of Volunteers there was no chance of victory. Over the preceding eight hundred years, there had been many uprisings, and all of them had failed. In the face of these last-minute calamities, the 1916 Easter Rising would go ahead and become a success, albeit a disastrous one.

LASTING ONLY one week, the Rising concluded with the superiorly equipped British forces securing an unconditional surrender.

The surrender.

The story within this faded photo of the surrender includes more than the obvious. There are three men in the photo: Pádraic Pearse, is standing erect wearing his IVF cocked-hat and what looks like a great-coat; Pádraic is looking at the English Brigadier-General Lowe; Captain Wheeler, in the left foreground, is standing next to the General. However, there is a fourth person in the photo – Nurse Elizabeth O'Farrell. She's standing to Pádraic's right; her feet can be seen just ahead of Pádraic's. Pádraic is in his IVF uniform, a cocked hat, tunic, and trousers: it is Elizabeth who is wearing the great-coat. The quality of the photograph is poor, making Elizabeth's coat and Pádraic's uniform look like one.

Nurse Elizabeth O'Farrell.

Elizabeth was a member of *Cumman na mBan*, an auxiliary unit of the IVF. She had been in the GPO with Pádraic throughout the week of fighting. Once the decision to surrender had been taken, Pádraic recruited Elizabeth to be the one to approach the

British military authorities. White flag in hand, having the trust of Pádraic and gaining the confidence of General Lowe, Elizabeth played a vital role throughout the two-day surrendering process.

The 1916 Easter Rising casualties were: British dead 116, rebels and civilians 485; British injured 368, rebels and civilians 2,217. Thirty-five-hundred were arrested. Ninety were sentenced to death, seventy-four of whom had their verdicts commuted to life in prison. Fifteen-hundred were interned in British gaols.

All seven members of the Military Committee were captured: Thomas Clarke, Pádraic Pearse, James Connolly, Eamonn Ceannt, Seán MacDiarmada, Thomas MacDonagh and Joseph Plunkett. Six of the seven were sent to Kilmainham Gaol; Connelly was injured and held in a temporary hospital at Dublin Castle. All seven were tried by field general courts-martial and condemned to death; they were the ones who had signed the *Irish Proclamation*.

Con Colbert.   *Ned Daly.*   *Seán Heuston.*   *Michael Mallin.*

John McBride.   *O'Hanrahan.*   *William Pearse.*

Markievicz.   *Éamon de Valera.*

Eight other men and one woman were likewise condemned to death. Seven of the men would be executed: Con Colbert, Ned Daly, Seán Heuston, Michael Mallin, John McBride, Michael O'Hanrahan and William Pearse. The woman, Countess Markievicz, and the eighth man, Éamon de Valera, would have their sentences commuted to penal servitude for life and be sent to English gaols.

On the morning of 3 May, Thomas Clarke, Pádraic Pearse, and Thomas MacDonagh were the first to go. The following day, Ned Daly (Tom Clarke's brother-in-law), Michael O'Hanrahan, William Pearse (Pádraic Pearse's younger brother), and Joseph Plunkett were executed. On Friday, it was John McBride's turn.

British civility of not having executions on weekends delayed the execution of the remaining men. Monday, 8 May arrived, and four more were put to death: Éamonn Ceannt, Seán Heuston, Michael Mallin and Con Colbert.

Seán MacDiarmada and James Connolly were executed on Friday, 12 May. James was brought from the Castle hospital to Kilmainham. He was carried in through the gaol's rear gate where the firing-squad was lined up. He was put sitting in a chair, bound and violently dispatched to join his comrades. Like Seán and the other executed leaders, his body was carried to Arbour Hill, placed in an unmarked pit, covered with lime and buried.

Roger Casement. Thomas Kent.

Thomas Kent was also executed; his death was by firing squad in Cork on 9 May. After a long, disparaging trial for treason, Roger Casement, an Englishman, was hanged in London on 3 August.

Markievicz, the only woman sentenced to death, had her judgment commuted because of her sex. Éamon was an IVF Commandant – he was not expected to receive clemency. It was only by the combination of four twists of fate that Éamon escaped the firing squad.

Firstly, De Valera was born in New York in 1882 to Catherine Coll, an Irish woman from Knockmore County Limerick, and Vivion de Valera, a Spaniard from Cuba. Éamon's father died in 1885, and Éamon was sent back to Knockmore where he was raised by his grandmother. Éamon's birthright to US citizenship brought US interests to his trial.

Secondly, over the two-day surrendering process, Éamon and his IVF Battalion were some of the last of the rebels to capitulate. His court martial and sentencing was delayed until 8 May – twelve of his comrades had already been executed since 3 May.

Thirdly, by the time De Valera was sentenced on 8 May, heavy US and internal British political pressure, plus increased local Irish pressure from John Redmond's IPP, were screaming for a halt to the executions. In response to this pressure, General Maxwell, the British General in charge, had advised Westminster that Seán MacDiarmada's and James Connelly's executions had been scheduled for 12 May and that these two executions would conclude his harsh demands for immediate reprisal for what Maxwell claimed were war-time treasonous acts.

Fourthly, when Maxwell examined Éamon's file, he found no Fenian background, only details of his IVF affiliation. Éamon did not appear to be dangerous or of any great import. A supplication made by the US at his delayed trial, broad political pressure, and this lack of Fenian background, combined to save De Valera.

The sixteen executed men had seen the Rising as a blood-sacrifice, and they knew the blood that would flow would include their own. They knew the Rising would not achieve their goal in the immediate future, but they were confident that it would re-ignite Ireland's centuries-old pursuit of freedom from England.

Their confidence was proven well held. In December 1921, after a five and a half year struggle, culminating in the *Irish War of Independence* and finally, an *Anglo/Irish Treaty*, the twenty-six county Irish Free State or Saorstát Éireann was established. Controversially, six Ulster counties were excluded in the Treaty; they would remain under devolved British Government control. Sadly, the Treaty resulted in the *1922/23 Civil War* – the Free Staters under Michael Collins, against the Republicans under Éamon de Valera. Michael was killed during an IRA ambush at Beal na mBlath outside Cork City, however, the Free Staters emerged victorious. Ireland's six Ulster counties remained under British control – the heartbreak of the partitioning of Ireland became a tragic reality. Éamon would survive to play a major role in Ireland's politics until his death in 1975.

****

Grace & Joseph

As we gather in the chapel here in old Kilmainham Gaol,
I think about the last few weeks, oh will they say we failed.
From our school days, they have told us we must yearn for liberty,
yet all I want in this dark place is to have you here with me.

Oh Grace just hold me in your arms, and let this moment linger,
they take me out at dawn and I will die.
With all my love, I place this wedding ring upon your finger,
there won't be time to share our love, so we must say goodbye.

Now I know it's hard for you, my love, to ever understand,
the love I bear for these brave men, my love for this brave land.
But when Pádraic called me to his side down in the GPO,
I had to leave my own sick bed, to him I had to go.

Now as the dawn is breaking, my heart is breaking too,
as I walk out on this May morn, my thoughts will be of you.
I'll write some words upon the wall so everyone will know,
I loved so much that I could see his blood upon the rose.

Grace – Frank & Sean O'Meara (1985): Copyright held by Asdee Music.

THIS FRANK & SEAN O'MEARA BALLAD CAPTURES one of the most poignant episodes of the 1916 Easter Rising. It memorialises the love and marriage of Grace Gifford (1888–1955) to Joseph Mary Plunkett (1887–1916), and Joseph's execution on 4 May 1916. The Rising has many moving chapters, but Grace and Joseph's story is perhaps the most heartbreaking.

Grace was introduced to Joseph by her sister Muriel and Muriel's husband, Thomas MacDonagh. They became engaged in December 1915 and planned to marry on Easter Sunday the following year. It was to be a double wedding that would include the marriage of Joseph's sister, Geraldine, to Thomas Dillon.

Grace Gifford & Joseph Mary Plunkett.

They were all members of the *Gaelic League*. However, Joseph and Thomas were also members of the IRB's Military Committee: Joseph was Director of Military Operations, and Thomas was Commandant 2nd Battalion of the Dublin Brigade. With the committee's coincidental decision to start the Rising on the same day as the scheduled nuptials, Joseph and Grace decided to defer their wedding. Not being directly involved in the planning of the Rising, Geraldine and her intended decided to go ahead with their's as planned. Ironically, with the Rising's eventual one-day postponement, Grace and Joe could have been married as arranged. Joe's mind would have been elsewhere during the ceremony, but it would have given the couple one day to celebrate their marriage – sadly they were to be denied even that.

Joseph had glandular tuberculous as a child, and as a consequence, he had health issues all his life. Despite his fragility from some neck surgery immediately before the Rising, he left his sick bed on Friday, 21 April to join his comrades. After the Easter Rising and the brave, albeit hopeless week of fighting, the inevitable surrender, the mass arrests, and the impetuous military court dead-sentencing, all that remained to complete the tragic event was the willingly-accepted executions of the seven leaders and the other nine condemned men.

Knowing he was to be executed on 4 May, Joseph told Grace he wanted to marry her before he died. Grace agreed and went out to buy the wedding rings on the afternoon of 3 May. Rings in hand, she arrived at Kilmainham Gaol at 6 p.m. She was kept waiting until 9:00 p.m. One can only imagine her state of mind during those three hours. The prison Governor had given permission for the wedding. Why the long wait? Her brother-in-law, Thomas MacDonagh, had been executed that morning, and Joseph was to be executed at dawn. The damp coldness of Kilmainham Gaol was too much for even a healthy man. What must the cold, wet cell be doing to her ailing Joseph? Was Joseph already dead?

Finally, Grace was led to the small, candle-lit gaol chapel; the prison used gas light, and that evening there was a breakdown of the system. Joseph was brought into the chapel in handcuffs. The manacles were removed for the wedding ring ceremony and the signing of the marriage register. Father McCarthy, the gaol's chaplain, performed the solemn nuptials with two British soldiers acting as witnesses. Once the service was complete Joseph was cuffed, led back to his cell and made ready for execution.

Kilmainham Gaol Chapel.

Grace left the prison and went to a nearby house in Thomas Street where she mourned her soon-to-be executed husband. In the early hours of the morning, a military car came to where she was. She was instructed to accompany the British soldiers back to Kilmainham. Grace and Joe were allowed a short ten-minute meeting in Joe's cell in the presence of some guards. With Joe's house keys in one pocket and a lock of his hair in another, and having said their final agonising goodbyes, Grace was escorted out of the cell and sent back to where she was staying on Thomas Street. She asked about collecting Joe's remains but was told, without explanation, that it would not be possible for her to do so.

Joseph was the last of the four men to be put to death that morning. He had removed his spectacles and wedding ring before he was led out to the prison yard for execution. He asked the priest in attendance, to give the spectacles to his mother and his ring to Grace. His last words were; "Father, I am very happy. I am dying for the glory of God and the honour of Ireland."

During the *1922–23 Irish Civil War*, Grace was imprisoned in Kilmainham Gaol – in a cell not far from where she had said her final goodbye to Joseph. She died a widow in December 1955.

****

Willy and The Proclamation

I MET WILLY O'BRIEN SOON AFTER I STARTED WORKING. He was a proofreader at Alexander Thom. Willy was a handsome, well-kept gentleman in his late sixties, about five-foot-ten, and his shoes were always polished to a shine that could almost be used as a mirror. He had a bright complexion and seemed to be smiling all the time. He had thick white hair, wore gold-rimmed spectacles and spoke like my Da, soft and gently. My Da had told me how as a young active member of the IVF he'd played his part in the 1916 Easter Rising. What I learned from Willy directly regarding one particular role he had played was soon to astound me.

I'VE BEEN instructed to report to Willy and hold copy.

"You're Gerry Kavanagh's son; am I right?" says Willy.

"Yes, Mr O'Brien."

"It's nice to meet you. Your name is Niall; am I right?"

"Yes, Mr O'Brien."

"Your daddy, was a good man, and it was all too early for him to be leaving you and your mammy, far too early; am I right?"

"You are, Mr O'Brien."

"Well, Niall, sit down here beside me, and we'll get started."

"Proofreading is all about getting it right. We've got to follow the copy. And so's you can see how important proofreading is, I'm going to tell you about the *Irish Proclamation*. Pádraic Pearse proudly read it to the Irish people outside the GPO in O'Connell Street on Easter Monday of 1916."

With that, Willy opens his desk drawer and carefully extracts an original copy of the historic document. It's yellowish in colour and folded to quarter size.

"Take a good look at this, Niall," says Willy. "And while you're looking, I'll tell you all about it."

217

The gist of what Willy O'Brien told me is as follows.

THE IRISH PROCLAMATION was written by Pádraic Pearse, with some late input from James Connelly. On Monday, 17 April 1916, the wording of the document was agreed to and signed by six of the seven signatories; Joseph Plunkett, the seventh signatory, was in the hospital for neck surgery and would sign later.

James Connelly was given the responsibility for the critical task of typesetting and printing the explosively secret document. It was his job to make sure the *Proclamation* posters would be ready for distribution for the planned 1916 Easter Rising the following Sunday.

James had a hot metal letterpress printing shop hidden in the bowels of Liberty Hall at Butt Bridge. His press was able to print poster size, and he had sufficient paper. However, with the large amount of text contained in the document, his small caseroom didn't have sufficient quantities of the large Double Great Primer Antique No.8 typeface required to typeset the edict. Normally, James would have used the services of Joseph Stanley's *Gaelic Press* in Liffey Street, but some weeks earlier Joseph's offices had been raided, and all the equipment was confiscated. James recruited Michael Molloy, a compositor, and a member of the IVF, to scour the city's caserooms and gather up what was needed. The required type was quickly secured and brought to Liberty Hall. A second compositor would be required, and that compositor was Willy O'Brien. Chris Brady, an ICA man, was the printer.

As a result of Éoin MacNeill's pivotal countermanding of the Sunday 'manoeuvres', the Military Committee had had an emergency meeting; they decided to go ahead with the Easter Rising but pushed in back to Monday. James Connelly called his printing crew into his office. He told them that under sworn secrecy they were to complete the *Proclamation* in time for distribution on Monday. During this brief meeting, Joseph Plunkett came in and put the final signature on the document.

Easter Sunday morning found Michael, Willy, and Chris back at Liberty Hall ready to complete their important task. Michael commenced setting the main text of the *Proclamation* while Willy worked on the starting and ending display lines.

218

Hand typesetting.

As Michael was typesetting the third paragraph, he ran out of the letter *e* twenty-five times, and the letter *t* five times: he couldn't complete the paragraph, nor the three remaining paragraphs, without those *e*'s and *t*'s. After discussing the problem with Willy and Chris, they came to a decision. They'd have to print the poster's top-half first, and then overprint it with the bottom-half.

Michael would finish the third paragraph using an available, smaller looking typeface for the missing *e*'s and *t*'s; he'd spread out their usage as he felt best. They'd then add Willy's top display lines and print the top-half of the poster. After the first printing, they'd dis the text type back into the typecases, typeset the remaining three paragraphs, then add the bottom display lines, and overprint the bottom-half onto the preprinted top-half.

There are many reproductions of this document, all of which, in one way or another, fail to capture the authenticity of the original. It was printed letterpress on a thin, yellowish poster stock. One-thousand copies were produced. If you were to examine any one of the few remaining copies you'd find lots of peculiarities.

The last three paragraphs and the signatories at the end, which were overprinted onto the first printing, are off alignment. In many of the many of the few remaining originals, there is too much space between the last paragraph of the first printing, i.e., the third paragraph, and the first paragraph of the overprinted bottom-half.

All the wrong font *e*'s and *t*'s are in the third paragraph. In the paragraph's fourth line, Michael decided to also use the smaller substitute font for the letter *i* along with one of the wrong font *t*'s in the word *it*; he decided the word would read better that way.

The *Proclamation* does have two compositor errors. Both errors are in the last paragraph: there's an inverted *e* on line one, and the words, *worthy of,* on the fifth line are typeset, *worthyof,* without a word space. These two errors, while being egregious, are surely excusable: the pressure on Michael was tremendous.

POBLACHT NA H EIREANN.

THE PROVISIONAL GOVERNMENT
OF THE
IRISH REPUBLIC
TO THE PEOPLE OF IRELAND.

IRISHMEN AND IRISHWOMEN : In the name of God and of the dead generations from which she receives her old tradition of nationhood, Ireland, through us, summons her children to her flag and strikes for her freedom.

Having organised and trained her manhood through her secret revolutionary organisation, the Irish Republican Brotherhood, and through her open military organisations, the Irish Volunteers and the Irish Citizen Army, having patiently perfected her discipline, having resolutely waited for the right moment to reveal itself, she now seizes that moment, and, supported by her exiled children in America and by gallant allies in Europe, but relying in the first on her own strength, she strikes in full confidence of victory.

We declare the right of the people of Ireland to the ownership of Ireland, and to the unfettered control of Irish destinies, to be sovereign and indefeasible. The long usurpation of that right by a foreign people and government has not extinguished the right, nor can it ever be extinguished except by the destruction of the Irish people. In every generation the Irish people have asserted their right to national freedom and sovereignty: six times during the past three hundred years they have asserted it in arms. Standing on that fundamental right and again asserting it in arms in the face of the world, we hereby proclaim the Irish Republic as a Sovereign Independent State, and we pledge our lives and the lives of our comrades-in-arms to the cause of its freedom, of its welfare, and of its exaltation among the nations.

The Irish Republic is entitled to, and hereby claims, the allegiance of every Irishman and Irishwoman. The Republic guarantees religious and civil liberty, equal rights and equal opportunities to all its citizens, and declares its resolve to pursue the happiness and prosperity of the whole nation and of all its parts, cherishing all the children of the nation equally, and oblivious of the differences carefully fostered by an alien government, which have divided a minority from the majority in the past.

Until our arms have brought the opportune moment for the establishment of a permanent National Government, representative of the whole people of Ireland and elected by the suffrages of all her men and women, the Provisional Government, hereby constituted, will administer the civil and military affairs of the Republic in trust for the people.

We place the cause of the Irish Republic under the protection of the Most High God, Whose blessing we invoke upon our arms, and we pray that no one who serves that cause will dishonour it by cowardice, inhumanity, or rapine. In this supreme hour the Irish nation must, by its valour and discipline and by the readiness of its children to sacrifice themselves for the common good, prove itself worthy of the august destiny to which it is called.

Signed on Behalf of the Provisional Government,

THOMAS J. CLARKE.
SEAN Mac DIARMADA.   THOMAS MacDONAGH.
P. H. PEARSE.   EAMONN CEANNT,
JAMES CONNOLLY.   JOSEPH PLUNKETT.

The Irish Proclamation.

While Michael's skills were being tested with the text, Willy had his own challenges with the display lines. The font chosen for the second and fifth lines of the top-five display lines, *THE PROVISIONAL GOVERNMENT*, and *TO THE PEOPLE OF IRELAND*, required six capital *O*'s and seven *E*'s: only two *O*'s and six *E*'s were available. Willy found four capital *O*'s from another type font that did the job well enough. Despite tearing the place apart searching, he could not find an alternative for the peculiarly serifed capital *E*. Talking the problem over with Michael, the infrequently used compositor's 'resin trick' was identified as being the way to go. Willy did have a capital *F*; working hard with the resin it would be possible to build a bottom cross-stroke onto the shank at the foot of the *F*'s down-stroke. After an hour or so of artistic endeavour, Willy resolved the dilemma. It was not the best of a job, but it would have to do.

The other problem incurred by Willy was in the fourth line of the top display lines: it was the main headline of the poster, *IRISH REPUBLIC*. Willy discovered he didn't have a capital *C*.

This quandary was to be creatively resolved. Taking a capital *O*, Willy turned it on its side; then, using a steel punch he smashed out the centre section of the right side of the sidewise *O*, making it look like the required capital letter *C*. Like the capital *E* in line five, it wasn't perfect, but it did the job. Willy O'Brien, one can correctly say, was the man who put the *C* in the *IRISH REPUBLIC*.

"So THERE you are," concludes Willy with a smile. "If we hadn't changed that *O* into a *C*, we'd all be living in the Irish *Republio!*"

Looking closer, I examine the *O* turned *C*. At first glance, it is a *C*, albeit an odd looking one: the cap height is too low; its right opening is shorter than it should be; the opening's top end-stroke extends too low, and its bottom end stroke is concave.

"That's a great story, Mr O'Brien," says I in awe.

"There's another one-letter-wrong story that upset a lot of people," continues Willy, as he extracts a dog-eared folded newspaper from his treasure trove of a desk drawer.

Willy turns to page one of the *Gateshead Municipal News* dated 11 October 1928. There is a photograph of King George and Queen Mary passing over the Tyne Bridge. The picture's caption reads, *"King George and Queen Mary pissing over the new Tyne Bridge connecting Newcastle-on-Tyne and Gateshead."*

"They were passing over the bridge!" declares William. "Not pissing over it. The caption was probably typeset by a good Irishman who had a well-placed grudge against the royalty."

****

HAVING BEEN a hot metal compositor myself, and while being conscious of the fact that I've some nerve making the following comments, I feel obliged to express my professional opinion regarding the typesetting of the *Irish Proclamation.*

I do think Michael Molloy could have done a better job of spreading out the use of those twenty-five wrong font *e*'s. They're all in the third paragraph, and it's a ten line paragraph. Michael concentrated their use in only five lines: one in line two; two in line five; eight in both the sixth and eighth line; and six in the ninth line. This concentration highlights their presence. So as to minimise this distraction, they should have been used two or three per line throughout the entire third paragraph. Better still, he could have spread those *e*'s throughout all of the first three paragraphs.

He did the same thing with four of the five wrong font *t*'s. One is in the third paragraph's seventh line, and that's good; but then, he put two of them in the third and fourth lines. And I also think his decision to have the fourth line's word *it*, with both characters in the smaller wrong font, was a bad choice. He should have set the word with both letters in the correct font, and then use the wrong font *t* in another word on another line.

Now . . . I feel a lot better having got that off my chest. And Michael; thanks for what you did. You not only typeset the *Irish Proclamation* for us all, but you also stood by Thomas MacDonagh in Jacobs factory during the fighting of the *1916 Easter Rising*. Please forgive me – being a compositor yourself, I know you know where I'm coming from.

****

Albert Hackett & Knockdowns

ALBERT HACKETT IS A STOCKY FIVE-FOOT-TEN proofreader. He isn't bald, but he's getting there. He has a hifalutin manner while at the same time being courteous, albeit in a strict businesslike way.

Just like Willy O'Brien, Albert does his work in what is referred to as the reader's box. There's a row of these boxes along the top wall of Thom's caseroom. Each box has separating wood sidewalls and a glass front wall; there is a glass, inwards-opening door on the left-hand side of the front wall. The boxes have a width of six feet and a depth of eight. They're about eight-foot tall and have open tops. The back four feet of the tiny rooms are filled, side-wall to side-wall, with a sloping reader's desk plus a set of shelves for reference books, dictionaries, &c. This leaves just enough space to house two tall stools, one for the proofreader on the right, and one for the copyholder on the door side, giving barely sufficient space for the door to open inwards.

Albert is working on an important rush job. His copyholder has gone home sick. Albert secures me as a substitute.

"Sit, boy!" barks Albert. "I want you to read this copy distinctly. No slurring your words," he continues. "Announce numerals clearly. Declare all punctuation, every comma, every full-point, new sentence and paragraph. Don't forget the colons, semi-colons, the opening and closing quotes, all the queries and exclamation marks."

"Don't you miss anything, boy!" he concludes. "We've an important job here, and each printed word must be right."

I'm sitting down and starting to read the copy aloud, when suddenly, Albert keels backwards, falls off his stool and with wild contortions he hits the floor, frothing at the mouth. I've never experienced anything like this. I'm stricken with fear.

Albert lands on the floor right behind me. With every contortion, he's wedging himself more and more between my stool and the door.

"Jays, what's wrong with ye?" I screech. I'm now standing on top of the proofreader's sloping desk. "Help! Someone help!"

Jimmy Smithers is nearby. He runs towards the box and my frantic plea for help. He tries to open the door. He can't.

"Albert is having a fit," shouts Jimmy. "Niall, get down and put something in Albert's mouth so's he won't bite his tongue off."

"I don't know how to do that. What'll I use?"

"Use that wooden pica gauge," instructs Jimmy, referring to the wooden pica measure I'm unknowingly holding in my hand.

Mick Smith and some more of the men, including Jerry Pollock, Cess and Jackie are outside to render assistance.

"Take it easy now, Niall," encourages Mick. "Just get down and do as Jimmy said. You can do it. Just put the gauge in his mouth and then try to push him over so as we can get him out."

"Go and call the ambulance," shouts Mick, directing his instruction to Jerry. "Tell them it's Albert having one of his fits. They know him, and they'll be here in a minute."

Albert's eyes are aberrantly wide open. As I climb down to insert the gauge into his mouth, his eyes are wildly moving and almost popping out of his head. With great difficulty, I manage to get the gauge into his froth-filled mouth. I'm able to push him over sufficiently to allow Mick and Jimmy get in and drag me out to freedom. It's all I can do not to burst out crying.

"Good man, Niall," says Jerry. Having made his ambulance call, he had returned to the scene. "You've probably saved Albert's life. For sure, you've saved the poor man's tongue," he continues, as he gives me an around-the-shoulders congratulatory hug.

I hold the mounting tears back, and like a man (I'm only seventeen), I suck them up.

"I hope he'll be OK. That's an awful thing to have wrong with you. I never knew he had epilepsy. Will he be alright, Jerry?"

"He'll be a hundred percent once we get him to the Mater Hospital and the doctors get a hold of him," replies Jerry. "And that's because of you, Niall. The right man in the right place at the right time. You should be proud of yourself. I know if the Duke, your father were here, he'd be as proud as punch of you, as indeed we all are," he continues. Turning to the men gathered around he adds, "Am I right, lads?"

"Right on," exclaim the gathered men.

The ambulance arrives, and Albert is taken out on a gurney.

"Oh, Niall," says Jerry, as the gathering starts to break-up. "When Albert comes back, and that'll probably be in the morning, don't say anything to him about what just happened. He doesn't remember anything about it when he gets those fits, and he doesn't like talking about it. Just leave it alone and pretend nothing happened. That's the best thing to do, and it's the way he likes it."

Sure enough, Albert is back in work the following day looking and acting as though nothing ever happened.

I TELL my Ma about Albert's fit later that evening.

"I'm proud of you," says Peg. "And Jerry is right. Your poor father is as proud of you as I am."

"Did I ever tell you why the men called your Da the Duke?" she asks, and before I can answer her, she tells me why.

"Your Da was a handsome man. Every morning he used nearly a bottle of Brylcreem in his lovely hair. He'd comb it back like a

Da's hair cream.

real gentleman, and no matter what the weather or no matter what he'd be doing, not a hair would ever be out of place. I always had a white starched shirt collar for him. There was never a morning I wouldn't be looking at him going out the door, and I'd be saying to myself, I married a gentleman."

"That's why they called him the Duke, and that's what he was. God rest you, Gerry," continues Peg. "He was my Duke, and I miss him every day."

I can't suck up the tears this time. I'm being reminded of how much I still miss my Da, and I'm seeing my Ma being a lonely woman mourning her dead husband.

"Now, stop your crying, love," says Peg, trying to console me.

"Go on up to your bed," says Peg. "You need a good night's sleep after what you've been through this day."

As usual, Peg's right.

Peg as a young woman.

"Goodnight, Ma," says I, as I lean over to kiss her. For the first time, I'm seeing her as a woman and not just my mother. I'm sad, and at the same time glad about what I'm looking at. I go up to my bed, cry for a while and finally fall asleep.

****

Tom the Newspaper Man, the Pawn List & Dis'in'

IT'S MONDAY MORNING AND IT'S THREE MINUTES to eight. I'm walking up Iona Road on my way to work, and it's raining heavy. I'm a tender seventeen years old.

"MORNIN' TOM," says I to Tom the newspaper man. He has a pile of newspapers shoved under his arm; they have been judiciously wrapped in a piece of blue tarpaulin so as to keep them dry.

"Damp," Tom replies, without as much as a glance in my direction. "Feckin' damp," he emphasises, as he opens the gate to his next client and splashes his way to the front door. All such deliveries require going to the front door and sliding the item in through the door's letterbox.

Tom is someone I've known for my entire life. He has a huge family. Peg told me he was responsible for making his 'poor wife' pregnant every ten or eleven months – and they've been married for a long time. With this ready and growing labour force at his fingertips, Tom & Co deliver morning and evening newspapers to an ever expanding number of homes in not only Cabra, Glasnevin, and Drumcondra, but also Cabra West, the Navan Road, and Phibsborough.

I often run into Tom on my way to work. If the weather is as it is this morning, pissing rain, he always answers my 'Mornin' Tom' with, 'Damp' plus his expletive, 'Feckin' damp'. If the morning has ice or snow, his response is 'Nippy' plus its expletive. If there's a hurricane blowing he renders a 'Blowy', blistering sun, a 'Hot', and on those occasions when it's a lovely morning he gives me a 'Nice one' plus its expletive 'Feckin' nice'.

227

Using my time-clock card, I have to punch-in before eight. It'll be five minutes after eight when the late horn blasts; I run the last leg and have just punched in when off it goes. No matter where I am, it shocks me, but when I'm right beneath the bloody thing, it comes close to giving me a heart attack.

"Mornin' Jack; mornin', Cess," says I, as I arrive at one of the imposition stones in the middle of the caseroom.

Jackie, Cess and I are assigned to the page makeup and imposition of the *Pawn List*. The *Pawn List* is a self-covered, saddle-stitched booklet distributed every weekday, and never later than midday. It's delivered to all the pawn shops and garda stations throughout Dublin City and its suburbs. It lists all items reported stolen on a preceding day or, as is the case with the Monday edition, over the weekend. It is a Monday morning, and as usual, the page count will be significant.

Pawn shops owners are obligated to report all incidents of listed items presented to them for trade. The thieves know about this, and that makes Friday the best day for stealing. Without the pawn shop managers having Friday's stolen items on their *Pawn List* until the following Monday, the thieves can boldly trade their Friday stuff on Saturday without fear of detection.

It looks like the thieves have been engaged over the weekend. I reckon the *Pawn List* will make as many as sixty-four pages – and that makes a heck of a lot of stolen stuff.

"How was the weekend?" syas Jackie. "Err a bit of skirt?"

"No skirt, Jackie," I respond. "You don't have to tell me about yours; more than you could handle. Right?" Before Jackie can answer, I ask Cess how his weekend was.

"I went to see *Ben Hur* in the Ambassador on Saturday with Tommy and Tony," Cess responds. "Charlton Heston was super, and the chariot races were brilliant."

"You guys don't know how to live," Jackie asserts. "A skirt a day keeps the doctor away. That's what I say."

And that's one of the many sides of Jackie: he doesn't know how to keep it in his pants. I've never met anybody so able in that department. He's amazing. Anyone, anywhere – he's constantly either talking about it or doing it.

228

"Shut the hell up, Jackie. Let's get this feckin' *Pawn List* out," says I, rolling up my sleeves; I notice that Mick Smith, Jackie's Da and our manager, is looking down at us from his nearby raised supervisory turret.

"Get moving," bellows Mick. "Press time now!" He's cracking the whip, and with the three of us together, it's necessary. We are only a few of years at the job, and we love it. We're learning about the printing and publishing industry, just like our fathers had.

The *Pawn List* makes sixty-one pages. We add three blank pages to make the needed cut-off of eights for printing. We complete the paging and formeing by nine o'clock. All eight, 8-page formes are out to the press room in the correct order, so as printing can start on one machine and then be perfected on another. It will take three letterpress machines working together to complete the printing, leaving sufficient time for Patricia Cowley and the girls to do their folding and finishing.

As always, before eleven o'clock the finished three thousand or so copies are loaded into the eight waiting vans, manned, revved-up and ready to go. Careful distribution analysis has told us we need eight vans to get the *Pawn List* delivered to all those pawn shops and garda stations before midday.

"Good work," says Mick. "In fifteen minutes it'll be tea-break time. Until then, get over there and do some dis'in'. Throw out any furniture that looks bad. We don't want anyone dropping a forme. Throw any bad lead into the pot for re-melt."

Looking forward to our morning break, we walk over to the cluttered-looking Distribution Room. The *Dis'in' Room* is where formes for stripping and breakdown are collected. Each forme is first cleaned of any remaining ink with paraffin-dampened scrubbing brushes. The formes are then unlocked, and the contents is methodically distributed to its proper place, ready to be reused for new work.

All type, other than foundry type, is sent for remelting, Monotype to the Monotype pot, and Linotype to the Linotype pot. Care is given to the gathering of all foundry type, often used for display lines such as chapter titles. Each capital and lowercase letter, each numeral, punctuation mark, and space are put back into their set of cases, depending on typesize and font.

Uppercase layout.   *Lowercase layout.*

Unlike the universally used QWERTY keyboard layout, designed to slow down the typist and avoid the knotting of the rising and falling arms of the most frequently used letters on the original Remington typewriter, the hot-metal typecase layouts are designed to maximise productivity while hand typesetting.

QWERTY keyboard layout.

For a long time, Remington's QWERTY typewriter had no serious competition; their keyboard layout became the accepted worldwide standard. This, despite the fact that the more efficient Dvorak keyboard layout was introduced in 1936. Today, the mechanical typewriter knotting problem no longer exists, but the use of the inefficient QWERTY layout does.

Dvorak keyboard layout.

Jackie, Cess and I will hear the 'Tea's up' call any minute now. All work will stop, and the workers will gather in their different favoured spots throughout the department to have their morning break, chat, and gossip.

****

Joe Sheehan – or Shite If You Like

"**T**EA'S UP," SHOUTS JERRY POLLOCK. Jerry is the wheel within the wheels. He's a compositor of many years' service, and if anyone wants anything to go right, it's essential that Jerry is on their side.

Jackie, Cess and I always have our morning break with Jerry.

"The barein' of the bum in the ice-bound bog is a bastard of a business," Jerry chants, as the three of us settle down with him to enjoy our morning tea and doughnuts.

Tea and doughnuts.

"I do declare," continues Jerry. "That bog is as cold as ice. I couldn't bear to put me bare arse on the seat for fear I'd stick to it." The toilet is the bog in the publishing and printing world.

"It's that ugly bollocks, Joe Sheehan," Jackie responds. "He always has the windows open. He does it so's we won't hang out in there. What a feckin' job! Shite should be his name, not Sheehan."

"You're right, Jackie," says Jerry. "He's an ol' shite alright. He keeps comin' 'round, sprayin' that smelly Jaye's Fluid all over the place. Only last week didn't he spray the stuff on me shoes. I told him to feck off, but I think all that Jaye's is makin' him deaf or somethin'. I don't think he even heard me."

"Is that right, Jerry?" says I. "Well, he did the same to Jimmy Smithers, and Jimmy nearly lost it. He went to Mick to complain, but Mick told him to stop moanin' and get on with his work. He said Joe was only doin' his job, and that but for him, we'd all be up to our arse in vermin."

"That's all very well," says Cess. "But there's got to be a better way. Someone should make that walkin' eejit stop sprayin' us."

"You're right, Cess," says Jackie. "And maybe that someone is us. I bet there's somethin' we could do."

Joe Sheehan has one shitty job. He's five-foot small, has a face as miserable as you can imagine, has little if any hair, and he's cursed with an Albert Pierrepoint type of disposition. He's an utterly awful sort of man, grunting his miserable way through his equally miserable life. Nevertheless, he's perfectly suited for the job. He's held it for many years; those who created the position and filled it with Joe must feel proud. Nobody and I mean nobody, would take that job other than Joe Sheehan.

His duties comprise of two tasks, both of which he executes just as well as Pierrepoint executed his; the pride and pleasure Joe gets from his work are evidenced by the constant, almost evil smirk on his face while he executes them. He displays as much sick satisfaction with one task as he does with the other. In no ranking order, let me tell you what Joe's tasks are.

Task number one consists of the daily spraying of the entire company with Jaye's Fluid disinfectant. Daily, Joe arms himself with his large, twin-canister backpack filled with the stuff; his trusty hose and sprayer are attached to the canister. There's a pumping device on the left-hand side, and he uses his right hand to direct and often misdirect the sprayer. He goes around pumping and pointing his way at everything, often including those individuals unfortunate enough to be in his path.

Task number two is even more insidious. Task two is made up of two separate duties, his bog cleaning and his truly sinister bog watching. Joe's bog cleaning tasks make the place consistently bright and shiny with well-maintained supplies of soap, hand towels, and toilet tissue. We can all somehow qualify a bog cleaner as being not an altogether lousy job, but a bog-watcher – now that's another thing entirely.

The company supplies a large, well-equipped latrine; but it has one most annoying feature. There's a small office at one end with glass walls on three sides, the fourth side being against the end wall; there's a stool in there and a small desk. That's where Joe spends most of his time. Sitting at his desk, he scrutinises the comings and goings of the latrine's patrons – Joe is the bog-watcher, much hated by all, especially the smokers.

The goal of this horrible part of Joe's duties is to minimise the length of time of each person's patronage of the latrine, and would you believe, to supply daily reports of any observations of abuse by its patrons regarding time spent performing their toiletry needs.

On colder days, Joe has the windows wide open; it doesn't take long for the place to be made, as Jerry describes, ice cold. On warm days the windows are locked tight; with the sun shining in and no cooling system, the latrine turns into a veritable oven.

Joe does his bog-watcher duties real well. Nobody comes in or out without him knowing about it. To help him on with his work each day, Joe has a well-designed, tabulated list of all employees: it's called, the DLR or *Daily Latrine Report*. The DLR's left-hand stub column is the Name column; it's followed by six sets of two columns, the Enter-Time and the Exit-Time columns; and then there's the right-hand column – the much-hated Comments column. Upon entering, and having been identified by Joe, the patron's time of entry is recorded in the Enter-Time column, and upon exiting the exit time is entered in the Exit-Time column. Anybody who, in Joe's reckoning, spends too much time in the bog has the fact noted in the Comments column. The six sets of time columns are there to accommodate those patrons who may have more frequent visits.

At the end of each day, Joe tots up the time expended by each employee. The DLR is then given to Mick for his edification and subsequent action as he deems fit.

With all the combustibles lying around, smoking is prohibited. Smokers, and there are many of those, often go into the bog for a smoke; they go to one of the twelve cubicles, to smoke and to do whatever else they might want to do at that time. It's been determined that anything over ten minutes constitutes an excessive time of the cubicle's use. This results in smokers, in particular, being victimised. It is the smokers who frequently receive the reviled Comment column entry.

Joe's job doesn't end with this disturbing reporting procedure – he plays a much more active role. He has the uncanny ability to be able to keep all cubicles under separate and complete surveillance at the same time. Whenever he discovers an abuse being perpetrated, he gets out of his office and goes down to the problematic cubicle. Then, with a clenched fist he bangs on the door, loudly grunting one or two admonitions as he does so: 'Time gentlemen!' 'What the hell are ye doin' in there?' and 'There are men out here waitin' to get in!' being his favourites. Muttering to himself, and undoubtedly feeling immense gratification, Joe then goes back to his glass bowl. These assaults always result in some angry responses from the accused: 'Fuck off out-a-dat!' 'Leave me alone, will ye!?' and 'For Jay's sake, get away from me!' are perhaps the most frequently heard rejoinders.

Excessive peeing time is considered to be an unnecessary reduction of paid-for working hours. It is an eight-and-a-half-hour work day; three or four visits a day and those minutes add up to a half an hour or more. That's the way management, and Joe see it – and when you look at it that way, you could say, who can blame them.

****

Now THAT you've heard all this, I'm sure you'll agree – Joe Sheehan or Shite if ye like, was one miserable son of a bitch. And those men put up with that sort of stuff! I suppose it has something to do with the fact that a lot of them had come from harder times – times when they were lucky to have a pot to pee in, never mind a bog like they had at Thoms. Thanks to the union, this incredible breach of privacy and human dignity was to end. Everybody was delighted, except of course for Joe – he was broken hearted.

****

Our Insurrection – The Planning

THE MORNING TEA BREAK IS OVER. AS ALWAYS IT concludes well before we want it to. Without any imposed supervision, the men get up and go back to work – Jerry is the first almost every time. We all love our morning break. Getting together and having a chat is a big part of our day.

"What are you workin' on, lads?" enquires Jerry.

"Nothin'," I respond. "The *Pawn List* is gone to press."

"I need help with this *Goff Catalogue*. It's comin' out me ears. I could use two of ye. Cess; you go over to Mick and see if that's OK. Jackie and Niall will stay here and start correctin' these galleys in the rack."

Cess goes over to Mick and having got the OK from him he shouts it back to Jerry.

"All right, lads," says Jerry. "Get at it."

"We're on it," Jackie replies.

Jerry at his frame.

We each get a galley out of the rack and place it on the frame. The corresponding proofs are waiting with their galleys. It's Monotype this time: greater care will be needed correcting these babies, especially so because they're set in 8-on-9 point. Unlike the *Pawn List*, which is set Linotype, each line being a single piece of lead, Monotype is one small piece of lead type per character, and there's anything from seventy to eighty characters per line. We'll need our composing stick and brass setting-rule as we make the required corrections.

Using the setting rule, each line needing correction is placed into the adjusted composing stick – twenty-seven pica is the measure of the *Goff Catalogue*. The corrected lines are then returned to their galley, ready for paging.

"I'M THINKIN'," says Jackie. "Joe's a lump of you know what. With a bloke like that, we've got to fight fire with fire."

"Shite is what we need," he continues.

"What do you mean, Jackie?" says I.

"I mean what I said – that's what I mean. Joe Shite is who he is, and shite is what we need to put manners on that ol' bollocks."

"I don't know what you mean," says I, getting frustrated at Jackie's lack of clarity.

"Well, let me ask you. What does Joe Shite treasure the most in his pitiable smelly life? Answer me that if you can."

"His kingdom down there. His feckin' bog and that glass bowl he lives in. That's what I think – that and his Jaye's Fluid."

"Dead right you are, Niall," confirms Jackie.

"And if I was to ask you," Jack goes on, "what would be the worst thing that could happen to that treasure of his? What would be your answer to that one?"

I pause for a moment to think about that one. Before I can respond, Jackie stops what he's doing; getting my full attention, he looks at me with a twinkle in his expressive eyes and an evil grin on his face.

"Shite! Loads of shite!" Jackie declares. "That's the answer. If we want to get the bollocks – and we do – let's shit on him. And when we do, we've got to make sure he knows why we're goin' to all that trouble."

While not grasping the details of how exactly we were to go about shitting on Joe, the thought of figuratively doing so is instantly appealing to me.

"That's all well and good, Jackie, but how in the name of Jays are you plannin' to shit on him?"

"That's what I've been thinkin' about. Tell me, Niall: how big is your shite first thing in the mornin'?"

I'm just beginning to get an idea of what Jackie might be planning in his creative mind, and it's starting to worry me.

"I don't know. Sometimes I don't shit at all, but most times I do. I'd say it might average at a half-pounder."

"And do you do it here or at home?" Jackie continues his pursuit of whatever the hell he's chasing. I'm not sure what it is, but it's becoming clearer very time Jackie opens his mouth.

"For fuck's sake, Jackie, where are you goin' with this? Tell me what the feck you're thinkin'!"

"I'm still thinkin' it through. It's got to be done just right."

"A half-pounder," Jackie rambles on, more to himself than to me. "I'm as regular as a Swiss watch, and I always do it in here. And mine is more like a pounder, maybe more. We need more shite, that's for sure,"

"Collecting it is the hard part," he continues. "Maybe Cess could help us out. It's only the three of us I'd trust with this sort of thing. It's got to be kept quiet, or we'll get our arses kicked. If me father were to hear about it, there'd be bloody murder."

"You can forget about Cess," I respond. "He's one of us, but he won't have anythin' to do with it. He wouldn't even piss against a wall, even if he was burstin', never mind shite."

"I suppose you're right, Niall. And that means it's up to you and me."

I don't have the full picture. I know Jackie doesn't have it either, however, I now know enough to be worried. Jackie is planning his very own Rising. It won't be against the Brits this time, but it'll be against as evil a foe, Joe Shite.

"Maybe, with it bein' only the pair of us, it'll be all the better," says Jackie. "No one else will know anythin' about it."

"And that's essential," says I. "Neither of us can afford to lose our jobs. Your dad might be able to save yours, but my Da is dead, and I'll be on my own."

"Absolutely, Niall. Mum's the word. No one will ever know it was you and me that put Joe Shite straight."

"OK, let's get to it," says I. "But let me tell you, Jackie: you're a genius the way you come up with this type of thing. It's goin' to be a pleasure gettin' that waster. We'll be doin' everyone a favour."

"You're right, Niall. A feckin' huge favour if you ask me."

"We'll do it on Wednesday," Jackie declares. "We'll have to hold our shite all day tomorrow, and then come in with a load on Wednesday. Together we might be able to put out more than two pounds of the stuff. We'll come in early. We'll get down to the bog, get it done and gathered up before Joe comes in. We'll lay it all out for him. No one will ever know it was us that did it; we'll act surprised and just stand there playin' dumb."

The truth is, I'm not as brave or as insane, as Jackie. As he's painting this picture of what our plan is emerging to be, I'm feeling sick – sick with not only averseness towards going ahead with the plan, but also in the stomach sick. Jackie notices this, and it's easy for him to do so – my green face tells him all about it.

"Now, listen up Niall," he says admonishingly. "Do you want to do this or not. Take that face off ye. The ol' bollocks deserves what we're goin' to do to him. It takes a lot of balls for anyone to do what we're goin' to do, and you should be seein' it as a calling or a sort of duty. As you said yourself, we'll be doin' everyone a favour. Are you with me or not, Niall?"

I gulp for much-needed air. Realising severe peer pressure, and a sense of being snared like some choking rabbit, I respond.

"You're right Jackie. Fuck it. I'm with you for better or worse. It's just that it's goin' to be an awful tough job. The thoughts of handlin' my own shite, never mind yours, is makin' me sick."

"Think of it as a duty," responds Jackie. "That's what I'm doin'. So suck it up: let's finish our plans."

"I'm alright now, Jackie." I lie. "So we're here on Wednesday, we've shit and gathered it up. Then what do we do?"

"You'll love this: I surprised even meself with this part. Usin' rubber gloves – I don't like the thoughts of handlin' that shite either – we'll divide it into thirteen piles."

"Why thirteen?" I interrupt.

"Because there are twelve cubicles and then there's Joe's office; that's why," responds Jackie, a big smile on his face.

Looking at Jackie in awe, I marvel at how his mind works.

"I see," says I, not able to see anything or say anything else.

"But that's not the best part," he continues. "Wait 'til you hear this. So's to make sure Joe gets the right message, we'll gather up thirteen lollypop sticks."

"Thirteen lollypop sticks!" I exclaim. "What the hell are they for?" Jackie's curious mind is someplace I've never been.

"We'll set three lines on the Ludlow in 12 point Gill Sans bold italic," Jackie goes on, positively giddy as he does so, and it's infectious; I start feeling giddy in anticipation along with him.

"The first line will say, *We Hate Joe Shite!* The second will say, *Feck off Joe!* And the third will say, *Stop Spraying Us!*" Jackie announces this with immense satisfaction.

"We'll take some hand-press proofs and cut them out so as they look like little flags. We'll put them on the lollypop sticks, and stick one into each of the thirteen piles of shite," Jackie concludes, "What do you think of that? I'm a genius, that's what I think!"

A genius in the strangest sort of sick way could be claimed, but Jackie having a weird mind is absolute.

"Jays, Jackie," I splutter. "You've thought this thing out, haven't you?"

"Yeep! I have," Jackie responds with pride.

"You bloody well have," I confirm.

Badly in need of a break, I walk away from Jackie and the intensity of our discussion. *What the hell have I got meself into?*

We continue to work on the *Goff Catalogue* corrections; there'll be lots more of it for us to work on when we're back again in the morning. We don't discuss the insurrection matter again until we're leaving work at five-thirty.

"Good night, Cess," says Jackie and me, as Cess quickens his step so as not to miss his bus home.

"Good night, Niall," whispers Jackie. "Don't forget – no shitin'. We've got a big day on Wednesday, and we don't want to screw it up. Mum's the word. I'll see you in the mornin'."

"Right, Jackie," I respond. "See you."

****

AT THIS juncture, it's appropriate to remind you and indeed myself, that to look at either Jackie or me, we were normal. We looked perfectly normal and might have even been considered by some to be abnormally pleasant young men. We liked dogs; we even went

239

to Mass on Sundays. And while our poor mothers had a lot to put up with, we loved them dearly. I always came home on Fridays with my sealed wage-packet and handed it to Peg; she'd open it, and after counting out the takings, she'd extract whatever she needed and returned the lightened envelope to me.

But listening to me tell you about Joe Sheehan or Shite if you like, and how we planned out this insurrection, I wonder; in hindsight, to have taken the matter to where it had arrived was screwball crazy!

****

Our Insurrection –
the Execution

T UESDAY IS ANOTHER LIVELY DAY; NOT AS MOMENTOUS as Monday, but as with most of my days, it has its moments. I meet Tom the newspaper man on my way to work. It's a nice day, so he gives me a "Nice one/Feckin' nice." The *Pawn List* is a piece of cake with only twenty-four pages. Jackie and I work most of our day correcting the *Goff Catalogue*.

We keep the word mum regarding our planned insurrection, even during our morning tea break. However, we do perform two important pieces of preparatory work.

Jackie has a lollypop in his mouth for almost the entire day. In the early afternoon, he comes over to me and whispers.

"I have eight lollypop sticks ready to go. Here, you take a couple and give the sticks back to me when you're finished. I'll be sure to have thirteen of them before I go to bed tonight."

I attack and enjoy the two lollypops; one is orange flavoured, and the other is raspberry. I give the naked sticks back to Jackie.

"Great, Niall. We're gettin' there," he declares, giving me a knowing wink of comradeship.

Jerry had talked about Jackie's behaviour throughout the day.

"I wonder what's up with Jackie?" says Jerry. "He's been suckin' those lollipops like mad. And he's not workin' well."

"Are you alright Jackie?" says Jerry. "What's with all those lollipops you've been suckin'? Are you gettin' sick or what?"

"No, Jerry," replies Jackie. "Everything's fine. Nothin's wrong; I just feel like suckin' somethin' sweet today."

The second piece of preparatory work involves the securing of hand-press proofs for the flags.

"Niall, come over with me to the proofin' press," whispers Jackie, trying hard not to let Jerry hear.

"I'm goin' to the bog," I respond out loud. "Do you want to go, Jackie?"

"Just what the doctor ordered," replies Jackie.

"You can keep nix while I'll pull the proofs," he continues as we make our way to the proofing-press.

The hand proofing-press is just below Mick's supervisory turret, beside Paddy Murphy's large-forme proofing press.

"I hope your Da is not in his office," says I.

"That's why I need you," Jackie replies. "You give me heads up if he or Paddy notices what we're at. I only need five pulls. I've set the three lines; they're hidden beside the press ready to go."

Happily, Jack's Da is not in his turret. And Paddy is proofing a big 32-page forme – he's far too engaged to pay any attention to our furtive activity. All six pulls are taken without detection – an additional pull is taken to cover any spoilage. Before rolling the proofs up, and so as to prevent the still wet ink from smearing, Jackie judiciously dusts them off with some chalk dust.

"Throw those Ludlow slugs into the meltin' pot, Jackie," I instruct. "Destroy the evidence."

Mission accomplished, we return and get on with our work.

Going home that night, Jackie, with the roll of you know what under his arm, plus a pocket full of lollypop sticks, says his usual, 'Good night, see ye in the mornin'. I return my standard salutation, but not before we have a whispered brief discourse.

"I hope you didn't shit," Jackie whispers. "I didn't; did you?"

"No," I whisper back. "Don't worry about it. I'll hold on to it tonight, and we'll be more than ready in the mornin'."

"That's feckin' great, Niall," Jackie replies, delighted with my response.

"We'll be ready to go, in more ways than one, if you know what I mean," he continues, laughing out loud. I join him in his laughter as we part ways.

We'll be as prepared as we could ever be.

Now, if only tomorrow were Thursday and our insurrection was all behind us, I ponder as I walk home to my dinner. It'll be sitting waiting for me, courtesy of Peg. Now there's a woman with a heavy load – me!

IT'S INSURRECTION day. I'd set the alarm clock so as I'd arrive at work before seven-thirty. There's no Tom, the newspaper man en route. I'm not surprised to see Jackie at the company gate waiting for me.

"Mornin', Niall," says Jackie. "Haven't we a day ahead of us?"

"Indeed and we do, Jackie; indeed and we do."

"We're all set with the flags," Jackie confirms, pointing to a bag he's carrying. "The rubber gloves we'll be needin' are in there, too."

We go straight down to the bog, and without going into unnecessary, disgusting detail, we do what we have to do. We augment our established plan with one minor addition of detail. We agree that the twelve toilet-closet piles of shite should be neatly placed on top of the downed seat covers.

There are only a few early-bird employees in the company at this early hour. The entire operation goes according to plan. We delay the distribution of the thirteen piles and the insertion of the flags until the last minute. Like clockwork, Joe is sauntering down to his bog at a minute or two before eight.

"I want to enjoy this," says Jackie. "Let's get behind those forme racks opposite the bog. I want to see Joe's face when he finds out what we've done to him.

"Once he comes out, we'll nip 'round through the machine room and get back to our stone like we know nothin'," Jackie goes on. "Joe is sure to start roarin'. He'll run up to my Da and report it. We'll just play total innocent and act as surprised as everyone else.

"In a minute or two everyone will know about it; and when they do they'll be shocked. But as we know, in another one or two minutes they'll see the beauty of it all. And wait 'til you see, all bar Joe and me da will be rollin' 'round laughin'."

It's one minute to eight as Joe swags his way into his kingdom. There's a minute or two before anything unusual is heard; Joe always goes to the windows first, to open or close them depending on the prevailing weather.

The first sound of Joe's discoveries is a sort of agonising groan; 'Ohhh! Ahhh! Ohhh!' followed by a loud 'Bang!' This is promptly followed by the noise of all the other eleven cubicle doors being opened and banged shut. Each bang is interspersed with its own 'Ohhh! Ahhh! Ohhh!' but at a higher and higher decibel level as he moves from one cubicle to the next. Joe's understandably tortuous response to the crime perpetrated against him, concludes with the noise of his office door being opened, followed by a final 'A-A-A-A-A-A-H-H-H-H-H-H !' of epic height.

"Jaysus help me! Look at me toilet!" roars Joe.

We listen in awe and wonder rather than with any real sense of satisfaction. We're feeling some sort of satisfaction, but the awe and wonder are winning out.

Just as we anticipated he would, Joe comes dashing out of the bog looking demented. We notice he has one of the lollypop flags in his hand. Satisfaction is now the winner. The look of agony on Joe's face is well worth all the shite we'd shovelled.

"Ohhh! Ahhh! Ohhh!" screams Joe, as he runs like a madman towards Mick's turret, waving the tiny flag in the air as he goes.

"Mick! Ohhh! Ahhh! Ohhh! Mick!" Joe roars, as he scampers up the caseroom floor.

Jackie and I quickly make our way back to our stone and dive into the Wednesday *Pawn List*. We arrive just as Joe is screaming his way up the turret's steps to a perplexed Mick.

"What the hell's going on with you," enquires Mick. He has never seen Joe, or anyone else for that matter, look so distraught. The flag Joe is waving makes it all the more perplexing.

"Me toilet, Mick," Joe loudly splutters. "There's shite all over the place. And look at this flag, and there's one of them in each of me cubicles. And isn't there one in me office as well!"

"Show me that," demands Mick, as he grabs the flag from Joe.

There's a seminal moment of silence as Mick examines the flag and its message. I see him look in Jackie's and my direction.

"Jackie . . . Your dad is givin' us a look," I whisper. "I hope to Jays he doesn't suspect it was us."

"Don't worry about it," Jackie responds. "It's me he's lookin' at; he always blames me. We had nothin' to do with it. Think that. We're in the clear. Let's ace this *Pawn List*. That'll help take our minds off it."

The effects of our insurrection are already moving fast.

"Holy malowly," says Jimmy Penny as he comes back from his usual early morning patronage of the bog. "Mehe-Mehe-Mehe! Wait 'til you see what's down there. It's a riot."

"What's up, Jimmy?" says Jackie, looking confused and innocent.

"Just wait 'til you see," laughs Jimmy P. "A bleedin' riot, I swear to God. The funniest thing you ever saw in your life. Poetic justice I'm tellin' ye, poetic bleedin' justice."

Before Mick has come back from the bog, minus Joe, the message has travelled far. Contagious laughter spreads with the knowledge and can be heard all over the place. Mick is sitting up in his turret, looking as grim as I've ever seen him look.

"Deservin'," I hear Jerry Pollock say from across the room as he joins in the infectious laughter.

"I told you, Niall," Jackie murmurs. "We've done them all a feckin' big favour. We're heroes, even if no one will ever know it was us that done it."

"You're right," I reply. "But what's your dad goin' to do. That look he gave us isn't good. Let's play it cool and act normal."

"Mick," I shout, innocent as a virgin. "The *Pawn List* will be finished in a bit. What have you got for us to do? Will we go to Jerry and work on the *Goff Catalogue*?"

Mick looks up: the moment our eyes connect, I know he knows that his son and I are the guilty ones. Mick knows it was us and even worse than that; he knows I know he knows. Jackie is his own flesh and blood, and despite everything, Mick loves Jackie. Mick is caught between the rock and the hard place. Undoubtedly, he has noticed the popularity of the crime. This plus my recent rise in popularity regarding Albert Hackett's fit gives Mick cause for some demanding considerations. He'll have to think more about it before taking his final decision regarding what he'll do.

"Get over to Jerry," Mick grunts, giving me his knowing eye.

"Jays, Jackie," I moan. "Your dad knows, I swear he knows, and he knows I know he knows. What the hell are we goin' to do?"

"The feck he knows," Jackie replies. "And even if he does, don't get your knickers in a knot. We didn't do it. We're in the clear! I

245

told you. Think that. It'll be OK. I know my Da. He could end up beatin' the hell out of me, and he might give you a hard time lecturin' you, but we're sound."

"I love your confidence," I reply. "Let's get this *Pawn List* out, and get over to Jerry like your dad said. I don't know about you, but I'm on my knees for the rest of the day. If ever we needed the help of the big guy in the sky, it's now."

"The devil looks after his own, Niall," replies Jackie, with a devilish twinkle in his eye.

****

OTHER THAN for Joe not going around spraying his smelly Jaye's Fluid, and for the fact that his bog watching was not up to its usual level of efficiency, the balance of the day went by quickly without further incidence of note. Thursday and Friday did get sprayed, but with a noticeable reduction in Joe's normal aggressive manner – nobody got sprinkled with the stuff; and while Joe's bog watching duties were slowly moving back to par, he somehow displayed a lack of his normal enthusiasm. However, during that three-day reprieve period, Mick's frequent, cold, accusatory glances at Jackie and I were speaking far louder than any verbal communication could have. There was no doubt in my mind – Mick was on to us.

****

Our Insurrection – the Punishment

IT'S MONDAY MORNING. AFTER WE GET THE *Pawn List* to press, Mick calls Jackie and me to his turret. It has taken five days for him to arrive at a decision regarding how he would handle the situation.

"Sit down there the pair of you," orders Mick, pointing to two small chairs in front of his desk. He settles himself into his taller, plush office chair on the other side of the desk.

Jackie and I are convinced that Mick knows. A lot of young apprentices have passed through his hands over the years, and he's been the manager of the department for a long time. Mick knows his only son real well, and he knows a lot about me. His experience and acquired intuition equip him well.

"Now . . . Have either of you two anything to say to me?" Mick asks. He's wearing glasses; they're hanging off the end of his nose, and his two piercing eyes are darting from one of us to the other. "Before you start – I've the patience of Job, but don't you test me."

"What do you mean, Da?" Jackie pleas innocently. "Did we screw up the *Pawn List* or what?"

"Feck the feckin' *Pawn List!*" Mick responds, almost whispering. "It's last Wednesday's debacle I'm talking about!"

I'll let Jackie take the lead. I'll just sit here and try my best to back-up whatever he says.

"What debacle are you talkin' about, Da?" asks Jackie, with a look of bewilderment.

"The bog debacle!" responds Mick in that ominous whisper of his, making it all the louder to his captured audience. "The feckin' bog debacle, that's what I'm talking about! And I warn you, don't test my patience."

"Ah sure look it!" responds Jackie. "It was the funniest thing any of us ever saw. The whole place is still laughin' about it."

"Is that right, now," Mick responds. He has his glasses back up on his nose, and he's leaning back in his chair with a kind of smiling grimace on his face. "You don't see me laughing, do you, bucko? And by the time I'm finished with you, it's not laughing you'll be; I can tell you that right now."

"I know it was you two that did it," snarls Mick. "You deserve all you're going to get and more. And don't either of you say one word, or I declare to God I'll do something I'll regret."

"And what do you have to say?" he continues, addressing me directly. "Sitting there like the little brat you are. What do you have to say for yourself, Mr Niall Kavanagh? I can tell you; your father is turning over in his grave looking down here and seeing the devilment you've been up to. And your unfortunate mother . . ." Turning quickly towards Jackie, he adds. "God knows I know what she has to put up with."

The prayers I've offered up, don't seem to be payin' off. We try to maintain our denial of guilt by looking pitiful. With an expression of hurt plastered on my face, I try to respond.

"We only joined in with everyone else havin' a good laugh," I lie. We had indeed joined in the laughter, but we had done a lot more besides – and all three of us know it.

"Joe's a pain in the face with his stinky sprayin'. And his bog-watchin' drives us all mad. Maybe somebody went a bit far with it, but as Jimmy P said, it was only poetic justice."

"Poetic justice, be damned!" responds Mick. "The pair of you nearly killed the man! And I know it was you two. Don't! Don't open your mouth, neither of you."

We don't open our mouths. Ensuing an agonising minute, Mick stands up, walks around to our side of the desk and announces his decision about what he had planned to do with us.

"Right, me bucko's," snarls Mick. "This is what's going to happen."

We sit with sickening anticipation. No matter what Mick's justice lays out for us, we'll suck it up and take it. With little or no subjectivity we'll accept the sentence duly administered, and hopefully, put an end to the matter.

"This begins and ends here!" Mick declares. "After I've finished laying out what I've lined-up for you two, we'll not discuss it further. I want to tell your mothers, but I've decided not to; it would wreck them entirely, and I won't be the one to do that."

The primary concern I'd been living with was that Mick would tell Peg about our exploits. What we just heard him announce is a welcomed relieve. *My prayers are startin' to work.*

"Now, listen carefully to what I'm saying," Mick demands. "I'll say it once, and I advise you, pay attention to every word."

"Starting this coming Saturday, and for the next three months, I want you two buckos to report to work every Saturday night at seven o'clock and stay here until ten. I've arranged for the night watchman to let you in and out. Except for the watchman, who'll be keeping a close eye on you, you'll be on your own for those three hours. Your punishment for what you've done is that you'll make that bog sparkle: floor-to-ceiling, wall-to-wall, sink-to-sink, every mirror, urinal-to-urinal, cubicle-to-cubicle, all the doors, and most important, Joe's observation office."

Mick takes a break in his sentencing, not for his own need, but so as to make sure the words he had spoken had sunk in.

"Do you understand what I'm telling you?" growls Mick.

"Yeah," Jackie and I respond. We're already feeling the weight of the sentence. As much as the thoughts of that nasty hard labour pain us, the thoughts of every Saturday night, the most fun-filled night of the week, being wiped out pains us even more.

"Every Saturday, buckos," Mick growls. "For three long months! Maybe that will put manners on you. And I don't want to hear a word about this from anyone. If I do, I'll lengthen your sentence by three more months. It's between you two and me. The watchman and I have discussed it, and he'll keep his mouth shut."

"Now, get the hell out of my office and get back to your work. I've had my fill of you," Mick gruffly concludes.

"It was well worth it," says Jackie, as we both descend the turret's steps. Jackie seems to have no regrets.

"It could be a lot worse. Our mothers will know nothin' about it, and that's feckin' great. And do you know what, Niall? My Da is a good bloke, and he's smart. I'd have done somethin' the same

249

to us if I was him. In a way, we deserve a medal, but my Da had to do somethin'. What do you think?"

"I suppose so, Jackie. The Ma not knowin' is super, but all those Saturday nights. That's feckin' brutal. Fuck Joe Shite, that's all I can say."

"Fuck him," Jackie confirms.

****

JACKIE AND I got to know each square inch of Alexander Thom's latrine. Three months of Saturdays and many hours of hard labour made sure of that. Those Monday mornings gave a good kick-off to Joe's week. Pleasantly mystified, he would come in and marvel at what he thought was his work. It was our work, but only Mick, the night-watchman, and Jackie and I knew that.

We missed out on three big parties, one of which we heard was a real blast, a Halloween Tramps Ball Party. We heard about some bloke turning up dressed in a costume that looked like a hairy scrotum with only one of the two testicles dropped. Written across the front of the costume was, 'The Tramps Other Ball'. We also missed out on seven dances. Jackie was deprived of God knows how many skirts.

Sadly, Jackie died a young man. He was only thirty-five when it happened. That crowning glory of his, winning the Eurovision Song Contest, ruined him altogether. He lost the run of himself, and to cut a long story short; his wife left him. That and the fact that his daughter stayed with his wife wrecked him. I was best man at Jackie's wedding. We had been through a lot together, Jackie and me.

****

Rory Doyle & Dolly Fawcett

CESS WHITTY AND JACKIE SMITH HAVE BECOME my close friends. Their friendship is very significant to me: my father's death, the move from Erris to Mannix, leaving school, and starting work, had all combined to make a huge void in my friends department. Cabra and my childhood contacts were still there, but the few miles between us was a wall to any continuance of any meaningful friendship. Cess and Jackie fill the void at this precarious time in my life.

I'M EIGHTEEN. In terms of apprenticeship time served, Jackie is a year ahead of Cess and I. It's a seven-year apprenticeship; Jackie is in his fourth year while Cess and I are in our third.

Bolton Street College.

Each afternoon during the first years of working, Cess and I spend our time attending class at Bolton Street College of Technology's, Publishing and Printing Department. Our professor is Rory Doyle. He smokes a pipe and wears a hideous dickey-bow. Rory is a pompous man, and he's a bully.

251

Freddie Moraghan and John McCabe sit beside me in class. John is a quiet type of bloke. Rory frequently picks on him to answer many of the random questions he throws out.

"Come on Mr McCabe," taunts Rory. "Stand up like a man and tell the class when and where Johannes Gutenberg, inventor of moveable type was born? Like a man now, come on, tell the class."

"In Germany, sir," answers John.

"And might I ask, in what town in Germany did the fortunate birth take place?" growls Rory. "The town, country, and date of birth are required. Germany doesn't cut it. Take it like a man now. In what town in Germany, and when was the man born?"

"I don't know," replies John. He's dying of embarrassment.

"You don't know!" roars Rory. "That response doesn't cut it either! What are you doing in my class? Do ye know the answer to that? Wasting your own time and mine! That's the answer!"

I want to punch Rory Doyle right in his face. Instead of doing so, I find myself jumping up out of my chair.

"Why can't you give it like a man?" I bark. "Then John could take it like one. Leave John alone! You're always pickin' on him."

A cold silence engulfs the classroom. I'm standing up with and for John, and there is Rory, glaring at me from eyes of intense anger. He leaps from behind his desk to the classroom door; opening it wide, he shouts at me.

"Get out of my classroom, you impertinent brat. Get you and all your belongings out of here. Now!"

With the closing door being slammed shut behind me, I find myself in the corridor and very worried. The door suddenly opens.

"Give me your attendance book," Rory snarls.

I take the attendance book out of my satchel. Rory snatches it from me, and once again he slams the door shut.

A minute passes, and the door is reopened.

"Take this and get yourself out of this college," Rory shouts, as he throws the attendance book at me. Rory has written across the current two-page spread in large red capital letters; *DISMISSED FROM CLASS FOR GROSS IMPERTINENCE.*

When I report for work the following morning, that attendance book will have to be signed by Mick Smith. Only Christ knows what my behaviour will bring down on me.

"And what did you do to deserve this!?" exclaims Mick. I had given him the attendance book. *Be honest about what happened* – that is my decision regarding how to handle the predicament I'm in. I tell Mick exactly what occurred.

"Mr Doyle is always bullyin' John," says I. "I know it might have been the wrong thing for me to do, but I just couldn't stand it anymore. John was nearly cryin', and I bet he knew the answer. It's only because of the way Mr Doyle goes at him. John gets all uptight, and he blushes and all. Someone should tell Mr Doyle; the way to encourage John is to be nice to him, not roar at him and embarrass him in front of the whole class."

"Did Mr Redding get involved in any of this?" says Mick. Mr Redding is the head of the publishing and printing department.

"I don't know," I reply.

"There are ways to do things. What you did isn't one of them. The teacher, what's his name, Mr Rory Doyle, is the authority in the classroom. If you've a problem with what he does you've got to report it to Mr Redding or me, not fly off the handle, starting a near fisticuff in the classroom."

"I'm not approving what you did," continues Mick. "You were very impertinent. Mr Doyle could do nothing but dismiss you."

"I know that now," I respond.

"Did you tell your mother about this?"

"No. I didn't want to upset her."

"It's probably better you didn't. I'll call Mr Redding and see what's what. In the meantime, you get your arse down there and get that *Pawn List* ready for press."

Mick calls me into his turret later that morning.

"I want you to write a letter to Mr Doyle. Copy Mr Redding and me. Apologise to Mr Doyle and promise him you'll never give him cause for your dismissal again. Say nothing else."

I do as Mick instructed. Before I go to class that afternoon, I first deliver a copy of the letter to Mr Redding.

"Now let this be a lesson to you," says Mr Redding. "I'll expect to hear no more about this and only good reports of your improved behaviour from Mr Doyle. Off to class with you now."

I go to Rory and give him the letter. He reads the epistle and announces his reluctant acceptance of my apology. He instructs me to take up a new back-of-class position. I notice John's location has also been changed. He's been moved to the front row.

Oddly enough, Rory and I soon become the best of buddies; and as for John McCabe, Rory is noticeably nicer to him. My boldness in expressing myself paid off. Rory becomes a better teacher, and John and I become better students.

ONE OF Dublin's brothels is next door to Bolton Street College. It's called the *Continental Café,* and Dolly Fawcett runs it. Freddie Moraghan and I often stand across the street, watching Dolly's clients come and go. Our interest in the place never includes going in, the truth being that the thought of picking up a dose of crabs or herpes dismisses all its otherwise pleasantly thought-provoking attractions. The titillation of watching the comings and goings of the clients is what we enjoy.

College on the left, Dolly's on the right.

Patrons come to the usually closed door, knock, and after a minute or so of waiting, which always includes the clients' furtive glances up and down the street, the door opens and in they go. We see them slipping out in a similar manner. It always amazes me that after what I imagine they've been through, they look the same as they did when they went in. One time we saw a priest go in. Rather than thinking the worst, I choose to think that maybe one of the girls was sick or dying, but then, one never knows.

Now and again, the girls come out and stand at the door. Looking like you'd expect, they just stand there, usually smoking a cigarette. They always have a mischievous grin on their well-worn, heavily made-up faces. Once, one of them brazenly winked and waved at us; shocked and uncomfortable, Freddie and I quickly turned away and ran back into the college.

****

The Brazen Head & Brendan Behan

"WELL LADS," SAYS JACKIE. "ANOTHER WEEKEND, a few more skirts, and another chance to make it the big one."

"Can either of you think of an'in' for us to do?" Jackie continues. "Is there an'in' goin' on?"

As always, the weekend gives us hopes for fun and frolic. The lack of response from Cess and I gives Jackie the sad news that nothing is going on.

"We've got to change this, lads," says Jackie. "We should be able to organise somethin' for every weekend."

"Let's meet at *The Brazen Head* tonight," suggests Cess. "I'll ask the lads to come. They all live 'round where I live in Kevin Street, and they're always up for a couple of pints. I'll get Tommy to bring his banjo. Johnny C and I will bring our guitars. A couple of pints and a ding-dong – that'll start the weekend off for us."

"Sounds great to me," says I.

"How many of your friends will be comin'," asks Jackie.

"Seven," answers Cess. "We three will make it ten."

"Another two and we'll be like the apostles," says Jackie. "Any chance of Peter and Paul joinin' us."

"If they did come, they'd be gettin' the best pint in all of Ireland, I can tell you that," says Cess. "*The Brazen Head* has been around for a long time. After nearly eight hundred years of pullin', it's not surprisin' they've got their pint right."

I'm tempted to argue with Cess's 'best pint in all of Ireland' claim, but I decide to let it go. *The Gravediggers pint is the best. I'll bring them up to me Uncle John later on. After they down a couple of his pints, there'll be no argument.*

255

I'VE INVESTED in a Heinkel Scooter. Peg is not pleased.

"You'll never change," says Peg. "Scooting around on those two wheels of yours at forty miles per hour. You'll be the death of me, not to mention yourself."

My Heinkel.

"I've got to have wheels, Ma," I reply, as I button up my leather jacket and balance my green tweed cap on the Kildare side.

"Don't be worryin', Ma," I continue. "I'm always careful."

"Careful muryaa!" replies Peg. "And wasn't young Pádraic down the hill careful, and didn't he end up in the Mater with broken legs and God knows what else."

"Well, Ma," says I as I'm walking out the front door. "I'm off to meet Cess and a few of his friends. I love you, and I promise I'll drive careful. Don't be worryin' about me."

"All right then," replies Peg. "But I want you to do me a favour. Wait a minute and let me get something for you."

Peg runs upstairs and is back down before I can reply.

"Here," says she. "Let me pin this into your jacket. The Blessed Virgin will take care of you."

The medal.

Peg unbuttons my jacket and pins a medal of the Immaculate Conception to my inside breast pocket.

"Now," declares Peg. "She'll look after you."

"OK, Ma," I respond. "If it makes you happy."

As I mount my trusty Heinkel, I'm thinking about what Peg had said. Recently, a young neighbour my age had been in a bad motorbike accident. *I've got to remember that. The two wheels*

256

make the chances of gettin' away with an accident pretty small. I've got to be careful. The medal mightn't stop me from crashin', but it can't do me any harm.

The Brazen Head is the oldest operating pub in Ireland – it opened its doors as a hotel and inn in 1198. I've heard about it, but this is my first visit to the historic place. It's located just below Saint Audeon Church on Bridge Street, close to the River Liffey. I park the scooter and go in.

The Brazen Head.

The pub's courtyard entrance gives me a good idea of what to expect. I open the unbelievably low door and go into a darkened low-slung ceiling room. At a small bar there's a lone drinker hugging a pint of Guinness; in the dim light, I'm not sure, but the man on the barstool looks familiar. Cess and a couple of his friends are in the back of the room sitting around an unlit fireplace.

"How are ye, Cess?" says I. "This place is as it was when it opened eight hundred years ago. I hit my head comin' through the door. I love it. It makes me feel tall."

"There you are, Niall," Cess replies. "Say hello to Tommy and Tony. The rest of the lads will be comin' later."

Cecil Whitty.   Tommy Greeley.   Tony Cunningham.

Cess is a fit, stocky bloke, about five-and-a-half-foot short. He wears glasses and has a unique set of facial features: small eyes set close together; a smiling, kind mouth; a pointed chin; and all this

257

crowned with a mop of brownish hair. Cess plays the guitar, is a good singer and has a great personality.

Tommy looks a lot like a six-foot tall Groucho Marx without the glasses and moustache. He's as witty as his lookalike: his bushy eyebrows, not as dark as Groucho's, but just as thick, together with his twinkling eyes and infectious smile makes us all laugh. His wit is as good as his comedic lookalike's; there are many times I get pains on my sides from the laughter his natural wit and humour create. He knows and sings as many songs as Cess and plays the banjo real well. Tommy is a jeweller.

Tony is as fit as a fiddle. He's into tennis and keeps himself in great shape. Tony is five-foot-ten, has blonde hair and looks a lot like Kirk Douglas. He walks like Kirk and does all in his power to sound like him. Tony is a printer's engineer with *Independent Newspapers*.

"I think I recognise that bloke at the bar," says I. "Do any of you know who he is?"

"That's Brendan," whispers Tony. "He's often in here."

"Yeah . . . That's who he is. He looked familiar. That's Brendan Behan alright."

"The last time I saw him I was nine years old," I continue. "I was with my Ma in the Richmond Hospital's clinic, queuin' up to go in to see Dr Abrahamson for her cortisone injection. Me Ma has Addison's disease; back then she had to go in for her shot every week. We were sittin' there when in barged Brendan, scuttered drunk. Beatrice, his wife, was on one side of him and Kathleen, his mother, was on the other, each of them tryin' to hold him up. He kept roarin', 'I'm a drinker with a writin' problem'."

"I know his *Auld Triangle*," says I. "Let's sing it."

"Go for it, Niall," urges Tommy.

That's all I need, a little encouragement. I take a deep breath, hum the solemn chorus as best I can, and follow with Brendan's equally solemn ballad.

As I'm singing, I look over at Brendan. He just sits there on his barstool with his back turned. The only acknowledgement from him is when I finish singing.

"A fuckin' grand song!" Brendan loudly declares, to Matt the barman, not me. "I've heard it sung better; but I tell ye, Matt – the man dat wrote that fuckin' ballad is a fuckin' genius. Now, give me another pint, quick. I've always said sobriety is an overrated condition, and let me tell ye, Matt – I'm fuckin' right!"

Jackie Smith and Cess's other five friends begin arriving: Johnny Charlton, a wine waiter at the Russell Hotel on the corner of St. Stephen's Green and Harcourt Street; Arthur Birney, who works in Guinness Brewery on Thomas Street; Johnny Reilly, an inventor of things electric; Brian Donaghue, a worker at the GPO on O'Connell Street; and Joe McKeown, a car mechanic. Other than for Jackie who is twenty, we're all eighteen years old.

Cess and Johnny C have their guitars. With two guitars, Tommy's banjo and ten young Dubliners drinking pints of Guinness, it takes no time at all for the ding-dong to start in earnest. We sing our way through the evening and arrange to meet again at *Mulligans* in Poolbeg Street the following night.

"That was a great session," says I, as we all respond to the barman's closing-time call, 'Time gentlemen, please.'

"Jackie was right," I continue. "We should talk about ways we can organise havin' somethin' goin' on for the weekends."

"Yeah," responds Cess. "When we meet at *Mulligans* tomorrow, maybe the ten of us can come up with some ideas."

****

BRENDAN BEHAN was born in Russell Street on the northside of Dublin, on 9 February 1923. He would become the quintessential Dubliner and one of Ireland's more outrageous, great writers.

Brendan Behan.

At sixteen years old, having been a *Na Fianna Éireann* boy scout since he was eleven, Brendan moved on to become a member of the IRA. He became active in the IRA's campaigns of armed opposition to Britain's continued occupation of six of the nine counties of Ulster. In 1939, during his failed attempt to execute an unauthorised solo blowing up of Liverpool Docks, Brendan was arrested by the English Special Branch and sentenced to three years in Hollesley Bay Colony Borstal in Suffolk, England, a tough youth detention centre.

He returned to Ireland in 1941. It didn't take long for him to renew his IRA activities. In 1942 he was arrested, tried and sentenced to fourteen years in Mountjoy for the attempted murder of two Garda Síochána detectives. He was released along with many other IRA interns under a general amnesty issued by Éamon de Valera in 1946. Brendan was twenty-three: his four years in gaol put an end to his active IRA membership. Fortuitously, his prison time kept him away from alcohol and helped to inspire him towards becoming a serious writer.

From an early age, he had been a brash, out-spoken, compulsive drinker. Out of gaol, he was quick to reacquaint himself with the demon drink. He became a frequent patron of many pubs throughout the city: *McDaids*; *Davy Byrnes*; *The Bailey*; *The Old Stand*; *Mulligans*; *The Brazen Head*; and the *Harbour Lights Bar*. When he was in his mid-twenties he suffering from the effects of an undiagnosed case of diabetes – drink and diabetes, a deadly blend. By his early thirties, his excessive drinking and now diagnosed diabetes, made him a critically ill, diabetic alcoholic.

Despite his illness, his writing success started in 1954 when his play, *The Quare Fellow* opened at the *Pike Theatre* in Dublin. It opened at the *Theatre Royal Stratford East* in London in May 1956; it was so well received that it had to be transferred to the larger capacity *Comedy Theatre* on the West End in July.

Brendan enjoyed being the celebrity he had become. While Ireland was somewhat jaded with his bombastic behaviour, his vulgar language, and his often drunken persona, what Brendan brought to his new English audiences was both novel and very entertaining. He did his best to keep sober, but being the alcoholic he was, there were far too many times when he failed miserably. He attended a lot of the performances of *The Quare Fellow*. People got tickets in the hope of hearing him jeer the actors from the stalls or see him try to supplement the performance with a song or maybe a spur-of-the-moment hornpipe in the aisles.

In 1958, Brendan's work achieved worldwide acclaim: *The Quare Fellow* opened at the *Circle in the Square* on Broadway, New York; his autobiographical novel, *The Borstal Boy* was published; and *An Giall*, the Irish language version of his second play, *The Hostage*, opened in the *Damer Theatre* in Dublin. Later that year the English version of *The Hostage* played at the *Theatre Royal Stratford East*, and in 1960 it opened on Broadway, NY.

Brendan was widely praised in New York. In late 1960 he triumphantly went to the USA to enjoy his laurels. When he landed at Idlewild Airport, he was met by a receptive, welcoming press and public. Brendan declared that the USA was his 'new found land', claiming that New York was his 'Lourdes'. He was sober, but stayed that way for only two months; sadly, once again the drink got the better of him. His many drunken brawls and arrests, including his semi-naked escape from a hospital after waking up from a diabetic coma, combined to give him a notorious reputation. The New York media and public enjoyed Brendan when he was drunk – a lot more than they did when he was sober. His habit of interrupting his plays, from which he had been banned in the West End of London, made him the toast of Broadway. He was even invited to President Kennedy's 1961 inauguration. Conversely, he was dishonourably banned from taking part in the New York Saint Patrick's Day Parade for presenting a negative drunken image of Irishness.

He returned to his Dublin, by boat, in 1963. In 1964 while he was drinking his last pint of Guinness in the *Harbour Lights Bar* on Echlin Street, he collapsed. He was rushed to the Meath Hospital in Heytesbury Street where he died. Brendan was forty-one.

****

Mulligans, the GOSS
and The Ivy Folk

COMPARED TO THE BRAZEN HEAD WHICH OPENED in 1198, the *John Mulligan* drinking establishment is one of Dublin's newer pubs. *Mulligans* opened its doors in 1782.

The John Mulligan Pub.

Located on Poolbeg Street, right in the heart of the city, and being the prototypical Dublin pub it is, it's seldom you'll observe a face or heard an accent in *Mulligans* without it having Dublin written all over it. Whenever I visit, I'm consumed with the sense of the haunting presence of Dublin's past. While *The Gravediggers'* ghosts are personal for me and are full of family relativity, the *Mulligans* ghosts are pure, parochial Dublin. I don't know whether or not they've even darkened *Mulligans* door with their shadow, however, one night when I was in there, I felt like I was rubbing shoulders with Harry Boland and Michael Collins! Another night I'd have sworn that Wolf Tone himself, or maybe it was Robert Emmett, was standing right beside me.

Many Irish literary giants have bent an elbow in *Mulligans*. James Joyce frequented the place and used it when he had his Leopold Bloom sitting at the bar sucking a pint. Regularly, the

Irish poet, Patrick Kavanagh dropped in and scribbled a few lines. Brendan Behan, after having his fill of the more intellectual clientele found in *Davy Byrnes* and *McDaids*, often ended up in *Mulligans*.

Putting Brendan and Patrick together, brought out the worse in the both of them. They never got on well – some might go so far as to say that they held a distinct mutual hatred for each other. But, friend or foe, Patrick did attend Brendan's funeral in Glasnevin Cemetery in 1964. Brendan's old mate, Mattie O'Neill gave the graveside oration ending with a solemn, 'We shall never see his like again'. Patrick was at the back of the crowded graveside and was heard to say, 'And thanks be to God for small mercies'.

Patrick would die three years later: a real culshie, he was born and buried in the township of Mucker, County Monaghan. Much unlike the extroverted, life-loving Brendan, Patrick had a reclusive, genteel type of poetic disposition. He was never the life and the soul of the party. Apart from some of his poetry, seldom if ever did he portray any real fondness for being alive.

Due to his own premature demise, Brendan wasn't able to attend Patrick's funeral; had he been around at the time, I'm sure he would have made an effort to be there. Undoubtedly, he would have had some equally sarcastic, but much more vulgar, parting words for Patrick – maybe something like, 'The fucker from Mucker' or 'He was only a Monaghan wanker'.

"I THINK we should start a club or somethin'," says Cess.

As arranged the previous evening, all ten of us are sitting in *Mulligans*, downing the first round of the night's pints. Cess is steering the conversation towards the planned discussion regarding how we would be best able to assure ourselves of having something to do on the weekends.

"Wine, women, song," says Jackie. "That's what it's about."

My little Latin came to mind: "Vinum, feminae et cantus; sounds good to me. And settin' up a club to help us get as much of it as we can is a good idea."

"That could be the club's motto," says Cess. "It sounds great – Vinum, Feminae, Cantus."

"We'll have to think of a good name," says Tommy.

"Maybe we could call it a Grand Order," says Cess. "*The Grand Order of Shameleons & Sharamalites*. What do you think?"

"What in the name of Jays is *Shameleons & Sharamalites*?" Tony enquires, on his own behalf and also on behalf of his equally confused friends. *The first word sounds somethin' like the lizard that changes its colour, but as for Sharamalites, I haven't a clue.*

"I just made it up," answers Cess.

"For Jay's sake, Cess," says Tommy. "You can't just make up words like that. They've got to have some meanin'."

"But, it sounds great, doesn't it?" responds Cess.

"It does," I agree. "But sayin' it with a pint in your hand might choke you. We could abbreviate *Grand Order of Shameleons & Sharamalites* to GOSS. Talkin' about pints, whose round is it?"

The Grand Order of Shameleons & Sharamalites, aka the GOSS, is founded, just like that. We elect Cess as Grand Master and Brian Donoghue as Chancellor of the Exchequer, all the other members being labelled Knights. A five shillings per week membership fee is agreed to, all proceeds being held by Brian and made available as an immediate start towards securing the required funding for the attainment of the GOSS's goals, namely, to obtain the maximum amount of wine, women, and song for its members.

Much well-lubricated discussion follows.

"We should organise parties," suggests Tony. "Just like the one we went to in Harcourt Street. We can rent places like that. There're rooms over the fish market in George's Street, and there are loads of basements along Baggot Street and Mount Street."

"Yeah," Jackie agrees. "We had to pay a half-a-dollar at the door to get into that party. We could charge the same. That would cover our costs and build up the funds."

"The girls should be let in for nothin'," says I. "All the blokes will have to pay, but the girls get in for nothin'."

"You're right, Niall," says Tommy. "At the Harcourt Street party, I saw some smashin' lookin' girls turned away at the door because they wouldn't pay. Penny wise pound foolish, if ever I saw it."

"What about organisin' dances?" says Tony.

"Jays, Tony," comments Tommy. "You're soundin' brilliant. You're comin' up with great ideas. What's wrong with you?"

264

"I think it's the Guinness," replies Tony. "After a couple of pints I always start thinkin' like a prodigy."

"Well, keep drinkin', Tony," says Cess.

"And aren't we always gettin' together for a sing-song," says Tommy. "Why don't we put together a folk group? We know loads of ol' ballads? We could call the group *The Ivy Folk*. Most of us live 'round the Iveagh Flats. We could spell Iveagh like the plant. That'll make it sound good and look better."

"Yeah, sounds great to me," says Jackie. "With the GOSS, parties, dances and *The Ivy Folk*, we'll never have a dull day."

****

JACKIE'S PROPHECY held true. We pursued the GOSS's pointed objectives with great success. All the members were given lots of opportunities to secure a heck of a lot of wine, women, and song – opportunities which, for the most part, were taken full advantage of.

We designed a membership card. A GOSS crest was decided upon. A shield, divided in three was placed on the card's front cover: a half-filled wine glass representing Vinum was placed in one-third of the shield; a bitten apple for Feminae in another; and a clef representing Cantus in the remaining third. Printed in gold on a dull, black 75lb card stock, the shield had a scroll with GOSS on the top and another scroll with Vinum, Feminae, Cantus at the bottom. Inside, printed in black Gothic Old Style on a pasted white antique 80lb text stock, we declared the names and titles of the proud GOSS membership. The card made it official; *The Grand Order of Shameleons & Sharamalites* was firmly founded.

Over the years, the many parties and dances the GOSS organised, supplied us with the perfect environment for the fulfillment of its goals. Not only that, it funded our ability to secure many summer home rentals. Skerries, a seaside town, north of Dublin city, was chosen as the ideal spot. We choose a beachfront property close to the *Gladstone Pub*. Those summer days were filled with more opportunities than we could ever hope to have. Our security deposit was never something we got back: the almost every night party scene made any such return expectations pretty remote. The funds were also used for a wonderful month's vacation tour on the French and Italian Riviera.

The Ivy Folk: Johnny Charlton, Tommy Greeley,
Mary Greeley and Cess Whitty

Not being the best singer, I became Manager, while Tony became Road Manager. We recruited Tommy's sister, Mary to join *The Ivy Folk*; we soon became one of Ireland's leading ballad groups. We had three successful records on the Pye label, appeared on three television shows, and were part of the Christmas, *Gaels of Laughter* show at the Gaiety Theatre a number of times. *The Ivy Folk* played in pubs and concert halls all over Ireland and England.

****

The Donnybrook –
Tiny Tommy & The Creatures

Row, row, row your boat,
Gently down the stream.
Merrily, merrily, merrily, merrily,
Life is but a dream.
      Row, Row, Row Your Boat – Eliphalet Oram Lyte (1852)

"**A**ND WHAT ARE WE GOIN' TO DO NOW?**"** I enquire of Tony. "We've made a shit load of money, and that's good, but look at the place. It's a feckin' wreck!"

The *Commercial Rowing Club* clubhouse is indeed wrecked. Blood is splattered all over the place, there are holes in the walls, the barroom door has been dragged off its hinges, and the large mirror over the bar is smashed. With these initial observations alone, the clubhouse more than qualifies itself as being officially wrecked. And there's no doubt – we'll be held responsible.

Commercial Rowing Club.

"After that smack in the gob you got, Niall, yer lookin' the same yourself," says Tony.

Tony's reference to my swollen, bloody lip reminds me that I'd been smacked pretty hard. I'd been in the thick of it, trying in vain to calm things down when I ran into a perfectly thrown punch from a perfectly rotten big fat fucker. I didn't realise it then, but

267

blood had poured from my mouth, splattering all over the place and destroying the new fancy shirt I'd bought only that morning.

"That bouncer we hired wasn't worth a damn," says I. "Have we paid him, Tony?"

"No, and we're not goin' to. That bastard should be payin' us! Did you see him? He was gone runnin' up the driveway to the Phoenix Park Gate before the second punch landed. A coward if you ask me, and not worth a shite. We'd have been better off hirin' Mother Teresa as a bouncer rather than that jerk; I'm tellin' ye."

Tony and I have just turned twenty. Feeling like two old men, we're sitting down together on the now empty clubhouse floor. Leaning against the wall, we try to gather our confused thoughts. Only a few minutes before, over three-hundred-and-fifty people were dancing around to the insightful sounds of *The Creatures*, a new up-and-coming Dublin rock'n'roll band we'd engaged for one of our GOSS fundraiser dances. I'm a member of the *Commercial Rowing Club,* and we had paid the club's modest rental fee for the night – all the bar's drink sales would go to the club, and we'd take the admission monies.

The Creatures.

The Creatures cost us fifty pounds; with three hundred and fifty paying attendees at five shillings per head, this left about fifty pounds for the GOSS. Liam McKenna, the group's leader, had asked for one hundred pounds. Tony and I worked him down to fifty by some heavy bartering; we offered Liam and his group free entrance to the next four parties the GOSS would be having. That plus the agreement to prepay clinched the deal. The GOSS's parties have acquired a reputation around the town. Some, for instance, our mothers, might say a bad reputation, but to all those who are lucky enough to be invited, our parties are considered to be splendid. Loads of craic[1], with all three of the GOSS's goals – vinum, feminae, cantus – in more than ample supply.

"Are you two lads alright?" squeaks out tiny Tommy.

"Yeah," I answer, startled to see Tommy appear from beneath an upturned table.

"Are you OK, Tommy?" I enquire.

"Yeah," he grunts, as he struggles to get his tiny body erect.

Tiny Tommy is one of *Commercial Rowing Club*'s best coxswains. He's a dwarf: he's maybe an inch over two-and-a-half foot standing up, and he talks just like you'd expect him to. When the fracas started, he'd been in his usual spot, sitting at the end of the bar – and I mean *on* the bar at the end – downing pints and talking to anyone who would listen to him.

"You were brilliant, Tommy," says I. "You flattened two of them when you jumped off the bar. Brilliant, bleedin' brilliant."

"If I were just a bit taller I would've taken out the lot of dem. W'at a bunch of bastards. And we know who they are. Der dat bunch of bowsies from Crumlin. We'll get dem – mark me words," Tommy goes on. "It was when one of dem knocked over me pint dat I got mad, and ye know, w'at with the way I am, I'm no good in a fight, but I couldn't control meself."

"I'm burstin' for a piss," Tommy abruptly interrupts himself. "Will one of ye carry me into the toilet, please?"

"Sure," I answer. "Just wait a minute, and I'll be with you." Dismissing the donnybrook horrors for a moment, I walk to the bar and equip myself for the urgent task at hand.

Tiny Tommy is a grand little fella with great wit and spirit. He must be somewhere in his late-thirties. In the club, it's common practice that anyone present at the time of Tommy's toiletry needs lifts him up, carries him out and lets him do his thing.

This peculiar activity seems to be exactly that, but to us, it isn't at all. We gladly do it, and we never give it a second thought. There are three deep steps on the way to the toilet; with his short crooked legs, Tommy is unable to negotiate his way. That and the fact he can't reach the minimum required height for a safe pants-dry pee prohibits him from being able to complete the task by himself.

"Right, Tommy," says I. "Let's go." I've returned from the bar, fully equipped and ready for action.

"T'anks very much, Niall," says Tommy, as I bend down to pick him up.

"A pleasure, Tommy," says I. "Up you come."

I carry him in my arms into the toilet just like I've done many times before.

"Now don't forget, Tommy: always–"

"I know," he interrupts. "Always wag yer wagger well in winter." And those words are his own. Each time we bring him out to pee, he lilts them.

"Are you finished, Paddy?" I enquire, after a full minute of hearing him relieve himself.

"Yeah, now give it to me," Tommy demands.

I'm equipped and ready to meet his ultimatum; I pass him the piece of tissue I had taken from the bar. Tommy is now carefully wiping his dampened penis dry. He's the only man I know who wipes his penis with a tissue after peeing; the rest of us shake it, button up and go – but not Tommy – he looks after himself really well.

"I'm finished now," he declares, dropping the soiled tissue into the toilet bowl. "Ye can bring me back. T'anks, Niall."

"You're welcome, Tommy," I respond, flushing the bowl with my left foot before we leave – my hands are full of Tommy.

We make our way back to where Tony is sitting on the floor, just where we had left him, only now he's looking startled.

"What's up with you, Tony? You look weird. What's wrong?"

"The fuckin' money!" Tony roars as he springs to his feet. "We left it in the cash box at the front door! Did you take it? I hope to Jays it's still there!"

I don't exactly drop Tommy, but I quickly put him down and run after Tony.

"Is it there?" I ask, panting with anxiety.

"I can't find it!" responds Tony, as he feverishly crawls around the floor looking for the money box.

"I left it right here," he continues, pointing to a shelf underneath the small table we had used to receive the entrance fees. Tony was taking in the money when the donnybrook started.

"There was a hundred feckin' quid in that bleedin' box!" Tony asserts, continuing his desperate search. "Where the fuck is it?"

Tommy has waddled his way across to us.

"T'ose Crumlin bowsies took it," interjects Tommy, sounding like a philosopher, a tiny one but equally profound. "I bet ye I'm right! T'ose types of dirty feckers would steal the eyes out of yer head if ye weren't lookin'!"

We stop our frantic search. Tony turns around. Sitting on the floor with his gob hanging open, he gapes at me.

"Jays, Niall. Tommy is right! I remember seein' that big fat bollocks who smashed you, standin' in here. I dropped everythin' when the trouble started and ran in to help ye. I got one good one into his fat stomach, and that stopped him from goin' at ye again. And then, he and his mates turned and ran for the door – I remember clearly now. That bastard stole our dough!"

"That was a blast!" Liam McKenna says gleefully. He and the rest of *The Creatures* together with four of their girl groupies have returned to the scene of the crime. Like everybody else, they'd scattered from the flying fists to escape injury. *The Creatures* have their gear up on the stage; they had no alternative other than to stick around, out of harm's way and wait for things to quieten down.

"Blast me arse!" says Tony. "Will you look at the place? And those Crumlin fuckers stole the takin's!"

"Do you guys know any of them?" I ask Liam.

"I know that big heavy dude," he replies. "His name is Brian, and I know where he hangs. He's on Durrow Road in Crumlin, just down from Clonard where I live."

Turning towards his buddies, Liam sought confirmation.

"Isn't that head the one and the same? Wasn't he at the gig in the Glasnevin Tennis Club last week, making a show of himself?"

"Right on, Liam," replies Fran, the drummer. "I remember the dude. He was pissed out of his friggin' mind, fallin' all over the place. Yeah man, I remember him," he continues, as only a rock'n'roll drummer would.

While Liam and the drummer are saying all this, I remember seeing the 'dude' at the Tennis Club. Tony and I had dropped in so as to check out the size of the crowd we might expect the following week. The fat bloke, Brian, was scuttered drunk, making a fool of himself. We'd stayed for a bit and had a dance or two before leaving. Strangely, I also remember that attractive blonde girl; I asked her to dance and got rejected. "No thanks," she pouted. "There's more fish in the sea," I replied. Turning to one of her friends, I succeeded in securing the favour, and with my ego crushed, off I danced away from her. That was the first time I ever laid eyes on Teresa Flynn.

"Well," Tony says, picking himself up from the floor, "when we catch up with him, he'll be really out of his fuckin' mind, out of his mind with pain from the lambastin' we'll be givin' him."

"And he'd better have our money. We'll beat it out of him," I add with venom. "Who's goin' to pay for puttin' the clubhouse together again? Us, that's who!"

"Woo, man," chimes in Frank Boylan, the bass guitarist. "Didn't we pick the righty-tighty time to get prepaid? Way to go, Creatures!"

"Screw you and the train you came up on," I respond. "This is not funny. We've been taken to the cleaners. You and your smart arse are the last things we want to be listenin' to. You've got your money, now shut the fuck up!"

"And ye've had a short night earnin' it too," says Tony. "It's only eleven now, and we booked ye 'til one. So do as Niall said; shut yer cakehole! Right!? There's a good chance we might be askin' ye for some of the money back! Right!?"

By the end of Tony's livid response, his nose is almost touching the bass guitarist's nose. Sensibly, Frank backs away, ever so slowly.

"Woo, man," he repeats. "No offence man. Peace, man."

It is early in the 1960s, the decade that would bring flower power, the anti-Vietnam War movement, bra-burning, hippies, bell bottoms, tie-dyed tee-shirts, long hair, psychedelic music and a load of other stuff. Some of the stuff is wonderful: the Civil Rights Act; the first man on the Moon; the Beatles and the Rolling Stones; the microwave oven; seatbelts; contact lenses; and with the help of Hela cancer cells harvested from the cervix of Henrietta Lacks, human polio vaccine trials. However, some of what the 1960s brought was bad: the acceleration of the use of illicit drugs; the worst of the Vietnam War, which dragged on for twenty years until April 1975; the erection of the Berlin Wall; the Cuban Missile

Crisis. There was a string of assassinations: John Kennedy, Martin Luther King, and Robert Kennedy. Then there was the escalation of the troubles in the six northern counties of Ireland.

The Creatures represent the Irish face of the hippie movement pretty well. We know little about the rest of the group, but we do know Liam. We often meet up with him in *O'Donaghues* on Merrion Row. He always has a song to sing or a story to tell. He's very smart and much better educated than any of us. He loves music in all its forms. He gives us a good glance at what this flower power stuff is about and how these times are affecting our world. Liam, like his buddies and many of the group's fans, is considered to be way out – talking, dressing and behaving in ways that disturb most people and test us all. This often results in their isolation. Through the many conversations we have with Liam, we learn that isolation is not only to their detriment, it is also to ours. Wisely we choose to get together, in peace, as Liam would say.

"Frank isn't cruisin' for a bruisin'," says Liam, trying to cool things down. "None of us are. All *The Creatures* are for peace," Liam continues, looking at all of the group and groupies. Turning back to look at Tony and me, he goes on. "Niall and Tony have enough on their plate sorting out this load. We're sorry for the clouds, man. We'll just go, pack up and cut out."

"OK, Liam," I answer, glad for the diffusion of what had almost become the number two donnybrook of the evening.

Tony and I are uptight and understandably so. Liam was quick to see it, and by stepping in the way he did, I'm reminded of just how smart he is. *The Creatures* and their groupies walk up the clubhouse floor to the stage and start packing their gear.

"You got to be more sensitive, man," I hear Liam say to Frank. "Use your lugs, man. Listening is what it's all about."

"Niall, give me a ring mañana," Liam shouts, as he and his merry band walk out of the clubhouse with their gear. "Let's see if we can help you get that Brian dude, OK?"

"You were great tonight, Liam, and you got the place hoppin'," I shout back. "Your draw was super. Tony and I, along with Tommy here, will sort things out and it'll be OK. I'll give you a call tomorrow. You might be able to help us track down that big bollocks. Thanks, Liam; and Frank – no hard feelin's, right?"

"Yeah," adds Tony. "No hards, Frank.

"Sure, man," Frank the bass guitarist says. "Peace, man."

****

Yarn #50 Footnote
[1] Loads of Irish fun and frolic.

The Donnybrook – Paddy the Barman & the Force

WHILE TONY AND I ARE TRYING TO GET TO GRIPS with our stolen money situation, and that tension-filled discourse with *The Creatures*, Paddy the barman had quietly returned to the clubhouse. Paddy Brown, a comfortably retired Garda Síochána, is about sixty. The club pays him handsomely for attending the bar, and most importantly, for handling the after-hour drinking the club frequently engages in. The local Parkgate Garda Station is just up the road. Almost every night you can find two or more of the off-duty gardaí sitting at the bar. It's often after hours you'll find them, sucking on their pints and knocking back small ones. Paddy's presence, it appears, gives them absolution for their sins. Paddy is a County Cork man.

"Holy Mother of God," Paddy moans, as he goes into his bar and sees the smashed bar mirror, chairs and tables thrown pell-mell around the barroom, and the bar room door off its hinges lying on the floor.

"Begorra now, and isn't dis an awful mess," says Paddy, his hands on his hips and looking very dour. "It'll be a while for me to get me bar back lookin' like the way I had it. And will ye look at me mirror, smashed to pieces, lyin' all over the place."

He's directing his laments to tiny Tommy who has come up beside him to commiserate. Looking over at them, I can't stop myself from quietly laughing. Paddy is six-foot tall and tiny Tommy, standing next to him looking less than the two-and-a-half-foot that was given to him – it's comical.

"Now don't you be makin' it worse dan it is, Paddy," says Tommy consolingly. "You'll upset yerself, so ye will. We'll get the place back lookin' the way ye like it in no time at all. And sure isn't me cousin, Martin, a glazier. I'll have him here in the mornin' measurin'. He'll have yer mirror back up der shinin' at ye before ye know it."

"Dat'll be a big help, Tommy," replies Paddy, still mournful, but beginning to see some light at the end of his dark tunnel.

"Tommy me ol' flower," says Paddy. "Ye're always der to brighten me up. Let me get at it now. I'll clear yer spot on the bar, and perch ye up out of harm's way while I tidy the place."

Picking tiny Tommy up, Paddy walks over to the end of the bar, clears it and puts his good friend on his throne.

"And if ye want to go to the toilet, Tommy, let me know. I'll bring ye out," says Paddy. "I'll pull ye one in a minute," he adds.

"Oh, now don't be botherin' yerself about dat, Paddy," replies Tommy. "Whenever ye're ready will be soon enough, although, to tell ye the truth, one of yer beautiful pints would go down well right now – after all we've been through, if ye know w'at I mean," Tommy continues, sending a mixed, yet clear message. "And didn't Niall help me to the toilet only a few minutes ago. I'm all set in dat department."

Paddy gets the coded message and immediately commences the first of what is always three pulls of the Guinness tap, the results of which always produce one of his beautiful pints.

While Paddy judiciously pulls the pint, Tommy sits on the bar taking it all in, enjoying every move. He can be heard muttering at the appropriate audio level so as Paddy would be able to hear him; after all, it is for Paddy's benefit Tommy is muttering. "Ah, will ye stop Paddy! Sure der's too much to be done. For the love of God Paddy. Aren't ye an awful man! Oh, der's no stoppin' ye! A Cork man for yer life. W'at am I goin' to do with ye?"

"There ye go, Tommy," says Paddy, having completed his performance. "Get dat into ye. I'll get on with me tidyin' now."

"Ye're an awful man, Paddy Brown," says Tommy, as he caresses the pint with his well-trained hand, placing the pint close beside him on the bar. "Ye shouldn't be botherin' yerself with me," he continues, "but t'anks very much, Paddy."

Before Tommy drinks any pint of Guinness served to him, there's a ritual to be performed – a type of respectful quality control ceremonial often used by Dublin's more expert Guinness drinkers. The pint, having been pulled by Paddy, requires no such inspection. However, Paddy and Tommy enjoy the ritual's staged performance so much, that Tommy always does it anyway. Taking a shilling from his pocket, Tommy taps the side of the glass three times with the edge of the coin – clonk-clonk-clonk. Had the pint been badly pulled, or had the Guinness itself been off in any way, the shilling-quality-control test would have produced an easily recognised, foreboding clink-clink-clink.

"A perfect pint, Paddy!" he proclaims, as he lifts the glass to his equally well-trained and parched mouth. "Never a clink from one of your grand pints, Paddy – always the perfect clonk! Me life on ye, Paddy. Sláinte!"

It will take Tommy precisely eight trips to his mouth, and a half-hour or so will pass before the entire pint is gone. When finished, the emptied glass will have seven distinct head-ring marks all the way down to the end, leaving the evidence of a perfect pint respectfully consumed.

Tony and I observe all of this as we're struggling with the downed barroom door.

"Have you got a hammer and screwdriver, Paddy?" Tony enquires. "We'll fix the door while you tidy up the bar. Have you a loan, Paddy?"

"I do now, yes," answers Paddy, as he does his own struggling with the broken mirror, and the upturned chairs and tables. "Der's a toolbox in the back. I'll stop w'at I'm doin' for a minute and get it for ye. Now . . . And was the door badly damaged?" he continues, as he walks over to Tony and I.

"No, Paddy," says I. "No real damage. The hinges have to be reset, and that won't be any problem once we have the tools."

"Well, dat's good news," says Paddy. "I'll go now and get dem for ye."

He quickly comes back with a tidy, well-stocked toolbox.

"Lads, I was thinkin' now," says Paddy, as he lays the toolbox down. "I shouldn't have left Tommy and the two of ye here with all the fracas. And I'm sorry I did dat. Ye see, I'm more dan able to throw a punch, but I'm afraid to, w'at with all the trouble I've brought on me wife and family. Ye see, when I get into a fisticuff

I lose the run of meself. Sure wasn't it dat dat got me a forced early retirement. I nearly killed a young man. He well deserved the beatin' I gave him, but I'd no right to punch him the way I did. I nearly killed him. And I was lucky to hold on to me pension when they let me go. It was an awful t'ing, to be sure. Dat's w'at made me run out and get away from it all, 'til it was over. Dat one punch, and I'll be livin' with it for the rest of me life. It's the one black blot on me otherwise sweet life."

"Paddy!" interjects Tommy. "If I were tall enough I'd jump down off dis bar and give ye a good kick in the arse. Would ye shut up out-a-dat! Ye did the right t'ing, and wouldn't I have been right behind ye if I had the legs to carry me."

"No, Tommy," responded Paddy. "I should have stayed–"

"I won't have any of dat now, Paddy," Tommy interjects again. "Ye're the best man I know. Cut in out now or–"

"Tommy is right, Paddy," says I, jumping into what was Paddy's confession. "You did do the right thing. Tony and I sorted it out without you, and we never for a minute thought you were bailin' out on us."

"No way," adds Tony. "Ye're sound, Paddy. We know who those bastards are. We'll tidy this place up, and then in the mornin' we'll go and get that fat bloke and our stolen money."

"What!?" exclaims Paddy. He hadn't known the money had been stolen, and he's alarmed to hear about it.

"The bowsies stole yer money! Now dat changes t'ings," says Paddy. "Changes t'ings entirely, so it does."

"It feckin' well does," Tony asserts. "And don't you worry about it. We'll get the money back, and while we're doin' it, we'll give them all a good lambastin'."

Paddy suddenly transforms into what he once was, a proud garda. Appearing and sounding utterly different, he pauses and then stretches himself up to his full height; looking first at Tommy and then towards Tony and me, he takes control.

"This criminal situation demands some good Garda Síochána intelligence," proclaims Paddy. "Now . . . Are'ru two lads sayin' you know who committed the crime? Is that correct?"

"Yes," I answer. "They're that crowd from Crumlin. The big fella's name is Brian, and he lives on Durrow Road in Crumlin."

"Now . . . Are'ru sure about that, Niall?" Paddy questions. He reminds me of a county Cork version of Perry Mason – in full control and putting all of the pieces of the crime together.

"Definite, Paddy. We're positive. Aren't we, Tony?"

"Absolutely!" comes Tony's confirmation. "It was those bastards for sure."

"And are'ru tellin' me they're from the Crumlin area? Now is that correct?" queries Paddy, very deliberately.

"Yes," I confirm, feeling as if I was in the witness box.

Paddy spends a full long minute walking up and down; head bowed, arms folded and looking so much like Perry that I worry about addressing him as such. Tommy, Tony and I know our place; we stay silent, as Perry, or should I say, Paddy, suddenly stops walking. With a surprising big grin on his face, he slowly shares with us the results of his professional deliberations.

"Gentlemen," he starts. "If you would now be so kind, you can leave all this stolen currency matter entirely to me and my good friends in the force." With arms unfolded and his head held high, Paddy recommences his walking.

"You see, I just happen to know the sargeant in charge of such crime up there in Crumlin, and I might add, very well. He is, in fact, married to a niece of mine. We in the force have our ways of gettin' things done if you know what I mean. We in the force have found there are more ways of killin' a cat than feedin' it buttermilk! There are lots of ways you can go about it. These misguided young men who were foolish enough to perpetrate this crime, well, let's say they've made a grievous mistake. We can understand and hopefully forgive fisticuffs, but gentlemen, stealin' is another t'ing – and the law will prevail!"

We all want to stand up and applaud. Instead of doing so, all three of us just look at Paddy as if indeed he was Perry Mason. In unrehearsed unison, we shout out.

"Me life on ye, Paddy."

"God, Paddy," adds Tommy. "Dat was well said. The force is weaker for not still havin' ye. Ye're a powerful man, Paddy."

"T'ank ye, Tommy," Paddy responds. "Sure and it's nothin'. I'm only doin' me job, and it's t'ankful I am to ye all for givin' me the chance to make up for runnin' out."

The Paddy we know had returned. Between his recovering 'ahems' while clearing his dry throat, I think I see him blush.

"Right on, Paddy," says I. "That'll be great. We were plannin' to handle it ourselves. Liam, *The Creatures* lead singer, was goin' to help us. He knows the fat bloke and where he lives. We'll leave it to you now. With all your experience, you'll get it done quicker and better than us."

"Thanks, Paddy," adds Tony. "With you on our side, we're bound to get it into the net. And Paddy, we'll look after you. Won't we Niall?"

"Sure we will," I confirm.

"No need for any-a-dat, lads," says Paddy. "It'll be my pleasure to help ye. Now let's finish up here and let me lock up the clubhouse. Der's a rowin' meet tomorra mornin'; we don't want dem crews comin' in here and seein' the place a mess. Tommy will get his cousin over, and he'll get the new mirror up over the bar. It'd be grand if it were up before drinkin' time tomorra night. Do ye think der's err a chance, Tommy?"

"No problem, Paddy," answers Tommy. "I was only talkin' to Martin durin' the week, and he was tellin' me dat work was slow. He'll help us out; der should be no problem in makin' it happen. I'll call him in the mornin' bright and early, so's he can get at it."

"Grand," says Paddy. "Let's get dis place lookin' respectable."

With some difficulty, Tony and I finish the rehanging of the barroom door. We quickly go at the tidying up of the dance floor. Spilt blood is wiped away, and the chairs and tables that were scattered about are up-righted. By the time we're finished, the only remaining eyesores are the half dozen holes in the wooden-panelled walls. They aren't big, but at this point, we can do nothing about them.

Paddy appears out of the barroom with Tommy in his arms.

"Dat's enough for tonight, lads. Once we've locked up, I'll bring Tommy home. Ye lads should come back in the mornin' as early as ye can. We'll all put spit and polish on dis place so's no one will ever know w'ats happened."

"I'll be talkin' to my friend from the force, the sergeant before I go to bed tonight," Paddy continues, returning to his official garda mode. "We'll discuss the stolen currency matter together in great detail, and gentlemen, do not be surprised if the situation is resolved to all of our satisfaction by tomorra night. Garda Síochána intelligence and the right way to go about it are what is required, and gentlemen, that's what we have here."

"No one would ever t'ink, only a short while ago, dis place looked like the wreck of the Hesperus," says Tommy, a big smile on his face. "We'll have it lookin' like a new pin in the mornin'."

"Thanks for all your help, Paddy. You too, Tommy," says I.

"Yeah," adds Tony. "Where would we be without you?"

"No problem, lads," says Paddy, speaking on behalf of himself and his tiny friend. "Let's lock up now and be on our way."

Out we walk, all together like Brown's cows. We lock up, and Paddy, with tiny Tommy in his arms, makes his way to his Morris Minor. In they climb, and with no seatbelt laws at the time, Tommy is placed on the carefully piled cushions in the front passenger seat. Tommy always insists on sitting in the seventy-five percent seat, and he's equally firm about being able to see out. Winding down his window as he pulls out of the driveway, Paddy shouts his goodbye.

"We'll see ye in the mornin', lads. Get home safe. And keep yer pecker up. The sergeant and I will do our job."

"Good night, lads," we hear Tommy holler, as they both exit the club's driveway.

"What a night?" exclaims Tony. "And wasn't Paddy terrific? I'll tell you one thing. I wouldn't want to be that Brian bloke. We don't know, and we might never know what's goin' to happen to him, but by Jays, one thing is definite: Paddy and the force will be on him heavy. I hope they beat the shite out of him."

"Right," I reply as we walk over to my trusty steed, my Heinkel motor scooter.

"Get your leg over, Tony. I can't wait to get into bed. I'm bollixed. My Ma will be at me fierce when she sees my lip. I can hear her now: 'Always with your fighting; I don't know what I'm going to do with you.' I hope she's asleep when I get home. That'll give the lip time to go down."

"Drop me off, Niall, and head home," says Tony. "We've got to be back here early. Can you pick me up? I reckon a little after eight would be right."

"OK, Tony," says I.

I drop Tony off, and I'm pulling into 1 Mannix Road soon after. I'm careful to turn off the engine at the top of the hill, and quietly roll down to the front of the house so as not to wake my mother. That is the standard drill when coming home late. The Ma sleeps in the front upstairs bedroom.

****

The Donnybrook – a Quirky Bed & Sausage Sandwiches

G RATEFULLY, PEG IS SOUND ASLEEP. Quitely creeping up the stairs to my bed, I hear Conor moving in his bedroom.

"Is that you, Niall?" he whispers.

"Yeah, Conor. Go to sleep. I want to go to bed," I whisper back.

"Clare called."

"Did she now? I'm glad I wasn't here to listen to her. She's drivin' me mad. She's at me to go over to London with her."

"I hope you don't go, Niall. If ye do, I'll be havin' Ma at me like she's always at you."

"Go to sleep, Conor. I don't plan to be goin' anywhere soon, other than me bed. I'm banjaxed. Good night. Nighty night, sleep tight, don't let the bugs bite."

I take my shoes off before passing my mother's bedroom. I need Peg chiding me like a hole in the head. Being particularly careful on the third to last stair tread, I had negotiated the squeaky stairs successfully. All the treads squeak a bit, but the third to last one is a snare altogether. I'd often thought that my mother laid it out that way so as to trap me when I'm sneaking in late at night, or as is more often the case, in the wee hours of the morning. Conor had heard me, but Peg, my darlin' mother had not.

Closing my bedroom door, I make sure to hold the inside door handle firmly until the door is against its jam, and the faulty catch is perfectly in line with the jam's receiver. I carefully release the handle and engage the catch. As I'm doing this, I think of how well we had done putting the barroom door back up and putting the

283

clubhouse back in shape. *We'll have it as right as rain in the mornin'.* Switching on the bedside light, my clock tells me it's a little after one. I set the alarm for seven a.m. There's one more hurdle before I can climb into my bed and go asleep.

My bed is a comfortable one, but as with my bedroom door, it has its quirks. If, as is the case right now, I'm obliged to mount it without making noise, a noise sounding like and as loud as a cat being squashed to death, there's a certain demanding way to go about it. Over time and the many occasions this demand has presented itself, I've discovered I can do so by placing a book beneath the bed's left leg at the headboard end. Not just any book – it has to be my copy of Robert Louis Stevenson's *Treasure Island*. This I do with the usual meticulous care.

Before I get into bed, I take the blood-stained shirt off and hide it in my backpack. *I don't want to encourage Peg. She'll probably see my lip, and that will give her more than enough ammo.* It isn't that my mother is anything like nasty. She's not. However, she knows me well, and that's the problem. I'm a selfish brat, always thinking about what is best for me and not so much for those around me, least of all, my mother. She knows it, and she's always there to remind me. She holds the eternal hope that I'll change. There was a time when she thought she had the makings of a priest in me, or maybe even a bishop. There's little if any chance of that happening, and she knows that too.

Ye can't fool yer mother was my second to last thought as I fell asleep. *Tomorrow is another lifetime and isn't it great that each day is brand new – another chance to make it the big one.*

AT THE instructed moment, the alarm goes into action. I promptly reach out to silence the noise. Like always, I had slept in the nude. Peg complains about that: "Look at you, going around the house naked, showing your derriere, and your little brother looking at you." I put on my underpants and sneak my way to the bathroom; my mother is still asleep.

Another day another dollar, I ponder, peeing and stretching as I do so. *A quick shower, and I'm out of here.* I turn on the shower, and as it warms up, I look in the mirror over the sink and review the lip condition. While the swelling has reduced somewhat, clear evidence of a battle endured remains. *No hidin' that from Peg.*

Ablutions complete, I sneak back to my bedroom, dress quickly and make my way downstairs. I'm almost out the door when I hear my mother shout.

"Is that you, Niall? Let me come down and make you some breakfast, love."

"No, Ma," I reply. "I'll pick up a sausage sandwich at the Esso station. Stay in your bed and don't be worrying about me. I've got to meet Tony at eight. We've to do somethin'."

"I love you, Ma, and I'll see you later on," I shout, as I close the door behind me, but not before I hear Peg say, "You're always going somewhere. Will you not stay and sit with your mother for a minute? Let me get you a bit of breakfast."

As I mount my Heinkel, I look back and holler. "Don't be worryin' about me, Ma. Love you, and I'll see you later."

I had escaped before she could see me and my swollen lip. I rev up and move on to pick up Tony. There's work to be done, and the sooner we get to the clubhouse the better.

Tony is waiting for me at the corner. He lives in the Kevin Street flats. He always waits there. That avoids me from having to park the bike and go all the way up to the third floor to get him.

"Mornin' Tony," says I, pulling up to him. "Cock your leg over and let's go. I'm starvin'. Would you like to stop at the *Esso* station and grab a sausage sandwich?"

Sizzling pork sausage.

"Mornin' Niall. A tasty sausage sandwich and a cup of tea will be brilliant. It'll get us ready for the job ahead of us."

We set off, and on the way, we stop at one of the many Eastern States Standard Oil petrol stations throughout Dublin city. They all seem to be owned or run by Eastern Indians, just like the city's hundreds of Fish'n'Chip shops, all run by Italians.

"And what may I ask, do Indians know about sausage?" says I, as we walk into the lovely smell of cooking sausage. "I thought they were only into curry and tandoori chicken and all that stuff."

"Makin' money," replies Tony. "That's what they're into."

"I suppose you're right. But how come we never see Dublin blokes like us do that? We're all slow at the mula makin' business if you ask me. It should be you or I or one of the lads who's behind this counter. We're all too slow; it's probably somethin' to do with us bein' too fond of the craic, singin' and the gargle."

"But, Niall, would you change it for the world? All work and no play makes a dull boy."

"There is that, Tony," says I, as we come up to the counter.

"Good morning, men," says the smiling Indian gentleman, greeting us warmly. "And how may my good wife and I serve you this lovely morning?" he politely enquires. His attractive, good wife is standing next to him in her Indian garb ready to pounce, as indeed he is, to our every need. *They know how to make ye feel welcome,* I ponder, as another reason for their success comes to mind.

"Thank you, sir," answers Tony, returning the politeness shown. "Two sausage sandwiches and two cups of tea, please."

The wife turns away to attend to our order, but not before she bows slightly to us and smiles.

"It is our pleasure, gentlemen," says the husband. "My wife will get that for you. That will be two-shillings-and-four-pence please," he continues, as he rings the tally up on his spotlessly clean register.

Before we are given our change and receipt, back comes the wife with the sausage sandwiches and tea on a small cardboard tray –two paper napkins are neatly placed to the side. *Jays, they know how to do it.*

"It's been a true pleasure serving you," says the husband. "Please come again. You'll find the sauce, milk, and sugar behind you. Good morning, gentlemen; have a good day."

I take the tray and find myself bowing back to the couple.

"Thank you very much, sir, and a good day to you both," says I as we turn to the tidy serving station.

"Now, that's the way to do it, Tony. We'd be all better off if we learned from these foreigners. And it'll be our own fault if we don't. Hats off to them. I think they're great, comin' over here and gettin' into it like they do."

"Yeah, Niall, and look at the grub. It looks delicious."

We attend to our tea, and with tray in hand, we walk out, sit on the Heinkel and have our breakfast. After the tasty repast, Tony in his customary manner farts loudly.

"Sorry about that, Niall. More room out than in."

"Right," says I. "Let's get to the clubhouse."

We mount and are driving up the Commercial Rowing Club's driveway soon afterwards. Tony continues farting all the way there. I'm glad to be sitting up front.

****

The Donnybrook –
Tidying Up & the Meet

T HE CLUBHOUSE FRONT DOOR IS OPEN. It's a little after nine; we're pleasantly surprised to see that Tommy's cousin, the glazier has arrived. The earliest replacement of the bar mirror looks good.

We're doubly surprised to see that Paddy and the glazier are not alone. A woman is with them, working away on the cleaning as only a woman can.

"Good mornin' to ye," Paddy greets us. "I'd like to introduce ye two lads to my good wife who's always der for me. Dis is she, and I'm proud to say she's a County Cork girl."

"Her name is Maureen," adds Paddy proudly, as he nuzzles-up next to the love of his life, his left arm wrapped around her ample shoulders. Maureen looks embarrassed and uncomfortable with the platitudes given to her by her loving husband. She's standing beside him in her floral apron while with her left hand she fidgets with her apron ties.

"I'm happy to meet you, Maureen," says I sincerely. She's way smaller than Paddy – about five-foot-four. Up close to her and shaking her hand, I can clearly see one of the undoubtedly many reasons why Paddy had fallen in love with Maureen – her eyes. They are sparkling light blue.

"Paddy is a great man," says Tony. "And here you are, just like him, helpin' us out. You're kind to do it, Maureen."

"Ah sura, will ye go-way-out-a-dat?" Maureen responds. "Aren't I only doin' w'at any woman would do, standin' by her man. We'll have dis place sparklin' in two shakes of a lamb's tail, so we will. I'm nearly finished out here already, and I'll be into Paddy's bar in a minute."

"Martin, Tommy's cousin, is in at the bar measurin'," Paddy chimes in. "He'll be finished soon, and den it'll be off with him down to Dawson Street to the glass shop. He just told me it'd be no problem for him to have the new mirror up by mid-afternoon. Now, and isn't dat grand news?"

"Paddy, would ye be after tellin' dem w'at the sergeant said to ye dis mornin'?" Maureen interrupts. "Ye haven't forgotten it, have ye?"

"It's good news, lads," Maureen continues, turning to Tony and me. "Isn't dat right, Paddy?" she says, poking Paddy.

"That's correct, Maureen," Paddy responds. "And t'ank ye, darlin'. I planned to inform the lads about dat important matter after the introductions."

Paddy releases his arm from its loving hold of Maureen's shoulders. Stretching up to his full height, his garda mode that had impressed us so much the evening before, once again consumes him.

"As arranged, the sergeant and I had an in-depth discussion on the case before goin' to bed last night," declares Paddy, his arms firmly folded as he starts to stride up and down.

"The good sergeant gave me a call early this mornin'. The results of our discussion are, as we speak, in progress, as we say in the force. He told me, in the strictest confidence I might add, that in pursuance of his investigation, he has ascertained dat the suspect is well known to the entire force. He indicated to me, and again I empathise in the strictest of confidence, dat last night's crime has given him the hoped for and appreciated opportunity to pursue and apprehend the one and the same suspect."

Paddy pauses, unfolds his arms, and gives one of his throat-clearing 'ahems'.

We are all once again mesmerised by his performance. I glance at Maureen: there she is, standing with her head tilted, arms folded, looking up at her man with adoring respect and pride. She has a look of solemn adoration on her face.

"The sergeant did not inform me of the exact manner of the apprehension he intends to employ," Paddy continues. "As I said to yee last evenin', we in the force have our ways of gettin' t'ings done. And done they will be. The good sergeant informed me dat the matter should be concluded promptly and dat he'll call me with the results of the pursuit, not later dan dis very afternoon."

"Jays, Paddy," exclaims Tony, "that's awesome."

All present want to applaud, and it's only Tony's comment that stops it happening.

"I'm tellin' you, Maureen, Paddy is the best man I know," I blurt out, wanting to kiss them both.

"Ah, and sure isn't he only doin' his job," says Maureen, as she tries hard to shake the magic of the moment out of herself. "Isn't dat right, Paddy, love?"

"Right as God's rain, Maureen me darlin' – dat's w'at it is."

Interrupting the love fest, Tommy's cousin, Martin the glazier comes out from the bar.

Martin the glazier.

"I'll be leaving ye now, sir," says Martin, directing his announcement to Paddy. He has a butt of a pencil stuck behind one of his ears and is wearing a well-worn hat perched on the side of his head. He's in overalls. The undoubtedly accurate measurements he had taken and written down on what looks like the back of a packet of cigarettes, is held tightly in hand. He looks the right man for the job.

"I'm off to the glass shop now, sir. And I'll be back before ye know I've gone. I'll have that mirror up for ye in a jiffy, sir," Martin concludes, as he runs out the door to his van.

"Now, dat's w'at makes old Érin great!" says Paddy. "A hard workin' man doin' the best he can. I'm not at all surprised dat Martin is Tommy's cousin. Sure wouldn't Tommy be just like him, only for the way he turned out? Tommy is a great little helper, ye know. Doesn't he help me out whenever it gets busy at the bar, wipin' and cleanin'. Der's times he even dries the washed glasses, and it's a fine job he does too."

"Paddy, for the love of God," Maureen interrupts, steering the conversation and our energies back to the task at hand. "Enough of dis chattin'. It's cleanin' we should be doin', not chattin'."

"Ye're right, Maureen," answers Paddy. "Now lads, Maureen and I will get into the bar and make everythin' shine. Ye two see w'at can be done about dem holes. Apart from the holes in the wall, I t'ink we're almost done. The bar needs a bit of spit and polish, but once the mirror is up, I don't t'ink anyone will be able to notice any of the mess dis place was in only a few hours ago."

We hear the early bird members of the *Commercial Rowing Club*'s rowing crew pull up outside. It's a friendly meet, not a full regatta. The visiting *Neptune Rowing Club* crew will be arriving soon. They'll all be kept busy for an hour or so taking down the shells from the racks, cleaning them, and deciding on the oars and blades to be used. Depending on the way the river is flowing and how the breeze is blowing, the choice of blade is critical; it often decides the win or loss of a race. The final call is the coach's with much influence from the coxswain; that usually brings about some, and sometimes a lot, of contention. The coxswain will follow the plan outlined by the coach, however, once the boat is fully manned and afloat the coxswain becomes the captain of the vessel.

The choice of oar and blade.

Tommy isn't coxing this morning. Paddy, who usually picks him up and brings him to the club, got him to agree that he needed the sleep and had left him in his bed.

While all the rowing stuff is going on outside and the slick cedar shells are being carried down to the river, the donnybrook clean-up crew are hard at work inside. By the time the rowing crews start drifting into the clubhouse, we've almost completed the task. We only need the new mirror up to make the place look the way we want it to be. The holes in the wood-panelled walls have been pulled out as best we can. They're still there, and two of them are pretty obvious, but we hope, only if you were looking for them.

"Now lads . . . Dat's a job well done," says Paddy, expressing well all of our satisfaction. "The mirror will be here soon. All we need is to hear from the good sergeant and we'll be smilin' like Cheshire cats. Am I right?"

"Be Jays you are," Tony responds, and with that, the phone behind the bar rings.

****

The Donnybrook –
the Law Prevails & Garda Ryan

"**N**OW DER YE GO. DIDN'T I TELL YE NOT TO WORRY**,**" says Paddy, as he turns and runs for the phone.

All three of us follow him. I notice Maureen is feverishly fingering a string of beads with a crucifix at one end: it's her rosary beads. A lot of older women never go anywhere without their beads in their pocket; Maureen didn't forget to bring hers. She's in hot pursuit of having God's mother put in a good word with her Son for her faith-filled hopes of good news. We younger Dubliners have drifted quite some ways from such faith, nevertheless, looking at Maureen, I drift back a piece.

Maureen's rosary beads.

"*The Commercial Rowing Club*," announces Paddy as he grabs the phone off its base. "Paddy Brown speaking."

We're all listening intently.

"I was expectin' yer call, sir, and t'ank ye very much, sir."

"Of course, sir."

"Yes, sir."

"Yes, sir."

"Of course, sir. I understand, sir."

"Absolutely, sir. It won't go any further dan dis, sir."

There's a pause in Paddy's responses for one long minute.

293

"Well . . . would ye ever–"

"Ye're absolutely right, sir."

Another pause, this time for a long ten seconds or so.

"Sure dat's not necessary, sir."

"Well, ye're bein' more dan kind, sir."

"Yes, sir. I'll make sure to emphasise dat, sir."

"Sir, it's been an honour to serve with ye."

"I'll do dat, sir, and you please say hello to me niece, sir."

"We will, sir, and sure maybe, if ye have the time, sir, ye could honour us with yer presence here at the rowing club."

"Dat'll be grand, sir. When ye have the time, sir."

"As I'm often heard to say, sir, the law will prevail!"

"T'ank ye, sir, and may He bless you too, sir."

Paddy returns the phone to its base. Turning towards his audience, and with a big grin on his face, he jumps up in the air.

"The law prevails! Just ye wait 'til ye hear all dat I'm goin' to tell yee. Yee won't believe it, but it's the truth! As true as God made little apples, dat's w'at it is."

Our exasperation has moved up a notch and is now near to damaging our hearts.

"For God's sake, Paddy. Will ye tell us before ye kill us altogether!?" pleads Maureen, looking at Tony and me, rosary beads still in hand. She then looks back at the man of her life, who is coming close to being attacked by the woman he loves so much.

"I'm sorry, darlin'," says Paddy. "Come on up here now. I'll pull yee two lads a good pint, and I'll have one along with yee. We do, though I say so meself, deserve it. And Maureen, will ye be havin' a small one? I know well ye're not a drinkin' woman, but it might be good for ye now, w'at with all the excitement."

"Yes, Paddy," answers Maureen. "Ye can give me a small Jameson. Ye're right. I'm nearly at death's door with ye. Maybe a small one will cool me down."

"Good. Now I'll tell yee all the full story."

We barrel up to the bar, and as instructed we place ourselves on three of the ten bar stools now neatly lined up against the shining bar counter.

Paddy's informative monologue, which goes on for a long time, is preceded by an agonisingly lengthy prologue.

"We've done for the inhabitants of Baile Átha Cliath w'at the sergeant has defined as being a meaningful service – for not only the city of Dublin but in fact for the entire country.

"However, and before I say another word, I'm solemnly bound to secure from yee all – dat includes you, Maureen me love – yeer solemn promise dat any words out of my mouth will be strictly for yeer ears, and dat those words are divulged to no other livin' soul. Do yee have dat fully understood, and is it solemnly agreed to?"

"Yes, Paddy love," Maureen confirms. "From your mouth to God's ears and ours, and to not another livin' soul."

"Yes, Paddy," says I. "You've got our word."

"The good sergeant's honour is at stake, not to mention my own and yeers, and I might add, the honour of the entire force. Any breach of dis oath could lead to unknown grave consequences. I'm honour bound to emphasise dat."

"Right, Paddy, love. Now . . . Will ye for God's sake tell us?"

"I will, and I t'ank ye for yer patience and understandin'," says Paddy, as he winks lovingly at Maureen. "And ye can put yer rosary beads away now, darlin'. Yer prayers have been answered."

Maureen puts her beads back into her apron pocket.

"T'anks be to the Blessed Virgin Mary," says she, reverently making the sign of the cross as she does so.

Paddy's prologue is complete. There are a few interruptions to his following monologue – a few 'Jays' and such from Tony and me, and Maureen adds some 'Holy Mother of Gods', 'I don't believe its', and one or two 'Right, Paddy, go-ons'. Drifting in and out of the more familiar Paddy and the not as familiar garda-mode Paddy, they both join to tell us the story.

"It would appear that the now in custody, Mr Brian O'Sullivan – dat's his full name – has been under surveillance, as we say in the force, for some time. His checkered past is well known. He spent most of his early youth and teens in Artane Boys Reformatory with the Irish Christian Brothers and was later to graduate, so to speak, to Borstal and Patrick's Institute in Mountjoy. It was misdemeanours, like stealin' bicycles, stealin' from the poor box in the church, knockin' off hard boiled sweets and bars of chocolate and such dat put him in Borstal. When he got out, the force had dir eyes on him.

"Der were strong suspicions dat he and his friends were involved in a lot of, as we say in the force, more serious crime. The force knew dir MO – dat's short for modus operandi – Latin, ye know. House breakin', knockin' down people and takin' dir money, stealin' women's handbags and such was w'at the force suspected dem of doin'. Most of dese crimes were perpetrated in Dublin, but the bowsies often spread dir evil ways out into the country towns, Athlone, Clonmel, and Dundalk to mention a few.

"After our discussion and havin' slept on it, so to speak, the good sergeant marshalled his men. He decided that the evidence we supplied was w'at he was waitin' and prayin' for. Sufficient evidence to apprehend and commit is w'at it's called in the force."

Paddy pauses. The three pints, and Maureen's Jameson which looks more like a good double to me, are ready to be served. Paddy lifts them over to his shining bar counter. Serving Maureen first, he places the beautifully prepared refreshments for our pleasure.

Grabbing hold of the glasses, we toast each other. "Here's to good friends and to you, Maureen," declares Paddy. "The girl I'd dye me hair for. Sláinte agus Dia linn uilig anseo![1]"

Feeling all the better for having done so, we take the first of the day to our mouths. Wiping the remnants of the pint's head from his upper lip, Paddy continues with his monologue.

"The sergeant and four of his best men proceeded to the suspect's house of residence in Durrow Road. It was O'Sullivan's mother dat opened the door. The sergeant presented the required search warrant, and after the poor woman had stopped cryin', she told dem that the suspect, who for the woman's entire life had tormented the soul of her, was up in his bed sleepin'. With no hesitation, all five members of the force mounted the stairs. With the help of the mother, they identified the culprit's bedroom.

"They rushed in. The culprit had to be shaken out of his undoubtedly drunken sleep, and when he did wake up, he sat der scratchin' his head with one hand while tryin' to hold himself sittin' up with the other. His hands were quickly brought behind his back, and the handcuffs were slapped shut so's to make sure he wouldn't try to make an escape from custody.

"The minute the force entered the room they observed the evidence. Sittin' der on the bedroom dresser was the money box.

Der it was, as plain as day, sittin' out for all the world to see. On first examination, yer money was found to be all der.

"And would ye believe it, wasn't der a lot more evidence. Evidence linkin' Mr O'Sullivan to many more crimes. Searchin' through his drawers and under his bed, the force found jewellery, watches, wallets, silver candlesticks and the like, hidden away.

"Mr O'Sullivan was only wearin' an ol' shirt at the time, so they made him put on a pair of trousers and a pair of shoes. They den dragged him down the stairs and wasn't he thrown into the back of the Black Maria. And isn't he now locked up in custody awaitin' arraignment in court dis very afternoon!"

The Black Maria.

One of Maureen's, "I don't believe its" interrupts Paddy. Tony and I add a couple of our own, "Jays."

"And, lads," Paddy continues. "Dat money box of yours is, as we speak, on its way here by courtesy of the good sergeant and one of his motorbike garda!"

"It's not!?" says I in disbelieve.

"Yes! It damn well is!" confirms Paddy, grinning from ear to ear. "As ye've heard me say many times, we in the force have our ways of doin' t'ings, and ye must keep this part of the story, as indeed all of it, in the strict confidence ye took an oath to behold. The sergeant saw no reason why ye two honest lads should have to be involved any further in the matter. He thought it only proper, and it could be seen as a type of reward to ye both, for ye to get the stolen money back without havin' it tied up for God knows how long in the courts. Now . . . Isn't dat good news?"

"Ye're a brick, Paddy," says Tony. "The best man the force ever had. Me life on ye, Paddy."

Maureen is falling in love with Paddy all over again.

"Paddy, me darlin'," Maureen swoons. "I married well when I married you. I'm so proud of ye," she continues and starts to cry.

"Now would ye all be gettin' a hold of yerselves," says Paddy. "I'm as proud of you, me darlin' Maureen, as you are of me. We've all done a grand job. So stop yer ol' whingin' and drink up yer Jameson now. Sure and isn't it laughin' we all should be."

The mellow-dramatics are given a timely conclusion when Martin the glazier comes bursting through the barroom door.

"I've got the mirror in the van outside," he declares. "Me two sons are with me to help carry it in. We'll have it up der over the bar in no time at all."

"And aren't you one reliable glazier?" says Paddy. "I'll clear up here now, and I'll make room for ye to do yer work. I'm goin' to be sure to tell yer cousin Tommy, how decent a man ye are. Make no mistake; if I or any of me many friends for dat matter, ever have a need for a glazier, it'll be yerself we'll be callin'."

"Thank you, sir," replies Martin. "Let me go and get to work."

We all walk out after Martin, eager to view the new mirror that would crown our hard work getting the clubhouse back in shape. As we reach the front door, a motorbike garda pulls in from the Clondalkin Road and comes roaring up the driveway, screeching to a halt.

"Well . . . It feels like we're havin' all our birthdays at once," laughs Paddy as the garda dismounts his motorbike.

Rummaging through his dispatch pouch, the garda takes out the money box. Straightening himself up to his full height, he makes a military-like about turn towards us; he then marches across the driveway to where we're all standing and eagerly awaiting the opportunity of welcoming him.

"Good day to you all. My name is Garda Sean Ryan," he announces. "I have been instructed to deliver to one Mr Paddy Brown an item upon my person. Would I be correct in assuming one of you persons is the one and the same Mr Paddy Brown?"

"You would be correct, sir. It is I," Paddy asserts, holding out his right hand.

"It is a pleasure to meet you, sir," responds Garda Ryan as he grasps Paddy's out-stretched hand and shakes it.

"You're held in high esteem by the force, and it is only for protocol I must ask you for some identification before handing you the item," he continues. "I know, you'll understand, sir."

"And indeed I do, sir," says Paddy, as he removes his bulging wallet from his back trousers' pocket. He quickly extracts his driving licence and presents it to the now smiling Garda Ryan.

"That's fine, sir," says the garda, returning the barely looked at licence. He then unbuttons his top breast pocket and extracts a docket book. Each docket is in duplicate, and the top docket has been prescribed. The required carbon paper is neatly placed so as the copy would record any further inscription on the top sheet.

"If you'd be so kind and sign your name, and by so doing verify your receipt and acceptance of the item I will now give to you, sir," says the garda, as he passes the docket book to Paddy.

"Thank you, sir. I will, as indeed it is required and proper."

Paddy signs his name, passes the docket book back and in turn is the recipient of the item, the money box. Garda Ryan then takes the top sheet of the executed document and hands it to Paddy.

"The sergeant has asked me to extend his best wishes to you and to your wife, sir," the garda says, acknowledging Maureen with a smiling glance. "I'll be leaving you now, sir," he concludes. He gives Paddy a salute, a salute that Paddy returns with gusto, and with so much pride that looking at him, I thought he'd burst.

Garda Ryan marches back to his motorbike. He's driving out of the clubhouse driveway as we all share in a celebratory hug.

Paddy passes the money box to Tony.

"Now, Tony; let you and Niall check out dat it's all der. The sergeant said it was, and dat's good enough for me, but check it anyway, to be sure."

"We will, Paddy," replies Tony.

"All our birthdays and our weddin's too," says I.

"Go on now and check yer money," Paddy replies with a big smile on his flushed face. "Maureen and I will go in to see if we can help Martin and his boys with the mirror."

"Now, Maureen. If only our crew beat those Neptune fellas," says Paddy as he walks back to his barroom with Maureen hanging adoringly on his arm. "If dat were to happen, dis day would be made a grand day, a grand day indeed."

All the money is there, Martin gets the mirror up, and the *Commercial Rowing Club* does beat the Neptune fellas. The day ends up being a grand day indeed.

And the night isn't bad either. Tony and I join up with Cess, Jackie Smith and Tommy Greeley at the clubhouse bar. As usual, tiny Tommy is on his throne. Paddy, in high spirits, is behind the bar with his sparkling new mirror. Victor Lloyd, the club's president, is there to cheer on the winning crew. Victor was my patron when I joined the club; he was dating my sister Geraldine at that time. My mother had begged him to try and get me interested in the sport and out of what she defined as being 'the dangerous going-ons he gets himself into.' Victor was to marry my beautiful sister Geraldine later.

The secrecy held by Paddy, tiny Tommy, Tony and I is held absolute. No one else knows anything about the donnybrook. We're standing at the crowded *Commercial Rowing Club* bar, pints are flying, and the craic is ninety. For Tony and I, the last twenty-four hours have been exhausting. We'd been through a lot. In the end, it all turned out well, however, the high spirits of the winning crew and those around us is almost too much for us.

"What are those holes in the wall all about?" asks Victor.

Paddy, the barman, is quick to respond.

"What holes would ye be talkin' about, Mr President?"

"The ones out there in the wall, Paddy," Victor answers.

"Do you know those holes in the wall out der, Tommy?" Paddy asks, directing his cloaked enquiry to tiny Tommy on his throne.

"No, Paddy," answers Tommy, as he shifts himself, while at the same time winking at me. "I've been out to the toilet twice tonight, and I didn't notice any holes in the walls at all."

Tony and I stick our heads into our pints and say nothing.

"Well, I saw one of them as I was coming in, and I saw another one up near the stage on my way from the toilet," Victor asserts.

"God bless yer eyesight, Mr President," says Paddy, as he looks up from his washing of glasses. "I'll come in tomorra a tad early, and I'll look at dem. Don't you worry yerself. I'll get dem fixed for ye."

We are in the clear; all evidence of the donnybrook has been adequately hidden. And the hard earned money, once lost but now found, is safely in the GOSS bank account waiting to fund the next series of GOSS parties and the great times we'd have.

"Four more pints, Paddy," says Tony "When you're ready."

"We'll go after this round, right, Tony?"

"OK, Niall. I'm bollixed tired."

"What are you two talkin' about?" Tommy Greeley enquires. Paddy is behind the bar, and as usual, he can hear and is carefully listening to every word uttered.

"Nothin'," says I. *A solemn oath is a solemn oath.* Picking up my pint, I make the fourth of eight head rings. *Four down and four to go.*

****

IT WAS weeks before we heard about what happened to Brian O'Sullivan. He was given a year sentence in Mountjoy Gaol.

"He deserves it," Tony said to me.

"He fuckin' well does," I confirmed.

He never stopped his stealing. We would later learn that he'd been somehow involved in the August 1963, Great Train Robbery in England, a heist worth £2.6 million ($7 million at the time, and more than $50 million or £35 million today).

The Commercial Rowing Club has changed somewhat, but it's still lying there where I left it. You can easily find it up near the Phoenix Park beside the ever-flowing River Liffey. Tiny Tommy, Paddy Brown and Maureen, as well as Victor, are gone. I do not know what happened to Liam and *The Creatures*. However, the memories of them all, and what those memories mean to me, are very much alive.

Dia linn uilig anseo, agus dóibh siúd go léir nach bhfuil.[2]

****

Yarn #54 Footnotes
[1] Good health, and may God be with all here!
[2] May God bless all here, and all those that aren't.

One Weekend in February 1964 –
Ma Rockett & The Metal Man

One weekend in February, nineteen-sixty-four,
*   three friends and meself, we went down to Tramore.*
There 'neath The Metal Man by the cliffs we did lay,
*   soakin' the sunshine that belonged to late May.*
The wind and sun's shadows set our heads ablaze,
*   as there on the grass, by the sea we did gaze.*
Just like the sad sailor, still up on his tower,
*   pointin' out his lost brothers, and lookin' so dour.*

*   To Lie on the Grass by the sea, the sea,*
*   to lie on the grass by the sea.*
*   The wind blows the grass and it tickles me,*
*   the wind blows the grass by the sea.*
*   A ladybird lands on the back of me hand,*
*   the birds in the air sang a song 'twas so grand,*
*   To lie on the grass by the sea, the sea,*
*   to lie on the grass by the sea.*

Two fields to the roadway, we were hungry and dry,
*   couldn't wait any longer, we thought we'd soon die.*
We went to Ma Rocketts, laid out the half-crown[1],
*   two pints and a third one, by the fire we put down.*
Then into Ma's kitchen, we ate a crubeen[2],
*   we stared at a supper like we'd never seen.*
A basin of crubeens, another of spud[3],
*   we tried hard to consume them – if only we could.*

And not havin' a place to lie down for the night,
*   Ma offered her hay, and we told her we might*
and we did. And next mornin' we woke with the birds,
*   we were soon again noddin' when we heard ol' Ma's words,*
"Come into yer breakfast, ye'll be late for Mass."
*   She looked smaller than ever down there on the grass.*
She'd been up for hours, tidyin' up the place,
*   grey hair all askew 'round her kind shiny face.*

302

Rollin' off the soft hay, we slid into our clothes,
  we greeted the day as bright as a rose.
Blue sky, not a scamall[4], not a shadow in sight,
  the kind of a day that you just couldn't fight.
Then into our breakfast, Ma's welcomin' door,
  eggs, rashers[5], tomatoes and sausage go leor[6].
And Ma in her apron, her hands on her hips,
  sayin' "Mass is fast comin', for God's sake call it quits."

Then after the Mass with its lecture so long,
  we went back to Ma Rockett, who'd done us no wrong.
There she was smilin', in her best Sunday black,
  so anxious to know when we would be back.
"'Twas so nice to have yees, ye're such lovely lads."
  Ma Rockett the angel, made us all feel the sads . . . to be leavin'.

To Lie on the Grass – Niall Kavanagh

I STARTED WRITING THESE WORDS that weekend, and after fifty plus years I think they might be just about finished. Cess, Tommy, Tony and I had a memorable time down there in Tramore, County Waterford.

****

IT'S EARLY 1964. THE ANXIETY OF WHAT ELSE might happen after Jack Kennedy's 22 November 1963 assassination is still very much present throughout the world, including Ireland.

JFK in Dublin.

I had seen JFK and his wife, Jackie parading by on Dame Street during their visit to Ireland in May 1963. The assassination had darkened the Christmas and New Year holidays. A good weekend away is what we need, and what Luke Kelly has just shared with us sounds like something that fits the bill. Luke and his friends, Ronnie Drew, Barney McKenna, Ciarán Bourke and John Sheehan are in the back music room of *O'Donoghues* pub on Merrion Row; Cess, Tommy, Tony and I are with them. We're playing our instruments, singing songs, drinking Guinness, and partaking in one of the many impromptu ballad sessions the pub is renowned for. Luke has told us of a pub in Tramore County Waterford, called *Ma Rocketts*, and that the famed Irish ballad group *The Clancy Brothers* had started their singing there. The thoughts of visiting are immediately appealing. Straight away we decide to go. Luke and his friends would later become the world famous *Dubliners*.

The Dubliners: Ciaran, Luke, John, Barney & Ronnie.

WE ARRIVE in Tramore just after eleven o'clock on what is an unusually spring-like, February morning. Seldom visited until 1853, when the Great Southern Railway made a branch line from Waterford City to the tiny town, Tramore quickly became the place to go for sand, sea and at Irish-like intervals, the sun. We spend some time strolling through the town's quaint, quiet streets. Small, well-cared-for, thatched-roof homes painted in white, adorn the winding streets. It's off-season, and the sleepy little township appears to have decided to have a lie-in this morning. The shops, and what seems to be an equal number of pubs, are thinking about opening, but they're in no rush about it. The few people we run into are of the same mind: nobody in a hurry to go anywhere and having all day to get there.

Tramore Town.

We stop and ask an old man to help us with directions. Leaning with his back resting against a wall, he looks very much a local. He has a white clay smoking pipe, stuck into his close-to-being-toothless mouth, and firmly supported with his right hand. He has a bent blackthorn walking stick held in his left hand.

"So it's Mary Rockett's place yee're lookin' for. Is dat right?" says the old man, speaking from a narrowly open mouth with the pipe still in it.

"Yes," Tommy replies. *We may have made a mistake in choosing him to help us arrive at our destination.*

"Well now," the old man continues, removing the pipe from his mouth. "Der's a number of ways yee could be goin' if it's Mary's place yee'd be wantin' to go to. Now . . . Let me see: yes, yes . . . Ah sure no . . . Dat would bring yee way out of yeer way. No, no . . . Now and dat might be the better way. Yes, dat would get yee der the quickest. Dat's the best way to go."

The old man discusses the matter with himself until they both arrive at the same conclusion. He returns the pipe to his mouth.

"Sure aren't yee all fine young men, and wouldn't yee be well able for it?" says he, pipe bouncing but skilfully held so as not to fall to the ground.

"Sure we are," answers Tommy. "We're ready, willin' and able."

"Right den," says the old man. Once again the pipe is removed from his mouth. "If yee were to turn 'round right now, and if yee were to walk down der to the trá more – dat's Gaelic for the big strand – now and if yee were to do dat, wouldn't yee be well able to see *The Metal Man*; he's up der at the end of the strand, standin' on his tower, lookin' out to sea. Ever since 1823, he's been pointin' to where he, along with his two brothers and 390 other poor souls, went down with the sailing ship *Sea Horse* into the icy-cold waters of Tramore Bay."

The Sea Horse.

305

"And wasn't it only himself and twenty-nine other men who came back up," he solemnly continues. "And for all those 363 poor souls who didn't – may they rest in peace." The old man completes his informative reverie by blessing himself: "In ainm an Athar, agus an Mhic, agus an Spioraid Naoimh, Áiméan. [7]"

"But arrah, and sure isn't Mary's place very close to *The Metal Man*," he declares, with a toothless smile and a lot of satisfaction. "All yee'll have to do is walk up to dat ol' sailor, and once yee're der, sure isn't Mary's place only two fields in from the cliffs."

"Thanks very much, sir," says Cess. We say our goodbyes to the old man by the sea and head towards the strand.

We now know where *Ma Rocketts* is. In addition, we've been reminded of the 1816 tragic capsizing of the *Sea Horse*. And we've been introduced to *The Metal Man*; once we're on the strand, we can see him, far in the distance, up high on his tower pointing out to sea. There are two other matching towers close by, both of which are unmanned. This is my first time in Tramore, but I've read about the *Sea Horse* and *The Metal Man*.

*Tramore's big strand: The Metal Man's three towers
are far in the distance.*

The Metal Man was erected in 1823 as a warning to other vessels and in memory of those who had drowned when the sailing ship *Sea Horse* tragically capsized in a violent winter storm on the 30 January 1816. The three towers were erected at the behest of the single survivor of three seafaring brothers, who were all part of the seventeen-man crew of the ill-fated *Sea Horse*. The surviving brother, symbolised by a metal sculpture of a sailor pointing out to sea, was placed on one of the towers; the other two towers were left unmanned, symbolising the two drowned brothers.

The *Sea Horse* had been chartered by the English Army to transport sixteen commissioned officers and 287 soldiers. They

306

were coming from Ramsgate Kent to their new assignment in Cork City. Seventy-one military family members were with them, 33 women and 38 children. Also onboard were the ship's captain, seventeen crew members, and one luckless naval officer passenger who had chosen to board the *Sea Horse* as his means of connecting with his own docked vessel in Cork. The *Sea Horse*'s onboard count was 393 souls.

Following two days of struggling with the raging storm's powerful winds and enormous waves, the *Sea Horse* was finally crippled and capsized in Tramore Bay. Only thirty survived the disaster: the captain, two crewmen, eight commissioned officers, and nineteen soldiers. Months would pass before the last of the bodies of the 363 lost men, women and children were washed ashore. Some of the drowned were never found.

The *Sea Horse* was one of a convoy of three ships. Astonishingly, that severe winter storm also capsized the *Boadicea*; 190 of the 324 onboard died when the vessel floundered on a shoal near Courtmacsherry Bay in Cork. The third ship, the *Lord Melville*, also struggled on a shoal near Kinsale, but it stayed afloat. However, eight men, four women, and a child tried to reach shore on a lifeboat; big waves overturned the boat, drowning all bar one of the men.

That violent, January 1816 storm claimed a total of 565 lives.

"*THE METAL MAN* looks far away, doesn't he?" says Tommy.

"He feckin' well does!" Tony confirms.

The multifarious way the old man had directed us is giving us some real concern. Being aware of the treacherous ways of Ireland's south-eastern coastline, an abundance of confidence is absent. Nevertheless, we now know where the old pub is, and we do want to get there. After a minute of pensive consideration, we do as the old man had suggested – we commence on our committed journey to *Ma Rocketts* via the trá more. There has to be another way by road, but being the adventurous type we are, off we go.

"Anyway, it'll be smashin' walkin' along the strand in the sun," says Cess, trying to brighten our spirits.

"You're right, Cess," says I. "This coastline beats the hell out of Skerries. It's beautiful, and the sand is firm for us to walk on."

It's three in the afternoon and being February, darkness will be coming soon. For now, the sun is low in a clear blue sky. It's giving a surprising amount of heat for this time of year. We pick up our step and proceed along the strand.

As we make our way, we take in the beauty of the ocean and the grassy dunes. We see flocks of black-backed gulls and curlews. Being from Dublin city, we're familiar with the bigger white seagulls and their bawling calls, but these smaller black-backed gulls almost sing.

Coming near to the end of the strand – it's over two miles long – the coastline changes to a gradually-rising, cliff-like seafront; there's little sand, and it's increasingly rocky. Our shadows, whenever the rising cliffs to our right permit it, stretch out to the sea. The early twilight plays with the incoming tide's colours; greens and blues in many shades, with the sea's white surf, softly splashing its presence.

Turning a bend, we see *The Metal Man*, still farther away than we'd like him to be, but much nearer than when we first saw him from the town.

The Metal Man.

The day quickly turns to night; the sky changes from bright clear blue to a dark and star-studded canopy. There's no sign of a moon. In its absence, the stars seem to be shining brighter than normal. We stop and lie down on one of the many big rocks to rest and capture the early night's magic. The Plough and the Big Dipper, along with all their buddies, twinkle down on us. We're treated to a long string of falling stars lasting for over five minutes.

It has become considerably darker. As we continue on our journey, we notice the cliff's rapidly increasing height. Disturbingly, we realise that the task of climbing to *The Metal Man* might be a tough one, and we also note that the incoming tide is well on its way. These realisations are of concern to us, but they're soon joined by the pleasant discovery that our new friend is close at hand. In a few minutes, we'll be right beneath *The Metal Man*.

We are in the dark, not for the first or last time in our lives, but this time literally so. Night's black blanket is upon us; it is only by the light of the stars that we can make our way on our difficult last leg of the old man's 'best way' to *Ma Rocketts*.

The night's sea, unlike the earlier part of the day which was like a warm summer day, is winter cold. In another situation, we'd say the sea is as calm as a mill pond, however, our circumstance is such that the incoming tide is starting to present itself as being perilous. We all slip in, up to our arse, a number of times. The frequency of Tommy's visits far exceed those of the rest of us; he's wearing leather-soled boots while the rest of us have rubber soles.

"Jaysus wept!" splutters Tommy, as he balances precariously on the slippery rocks covered with wet seaweed. "We're forever in the dark, but this sucks. If I could lay me hands on that ol' fella I'd strangle him. I swear I'd like to kill the ol' bollocks."

"Lads," says Cess, "listen up: we have to be careful. The tide is comin' in fast. We have to start up the cliff now. If we don't, we just might end up like *The Metal Man*'s brothers."

Cess, the old man of the group, is right, and we all know it.

"Will ye shut the fuck up, Cess!" responds Tommy. "Here we are in the dark, between the devil and the deep blue, soaked from the arse down, and here you are, tellin' us we're goin' to end up like that dead pair out there. Give us a break, will ye!?"

"No," says Tony. "Cess is right. Getting up the cliff is what we should be doin', and the sooner, the better."

"Right," says Cess, looking at Tommy. "So let's shut up, all of us. Stop roarin' at each other and let's get goin'."

Cess is a few months older than Tommy, Tony and I. We all accept him as being the sensible one. We happily treat him as a figurehead with the rights and responsibilities of leadership. Cess keeps us all in line.

Tommy looks away, then up at the cliff, muttering to himself. "I've a pain in me balls with Cess, always with his moanin', lookin' at the dark side."

The Metal Man cliffs.

We follow Tommy's gaze, each of us looking up at the foreboding precipice, each of us searching for the best way to get to the top, and out of Tramore Bay's deepening and increasingly treacherous cold waters.

****

Yarn #55 Footnotes
[1] A two shillings and sixpence Imperial Monetary System coin.
[2] A pig's foot.
[3] Potatoes.
[4] Cloud.
[5] Strips of bacon.
[6] Lots of.
[7] In the name of the Father, and of the Son, and of the Holy Spirit, Amen.

One Weekend in February 1964 – Ups and Downs, the Slide & All Alone?

THE CLIFF HEIGHT UPON WHICH *THE METAL MAN* perches is all of one-hundred feet. It's at the apex of a rising coastline cliff that starts near the end of the big strand. Some scattered clouds have joined the stars, reducing the already limited visibility, and preventing us from being able to see the last thirty feet of the climb. It looks like it has a relatively easy slope for the first fifty feet, after which it gradually gets steeper. Without a doubt, a difficult ascent, but we're confident that we'll be able to manage the climb.

"Right lads," says Cess. "Who's goin' first?"

This enquiry causes panic amongst us.

"I think the tallest of us should go first," I suggest. "That would give the longest stretch at the top as we go up."

Thinking of myself as being genius-like with this brilliant logic, I am amazed at Tommy's irate response – Tommy is the tallest.

"No way!" shouts Tommy. "The thoughts of me climbin' up this feckin' cliff is givin' me the willies. I think that ol' bollocks back in the town wasn't the full shillin'. What the hell was he thinkin'? Did he think we had wings or what? No, Niall . . . You can feck off. I'm not goin' up first."

Tommy's angry response puts a quick end to any chance of acceptance of the brilliant logic contained in my suggestion.

"Why don't you go first?" Tommy continues. "I remember seein' you climbin' in Skerries. You were great, wasn't he, lads?"

311

It's difficult not to take this as being anything other than a compliment, so I shut my mouth. And then I start to think. *Bein' first mightn't be a bad thing. The first one up wouldn't have the stones and shit loosened by the precedin' climbers fallin' on him.*

"What do you say, Niall?" says Tony. "Tommy's right about you bein' a brilliant climber."

Another compliment, and seldom if ever does anyone get one of those from Tony.

"I don't know," I reply.

"I think they're right, Niall," says Cess. "Will you go first? If we can't agree, we'll have to pull straws. And lads, look at the tide. It's comin' in."

That does it!

"OK, Cess! I'll go first," I shout. "I'll be first, Tony will be second, Tommy third and you can be at the end. Now for fuck's sake, let's get out of here."

A four-person free climbing of a hundred-foot cliff in a dark, cold night was never in our plans.

"*Ma Rocketts* had better be worth riskin' our fuckin' lives for, that's all I can say," says Tommy.

"Put a sock in it, will you!?" says Tony. "That's no way to start the climb. It's goin' to be tough enough without listenin' to you moanin' all the way up."

"I'll zigzag my way," says I. "In that way, the loose stuff won't be fallin' on top of the three of you."

"Good idea, Niall," says Cess. "We should have about eight feet between us – right?

"Yeep. Dependin' on the way I decide to go as I'm goin' up, that eight feet will allow me not to be worryin' about you followin' and the loose stuff fallin' down."

A quick calculation shows us that the top climber, me, would be about half of the way up when the last climber, Cess, would start climbing. With this understood we start our climb.

The first forty-odd feet is easy enough. The cliff face is predominately stone with plenty of foot and hand holds to choose from. Nonetheless, it's demanding at all times with changes of direction frequently required. Our wet lowers and the night's cold wind, which is getting colder as we proceed upwards, combine to make us a long way from comfortable. This and the fact that I'm coming close to being more than half way up, and don't know what is ahead, gives me a lot to be uneasy about.

"Niall, can you see the top yet?" shouts Tommy.

"No, not yet. So far so good. When I do reach the top, I'm goin' to kiss that sailor's arse, not to mention the tower he's standin' on."

It's strange how humour affects us in times of stress. We all simultaneously laugh out loud at this planned delay in the execution of my courting intent. The echoes of our laughter join in, and it takes all in our power not to fall due to the merriment of the moment. We'd stop laughing, but then the echoes from the cliffs and sea would continue, feeding us to laugh all the more. How ironic if we were to fall from the effects of genuine hearty laughter.

"Shut up, Niall, will you?" says Tony. "I nearly fell with ye."

"Yeah, Niall," grunts Tommy. "Concentrate on gettin' us up and off this feckin' cliff, never mind the craic. Time enough for jokin' when we're on terra-bleedin'-firma!"

"How does it look, Niall?" comes a nervous shout from Cess who has just started to climb.

"I can't see all the way up. It's gettin' steeper, but if it continues to go as it has, we should be up and off to *Ma Rocketts* in no time. I just want to get my breath. Let's take a minute to rest a bit."

I need the rest. The rough stone cliff has taken its toll on my hands; some of my fingers are starting to bleed. Resting on the cliff face, our laughter and all its echoes are replaced with the loud silence of where we are.

I look out at the calm, dark star-lit sea. The stars seem to have vastly increased in number and brightness. Some of those black-backed gulls are still out flying around trying to lengthen their day. The starlight hitting the gulls' white feathers makes them change to black and silvery blue. *As me Da once told me, 'To lengthen the day you've got to rob from the night.'* I glance at my watch; its luminous hands tell me it's a little after eight o'clock.

313

Black-backed gulls.

"Right, lads!" I shout, breaking the night's eerie silence. "We're wastin' good drinkin' time. It's eight o'clock, and closin' time is eleven. Are we ready to start up again?"

"Let's go!" comes the response from below.

"The thought of downin' a couple of good pints is killin' me," yells Tommy. "If you get us up this cliff, Niall, you won't have to put your hand in your pocket." And with that appealing offer from Tommy to lay out for my drink, we recommence our assent.

The cliff's incline is now close to vertical. The stone face continues and supplies the required holds, but as I move up, I notice there is more loose earth and stone starting to appear.

"For Jay's sake!" says Tony. "You're throwin' an awful lot of shite down on us!"

"Sorry about that," I respond. "As we go up, there's more and more loose earth. You've got to stay farther away from me."

Tommy and Cess had also been hit with some of the ominous falling earth and stone. I change direction, and that for now solves the problem. I'm getting near to the top; I can hear the noise of the wind blowing the grass above. The air smells salty, grass sweet. It's colder, but the thoughts of how near I am to the top gives me the warmth needed to continue.

I'm about twenty feet from terra firma when it all goes wrong. The firm stone face surface changes to loose stony earth. Looking up, I can see the outline of the cliff-top's windblown long grass framed in the star-filled night sky. I try to advance, changing directions to the left, then to the right. Each time I try to make a hand hold, the loose earth comes away and falls. The cliff-top now looks as far away as those stars.

I'm scared. In one moment, after a lot of exhausting failed effort, I see the absolute horror of what the situation is.

314

"We're bollixed!" I holler. "There's no way we can get up this fuckin' cliff! I'm only twenty feet from the top, but it might as well be a hundred feckin' miles. We've got to get back down."

The lack of response from Tony, Tommy or Cess is haunting.

"Do you hear me?" I roar. "We've got to get back down!"

"Jays, Niall, are you sure?" shouts Tommy.

"I'm tellin' you. The last of the climb is all earth and loose stone. There's no way we can do it. We're bollixed, and that's that. We just have to go back down."

"And goin' back down isn't goin' to be easy," says Tony. "What do you think, Niall? You and I will have the worst of it. Tommy and Cess are about half way down already. It's goin' to be much more difficult goin' down than it was comin' up. And I'm frozen. My hands are bleedin' and nearly fallin' off me."

"Niall, if we're as bollixed as you say we are, we'll have to go down," shouts Cess, sounding a lot like what he is, a leader.

"We've no alternative," he continues. "It's a little after ten now, we're all frizzin-well-frozen, and it's goin' to get colder. So let's start down. I'll go first, and I'll try to make the path as clear as I can. Once I'm down, I'll let you know. Then you come down Tommy, then Tony and Niall will follow. As we descend, we've got to make sure we clear any shit we find. That will make it easier for us all."

"Well . . . This puts an end to our couple of pints," says Tommy. "Less overtime for Arthur Birney, and a drought for us. I'd a bad feelin' about all this from the start. That ol' bollocks in the town was out to get us from the beginnin'."

"Shut up, Tommy!" demands Cess. "Let's help each other get out of this bloody cold. Otherwise just shut the fuck up! Right, Tommy!?" continues Cess, directing his leadership response to not only Tommy but to us all.

"I'm startin' down," says Cess. "Let's all keep our energies and thoughts on gettin' off this cliff. No moanin' and groanin' from any of us." Cess, as usual, is perfect in his timing and taking control of the situation.

I'm exhausted, I'm freezing, and I'm very worried. During all the serious discussion, I've repositioned myself in a manner that allows me to face outwards, my arse wedged into the cliff face. My backpack, cushions me nicely, giving some needed relaxation to my aching cold body. Listening to Cess and to what the plan is, gives me the bad news that I'll be perched up here for some time before making my descent, maybe for another hour or more.

I have a bird's eye view, albeit in the dark, of everything the night's starlight allows. The few accumulated clouds have been blown away, and my eyes have adjusted to the night's starlight. Looking down I can see Tony, Tommy, and Cess clearly. Cess is working his way down; he's being obsessively attentive to his self-inflicted obligation of cleaning his path as he goes. It takes him about half an hour to reach the bottom, a bottom that has risen to meet him; the tide is fully in, calm with little or no meaningful wave splashing, but it has significantly reduced the rocky shoreline. That will make our return to the big strand a wet and cold one.

"Are you OK, Cess?" I shout.

"Yeah, I've made it!" responds Cess. "The tide has come in, and that's a pain, but once we all get down, we'll be OK. I think there's enough shoreline for us to go on. We should be able to get up to the top just a little bit farther back."

"Tommy, you start down now," Cess continues. "Keep to the path I took – then you'll be smilin'."

"OK, Cess. Here I come," says Tommy. "If you see me goin' the wrong way, give me a heads-up."

"Don't I always," Cess responds in jest.

Once again the power of timely humour gives a small break from the pressures we're feeling. There are no echoes this time, and just enough humour to keep our spirits up.

Tommy's descent is about fifteen more feet than Cess's was. That means another half-hour plus before he'll reach the bottom. Then Tony will go, and that'll take another three-quarter of an hour. I'll be perched up here with my arse in the cliff face for another hour plus. The cold night air is eating into me. The thought of another hour's exposure adds a lot to my discomfort.

I'm freezing; to increase blood circulation, I shake myself. The stony earth holding me into the cliff face suddenly breaks away. I slide perilously for about ten feet until a godsend, solid piece of rock, catches me between my legs, stopping the deadly descent. The sudden halt tries to hurl me forward, but by some magical means, I'm able to hold on.

"What the hell!" roars Tony. He's just to my right. "Are ye OK, Niall? For Jay's sake, what happened!?"

We are near enough to each other to see the terror in our eyes.

"I was shakin' myself so's to get warm, and the feckin' thing gave way," I answer. "I nearly cut my balls off landin' on this rock. I feel like they're in my mouth. Christ almighty, what have we gotten ourselves into? Are you OK, Tony?"

"Yea, but for Jay's sake, Niall, no more shakin'."

"What the fuck happened?" yells Tommy.

"I nearly fell off this fuckin' cliff; that's what happened," I answer. "It's freezin', and I almost lost my manhood hittin' this rock I'm sittin' on."

My backpack is now pushing me forward. Quickly, and with great care, I move it to my front, securing the two bottom straps around two of my trousers belt loops.

"Are you OK, Niall?" shouts Cess.

"Yes. I'm worried about my unborn children, but I'm OK."

"For Jay's sake, Niall, stay still 'til it's your turn to come down," says Tommy. "None of us will have children, or anythin' feckin' else if we're not careful."

I've just been through a near death experience. As I sit on my perch, every fibre of my being lets me know about it. I piss in my pants, not just a squirt, a real Powerscourt. Uncontrollably, it pours out, down both legs and into my boots. *That's one way of gettin' warm. I hope Tony didn't hear the falls or smell me smelly pee.* I smell it, but the wind is dissipating the stink upwards.

"How old are we, Niall?" asks Tony, bringing me out of my personal urinary thoughts. "Are we twenty-one or twenty-two?"

"For feck's sake, Tony. What the fuck's up with you? We're nearly twenty-fuckin'-one! And if we ever get down from here, maybe we'll get to bein' twenty-fuckin'-two."

"I was just thinkin'," continues Tony. "How old was your dad when he died?"

"For Jay's sake, Tony, shut the fuck up! He was forty-nine! What's with all this age and dyin' stuff? Once Tommy gets down, you'll be on your way, and then I'll follow. So cut out all this crap. You're givin' me the willies."

"I'm nearly down," shouts Tommy, interrupting the depressing conversation Tony and I were having.

"It's not too bad once you get down a bit," Tommy continues. "But take it slow. I nearly slipped once or twice."

"You're doin' great, Tommy," shouts Cess.

It's eleven-thirty, and in the darkness I can just barely make out Tommy at the bottom, Cess cheering him on to the finish line.

"I'm down," shouts Tommy, "and thanks be to Jays for that. Come on Tony, move your arse and let's get the fuck out of here."

"Two down, and two to go," shouts Cess. "Tony, come on down! We're waitin' for ye! Then you, Niall."

Cess, once again, is doing his best to keep our spirits up.

"It'll be more than an hour before I start down," says I. "It'll be tomorrow before we're all out of this shite. Let's go, Tony. Are you ready?"

"Ready, willin' and I hope to fuck, able. You hang in there, Niall. I'll be as quick as I can. Good luck."

And with that, Tony turns and starts his dissent.

"I'll miss you, Tony, up here on my own. Forget about that as quick as you can stuff. Take it easy. You and I have the worst of it. You've got to be careful, particularly in the beginnin'."

The moment Tony commences his descent I'm consumed by a gigantic new wave of fear and apprehension. For the first time, I'm considering how exactly I'm going to get down. Ever since I slid to my new perch, holding on has been my only consideration. Now this, to me utterly new reality of actually descending is hitting me. I panic at the thoughts of even moving. My legs are straddling my rock, and it is only that rock that's keeping me up. I'm still facing outwards, and while my hands have some hold, my feet are just dangling in space.

The full realisation of my perilous condition plus the midnight cold wind, join to freeze me. I want to scream out, but I can't. I try, but nothing comes out. *Jesus wept! I can't even talk. I'm not*

318

goin' to be able to move, never mind climb down. For feck's sake Niall, relax, or you're goin' to die!

Desperately, I try to relax. I lean back against the cliff face as best I can and look up at the night sky. All the stars are twinkling at me, but this time I'm also seeing God up there, orchestrating everything. *Jesus, please help me. I promise you, if ye get me out of this, I'll, I'll do anythin' ye want. I swear I will. Please give me the strength to do what needs to be done to get me down safe.* I sit on my rock, stricken with fear of what might happen. Stinging tears running down my face makes me realise I'm crying, and just like my pissing, uncontrollably.

"Way to go, Tony," I hear Cess roar out.

In the preceding minutes, I had been in my lonely world. Cess's distant voice comes as a big surprise.

"Are you nearly down, Tony?" I amaze myself at hearing my own voice. *Ye never know, but maybe God did hear me. I have me voice back, and that's worth somethin'.*

"I've a little bit more to go," answers Tony. "You were right about the first part. I nearly fell a few times. Watch yourself. I've cleared as much as I could, but there's a lot of shit."

I badly want to share the horror of my situation, but I don't know how to. *I'm bollixed is a good way to start, but then what? Call for a helicopter, maybe? I just don't know.*

"Made it," hollers Tony.

"Brilliant," says Tommy. "Now, Niall . . . Come on down."

"And Niall, the tide seems to have stopped risin'," says Cess.

I pause before I try to share my dilemma with them. *I've got to tell them, and that's that. Just tell them straight; between us, we'll come up with somethin'.* My introduction goes as planned.

"I'm bollixed, lads," I blurt out. "I can't move from where I am, never mind climb down. My feet are danglin' in space, and I can't move left or right without fallin'."

"Niall, if you're messin', I'll kill ye!" Tommy shouts. "Come the fuck down!"

"Jays, Niall," says Tony. "Are you sure you can't move?"

"Lads!" interjects Cess. "We know Niall well enough to know he wouldn't be sayin' what he's sayin' if it wasn't true. So let's

319

decide what to do. What's happened, happened. We have to get whatever help is needed to get Niall off this feckin' cliff."

"Niall," shouts Cess, "are you able to hold on? Are you secure enough to hang in while we go and get help?"

"Yeah. The rock I'm hooked on is safe. I'm frozen, and that's what's hurtin' most. Going for help is the right thing to do. A helicopter would be great, but there's no chance of that. The best way to go is for someone to throw a rope down from the top and drag me up. What do you think?"

"That's what we'll do then," replies Cess. "I reckon it'll take us about an hour before we can get you the rope. But before we move, and don't get annoyed, but are you sure there's no way you can move from where ye are?"

"Positive. Ever since Tony started down, I've been lookin' at the shit I'm in. I can't move without fallin'."

"OK, Niall," says Cess. "We'll be as quick as we can,"

"You're an awful pain in the hole, Niall," cries Tommy. "You'd do anythin' for attention."

"Hang in there, Niall," says Tony. "We won't be long."

"See you, Niall," shouts Cess. "Let's go lads!"

From my bird-like position, I see the committed trio pick and splash their way through the rocky coastline back towards the strand and the closest possible climbing point to terra firma. They quickly disappear.

A bird's eye view.

THE NEW day is an hour old, and I'm now all alone, or at least I think I am. *What day is it anyway? Saturday. If ever I've been alone, this is it. And it'll be an hour before they'll be back with the rope. What'll I do with meself? I've got to keep warm and stay awake. I don't want to nod off and fall to me death.*

320

I start to do what I often do when I find myself alone. I start a poem. I imagine I'm safely up and lying on the grass.

To lie on the grass by the sea the sea,
to lie on the grass by the sea.
The wind blows the grass, and it tickles me,
the wind blows the grass by the sea . . .

The ever increasing cold, plus the disgusting stink of my pee, soon puts an end to the mental powers of concentration my poem demands. So's to generate some body heat, I use my hands to rub those parts of my body I can reach. *I wonder what me Ma is doin' right now. She's probably in bed, fast asleep. Exactly like I'd be if I wasn't stuck up here. Unless, of course, if Clare were with me; then it would be far from asleep I'd be.* Clare is all a young man dreams of – big voluptuous boobs, a smashing kisser, and a good mind. She's an art student at Martins College of Art & Design in London. I met her on the Silver Strand in Wicklow while she was on holidays with her family. Her home is in Wales. *I won't die wonderin'. I wonder where she is right now. Over in London messin' around with that arsehole, Frank Smythe, I bet. Win some, lose some. All's fair in love and war, and all that shite. Me Da knows where I am. He's up there with the big guy and sees what's happenin'. Hey Da, will you put a good word in for me?*

Suddenly, I feel a creepy sensation in my legs and feet. I can't reach down for fear of my top body weight hurling me forward. *What the hell!?* I gently shake my legs so as not to put extra pressure on the rock. The creepy feeling continues, if not intensifies. I look down at my knees, and to my horror I see hundreds of ants crawling all over me. I'm not alone! There are thousands of the little buggers, attracted by the scent of my pee, gathering together for a big ant feast, and I'm the main course.

OK, Niall. Take a deep breath. Let it out slowly. Right. The choice is to let them do what they like as far as me legs and feet are concerned or die. It's as simple as that. They'll stay down there for the pee, and they'll leave the rest of me alone. Jays, they'll be up 'round me flute. Fuck it! I can do nothin' about it.

The idea of opening my fly and holding myself so's to prevent the ants crawling into my meatus, hits me. That would be a good way to guard against any damage to that significant part of my developing manhood. I quickly zip down and grab him with my left hand. *Got ye! Nothin's goin' to happen to you. Screw those ants.*

The ants are the small, less aggressive Irish kind. Not like those big mothers in that movie, I once saw; Indians buried some cowboys up to their necks in an anthill, and the ants ate the poor buggers alive. The idea of slipping my trousers off comes and goes. I'm frozen with them on and would probably die of cold without them. The problem of having nothing to do but sit waiting for the rope to hit me is solved: my full attention is directed towards the single task of killing any and all ants with my one free hand.

It seems to take forever, and who knows how many ants die on that cliff face, when, as if from heaven, I hear the beautiful sound of a human voice right above me.

****

One Weekend in February 1964 – the Rope, Three Friends & Terra Firma

"**A**RE YOU OK, NIALL?" SHOUTS TOMMY. "I'm down here with my langer in my left hand, I'm bein' eaten alive by ants, I'm freezin' me bollocks off, and you ask me am I OK!" I shout my response. "No, I'm not OK! Did you get the fuckin' rope? Throw it down to me, quick for Christ's sake!"

The sound of Tommy's, Tony's and Cess's loud laughter is the immediate response to my impassioned demands.

"Stop the feckin' laughin', you eejits. I'm nearly dyin' down here. Throw down the bleedin' rope!!"

"Jays," says Cess. "What you said was the funniest. We've got the rope, and we're goin' to lower it down now. We've made a lasso; you can slip it over your shoulders and under your arms. Once you've got it 'round you, roar and we'll pull you up."

"And another thing, Niall," says Tony. "Put your langer away before you come up. We're sick enough laughin' at you without havin' to see your one-eyed monster."

Again, more raucous laughter from the three of them.

"When I do get up, I'm goin' to kick your arses," I yell.

"Thanks be to God you're OK, Niall," says Tommy.

"Well, I'm not up yet, so continue worryin'. Get that fuckin' rope down here. These ants are crawlin' all over me."

"Here it comes, Niall," shouts Cess.

I slip the lowered rope over my shoulders and under my arms, but not before I kiss it as lovingly as I had ever kissed Clare or Colleen for that matter.

"Pull me up. And for feck's sake don't let me fall."

323

"On the count of three," shouts Cess. "Niall, you'll be up here with us in a minute. Right lads – one, two, three!"

Up I go; pulled from my life-saving rock and dangling in mid-air. *I've a bit farther to go before I'm safe. In the meantime, I'm in God's hands and those of my three friends.*

"One, two, three!" Cess repeats.

Up I go again, still dangling in mid-air. *Well Da, thanks for puttin' the word in. And Jesus – I'll keep me promise. Knock, and as you say yourself, the door will be opened.*

"One, two, three!" says Cess for the third time.

"He's almost up, lads," continues Cess. "One more pull."

"Cess," I shout. "I'll stretch me arms up and out with this last pull. Grab them when you see me come up over the top."

"OK, Niall, I'll grab ye, don't worry. The last one, lads; one, two, three!"

The sight of the three of them on terra firma, with Cess's hands reaching out to grab me is, simply put, divine.

"Have you got a hold of him, Cess?" asks Tommy.

"Yes. Just give another tug, and he's safe. One, two, three!"

And there I am, kissing the grass the sailor's tower stands on. Rolling over, I look up and see *The Metal Man* standing on his tower. *I'll have to delay the kissin' of his arse. I had more than enough climbin'.* Instead of the promised kiss, I give him a nod.

Tommy, Tony, and Cess throw themselves on me. We all share in a childlike roll on the grass, congratulating ourselves on the entire group's survival.

I'd been on the cliff for more than five hours; I fully realise how lucky I am.

"It's nearly two o'clock in the mornin'," says Tony. "Where are we goin' to lay up for the night? I'm whacked from all the runnin' we did gettin' the rope."

"And Niall, thanks for puttin' your langer away," Tony adds. And on comes more uncontrollable laughter. This time, I join in.

"Jays," exclaims Tommy, interrupting the moment. "What's that fuckin' stink? Is it comin' from you, Niall?"

With the joy and excitement of being saved and finally back together with my three friends, I had forgotten about the ants, and also about pissing all over myself. The ants are still crawling all over me. I jump up. In the cold wind, I strip naked and run around like a flaming idiot, shaking the discarded clothes and beating myself with them in an insane effort to get rid of the many ants feasting on me.

"The feckin' ants!" I scream. "They're eatin' me alive!"

Surprisingly, all three of my friends take my ridiculous behaviour very seriously. Each picks up a piece of my discarded clothing and commences to beat the ants off me. In preference to handling that which he had disgustingly discovered was my damp underpants, Tommy takes his jacket off to use as a weapon,

"Jays, Niall," Tommy splutters. "The only underpants I've ever held is me own," he continues, as he hurls them to the ground and starts walloping me with his jacket.

Finally, I just stand there, exhausted. Bollocks naked, and with the greatest humility, I let my three friends divest my tortured body of those ants. With the kindest and gentility usually reserved for the most intimate of moments, Tommy, Tony and Cess, my three friends, wipe me down from head to toe. All three of them realise that I'm utterly distraught. This pure kindness is done before they realise what the hell they were doing.

"For Jay's sake, Niall; put your pants on," says Tommy.

Those words from Tommy breaks the spell of that extraordinary moment. I look at them all, and I start crying.

"Thanks, lads," I try to say. "You're good to me, and I not only owe you my life, but I love you very much."

"Ah! Shut up, and put your pants on," says Cess. "Wouldn't you do the same for us," he continues. "That's what friends are for, and maybe we're stretchin' it a bit, but what the fuck. Now get dressed, and we'll go and find some place for us to sleep."

I search around for my clothes and start to dress. The wind and shaking had done a good job drying them out. I notice that all of the lads are sniffling: the actual nature of what we had been through is settling in.

"Here's one of your socks," says Tony, throwing the piece of hosiery at me.

"And here's your bleedin' trousers," says Tommy. "Jays, there's that fuckin' stink again. It's comin' from your pants!" Tommy continues, throwing them at me.

"I peed in them," says I with embarrassment. "When I slid down it just came out. I couldn't stop it."

There is a formative moment of silence, broken by Cess.

"If any of us went through what you've gone through we'd have shit ourselves," declares Cess. "Am I right lads? Don't worry about it, Niall. You can wash your trousers, and that'll get rid of the stench. Put them on. This cold must be killin' ye."

The cold night air is close to doing just that. I quickly finish dressing. We gather up the rope and start inland to find a spot where we could lie down for the night and get some much-needed sleep.

"Give me that rope," says I, grabbing it from Tony. "I never thought you could love a rope, but I'm tellin' ye, I love this feckin' thing. Where did you get it from anyway?"

"That's another story," sighs Cess. "We splashed our way along the coast, and it wasn't long before we were able to cut up higher to the top. After a bit of lookin' around, we spotted a light. We ran our way to it as fast as we could, and it was a small cottage."

"Yeah, and we thought we were goin' to be eaten up by a fuckin' big Alsatian," adds Tommy. "The dog came runnin' at us, teeth showin' and roarin' like it thought it was a bleedin' lion!"

"Then an ol' man and his missus came out, and the dog turned into a little lamb, I swear," adds Tony.

"Anyway," continues Cess, "we told them the story. They must have been eighty years old if a day, and at first they didn't, or maybe they couldn't understand what we were goin' on about."

"Yeah," interrupts Tommy. "The pair of them made the ol' bollocks in the town look like Einstein."

"Anyway," repeats Cess, "they finally got the message. The missus went back into the house and came out with the rope. We knew that was as much as they could do for us. We asked if they had a phone, but they didn't. So we said thanks and ran like greyhounds back to *The Metal Man* and you."

"Well, all this is one for the books," says Tony. "Somethin' to tell the grandkids."

"And it proves the GOSS can get through anythin'," says Cess.

"Go GOSS Go!" I roar, and we all repeat the cheer in unison.

The image of me running around like a maniac, naked in the dark, underneath *The Metal Man* at two o'clock in the morning, and the three lads looking on in disbelief, comes crashing into my mind. I start to laugh.

"We don't have a photograph of us, but by Jays, we do have a great memory-graph. And that's goin' to last forever," says I. "I can barely believe it, so I suppose most people who'll hear about it won't believe it at all. But we know what happened, and I know it's goin' to have one heck of an effect on how I think about things from now on. We're growin' up, lads. There's nothin' like nearly dyin' to make you know you're alive."

"Oh!" I exclaim as we continue walking inland. "I started a poem. I think I'll call it, *To Lie on the Grass*. Maybe we'll be able to write a tune for it and give the *Ivy Folk* another ballad to sing."

JUST A field away, we find an old empty cow shed that suits us fine. It's dirty, but then so are we, and we're utterly exhausted – a match made in heaven you could say. We had not eaten all day, and almost simultaneously our empty stomachs let us know about it. With the light of the stars creeping in through the many holes in the cowshed roof, we rummage eagerly through our backpacks.

"What have you got, Niall?" asks Tommy. "I've a couple of Mars Bars. And I've orange juice in my flask."

"I've got a lump of chicken my Ma gave me when I was leavin' this mornin' or yesterday mornin', I should say," I respond. "And I've a bag of Tayto Cheese and Onion, a bit bashed up, but I bet they're good. I've nothin' to drink."

"And I've got two sandwiches," pipes in Tony. "I don't know what's in them, but we don't give a fuck, right?"

"We'll be eatin' like bleedin' kings!" says Cess. "I've a banana, an apple, a bag of raisins and a bottle of water."

We lay out all the stuff, and with surgical exactness, Cess divides our mouth-watering repast into four equal portions.

"We can all share the juice and water," says Tommy.

"Great, Tommy," says Cess. "We'll get this stuff down, and then we'll get the winks. Bon appétit, as the French man said."

"It'd be nice if we had four pints to wash it all down, wouldn't it?" says Tommy. "Let's pretend the juice and water are black."

"Hunger is the best sauce," says I. "That was delicious!"

We all lie back on our separate sleeping bags, and in no particular order, we belch loudly, laughing after each and every belch. This post-meal jollity ends with Tony rendering one of his renowned and much-feared farts.

"Ah!" moans Tony, with the greatest of satisfaction. "That felt good. More room out than in, that's what I say."

"You dirty bugger you, Tony," says Tommy. "Put a cork in it, or we'll throw you out of here."

Relaxing in our well-fed comfort, we all join in and nearly lock-jaw ourselves yawning.

"In the mornin', after gettin' the winks," groans Cess, his yawns interrupting his ability to communicate. "We'll go to *Ma Rocketts*. She won't be open. I suppose we can spend some time at *The Metal Man*. It'll be interestin' to see the cliff in daylight. Don't forget, Niall, you've to climb up and kiss the sailor's arse."

"Fuck it," says I. "I waved at him, and that'll do. I've had enough climbin' to last me a lifetime."

Snuggling into our sleeping bags, we're asleep within minutes.

My last thought before nodding off is of those black and white/silver gulls, flying around, trying to lengthen their day. The pee stench doesn't bother the lads or me. I fall into a deep and peaceful sleep muttering –

To lie on the grass by the sea the sea, to lie . . .

****

WE ALL slept soundly. We woke up to bright sunlight streaming through the holy roof of the cow shed – and there's intended double meaning there – the hallowed dirty shed had covered our weary bodies well.

We crawled out of our sleeping bags to greet the beautiful morning. The sun was low in what was a clear blue sky. The grass under our bare feet was damp from a blanket of morning dew stretching out as far as we could see. We discovered we had been sleeping in a field of precious 'dewels': with the low sunlight's angle, each dew-soaked blade of grass was sparkling.

The *To Lie on the Grass* verses I shared with you earlier, covers the highlights of the remainder of that weekend. Unfortunately, Ma Rockett is no longer with us. She's up in heaven, tidying up the place, cooking her famous crubeens, and welcoming all the newcomers who are lucky enough to have arrived.

Ma Rocketts in 1964.

And the pub is still going strong. It's changed some from when Ma was in charge, but it's still there to greet those who drop in. It's currently run by another Mary and her husband Paddy; Paddy is a grandson of Ma Rockett. Amongst other fine fare, they still serve crubeens. When I recently spoke to Mary, she told me that the business was 'a bit down.' So, for that reason, if for no other, I strongly urge you not to miss out on a visit. You never know, but you might find me sitting at the bar, having a pint and a big plate of crubeens and spuds. If you were to go, and I hope you do, try to make it for a weekend. A weekend, when the Tramore Horse Racing is on would be grand. But I'm advising you; when you do go, take the R675 on out to Newtown Glen Road – never you mind the trá more.

Ma Rocketts today.

****

English/Irish, Protestant/Catholic Stuff

They say that the lakes of Killarney are fair,
*   no stream like the Liffey can ever compare.*
If it's water ye want ye'll find nothin' so rare
*   as the stuff that flows down by the ocean.*

> *The sea, oh the sea, grá geal mo croí,*
> *   long may it roll between England and me.*
> *It's a sure guarantee that someday we'll be free –*
> *   thank God we're Surrounded by Water.*

Tom Moore made his waters meet fame and renown,
*   a lover of anythin' dressed in a crown.*
In brandy the bandy ol' Saxon he'd drown,
*   but throw ner a one into the ocean.*

The Scots have their whisky, the Welsh have their leek,
*   their poets are paid about ten pence a week.*
Provided no hard words 'gainst England they speak,
*   Oh Lord! What a price for devotion!*

The Danes came to Ireland with nothin' to do,
*   but dream of the plunder, ol' Irish they slew.*
"Ye will in yer Viking," said Brian Boru,
*   and he threw them back into the ocean.*

Two foreign ol' monarchs in battle did join,
*   each wantin' their head on the back of a coin.*
If the Irish had sense they'd throw both in the Boyne,
*   and Partition throw into the ocean.*

Surrounded by Water – Dominic Behan (1960)

OVER THE YEARS, while living most of my life out of Ireland, I have frequently been asked to explain what this ongoing English/Irish, Protestant/Catholic 'stuff' is all about. Regrettably, I never seem to have the energy or time to respond in a satisfactory manner, either for myself or the person making the enquiry. The problem is that a respectful, informative response takes more time than any normal conversational reply permits.

Nonetheless, the genuinely interested enquirer is always worthy of a thorough response. Feeling obliged to correct my many past failings in this regard, the way I'll now go about supplying that required apposite response is to share a few personal happenings which expressively pertain to the topic. This yarn and the three that follow should do the job.

****

IRELAND IS ONE-HUNDRED-AND-FIFTY-MILES WIDE and three-hundred-miles deep – roughly half the size of New York State. Comprised of thirty-two counties, it has four provinces: Ulster's nine counties are to the north; Leinster's twelve are to the east; Munster's six are to the south; and Connaught's five counties are to the west.

Map of Ireland showing its four provinces and Northern Ireland.

Much like its preceding eight-hundred years, for the first twenty-two years of the twentieth century, Ireland was considered part of the United Kingdom and governed by England from Westminister. In 1912, following many years of political pressure, a new *Irish Home Rule Bill* was successfully introduced and agreed to; it was scheduled to be implemented in September 1914. However, with the outbreak of World War I in August 1914, its enactment was postponed pending the war's conclusion.

The war ended in 1918, but by then, so much had changed that any real possibility of implementation of the *Irish Home Rule Bill* was considered impossible – by both sides.

331

In response to a) the disastrous success of the *1916 Easter Rising* and the years of continued armed conflict that followed, and b) pressures from Ulster's protestant majority – some powerful pro-British, protestant entities in Dublin and elsewhere throughout the south, added to these pressures – England enacted the *1920 Government of Ireland Act*. The Act purported to divide Ireland into 'two new and separate states': Ulster would become 'Northern Ireland,' and Leinster, Munster, and Connaught would become 'Southern Ireland.' Irish Protestants, especially those in the north, did not want to become part of an independent thirty-two county Irish State with its papist majority – they demanded that they stay part of the mostly protestant United Kingdom.

In July 1921, a truce in the *Irish War of Independence* was declared. In January 1922, after six months of heated, difficult discussions, the *Anglo-Irish Treaty* was agreed to: under the terms of the *Treaty*, Ireland would become an Irish Free State. However, the *Treaty* permitted the population of six of Ulster's nine counties (Antrim, Armagh, Derry, Down, Fermanagh, and Tyrone), if it so wished, the option of remaining under British control.

Despite the fact that two of the six counties, Fermanagh and Tyrone, had catholic majorities and had voted to be part of the Irish Free State, the six counties' overall protestant majority was quick to use its option. These six Ulster counties became the new Northern Ireland, with a limited self-rule government controlled from Westminister. The other three Ulster counties, Donegal, Cavan, and Monaghan, plus the twenty-three counties of what had been defined as Southern Ireland, became the twenty-six county Irish Free State. Following more than eight hundred years of British dominion, Ireland would become independent, albeit by paying a high price – the partitioning of Ireland. The terms of this conflict-ridden, controversial *Treaty* were scheduled to be implemented in December 1922.

The immediate consequence of the *Treaty* was the *1922-23 Irish Civil War*. It was a war that had *pro-Treaty* Irishmen fighting *anti-Treaty* Irishmen – men who had fought together to gain Irish independence, now turned their guns against each other. The *pro-Treaty* supporters led by Michael Collins had reluctantly accepted partition as a temporary sacrifice for peace and an end to the long,

332

armed struggle; they were confident that over time the Northern Ireland population would vote for a united Ireland. The *anti-Treaty* supporters led by Éamon de Valera rejected partition outright; they had fought for a thirty-two county independent Ireland and would not accept anything less, at any cost. While there was some fighting within Fermanagh and Tyrone, the *Irish Civil War* was primarily played out in the Free State.

As the *Civil War* was going on in the Free State, the protestant majority in Northern Ireland, heavily supported by the British Government, were putting together the pro-British, protestant controlled state the six counties was to become. The catholics in the new Northern Ireland, who were to a great extent anti-British, were blatantly marginalised – in housing, education, employment, and most significantly, in political representation.

The *Civil War* ended with the *pro-Treaty* side being the victor. Eight hundred of the *pro-Treaty* Irish National Army under Collin's (Free Staters) and more than two thousand of the *anti-Treaty* supporters under De Valera (Sinn Féiners) died in the hostilities. Approximately twelve thousand Sinn Féiners were imprisoned.

In 1923 the protestants in the North felt very confident about their new Northern Ireland State, and their confidence was well founded. The *pro-Treaty* supporters were the victors of the *Irish Civil War,* and they now governed the Irish Free State; they had agreed to partition.

ARTHUR MONTGOMERY is the Managing Director of Graphic Film Limited, a new Thomson Corporation publishing company located on Jervis Street, Dublin. Arthur and his colleague, Ted Webb from the Thomson's headquarters in London, have just finished one of their interviews for the position of Chief Estimator at the company. I aced it. It's early 1966, I'm twenty-three, and I'm feeling very confident that I'll be offered the job.

After the formal interview, Arthur, sitting back in his large desk chair, starts to chat. "What do you think about these new troubles in the North, Niall?"

Arthur's accent has identified him as being from Belfast, and Ted's makes it clear he's the Englishman he is. It's crystal clear to me that this explosive question is coming from a Northern Ireland man, and most probably a pro-British protestant to boot.

I hesitate before replying. *Don't screw it up, Niall. This bloke is not goin' to like what you've got to say. He asked the question, so to hell – and screw the job if he decides not to give it to me.*

"The growing conflicts in the north of Ireland are a continuance of the problems caused by Britain's wrongful, centuries-old occupation of the entire island," I start. "The sooner the British get out of the six counties, the better. Let Britain define plans for an orderly withdrawal, over say ten years, and let the entire Irish population sort it out. With all the protestant, pro-British manipulation by the current government in the six counties, it won't be an easy task. Having the island partitioned the way it is, is the basis upon which the current troubles exist, and they'll continue until we have a united, thirty-two county Irish Republic."

Arthur angrily stands up. The chair he's been sitting in crashes against the wall behind him. Leaning over his desk, and supported by his two hands that are now grasping my side of the desk, he looks into my eyes and whispers his icy-cold response.

"O'er my dead body! Northern Ireland stays with the crown!"

I must have aced the interview: despite the animosity generated, I am offered, and accept the job.

As Arthur inferred during our divisive, post-interview chat, the 'new troubles in the North' had indeed grown. The population was still over sixty percent protestant. Dr Conn McCluskey and his wife Patricia had founded the *Campaign for Social Justice* (CSJ) in January 1964, highlighting discrimination against the civil rights of the North's catholics.

Patricia & Conn McCluskey.

In March 1966, Ian Paisley, founded the *Ulster Constitution Defence Committee* (UCDC) to challenge the CSJ. The new *Ulster Volunteer Force* (UVF), a splinter group of the UCDC, was formed in April 1966. The UVF was an illegal organisation of 'heavily armed protestants dedicated to the cause'. In May 1966, the UVF declared war on the IRA. At that time, the IRA was not engaged in armed action. However, Irish nationalists were planning to celebrate the 50th anniversary of the *1916 Rising*; Unionists feared 'a revival of the militant IRA was imminent'.

Ian Paisley.

In June 1966, the UVF carried out three attacks. In the first, a protestant civilian died when UVF members firebombed a catholic pub beside her home; in the second, an innocent catholic civilian was shot dead; and in the third, the UVF fired on three uninvolved catholic civilians, killing one and wounding the others. The 'troubles' escalated to horrific levels, lasting for almost forty years and causing more than four thousand deaths.

****

AT 1:32 A.M. on 8 March 1966, I heard the blast. It was after one of my many late nights out. Having crept into 1 Mannix without waking Peg, I was taking a much-needed pee at the time. Wondering for a moment, what caused the explosion, I dismissed it and went to bed.

Nelson's Pillar before.

Courtesy of a CIE bus conductor, I learned of the source of the blast on my way to work later that morning. Dublin's Nelson's Pillar had been blown up. The IRA had done the job – a chore that

335

should have been done by any one of the many Irish Governments in power since the setting up of the Irish Free State in 1922.

I arrived at Graphic Film at a little after eight; the company's office was not far from O'Connell Street. Along with Brian Williams and Marion Grant-Freemantle, two of my new work colleagues, we went up Henry Street to O'Connell Street, just outside the GPO where Nelson was. Hundreds of people were there to see Horatio and his pillar scattered in a million pieces. Looking at it was shocking. My first thought was a surprisingly sad one: without the Pillar, Dublin would never be the same again.

Nelson's Pillar after.

Partition hasn't gone away; it remains with us to this day. Nor has the defeated, yet undeterred Sinn Féiners/IRA; their passionate pledge to continue their pursuit of a thirty-two-county, independent Irish Republic, by whatever means and no matter how long it takes, also remains. As does the resolve of Northern Ireland's equally zealous unionists, to stay part of the United Kingdom.

****

Go North Young Man

"**H**OW ARE YE, NIALL," SAYS JACKIE. "I'm runnin' out of daddy-stoppers. Would you like to come up to Belfast with me? We can get some up there."

It's late 1966, and the sale of condoms is outlawed in the Republic of Ireland. For those of us who need them, and Jackie is certainly one of those, 'Go North, young man' is the solution. In the six counties of Northern Ireland, condoms are available in all chemist shops.

"I've never been to Belfast, Jackie?"

"I go up, to stock up – once a year at least. It's a pain in the arse, but what can I do? I can't buy them down here. Thanks be to Jays for daddy-stoppers, that's all I can say. But for them, I'd be a daddy to a village of kids."

"When are you goin' up?"

"I'm on my last six-pack. We could go up on Saturday, stay over, do the shoppin' and be back late Sunday."

"OK, Jackie. It'll be interestin' to see what's goin' on up there. You bring your two-man tent. That'll give us a place to sleep."

Border checkpoint.

Jackie and I meet early Saturday morning and hitch-hike our way to the border. We're subjected to a strip search by British soldiers on the six counties side of the border. This nasty experience sets my expectations for my first visit to the six British-occupied counties of Ireland. There are armed soldiers all over the place. There's a rebellious, unfriendly atmosphere, and everyone looks sad. Segregation of the population in Belfast city is blatant.

Pro-Republic.

The Republic of Ireland's flag is green, white and orange. The tricolour's green symbolises the Irish catholics, and the orange signifies the Irish protestants, and ironically, the white represents peace and unity between the two. Many streets are identified by the colour green, and others by the colour orange. Walls and pavement kerbs, painted by the residents, loudly declare each road's allegiance.

Pro-British.

After some careful searching, we find a quiet field on the outskirts of the city – a secure enough place to set up our tent.

We'd seen a poster on a lamp post advertising a local dance, and have plans to attend.

"Let's get this tent up, clean ourselves, down a couple of pints and get a couple of skirts for the night," says Jackie.

"The poster said the dance is at the lodge. That means it's at an Orange Order Lodge. We'll probably be the only catholics there."

"Well Niall, ye don't check out the baptismal cert when ye're pockin' the fire," answers Jackie. "I don't give a damn if the skirt is catholic, protestant, jewish, or islamic for that matter. I bet a bit of strange will be good for us anyway."

"It looks like protestants don't mix with catholics," says I. "These northern people are different. Everywhere you go, you can see segregation. We'll have to size it up before we go into the dance. Maybe there's a boozer near the lodge. We can get a feel for what it'll be like when we're havin' our pints."

"Where is the lodge anyway?" Jackie asks.

"I haven't a clue. We'll have to ask someone for directions."

We stop at one of the lamp posts with the dance poster and wait for some local to pass.

"And why is it that yee two want to know about our lodge?" comes the gruff response to our request for directions from the first young local that passes by.

"We're visitin' and we'd like to go to the dance," I answer.

"Do yee, now?" the stranger says. "Yee don't look protestant to me. If I were yee, I'd think twice before goin'. Don't get me wrong: I've a few catholic friends, and I've no problem with yee, but most of my protestant friends can't stand catholics. All the 'troubles' make any friendship tough."

"What do you mean, we don't look protestant?" Jackie asks.

"Yee just don't," replies the stranger. "And if I can see it, believe me, most of the crowd that'll be at the dance will see it, and a lot clearer than I can."

"Jays. Sure aren't we all Irish?" responds Jackie.

"True, but here in the wee North, the majority consider themselves to be Northern Irish and protestant. That makes yee in the south different from us."

"But I'll tell yee," continues the stranger. "My name is Willy Sparrow, and I'm goin' to the dance. Why don't yee come with me? I'll get yee in. Just don't wave yer green flag. Think orange, and if yee do click with the girls, keep the conversation far away from politics and religion."

"Thanks a lot, Will," I respond. "That won't be a problem. As the sayin' goes, we're only here for the girls and the beer. Is there a boozer on the way? Jackie and me, Niall is my name, we'd like to buy you a Guinness or two. Am I right Jackie?"

"You are, Niall. And maybe even a third one."

"That's solid," says William. "The Cavehill is near the lodge. They serve a good pint of protestant porter." Willy is referring to the effects of Arthur Guinness, founder of Guinness in 1759, and his reproof of the United Irishmen in 1798. Catholics shunned the drink, and Guinness became known as the 'protestant porter'.

"Have ye a second name, Niall?" Willy asks as the three of us start on our way to the Cavehill Inn.

"Why do you ask, Will? John is my second name."

"Great. Use John tonight. Niall is a sure give-away that ye're catholic. I just want yee two to have a good time and not get into any trouble. That's the way it is. Jackie and John should keep yee both safe. OK?"

"Isn't it awful that we have to do such a thing," says I. "This protestant/catholic stuff is a load. I know what you're sayin', but isn't it awful that this little island of ours is the way it is. Maybe we'd all be better off if there was no religion."

"It's a way of livin' that has its problems," Willy replies. "But lads, when ye're in hell, ye've got to dance with the devil."

As always, after the second pint, things look a lot better.

"One more for the road," suggests Jackie. "And Will . . . These pints are a lot more than good enough. They're perfect."

"On behalf of us all, thank ye very much, Jackie. We in the North, do the best we can. How do ye find it, John?"

"Perfect, Will. But I'll tell you; enough of this chattin'. It's inside dancin' we should be. We should be in there with all those lucky girls waitin' for us. Let's down these three and go."

"You're right, Ni–John," says Jackie. "Let's see the bottom of these three, and then it's into the real bottoms, and tops too if you know what I mean."

"That's my Jackie," says I. "Can't keep it in his pants. He never has and he never will."

"There ye are, William," greets the large overfed bouncer at the entrance to the Lodge. "I don't know yer friends, William. Who are they? I'll have to see some identification. Ye know well, William – these days we can't be too careful."

"No need for that, Adam. Jackie and John are up from Dublin visitin' me. They're my friends, and I vouch for them. They're here on my invitation, and they're sound."

"William's word is fine with me," says the bouncer. "In yee go now and enjoy yerselfs."

"Well, that went well," says Jackie, as the three of us pay the required admission fee. "Adam looks like someone you'd want as a friend rather than an enemy."

"Trust me," comments William. "No catholic wants to be on the wrong side of Adam. He's stone orange."

"Skirts galore!" exclaims Jackie. "I don't know where to start. Would you look at them, all lined up waitin' for us. A sight for sore eyes, if ever there was one."

"Don't forget," William advises. "Think orange, no politics or religion. I've got to leave yee now and tie up with my mates. If I don't see yee, I'll know yee've hit it off with the girls. Good luck, and welcome to Belfast!"

"Good luck, Will," I answer. "Thanks for lookin' after us."

"Peace," Willy responds, as he cuts through the crowded dance floor to meet his friends.

"Now there's a good bloke," Jackie declares, alluding to Willy and how helpful he had been.

"Niall, it's time for us to start makin' our moves. Do you see that pair of beauties over there? The two in the red dresses?"

"I like your taste, Jackie. You take the redhead, and I'll take the blonde. OK?"

"Either way suits me. Let's go over and shake their glands."

"Jays, Jackie. Cut out the sex jokes, at least 'til we say hello."

"You're right, Niall. I'm a horny bugger. I'll try to control myself."

"Good evenin' ladies," says Jackie, with his hand outstretched. "May I introduce myself? My name is Jackie, and this is my good friend, John. We're at your cervix, ladies."

So much for Jackie's ability to control himself. Amazingly, and much like always, this incredibly offensive style of Jackie's wins the day.

"Jackie and John," says the redhead, eying us up and down. "My name is Sandra, and this is my best friend, Susan. So ye're into cervixing. Is that right? We love yer accent. Are yee Australian or what?"

"Whatever it takes," says Jackie. "I think we'd be anythin' you two want us to be. Am I right, John?"

"What do ye think, Susan?" says Sandra.

"They look good enough to me," answers Susan. "Let's see how they can dance. It's the moves that count. Isn't that what counts, Sandra?"

"It's all in the moves, Susan," says Sandra.

"Well, let me tell you, if it is moves you want, you've come to the right department," Jackie replies, grabbing Sandra by the hand.

"Give me a hold of you, Susan," says I. With more than a little surprise we kiss – a short yet promising kiss.

"I love yer moves, John," Susan says facetiously. "Let's get out there with Sandra and Jackie. Time enough for what looks like being an exciting night."

Little did we know how exciting the night would be. We're dancing for only a minute or two when a bomb explodes. It comes from somewhere in the back of the building. Windows are blown out; that and the deafening noise causes absolute pandemonium.

"Let's get out of here," shouts Jackie as the four of us, like everyone else, run to the exits.

Bombings.

Ears ringing, but otherwise OK, we're standing outside the lodge, huddled close together when a second explosion erupts.

"Holy Jays!" I exclaim. "The farther away from here, the better." Hand in hand, we run down the Cavehill Road, towards the Inn. Police, fire and army units are coming from all directions.

"If ever we needed a drink it's now," shouts Jackie. "Come on. Let's get in out of harm's way."

"Those fuckin' IRA!" says Sandra.

"A bit of excitement is always a good thing, but that was ridiculous," says I. "We've heard of this stuff, and we've seen it on the tele, but bein' in the middle of it is a whole different thing. Does this often happen, Susan?"

"Live in Belfast for a while, and ye'll know all about it," answers Susan. "Nearly every night something happens. If it's not some explosion, it's gunshots and killin's. Last week two men were found shot to pieces up the Crumlin Road."

Shootings.

"Well, we're all in one piece," says Jackie. "And there's love in the air despite everythin'. Am I right, Sandra?" Jackie continues, placing his hand high on Sandra's leg.

"Ye are, Jackie" answers Sandra. "Those IRA were out to remind us they're here. If they'd used their bigger bombs, we'd be dead or on our way to the hospital. Quick, get us a couple of Bacardi'n'cokes so as to settle our nerves, will ye Jackie?"

"Two pints of Guinness and two Barcardi'n'cokes," shouts Jackie. "Let's get them down, and then go celebrate our survival."

The togetherness we had created is intensified by the combination of the excitement of the unbelievable experience, and the joy of our survival. With uncommon abandonment, both couples indulge in passionate kissing.

"Sorry to interrupt the love fest, lads," says the server as he puts the drinks on the table in front of us.

"No problem," Jackie responds, detaching himself from Sandra. "We need to come up for air anyway."

"You're right, Jackie," says I. "And if you're not a gorgeous girl, Susan – what a kisser."

We finish our drinks and start to walk our way to where the girls live. We break into two appropriately distanced couples, Susan and me in front, and Jackie and Sandra in the rear.

Susan is leading the way, in every regard. We stop a few times to feed our growing passion. Susan's adept abilities make each stop increasingly satisfying.

We've paused at a shady, low garden wall.

"John," Susan sighs. "Look at ye down there. Let me help you."

343

"Sufferin' divine," I moan. "Susan, what are you doin' to me? Stop for a minute and come up here."

As she does so, she adeptly removes her panties.

"Would ye mind these for me, John," says she, pushing her panties into my jacket pocket. "With you and yer guy down there, I don't think I'll be needin' them."

"So there you are," shouts Jackie. Sandra and Jackie have come up to where we are; Susan perched on the wall, and me with my bare arse showing and my pants around my ankles.

"Now, how's that for a happy couple?" says Jackie. "Is there anythin' like it?"

"I don't think so," moans Susan. "What do ye think, John?"

"If there is, I can't imagine what it is," I answer.

"Put yer pants on," says Sandra. "If the RUC comes along ye'll be arrested."

We get ourselves together, and arm in arm, the four of us continue on our way. We're walking for some time when I notice that while there are homes and pavement to our right, to the left there are as yet undeveloped fields. We come to a bend right. The pavement forks gradually to the right onto a different road with more pavements and homes on both sides. The road we had been on continues to the left of the fork with no pavements or homes. The two girls suddenly stop.

"We can't go down this road," declares Sandra.

"Ye're right," confirms Susan.

"We'll go the old road and cut over the fields," asserts Sandra.

"Why can't we go down this road?" I ask.

"It's a protestant road, and yee two are catholic; that's why," answers Susan. "Especially after the trouble tonight at the lodge."

"You've got to be kiddin' me!" I exclaim. "And how do you know we're catholic?"

"Yee just look catholic," says Sandra.

"Jays!" exclaims Jackie. "We look catholic!?"

Neither Jackie nor I have rosary beads, miraculous medals, or pictures of the pope showing, and we had taken Willy's advice and not discussed religion or politics.

"That's ridiculous," says I. "We are catholic, but to hear you say we 'look catholic' is just crazy."

"Let's stop talking about it," says Susan. "It'll be fun to go on the old road anyway. Come on and don't be bothering yerselfs. Fuck all this catholic/protestant stuff, that's what I say."

"You're all mad up here," says Jackie. "I don't understand it."

"But it's enjoyable, isn't it, John," says Susan.

"That's for sure," I confirm, as I grab Susan and kiss her.

We make our way up the old road, across the fields and kiss our girls goodbye. Before we part, I return Susan's panties.

"WHAT'S THAT smell?" says Jackie, as we arrive at our tent site.

"It's shite," I respond in disgust. "We've got cow dung on our shoes." While we were walking across the fields, we had stood in some cow patties. We remove the stinky shoes and leave them outside the tent.

We're in our sleeping bags, getting ready for some much-needed sleep when Jackie approaches the difficult question.

"What's all this protestant/catholic stuff about anyway?"

"The Brits, Jackie. They screwed up the whole island. It has plagued Ireland for a long time, and it's still going on. At one time, it may have been an English/Irish thing, but not so much now. And it's not so much a protestant/catholic thing either. As William said, it has become more a way of life thing."

"How do you mean 'a way of life thing'?"

"If you let me, I'll tell you," I respond. "The way things are didn't happen overnight. It's taken hundreds of years."

Jackie almost lockjaws himself with a long, demanding yawn. "Fuck it, Niall. I'm bollixed. You can tell me in the mornin'."

****

How We Got
to Where We Are

Where is the flag of England? Go North, South, East or West,
wherever there's wealth to plunder or land to be possessed,
wherever there's feeble races to frighten, coerce or scare,
ye'll find the butcher's apron, the English flag is there!

The Maori often cursed it with his bitterest dyin' breath,
the Arab hissed his hatred as he spat at its folds in death.
The helpless Hindu feared it, and the Kenyan did the same,
and Irish blood stained it, with a deep and indelible stain!

It's waved on scenes of pillage, it's waved on deeds of shame,
it's waved over fallen marauders, ravished with sword and flame.
It's looked upon ruthless slaughter, massacre dire and grim,
it's heard the shrieks of victims, drownin' the jingo hymn!

Where is the flag of England? Seek lands where natives rot,
and where assured extinction, must soon be the people's lot.
Go search once glad islands, where death and disease are rife,
and greed of colossal commerce now fattens on human life!

Where is the flag of England? Go sail where rich boats come,
with shoddy and loaded cotton, and beer and bibles and guns.
Go where brute forces triumph and hypocrisy makes its lair,
in your question ye'll find the answer, it was, and still is there!!

The Butcher's Apron – Henry Dupre LaBouchere (19th Century)

"WE'VE LOADS OF TIME, NIALL," SAYS JACKIE. "Our train doesn't go until four. So go on, tell me."

Jackie and I are sitting in a café at the Belfast/Dublin Enterprise Express train station. The train is the most efficient way to commute between the cities, and we badly want to get out of Belfast and back to the sanity of Dublin. The train service had recently been reopened having been closed in 1964 due to increased troubles at the border crossing.

"All this protestant/catholic stuff began way back in the first half of the 1500s," says I. "Henry-VIII started it, and that's less than five hundred years ago. But the English/Irish stuff started four hundred years before that. The English King Henry-II, came across the pond in 1171, declarin' himself Lord of Ireland. That was the beginnin' of what's turnin' out to be close to a thousand years of occupation by the Brits.

"But, before I go on, it's important ye understand how the people on these two islands we're livin' on, got to where we are."

"Go on then, Niall. I know little about all that stuff."

"OK, Jackie, here we go." I take a deep breathe, and with all my energy summoned I begin Jackie's edification.

"Over nine hundred years ago, around 1000 BC, the Celtic tribes of Central Europe started to migrate all over continental Europe. Ireland and England were called the Prettanic Isles back then, and because of their remoteness, the Celts didn't bother with either of the islands 'til about 500 BC. Thanks to the Celts who introduced the discovery to Europe, it was the Iron Age. The Celts not only brought their iron, but they also brought their customs, their way of life and their language. With ever increasin' numbers, it didn't take long for them to dominate the Prettanic Isles' sparse native populations. Their arrival was gradual, spreadin' over many centuries. Unlike their continental migrations, which included brutal attack-and-conquer tactics, they settled in pretty peacefully and intermarried with the natives.

"The growing Roman Empire arrived on the shores of what we now call England in 27 AD. They enforced their Roman law on the Celtic-Britons and quickly became the rulers of the land. They renamed the island Britannia and gave Ireland the name Hibernia. The Romans never came to Hibernia, and they paid little attention to the parts of Britannia that are now Scotland and Wales. The majority of the population became Roman-Britons; all non-compliant Celts were pushed north to Celtic-Scotland or west to Celtic-Wales and Celtic-Hibernia.

"Saint Patrick brought christianity to Hibernia in the mid-400s. In the late 500s, Saint Augustine did the same thing in Britannia.

The populations of both islands spoke a kind of Celtic language and became predominantly christian.

"In around 500 AD, after the collapse of the Roman Empire, the Romans left Britannia. The Angles, Saxons, and Jutes from Denmark and Germany were quick to take advantage of the absence of the once feared and mighty Roman Empire; they crossed the North Sea and invaded Britannia. The Angles became the most dominant of the invaders. Pretty soon a new language started; that language would later become English.

"In the 800s and 900s, the Vikings and Danes invaded the two islands. In Ireland, Scotland and Wales, after a fair bit of fightin' with the local Celtic kings, a lot of them stayed, and just like the Celts, they settled in and intermarried. In Ireland, it was this mixed population that created a christian Celtic-Irish race.

"As this was goin' on in Ireland, a christian Anglo-Saxon race was developin' in England."

"So that's when the Irish/English thing started?" says Jackie.

"In a manner of speakin', you're right. But there was nothin' wrong with that. The settin' up of different nations was a natural progression that helped the populations of Europe live in harmony. It was happenin' all over; with all the different languages, and travel bein' difficult, that was the best they could do."

"Yeah," answers Jackie. "The fact that Ireland and England are two separate islands makes even more sense of what happened."

"Anyway," I continue, "in 1066, William, the Duke of Normandy invaded England to claim the English crown promised to him by the deceased Anglo-Saxon King Edward the Confessor. When Edward died, Harold Godwinson, an Anglo-Saxon, had claimed the crown, and that didn't sit too well with William; to wit, his decision to invade. At the Battle of Hastings, William defeated and killed Harold, England's last Anglo-Saxon king. William was crowned King William-I on Christmas Day 1066 and became the first Anglo-Norman King of England.

William-I.   *Harold-II.*

"At that time, Ireland was bein' ruled by a number of Celtic-Irish kings. One of them, Dermot MacMurray Kavanagh, King of Leinster, was deposed in 1166. He reached out across the Irish Sea to the Anglo-Norman King Henry-II, grandson of William-I, for assistance. Henry let Dermot put together a force of mercenaries led by a man named Richard Strongbow De Clare."

Dermot.   *Henry-II.*

"In 1169, Strongbow and his mercenaries arrived in Ireland. And they did so on behalf of Dermot; ironic, don't you think – it was the Irish themselves who first invited the English in."

"Is Dermot any relation, Niall?" asks Jackie.

"Probably, but I don't know. Anyway, it didn't take long for Strongbow and his men to reclaim Leinster for Dermot."

Strongbow.   *Aoife.*

"Strongbow, it would appear, got the hots for Dermot's daughter, Aoife. They married, and when Dermot died in 1171, Strongbow became King of Leinster. This caused Henry-II to freak out about the possibility of a rival Norman state developin' in Ireland. Pope Adrian-IV, the only English pope, had given Henry permission to invade Ireland as a means of strengthening Rome's control over the wild Irish christians – seemingly, Saint Patrick didn't do a good enough job. Anyway, with the pope's permission under his belt, Henry decided to invade Ireland, more for his own reasons than those of the pope. While establishin' the pope's control over the Irish christians, he would also establish his own authority and control over that upstart, Strongbow.

"Henry-II landed in Waterford in 1171, becoming the first King of England to set foot on Irish soil. This marked the beginnin' of English rule in Ireland. Waterford and Dublin were proclaimed royal cities, and Henry declared himself Lord of Ireland. He was acknowledged by most of the Irish Kings. They saw him as their chance to stop the expansion of Leinster into their smaller, weaker kingdoms.

John-I.

"In 1185 Henry-II gave his Irish territories to his son, John. When John-I succeeded as King in 1199, the Lordship of Ireland became the possession of the English crown. It would stay that way for the next three hundred plus years.

Henry-VIII.   Catherine of Aragon.

"In 1509, at the age of eighteen, the second English Tudor king, Henry-VIII was crowned. From the beginnin', Henry had an obsession regardin' havin' a son as his male heir. In the same year as his coronation, he married his widowed sister-in-law, Catherine of Aragon, the daughter of the Spanish King and Queen, Ferdinand & Isabella. In 1516, after bearing four stillborn children, Henry and Catherine had their first healthy child. However, it was a girl; they named her Mary. With Catherine's sixth and last pregnancy they would try one more time for that male heir; they failed in their effort. Once again their child, another girl, was stillborn.

"Henry started to panic: there was never a queen monarch of England. He badly needed a son. If Catherine couldn't give him one he'd have to get rid of her and marry someone else. Henry had many mistresses to choose from, and one of them was Anne Boleyn. Although the pope regularly granted annulments to royalty, Henry's request for one was turned down – primarily due to the objections of the powerful catholic court of Spain.

350

"'So . . .' says Henry to himself. 'To hell with the pope and all you papists. I'll start my own church, and then I'll be able to do whatever the hell I want.' And he did: in 1533, during the turmoil of the Protestant Reformation, Henry-VIII, for reasons other than religious, declared England's separation from the Roman Catholic Church. He started the Church of England and declared himself as its head. After almost twenty-four years of marriage, he granted himself an annulment, banished Catherine of Aragon, and married Anne Boleyn. All this was brought about by Henry's obsession regardin' not havin' a son as male heir to the throne.

Anne Boleyn.

"But would you believe it? Anne Boleyn, who was already pregnant when they married, gave Henry another girl – that girl would eventually turn out to be Queen Elizabeth-I. Anne miscarried two more children in her failed attempt to give Henry his son. That was too much for Henry: he went ballistic altogether. He thought of himself as being cursed and would never be able to have a son. He'd have to get rid of Anne and sow his seeds elsewhere. He contrived a case of adultery against Anne for which she was sentenced to death. She was beheaded in 1536.

"Henry had six wives. He'd die in 1547, but not before he had married a Jane, one more Anne and two more Catherines.

Jane Seymore.　*Anne of Cleves.*　*Catherine Howard.*　*Catherine Parrs.*

"Only two weeks after Anne Boleyn's execution, Henry married his third wife, Jane Seymour, one of Anne Boleyn's ladies-in-waiting. Bob's yer uncle, straight away Henry had his son, Edward-VI. But there was a terrible price to be paid: twelve days after the birth Jane died.

"Early in 1540, Henry married his fourth wife, the German Princess Anne of Cleves. It was a diplomatically arranged, vital marriage made to strengthen an alliance between the two most anti-papist protestant states in Europe, England and Germany.

"By all accounts, Anne of Cleves, unlike Catherine of Aragon, Anne Boleyn, and Jane Seymour, was notably unattractive. So much so that Henry claimed he never consummated the marriage. He declared that she 'looked not unlike a horse.' Having secured the required alliance and after only a short six months of marital misery, the marriage was annulled.

"While married to Anne of Cleves, Henry had started an affair with another Catherine – Catherine Howard. Immediately followin' the annulment of his marriage to Anne, Catherine Howard became Henry's fifth wife.

"After two years, the somewhat promiscuous new Queen Catherine was arrested for treason. She was accused of adultery with Henry's personal manservant, Thomas Culpeper. In 1542, havin' been found guilty as charged, Catherine, along and the boyfriend Tom were sent to the Tower and beheaded.

"Catherine Parr was Henry's sixth wife. They married in 1543. She died in 1548, one year after bein' widowed by Henry in 1547.

"As I've said, Jackie, all this protestant/catholic stuff started with Henry-VIII. He and his breakin' with Rome did it. Everybody had to stop being Roman Catholic, and pay homage to the English crown and the new Church of England.

"Using Thomas Cromwell as his front-man, he imposed a new anti-papal *Oath of Allegiance* law throughout England, Scotland and Wales. Once that was done, over he came to Ireland to do the nasty, declarin' himself King of Ireland. Anyone who refused to take the oath, and many catholics did, were branded as traitors, had their property confiscated, and were made subject to imprisonment, banishment and often death.

"After Henry's death in 1547, Edward-VI, Henry's only son by his third wife Jane Seymour, was crowned king at the age of nine. After a short six-year reign, he died in 1553. During his reign, and under the guidance of John Dudley, his advisor, he created a new state, actively supporting protestants and marginalisin' all catholic power and influence. Reforms were enforced in the new church, includin' the abolition of clerical celibacy, the abolition of the Mass, and having compulsory English for all services. Many catholic churches, abbeys, and monasteries were closed, their lands and properties confiscated and clergy banished.

Edward-VI.   *John Dudley.*   *Jane Grey.*

"Edward was ill for some time before his death. He and his advisors knew he was dying. Being the young, staunch protestant he was, he wanted his new state and church legacy to live on after he was gone. Under the royal succession laws of the time, Edward's heir apparent would be one of Henry-VIII's daughters, Mary first-in-line, and Elizabeth second-in-line. Third-in-line was a favourite cousin of Edward's, Jane Grey.

"On the basis that Mary and Elizabeth's mothers' marriages had been annulled, Edward considered his two half-sisters as being illegitimate and dismissed the legitimacy of their rights to the throne. Before Edward died, he wrote and signed an *Act of Succession* declaring that upon his death, Jane Grey, his cousin and a staunch protestant, would be crowned monarch; with Jane as Queen of England, his protestant legacy would be protected. Most importantly, his devout catholic sister, Mary would not be given the opportunity of backslidin' all his pro-protestant good works and revertin' England's church and state to its centuries-old, catholic, papist ways. Much to the dead Edward's disappointment, catholic Mary quickly gathered the required support and successfully claimed her realm on 19 July 1553. She was crowned as the first monarchical Queen of England and Ireland in October 1553. Both the deposed, uncrowned protestant Jane and John Dudley were imprisoned in the Tower of London and beheaded.

Mary-I.

353

"Mary reigned 'til her death in November 1558. She did her best to re-establish a catholic, papist state and church. She gained the nickname Bloody Mary by the hundreds of protestant executions she organised durin' her five-year reign.

"When Mary died, Henry-VIII's second daughter by Anne Boleyn, Elizabeth, became the second monarchial Queen of England, Queen Elizabeth-I. She would reign for almost forty-five years 'til her death in 1603.

Elizabeth-I.

"Unlike her sister, Elizabeth was as staunch a protestant as Edward-VI was. She immediately reinforced the *Oath of Allegiance* law and returned the country to bein' the protestant state it had been before Mary. Once again it was a bad thing to be a catholic. Under Elizabeth, there were more mass executions, only this time it was the catholics' turn for decapitation.

"After Elizabeth died, in came King James-I. He went at it hard, particularly so in Ireland. He expanded confiscation of Irish catholic land and pushed for full colonisation with protestant settlers from England and Scotland.

James-I.   *Charles-I.*   *Oliver Cromwell.*

"Charles-I followed, and thinkin' it couldn't get worse, in comes Oliver Cromwell, and it did. Cromwell introduced the Penal Laws and expanded colonisation even further. He did a great job of it up here in Ulster. The Irish catholics of the other three provinces were equally persecuted, but while all catholics lost their land and were denied their established way of life, Leinster, Munster, and Connacht rebelled against the imposition. Lots of them refused to change their religion. The late 1500s, 1600s, and

354

way into the 1700s are paved with the annihilation of Irish catholics and their way of life. Many Irish catholics were shipped as slaves to the colonies."

"What!?" gasps Jackie. "I've never heard about Irish slaves!"

"Well, it's true. Massive injustice was imposed on anyone not declarin' allegiance to the crown and the protestant Church. Irish land, language, and liberty were denied to the catholic Irish."

"Jays, Niall," exclaims Jackie as he suddenly stands up.

"What's wrong with you, Jackie?" He's looking as if he's in some sort of panic.

"Here we are, waitin' for the train, and you tellin' me all about this Irish slave stuff, and I've just remembered," he responds, gasping as he does so. "We haven't done what we came up here to do. The daddy-stoppers!"

"Hold your thoughts for a minute and let me get over to the chemist shop and get my supply," he yells, as he dashes away. "I'll be back in a minute. I want to hear all about that slave stuff."

"Go on, Niall," Jackie urges. He has returned with the important, and in his case essential, contraband. Having safely stashed the condoms away in his backpack, he's encouraging me to continue with his edification.

"Where was I?" I ask.

"The Irish slaves," answers Jackie.

"Oh yeah, the slaves. Ireland's history is filled with some shockin' things. The most shockin', and at the same time least referred to, is that of English-imposed Irish slavery. The first shipment of Irish slaves was in 1612, durin' the reign of James-I. Thousands of Irish catholics were shipped to Barbados and to English rubber planters on the Amazon."

"How do you know about this, Niall," asks Jackie.

"I first heard about it while I was takin' some Irish history night classes in UCD. Colm O'Loughlinn gave us a load of info on it."

"In 1625, King James-I issued a proclamation that all Irish political prisoners were to be transported to the colonies and sold as slave labour to the planters.

"The Irish had a tendency to die in the heat and weren't as well suited to the work as African slaves. And African slaves had to be bought. Irish slaves could be kidnapped if there weren't enough prisoners. This made the Irish the preferred 'livestock' for many English slave traders."

"Jays, I'm gettin' annoyed now," says Jackie. "All this shit was in the name of religion!?"

"Yeah. Religion, land, and power. And with the arrival of Oliver Cromwell and his Roundheads, things got a lot worse. Tens of thousands of Irish catholics were killed, and many more were sold into slavery."

"That big mad bollocks, Cromwell," Jackie adds. "He was an nasty bugger altogether."

"You're right, Jackie. It was Cromwell who instigated the ethnic cleansin' of Ireland. He demanded that all the catholic Irish resettle west of the Shannon or be transported to the colonies – 'To hell or Connaught.' The Irish catholics refused to relocate peaceably. A law in 1657 read, 'Catholics who fail to transplant themselves into Connaught within six months will be guilty of high treason. They'll be sent to America or some other parts beyond the seas. Anyone who attempts to return will suffer the pains of death.'

"Cromwell's soldiers were encouraged to kill the catholic Irish who refused to move, but they made so much on the slave trade it was worth their while to round them up and sell them.

"While the tradin' of Irish slaves tapered off a bit in the mid-1700s, England once again shipped out their Irish prisoners as slaves after the Irish Rebellion of 1798.

"Many never made it off the ships. In one case, a hundred and thirty-two Irish slaves were dumped overboard because the ship's food supplies were runnin' low. The insurance would pay for an 'accident', but not if the slaves were starved to death.

Workin' in the hot sun, the Irish slaves weren't as productive as the African slaves. And the Irish were catholic; to the protestant American planters, catholics were papists, and papists weren't even considered christian.

"Despite that, the planters began to breed the Irish slaves with the African slaves to make lighter skinned slaves. The lighter skinned slaves could be sold for more money. A law was passed against this, not for moral reasons, but because it was causin' the Royal African Company to lose money sellin' their African slaves.

It wasn't 'til 1839 that a law was passed by England endin' the slave trade.

"Ever since Henry-VIII, right up until *Catholic Emancipation* in 1823, Irish catholics throughout the island were treated, at best, as second-class citizens. Exclusively, government control and power were administered by England through planted protestants. For more than four hundred and fifty years, until the establishment of the *Irish Free State* in 1922, the protestant way of life ruled every aspect of law in Ireland. The English systematically regulated and limitin' the country's catholic population, their language, their way of life and the practise of their religion."

"And then there was the famine," says Jackie. "There was loads of food in Ireland, but the Brits shipped it over to England."

"Your right, Jackie," I confirm. "The population of Ireland dropped from eight million in 1845, to three million 1850. More than a million died of starvation. The others had to emigrate to the USA, Australia, and England to avoid a similar fate.

"And that's only a little less than a hundred and fifty years ago, Jackie. Only a few feckin' lifetimes ago!

"While the *1916 Easter Rising* was a disaster, it was also a success. It was the *Rising* that planted the seeds for the *War of Independence* and an *Irish Free State*. But, the settin' up of the Free State included the partitionin' of these six northeast counties.

"In Northern Ireland, the protestant majority intensified their commitment to the preservation of their protestant, pro-British way of life. Without any real supervision from Westminster, a protestant dominated government was set up. They gerrymandered the electoral structure assuring protestant control and the exclusion of all catholic influence.

"While all this was goin' on in the North, in the Free State there was never any form of retribution towards the protestant minority. In the Republic of Ireland, catholics and protestants live and work together in peace. The fear of the northern protestant population with regards to how they would be treated by the catholics in a united Ireland is unjustified."

"Wasn't Douglas Hyde, the first President of Ireland, a protestant," interjects Jackie. "And there's loads of protestant politicians in Leinster House, all elected by catholics."

357

"Robert Briscoe, the Mayor of Dublin, was jewish," I assert.

"And aren't two of our best friends, Cess and Arthur, protestant," Jackie adds.

"In 1921, Michael Collins and the boys weakened while they were negotiatin' with Westminster for a united independent Ireland. They were able to save three of Ulster's nine, but unfortunately, they couldn't break the stalemate regardin' the other six. Rumour has it that Michael finally settled the deal with a young Winston Churchill over a few drinks. And then that stupid *Irish Civil War* – Éamon de Valera and the Sinn Féiners going one way, and Michael and the Free Staters going the other way. That screwed up everythin', and we still ended up with a split country.

Michael Collins.   *Éamon de Valera.*

"Right or wrong, at this stage on this earth of ours, nations do exist, and it's just plain wrong that Ireland is divided the way it is. It is this reality that's the first of two realities needin' acceptance. The nonsense of the Northern Ireland protestants' expectation of any continuance of dominance of their way of life over their catholic countrymen is the other reality. We are all equal as Irishmen. Religion is not, and should never be the anchor upon which a country's laws and government are structured. All men are equal, and if religion gets in the way of that primary condition, away with religion is what I say. Those days are gone forever.

"The blood lust of the pope-led *Inquisition* was wrong. So too was the blood lust of Henry-VIII and the *Reformation*. What's goin' on in Northern Ireland today is equally wrong."

"Jays, Niall," Jackie responds. "You sound like Charlie Haughey. If you were up for election, you'd get my vote."

"Runnin' for office, me arse," says I. "What time is it? We should be goin' to the train. I can't wait to get out of this fuckin' place. Other than for Susan and Sandra, it's been a waste."

"Yeah. The girls plus this load of daddy-stoppers makes it all worthwhile," answers Jackie, smiling as he affectionately pats his hidden contraband, carefully crammed away in his backpack.

****

Will It Ever End?

"**W**ILL IT EVER END?" ASKS JACKIE. We've boarded the train, and are on our way back to Dublin.

"As my Da said, 'Heaven is upstairs, and the devil is down here.' One thing is for sure; it's lookin' like it'll get a lot worse before it gets better."

"So the gist of it is, the protestants up here are afraid that in a united Ireland their way of life is goin' to end," says Jackie.

"Yeep. That and the fact that the protestants and their Orange Order have allegiance to the United Kingdom, not to a thirty-two county Republic of Ireland. And isn't it understandable? For hundreds of years, they've benefited from bein' protestant and loyal to England. We've got to make them see that their fears of retaliation by catholics in a united Ireland are unjustified."

"The way the IRA is behavin' isn't helpin' that one," says Jackie. "I can understand the catholics in the North bein' pissed off with the way they continue to be treated, no power and stuff, but the bombs are only makin' the protestants more reluctant to unite with the rest of us. The bombs are a danger to their life, never mind their way of life."

"Right now the IRA are out to bring everyone's attention to the injustices the catholics are livin' under," I respond. "Sure, they fightin' for a united Ireland, but they are goin' about it the wrong way. Killin' people is never the right way."

"I think it's time for the Republic to get together with England and sort out all this shit," says Jackie. "Apart from everythin' else, it must be costin' the Brits a bundle."

"It is. And money, if nothin' else, will bring about somethin' like that. Not now, but someday soon."

"Well, Niall, you've told me a lot of stuff I didn't know."

"There's another great story, my Uncle Colbert, my Ma's brother, told me. He and his two brothers, Wally and Tom, were involved with the IRA fightin' the Black'n'Tans. It has little to do with what we've been talkin' about, but it does include Michael Collins and would you believe the Soviet Union.

Russian Czar's crown jewels.

"In 1921, the leaders of the new Soviet Union were severely low on funds. They secured a loan of 25,000 Irish pounds from Ireland's Michael Collins. The Russians used some of the Czar's Crown Jewels as collateral for the loan. The transfer was made in New York City between the Soviet Ambassador and the Irish Envoy in the United States, Harry Boland. The *Irish Civil War* had started, and Boland, although friendly with Collins and the *Free Staters*, sided with De Valera and the *Sinn Féiners*. When Boland returned to Dublin, he kept the jewels hidden in his mother's house. Boland was shot in Skerries in 1922. Before he died, he instructed his mother to keep the jewels hidden from the *Free Staters* 'til Éamon de Valera, and the anti-Treaty *Sinn Féiners* came to power. For years, Harry's Ma kept the jewels under her bed, but in 1938, just before she died, she gave them to the Irish Government under De Valera. They were placed in a safe in Government Buildings and forgotten about until 1948.

"When they were discovered, and after some negotiations with the Soviet Ambassador, it was arranged for them to be returned to the Moscow in exchange for the 25,000 Irish pounds initially loaned by Collins. The jewels were finally given back in 1950.

"There's one for ye, Jackie," I conclude. "The Irish Free State helped Lenin set up the Soviet Union!"

****

FOLLOWING THE 30 January 1972 *Bloody Sunday* killings in Derry, things went from bad to worse in Northern Ireland. So much so, the British decided to dissolve the Stormont Government in

361

Belfast and introduce *Direct Rule* from Westminister. Fifty years of protestant, gerrymandered government was finally considered enough. Under *Direct Rule*, things slowly started to get somewhat better; however, serious, deadly conflicts continued for another twenty-six years – up until the much welcomed *1998 Good Friday Agreement*. From the early 1960s through to 1998, more than four-thousand people had been killed, over 48,000 were seriously injured, and property damage was more than 1,000,000,000 Sterling.

Due primarily to the success of President Bill Clinton's measured intervention, and his insightful appointment of the skilled diplomat Senator George Mitchell as an independent mediator, the *Good Friday Agreement* was agreed to on Good Friday, 10 April 1998.

A ceasefire had been declared in December 1997; Mitchell was quick to take advantage of the cessation of hostilities. In pursuit of a peaceful end to 'the troubles', he adeptly organised a series of difficult meetings. He got the representatives of both the British and Irish Governments to agree to continue the meetings until an agreement was produced. Agents from all of Northern Ireland's different conflicting parties, excluding the stubborn and adamantly protestant, pro-British DUP, led by Ian Paisley, took part in the challenging discussions.

Finally, and despite the absence of Ian and his stubborn band, the *Good Friday Agreement* was finalised and made ready for two separate plebiscites by the citizens of both Northern Ireland and the Republic of Ireland. The essence of the Agreement was as follows: The involved paramilitary groups would disarm, and Westminster would remove British troops from the six counties; A Human Rights Commission would be established; The citizens of Northern Ireland would be granted the right to become citizens of the Republic of Ireland or the United Kingdom or both; Territorial claims by the Republic of Ireland to the six counties would be controversially released; Northern Ireland would stay part of the United Kingdom until, a) the majority of Northern Ireland's citizens voted to unite with the Republic of Ireland, and b) the majority of the Republic of Ireland's citizens voted yes to any such union.

The referendums were held on 4 May 1998 and resulted in both Northern Ireland and the Republic of Ireland returning an overwhelming yes vote for the enactment of the *Agreement*.

The DUP's loudly displayed intransigence by not being party to the *Good Friday Agreement* – to what they identified as being a shameful reneging of their heritage – was soon to reignite the temporarily appeased republican pursuits of a thirty-two county Republic. For another six years, many incidences of a return to 'the troubles' occurred; the horrific August 1998 Omagh Bombing with thirty-one deaths and 220 people injured came close to derailing all the potential good the *Good Friday Agreement* promised. The full effective implementation of the *Agreement* did not happen until after the signing of the *2006 St Andrews Agreement*: Ian and the DUP finally agreed to sit and negotiate power-sharing with all involved parties including representation of the catholic minority by the Sinn Féin/IRA party.

After the *St Andrews Agreement* had been reached, tensions eased. The ceasefire has, to a large degree, held. Some new splinter groups of die-hard republicans and loyalists have emerged; sadly, conflicts albeit infrequent and comparatively minor in nature, continue. That old English/Irish "stuff" is still with us – and it will continue until Ireland's thirty-two becomes one nation serving all its citizens equally.

Evidence of that Protestant/Catholic stuff is also still with us. Consider this statute of active English law as it stands today: a Roman Catholic cannot be made monarch of England or be married to the monarch of England without renouncing his or her religion and becoming a fully practising member of the Protestant Church of England.

****

Robert Maxwell –
My First Encounter

Have ye heard about the big strong man?
He lived in a caravan.
Have ye heard about the Jeffrey Johnson fight?
Oh, Lord what a hell of a fight.
Ye can take all of the heavyweights ye've got,
we've got a lad that can beat the whole lot.
He used to ring bells in the belfry,
now he's goin' to fight Jack Dempsey.

> *That is Me Brother, Sylvest. (What's he got?)*
> *A row of forty medals on his chest. (Big chest!)*
> *Killed fifty men in the west, he knows no rest,*
> *think of a man, hell's fire, don't push, just shove,*
> *plenty of room for you and me.*
> *He's got an arm, like a leg. (Lady's leg!)*
> *And a punch that would sink a battleship. (Big ship!)*
> *Takes all of the Army and the Navy, to put the wind-up, Sylvest.*

Now, he thought he'd take a trip to Italy,
and he thought that he'd go by sea.
He dove off the harbour in New York,
and swam like a great big shark.
He saw the Lusitania in distress,
he put the Lusitania on his chest.
He drank all the water in the sea,
and he walked all the way to Italy.

Me Brother, Sylvest – Traditional (1920s)

SOON AFTER I JOIN GRAPHIC FILM LIMITED, the company moves from Jervis Street to the Malahide Road in Coolock, one of the Northside Dublin suburbs. Within a year of the move, the company is sold to Robert Maxwell's Pergamon Press and renamed the

European Printing Corporation. Like most of Maxwell's early acquisitions, it's bought for a song, and in this case with the help of grants and tax breaks from the Irish Government. Maxwell's cited goal is to create a publishing unit in Dublin that would service all of his companies' typesetting and printing needs, and act as a distribution centre for his products; the new company promises employment to Dublin's increasing unemployed.

The company's Board of Directors makes some immediate changes. Robert Maxwell becomes Chairman. The rest of the Board includes a number of Irish media business celebrities. Dublin men are appointed to the top two management positions: Pat Kennedy as Managing Director CEO; and Ian Hunter as Finance Director. I'm promoted to Production Manager and given the task of Project Manager for the planned big expansion.

MAXWELL REGULARLY visits the plant, and today is one of those days. He arrives in a big, black, chauffeured Rolls Royce. Knowing all too well about his reputation for scaring the sherbet out of everyone he meets, Pat and Ian try to control his visits. Being Project Manager, each time Maxwell comes, I make sure Pat and Ian are brought up to date on the project's progress. By so doing, they're able to hold the dog at bay and away from me. However, this time Maxwell has instructed Pat to let me know he wants to talk to me directly: I've to stand by and await his call.

It's seven o'clock, and I've been waiting all day. Suddenly, Maxwell's burly six-foot-two, two-hundred-fifty-pound body fills my office doorway. "I have a plane to catch," he barks "Ride with me to the airport."

Robert Maxwell.

I grab my bulging project binder, and like a little lap-dog, I follow him to his car. A firm-faced chauffeur has the engine purring. In climbs Maxwell; from the cavern-like interior comes his booming, demanding voice.

"Quickly! Get in here! Damned public airline transportation, like time, waits for no man, not even for me."

I climb in. He's sitting on the luxurious leather interior to the left, facing forward. I turn to the right and plunk myself down, facing him, and as far away as I can get. The car is equipped with a radiotelephone. Before we have exited the company's driveway, Maxwell has the phone in his hand. It is the first of four calls he makes during our drive to Dublin Airport. The first is to someone he speaks Yiddish to, the second is in French, the third is in German, and the fourth is in some East European language I cannot identify. We're pulling up to the Dublin Airport departure area when, for the first time, he acknowledges my presence.

"Tell me, Project Manager. How confident are you regarding the success of these Dublin printing and distribution plans?"

"It's outlined in my latest update," I reply, opening my binder.

"Fuck the latest updates," Maxwell barks. "I want to know how confident *you* are about the success of the plans."

"One-hundred fuckin' percent, sir," I reply without hesitation. *To hell with it. If he can fuck, so can I.*

"Good, fucking good," Maxwell laughs. "Make sure I get copies of all your updates. Directly from you to me at Headington Hill Hall. If you need help in pushing this project through, let me know. Good, fucking good."

We're out of the car and standing outside the departure entry.

"Driver," shouts Maxwell. "Bring this man back to the plant."

"Yes, sir," responds the chauffeur.

Maxwell turns to me; extending his hand, he firmly grabs mine. "You have a lot of work to do," he says, shaking my hand firmly and smiling as he does so. "Eh, what is your name?"

"Niall Kavanagh. And you're right, sir. A lot of work."

"Good, fucking good," laughs Maxwell, as he turns away and disappears through the departure entry's swing doors.

ROBERT MAXWELL – the most extraordinary man I have ever met. His entire persona was, to say the least, erratic and always unpredictable. Everyone who had anything to do with him, in both his private and business life, immediately if not soon after that, felt threatened by the massive personality of this enigmatic man.

Everything he did or said seemed to depend on his Hilter-like, absolute certainty that he was feared. Securing respect and admiration from his staff, his 'friends' and even family, were of no consequence. In all his dealings, he depended on the other person's real fear of what he might do or say next. Regarding wealth, whether using his own or as was often the case, using someone else's, his regal-like ostentatiousness was unparalleled.

Maxwell was fluent in most of the European languages, spoke Yiddish and had personal relationships with many of the world's political, academic and business leaders. He always seemed to be in control and powerful. However, his incredible ability to generate that distracting fear was what gave him his real power. Few ever even tried to stand up to his outrageous audacity.

Like a lot of his kind, he did many good things during his life, but behind it all, and as would be clearly seen in the end, he was a megalomaniac. He had little other than a personal, self-serving purpose to everything he involved himself in. His early life brought him many experiences which, when combined might suggest that the man's complexity was well founded.

In 1923, Ján Hoch – Robert Maxwell's original name – was the first born child of a Hassidic family in the small town of, Slatinské Doly in pre-World War II Czechoslovakia. In 1938, having been encouraged by his mother to leave home and escape the growing anti-jewish sentiment in his town, he made his way to Budapest. He was selling trinkets on the streets of Bratislava in 1939 when Hitler's allies in Hungary occupied his homeland, and the Nazis marched into Czechoslovakia.

He had one younger brother and five sisters. In 1940, at the age of seventeen, Maxwell and two of his sisters somehow managed to escape the expanding holocaust and its death camps. His parents and four of his siblings were not so lucky. They were killed during the 1944 Nazi invasion. His father was shot dead by the Nazis in Auschwitz. His mother, younger brother and three sisters all perished in the gas chambers. Maxwell escaped to France where he joined the Czechoslovak army in exile. When France was defeated, he transferred to England and joined the British army as a private. It was then that Ján Hoch, as suggested by his commanding officer, changed his name to Robert Maxwell.

He was promoted to the rank of corporal and saw action in Normandy. His commanding officers were killed during the early part of the invasion. Taking command, he defeated some German forces near the beach. Being the man he was, he then went to his new commanding officer and asked for a medal and promotion. He didn't get the medal but was promoted to sergeant. This was a brazen display of the audacity that would become one of his many outrageous physiognomies. He'd later get his medal: he received the Military Cross from Field Marshall Montgomery. In 1945, he was promoted to captain. Attached to the British Foreign Office, he served in Berlin during the next two years.

He met and married Elizabeth Maynard, a French protestant, in Paris in 1945. Unlike her husband, Elizabeth came from a wealthy family. Robert and Elizabeth would have nine children. Michael, the eldest son, was in a car accident when he was fifteen; he never regained consciousness, and after seven years he died. Their sixth child, Karine, died of lymphoma at the age of three.

Elizabeth & Robert.

Soon after the war, Maxwell got into the media business. Using his language skills and his many contacts in the Allied occupation authorities, he became the British and USA distributor for Springer Verlag, a Berlin-based academic publisher. In 1951, funded by his wife's family, he bought seventy-five percent of Butterworth-Springer, a small scientific journal publisher. The company's name was changed to Pergamon Press. Maxwell's energies and contacts rapidly grew the business.

Oxford's Headington Hill Hall was to become Pergamon Press's headquarters. It was built in 1824 by the local brewery family, Morrill, who lived there for one hundred and fifteen years. In 1939, the Hall was used as a WWII hospital. After the war, it became a rehabilitation centre run by the Red Cross. In 1953, the fifty-one room Italian mansion was sold to Oxford City Council for a mere £13,700. This price included thirty-seven acres of land,

368

as well as its four lodges, its stables, and outbuildings. The Red Cross continued to use the Hall until 1958. In 1959, the council used twenty acres for Headington Hill Park and offered the rest on a twenty-one-year lease to the highest bidder. Robert Maxwell secured the lease with an offer of £2,400 a year.

Headington Hill Hall.

Pergamon Press moved in and was soon to become one of the world's major scientific and technical journal publishers.

Initially, Maxwell rented the estate purely as business premises, but soon he, his wife Elizabeth and their nine children took up residence there. Pergamon Press was relegated to the old stables and some outbuildings. He restored the mansion, which had become dilapidated. Often, Maxwell would refer to Headington Hill Hall as 'the best council house in all of England.'

The original Victorian stained glass window at the head of the inside entrance stairway, showing Samson at the gates of Gaza, was damaged during the war and was replaced by Maxwell. The new window had Maxwell himself as Samson; he has a pendant around his neck, depicting the head of Penelope and indicating that with every successful man, there's a strong woman. One would think that his Penelope was Elizabeth, but as would be understood from Maxwell's conversations regarding the piece, his Penelope was his mother, Hannah Slomowitz. Throughout his life, he held a deep guilt for leaving his parents and four siblings to die in Auschwitz. Survival guilt was Maxwell's heavy cross.

****

Robert Maxwell –
My Second Encounter

MY SECOND ENCOUNTER WITH MAXWELL WAS during his 1966 re-election campaign as Labour MP for Buckingham. He had been elected in 1964 and would continue to hold his seat until 1970. Early in their marriage, Robert had promised Elizabeth that, among many other things, he would one day be the British Prime Minister. Most of the 'other things' materialised; however, his six years as an MP put an end to his PM aspirations. He discovered that "I can't get on with men, or it might be truer to say, men can't get on with me." Ridding himself of his political goals gave him the required collective energies for growing his media empire.

PAT KENNEDY has just finished speaking to Maxwell by phone. Maxwell had ordered Pat to attend a meeting at Pergamon Press's headquarters in Headington Hill Hall, Oxford, at nine the following morning, and that the 'fucking project manager' was also to attend.

"But, Pat," says I, "it's four o'clock in the afternoon. How can we get there by nine in the mornin'?"

"We'll have to fly out of Dublin to Birmingham tonight, sleep over, hire a car, and get on the road to Headington Hill Hall by seven in the morning," Pat outlines. "It's an hour's drive to Oxford, and that'll get us there in plenty of time."

"And Maxwell did say he wants you there," Pat continues. "He made it clear. He was laughing as he said it, but what he actual said was, 'and bring that fucking project manager with you.' I can never make him out. Ever since you had that trip with him to the airport, he always refers to you as the fucking project manager."

Pat and I almost miss our late flight to Birmingham, but the demands of Maxwell would be met; the fear of the consequences of not meeting them always makes it happen, even when it seems impossible.

"What's this meetin' about anyway?" I ask Pat, as we're driving up to the main gates of Headington Hill Hall.

"As I said, I can never make that man out. I don't know what he's planning. Just let's get in there and get it over with."

As Pat and I are entering the driveway, we're stopped by two guards posted at the entrance gate. The estate parameter is reinforced with barbed wire. Video cameras are fixed to trees.

We park the car and are walking up the steps to Maxwell's mansion at a quarter-to-nine.

We're greeted by an exquisitely decked butler-type door guard.

"Welcome to Headington Hill Hall, gentlemen," he chants in perfect Oxford English, as he replaces the speaker on the door's telephone wall base. "Mr Pat Kennedy and Mr Niall Kavanagh of European Printing Corporation, I believe. Mr Maxwell is expecting you. Please come in and follow me."

The staircase.

The opulence of the enormous hallway with its graceful, grand staircase is dominated by the tall, colourful Samson at the Gates of Gaza stained glass piece at the top of the stairs. I've never seen such opulence. It's overpowering. Knowing whose home I'm in, I should not be surprised: everything about Robert Maxwell is designed to do what's happening. I'm in awe.

371

The doorman leads us to the largest boardroom I've ever seen. An enormous oval table with more than thirty chairs dominates the room. There are only two doors, the double door we'd just been led through and a smaller single door directly behind the head of the table. The chair at the head of the table is throne-like in size.

To our surprise, some of the chairs are occupied. Up to a moment ago, Pat and I had assumed that the meeting was a three man get-together with only Maxwell, Pat and me in attendance.

"There are name cards on the table," the doorman informs us. "Good morning, gentlemen," he concludes, as he makes a military type about turn and retreats to his post at the front door.

We search the table and find my name card to the right of the throne. I notice that as often happens with the spelling of my first name, the card reads, *Nile* Kavanagh, not Niall. Pat's name-card is somewhere in the middle on the left side of the table.

"What the hell is he at?" I whisper to Pat. "I'm only the 'fucking project manager'. He's shoving me up beside the throne. I'll be barely able to see you, Pat, never mind talk to you."

"I can never make the man out," says Pat. "It is what it is. Go to where he's put you. Relax, sit down and let's see what happens."

With a lot less relaxation than needed, I sit myself down in the assigned chair. Another fifteen or so men join us before the meeting's kick-off time. Other than for Pat, I've never met or spoken to any of the attendees.

Nine o'clock comes and goes, and there's no sign of Maxwell.

Near to half-past-nine, the single door at the top of the table suddenly bursts open and in he walks. He's dressed in a flowing white dressing gown and slippers; he looks like he's just got out of bed or perhaps like he's been up all night – I'm not sure. The one thing I am positive about is, Maxwell is one weird bloke. He might be a lot of other things, but weird he is, audaciously weird. There are two other men, correctly dressed, with him.

Maxwell drops himself into the throne chair to my left; his two buddies stand behind him, one on each side of his throne.

"We're going to postpone this meeting," he barks, scratching his ruffled hair. "I'll be back in no more than three hours."

Just like that – Maxwell, with little if any reasonable notice, orders twenty or so people to a meeting, turns up a half-hour late in a dressing gown, and outrageously announces that the meeting is postponed for another three hours. You would think that that's surely the worst it could get, but if you did you'd be wrong. It does get worse, and for me in particular, a heck of a lot worse.

"You," Maxwell says as he grabs my name-card.

"Eh, what's your name?" he asked as he looks at the card.

"That's not your name!" he roars, well above the sound of the attendees' mumbled confusion. "You are N-i-a-l-l Kavanagh, not N-i-l-e Kavanagh, damn it!" Turning to one of his two buddies he thrusts the name-card at him.

"Find out who is responsible for this and fire him," he rants. "What sort of people are we hiring? We're publishers, damn it! I won't have anyone who can't spell working for Pergamon Press!"

I feel mortified having my name mentioned within Maxwell's tirade. I want to crawl under the table and disappear. He'd secured a well-earned reputation for firing people for next to nothing. Often he'd do so on a mere whim or as a means of expressing his power to others. He seldom if ever had a consultation with the individual's manager, and gave little regard to the staff member's otherwise valuable contribution to the organisation.

Maxwell stands up. Reaching high in the air, he stretches himself. The waist tie-rope of his dressing gown opens. There, in front of us all, appears Maxwell's unattractive naked frontal.

A few seconds is not a long time, but these seconds, looking at Maxwell's genitalia, feel like a lifetime. He's in no hurry to re-tie his tie-rope. He finishes his stretching, and as casually as you could imagine, he covers it up. Smiling, he turns to me.

"Niall," he says. "You're the project manager. Am I right?"

"Yes, sir," I reply, utterly mesmerised by the man's boldness.

"I want you to come with me," he continues, as he turns and heads for the door. He addresses the attendees en route.

"Gentlemen, we'll be back in no more than three hours."

I give Pat a bewildered, begging glance as I grab my binder. Just like that little lap dog I had experienced myself becoming on my first encounter with Maxwell, I follow him out. Pat's answer to my panicky glance is an equally puzzled hunching of his shoulders, accompanied by a perfectly matched expression on his face. *So much for any assistance from that source.*

As the lap dog follows from behind, my thoughts expand to include real petrifying fear. *This guy is an absolute nut-case. He's just flashed us! What the hell is he goin' to do next? Why the hell does he want me to come with him? Where the hell are we goin'? Why is he goin' around in his dressin' gown and slippers?*

We walk through way too many hallways and rooms for me to remember. We climb a broad set of stairs, and after what seems like another lifetime of anxiety, we arrive at what appears to be an annexe to a bedroom suite. Not a word is spoken during this agonising trip. The lap dog wants to bark real badly, but being that lap dog, I just hang in there, quietly whimpering to myself.

"We have an election to win," announces Maxwell.

"You three sit here while I get ready," he instructs.

His two buddies and I do as we are told. We sit down and wait for Maxwell to reappear – hopefully, dressed and all cleaned up.

"The town of Olney awaits," Maxwell announces as he storms out, dressed in a dark blue, pin-striped suit, white shirt, and red tie.

It's 1966. I know that Maxwell, after an unsuccessful attempt in 1959, had been elected as Labour MP for Buckinghamshire in 1964 and that his seat was now up for re-election. *Jays! The mad bollocks is leavin' the meetin' to go out and do some campaignin'! Pat and all the others are back there, and this mad bollocks is just barrellin' off, leavin' them sittin' around for three hours. How the hell does he get away with it? He's one son of a bitch, that's for sure.*

More bewildered than ever, I join the gang of three – Maxwell is in front, his two buddies are behind, and I'm in the rear. We exit the mansion to where a Bentley plus chauffeur are waiting. In we pile, and off we go to what I assume will be the 'town of Olney.'

Maxwell's Bentley.

It takes us a little over one hour to reach the planned destination. En route, the Bentley makes one stop, a stop that not surprisingly adds, even more, bewilderment to my tortured mind. After about forty minutes driving, the stop occurs on a quiet stretch of country road.

"We'll change cars here," snorts Maxwell.

We all get out of the Bentley. Following our mad leader, we head for a modest, white four-door Ford Corsair, parked just in front of where the Bentley had stopped.

"Where is that mackintosh and cap I told you to bring?" Maxwell asks of the man standing by the Ford.

"In the front seat, sir," the man replies.

Maxwell bends into the car, takes out the cap and mackintosh and dons both. The mackintosh matches the Corsair perfectly, and the cap has seen better days. His image transforms from one of arrogant opulence to one of ordinary, one-of-the-crowd humility.

"How do I look?" Maxwell enquires of his captured audience.

"Perfect for the occasion, sir," one of his buddies responds.

"I agree," says Maxwell, as he climbs into the Corsair's front passenger seat. "You three get in the back," he continues, directing his buddies and me.

"Get in and drive," he orders the Corsair man.

Our final destination does turn out to be Olney's Market Square. There's a crowd of maybe a hundred surrounding a decked-out, open-backed lorry in the middle of the square.

"All of you stay in the car," orders Maxwell.

He opens the car door, and standing on the door frame he gives the crowd a two-handed Churchill-like victory sign. With the noticeable assistance of undoubtedly planted poster-bearing Maxwell supporters, the gathered crowd cheers. Maxwell dismounts the door frame and makes his way to the lorry, smiling and shaking hands.

He speaks for perhaps fifteen minutes. I'm so astounded with the man's nerve. As he's doing his thing, I just sit in the car, lost in my profound efforts to accommodate his overall outrageous behaviour. *The connivin' son of a bitch changed from his posh Bentley to this dirty lookin' Ford so as to fool the crowd into thinkin' he's one of the boys and not the multi-millionaire he is. And the old mac'n'cap trick! He's just too much. He's a wreck waitin' to happen. Jays help us.*

My worrying reflections on this unreal second encounter with Maxwell is rudely endorsed by Maxwell himself when he returns to the car.

"Let's get out of here," he instructs, as he throws himself into the front passenger seat and slams the car door shut. "That should help give me a resounding victory."

"I've a meeting to attend," he continues. "As fast as you can, driver; however, faster than you can is my preference."

The Bentley is waiting for us where we had left it. We exchange the Ford Corsair plus driver for the Bentley plus chauffeur. After discarding the ridiculous mackintosh and cap, Maxwell the MP quickly reverts to Maxwell, the media empire king. He's on the car phone straight away. As we pull up the driveway to Headington Hill Hall, he is still talking on the phone. We've been away for more than two and a half hours.

"Well, Niall," Maxwell says, as we're walking into the mansion. "Do you remain one hundred fucking percent sure of the success of our Dublin printing and distribution plans?"

Incredibly, this is the first and only time Maxwell has made any reference to me, or the project, during all the time we were together.

"Yes, sir," I reply. "One-hundred fuckin' percent plus."

"There's much competition for this project. If EPC succeeds in securing it, it will be your expressed confidence that has done it," is Maxwell's response. "Good, fucking good," he adds, as he starts to laugh. He's still laughing as we all enter the small entrance door to the meeting room.

"Good morning, gentlemen," Maxwell roars as he sits down on his throne. "The meeting will now come to order."

There's a gavel to his right; he gives the wooden sound-block a whack that does its job. All the attendees become super alert. They're delighted with the fact that after three hours of what must have been agonising waiting, something is about to happen.

"Despite many objections, and the many alternate plans submitted to me, I have decided that our new printing and distribution centre will be in Dublin," he announces.

You can hear a penny drop. Silence is often referred to as being golden, but right now it sounds more like a copper penny, not at all like gold – it's decidedly dull. If any of the attendees have something to say about Maxwell's announcement, they do not express themselves, or as is more likely, they don't have the balls to speak. Some of his British and French companies are present; I've no doubt that they have a lot of objections to the decision.

"There being no objections," says Maxwell. After a painful pregnant pause, he continues, "This meeting is now concluded."

I look over at Pat, and we both enjoy a moment of silent pride and pleasure.

I RELAY to Pat all that had happened during my three hours with Robert Maxwell; our return to Dublin gives me just enough time to do so. Pat tries hard to believe it, but like myself, he finds it impossible to do so.

"And the way he turned up for the meetin'!" says I, utterly exhausted from the energy I had expended, trying to itemise my ordeal. "He's a half-hour late, turns up in his dressin' gown and slippers, and then he flashes us all! What sort of a weirdo is he!?"

"The man is a nut case!" I continue. "And why, can you tell me, did he have me go along with him on his campaignin'?"

"He does all this type of thing so as to confuse everyone," answers Pat. "He gets us confused and then pushes his agenda through without dissent. He knew there'd be a lot of people at the meeting who would not agree with his decision; that was his way of getting his way without having to tackle anyone's objections."

"Turning up late and in his dressing gown was his first punch," Pat continues. "Flashing us was the second. The mystery of you being chosen to go with him while the rest of us sat there for three hours wondering what was happening, is the third. The knockout punch was declaring his decision without any expressed dissent."

We end up keeping our sanity by having two small Jameson before we land at Dublin airport and latching on to one absolute certainty: Robert Maxwell, the most extraordinary man I have ever met is close to being entirely insane.

****

FOR THE following two years, the Dublin printing and distribution plans continued to go back and forth with many delays being introduced by Maxwell. I spent almost the total of my working time for more than two years on the project. There must have been hundreds of other person-hours expended. Tragically, it ended up being a non-starter. In the meantime, Maxwell's typesetting needs for all of his ever growing scientific and technical journals were being satisfied for next to nothing: one of his companies, the European Printing Corporation, billing another of his companies, Pergamon Press – money coming out of one of his many pockets and into another. This type of manipulation of his finances was and continued to be, his modus operandi.

At the height of his media empire, Maxwell had over 400 companies worldwide. He was listed as the tenth richest man in the UK, with a net worth of more than $1.75 billion.

He was active in many philanthropic causes. He was chairman of the National AIDS Trust, was involved in the Commonwealth Games in Edinburgh, and provided the funding for an international conference on the Holocaust. He had an interest in two English soccer clubs – Oxford United and Derby County.

Maxwell's downfall came about by his unwise expansions and overly high payments for the acquisition of some of his assets. The real complexities of his business empire plus his secretive operating style, which no one including himself ever fully understood, was to blame.

In the early 1970s, his activities were subjected to a critical report by the Department of Trade and Industry. He lost control of Pergamon Press but would re-acquire the company in 1974. Parts of his growing business empire ran into difficulty in the financial downturn of the 1980s. He was accused of raiding the assets of some companies he owned, including the Mirror Group's pension fund. By the second half of 1991, the British Fraud Squad had compiled a lengthy dossier on Maxwell, and the exact position of his empire surfaced in the press.

Lady Ghislaine.

On 5 November 1991, Maxwell was cruising on his luxury yacht, Lady Ghislaine, off the Canary Islands. He was alone, other than for the yacht's crew. He was last in contact with the crew at 4:25 a.m. He was found missing later in the morning. His naked body was subsequently recovered from the Atlantic Ocean.

It has never been determined whether his death was caused by suicide, accident or murder. Many conspiracy theories exist, including those in which various intelligence agencies (including the Israeli Mossad) were responsible for his death. There is some evidence that Robert Maxwell might have been killed as a result of his threat to expose Mossad if they refused to supply him with the funds he needed to salvage his crippled media empire. It would appear that Maxwell's crazy activities included not only some serious business financial crime but also some global espionage.

After his death, Maxwell's debts were assessed at $3.5 billion.

****

Teresa – the Beginning

"**E**XCUSE ME," THE BLOND SAYS SHARPLY. "MAY I HELP YOU?" I'm passing through the small secretarial office to Pat Kennedy's office. It's been unmanned for some time. I want to discuss some aspects of our company's ongoing negotiations with Oifig an Phoist[1] regarding establishing the most efficient way of mailing single and bulk copies of Pergamon Press learned journals to Eastern Europe, the Soviet Union, and the Far East.

"I need to see Mr Kennedy," I reply, surprised by the blonde's presence, and somewhat offended by the stern tone with which I had just been addressed.

"Mr Kennedy is on the phone," is the blonde's curt response. "Your name and telephone number please?"

"Niall Kavanagh. My extension is 296. Who am I speakin' to?"

"Teresa Flynn," the blonde replies. "I'm Mr Kennedy's new assistant. When he's off the phone, I'll let him know you dropped by, and arrange a time for you to come back."

Teresa.

"And how do you spell your first name?" she enquires, as she glances up at me while writing a note to Pat on the top slip of her pink message pad.

"N-i-a-l-l," I respond.

"And is the matter urgent, Niall?

"Yeah. I'm held up with some journal distribution plans. I need to bounce a few ideas with Pat."

"I'm pleased to meet you, Niall," Teresa smiles. She extends her hand, and grasping it, I touch Teresa for the first time.

"Nice to meet you," I respond, as I find myself oddly astonished at how perfectly her hand fits into mine. We're not in any way conscious of it, but surprisingly, this isn't the first time we've met: Teresa is that girl who had refused my request to dance at the Glasnevin Lawn Tennis Club some four years earlier.

A lot of things had to happen for us to meet again. I had to join Graphic Film, and the company would have to move to Coolock. Rita, Teresa's mother, would have to be in an accident while riding her bicycle on the Malahide Road, near Collins Avenue; Rita broke her hip. Teresa, who was a paralegal working for Enda Marren, a solicitor on Marlborough Street in Dublin city, would then have to choose to leave her job so as to be nearer to her Ma during the long recovery. She'd then have to apply for and secure the position of assistant to Pat Kennedy, Managing Director of the European Printing Corporation.

TERESA AND I have become morning coffee break buddies, sharing much of our trials, tribulations, and boyfriend/girlfriend troubles with each other.

"What sort of a bitch is that?" I moan, as I sit down opposite Teresa at the coffee table. "I go to the trouble and expense of buyin' the tickets, I even get a box of chocolates and flowers for her and what does she do? One day before the dress dance, she tells me she can't go. I've even rented a monkey suit – even a dicky bow and cummerbund."

The girl I had asked to a dress dance has bailed out on me. Here I am, all decked out, ready to go, and now I've nobody to go with.

"That's awful, Niall," Teresa replies. "You're better off without that type of girl. She's rude."

"I don't even like the bitch. I hope she dies roarin'.'"

"What are you goin' to do with the tickets?"

"The dance is tomorrow night, for Jay's sake. No one would buy them. I couldn't even give the bleedin' things away."

"It's a shame to waste them, Niall."

"Now, and only if you like," Teresa continues. "I'm doin' nothin' tomorrow night. We could go together. That'll be better than just wastin' all that money you've spent. What do you think?"

Teresa's offer comes as a complete surprise. For more than a year, I've never seen or even thought of her as being other than a work-mate. She's someone I work with. Seeing her as being anything other than that makes me feel uneasy.

"Are you sure? What about Garret? What'll he have to say about it?" Teresa's boyfriend's name is Garret Woodcock.

"I've broken up with him," Teresa responds.

"You've been goin' out a long time. Why did you break up?"

"He hit me," is Teresa's surprising response.

"He hit you! That's awful; did he hurt you?"

"Yeah, he did. And it's not the first time he's done it."

"God, Teresa. You never told me about him hittin' you. If you had, I would have done somethin'. You could get him arrested for that. Does your Ma or Da know about it?"

"You're the only one I've told, Niall," Teresa answers, shifting uncomfortably in her chair, looking down at the coffee table and her firmly clasped hands. Teresa's hands are usually beautiful. Her nails are perfectly polished, and each of her fingers has a cute dimple at the knuckle.

"I'm ashamed to tell anyone," she continues. "The other time he hit me, I told him if he ever did it again I'd stop goin' out with him. So it's over. I'm havin' nothin' more to do with him."

"I think not! Havin' him arrested is what you should be doin'."

"Does he drink too much or what?" I continue. "No matter what you did or didn't do, he's a real arsehole for hittin' you like that. Where did he hit you, Teresa?"

"He tried to hit my face. I ducked, and moving back away from him, I toppled over the back of the couch. I landed on my bum, thumpin' the fireplace surround. It's all bruised. I can't show you that, but I hit my shoulder at the same time."

Teresa pulls the loose, long sleeve jumper she's wearing off her right shoulder and shows me the evidence.

"God, Teresa," says I, looking at her badly bruise shoulder. "Did you get it checked out? You might've broken somethin'."

"It's only a muscle bruise," Teresa responds, bending her arm. "I can move it with no problem."

Teresa's sharing of Garret's abuse is disturbing to us both. For me it's an absolute surprise: I'm genuinely upset for what happened to my friend and worried about how, if at all, I could help her. For Teresa, the fact that she had shared her secret with me, in what I know was an unintentional manner, makes her feel exposed and bruised in more ways than one. The tears are just about to start. *I can't handle women when they cry.*

I get a sudden, strong desire to punch Garret Woodcock right in the kisser. *What sort of a bloke does that to a girl?*

"Teresa," says I, grabbing her two beautiful hands in mine and making her look into my laughing eyes. "Look at me. I don't know Garret, but I've seen him a few times. He might be a good lookin' blonde and six-foot tall, but do you know what? Ever since I first heard that arsehole's name, I didn't like him. Just imagine, you could have ended up marryin' him, and then we'd be callin' you, Teresa Woodcock! And all your children would be little Woodcocks." Teresa bursts out laughing.

"Now, those bruises you've got will go away," I continue, "and I'm not makin' little of what that fecker did to you, but considerin' everythin', especially his name, I think you've had a lucky escape. What do you say?"

"Thanks, Niall. You're makin' me laugh. I never thought about his name – Woodcock – it's awful, isn't it? Not that I need it, but you've given me another good reason to be happy it's over."

"Right then, Teresa. Thanks for bein' my dance date tomorrow night. It won't come as any surprise to you, but if for nothin' else, there's a box of chocolates and a bunch of flowers in it for you. I hope you like Black Magic."

"I love them. And my Ma loves them too. I can go in a green dress or a blue dress. What colour would you like me in?"

"Blue looks great on you."

"Blue it is, then," Teresa confirms, gently squeezing my hand.

Neither of us is aware that we're still holding hands.

We look down, and for maybe four or five seconds we gaze at the beauty of what we had created – Teresa's two beautiful hands entwined in mine.

For us both, it's a shocking realisation. Its beauty shocks us. However, the shock of realising that of all the couples in the world that might be expected to create such loveliness, it was Teresa and Niall, the most unlikely couple, who had done so.

"Sorry about that, Teresa" I mumble, pulling my hands from hers and shifting uncomfortably in my chair, all embarrassed and confused. "I got caught up in the moment. I'll pick you up at your house at seven. We'll go in a taxi. I didn't realise I was holdin' your hands. I'm sorry for holdin' them."

"Thanks, Niall, and it's OK," Teresa responds, looking as embarrassed and confused as I am. "I'm upset, and you're only tryin' to help me."

"You're right, Teresa. We're makin' a big deal out of nothin'. We were just holdin' hands for a few minutes, for Jay's sake."

"You're right, Niall. We're only goin' to a dance together. It's not as if it was a real date. So let's forget about it."

"Seven is great," she continues, shaking herself and the awkward conversation away from the complex realities of what had occurred, and back towards the required dress dance logistics. "And Niall, there's no need to be spendin' more of your money on a taxi. We can go in my Mini-Minor."

"I didn't know you had a car, Teresa. I've the Heinkel scooter, but I can't have you swingin' your leg over that when you're all dressed up. And the wind would blow your hair out of shape."

"We can use my Mini if you like," Teresa responds. "But, do you know what? It might be great fun goin' on the bike. And you don't have to worry about my hair. With this Twiggy style of mine, the more it gets blown, the better." Teresa's hair is styled and cut short like the English model and actress, Twiggy, who's setting new fashion standards in the UK and Ireland.

I pause before responding to what Teresa had suggested. *She's surprisin' me. She's game for anythin'. Goin' on the bike would be a real lark. I'd never have thought she'd have thought so.*

"Are you sure about the bike? The weather has been beautiful this week. I hope it won't be rainin'."

"Sure I'm sure," Teresa replies. "And if it does rain, we can always use my Mini."

384

IT'S A beautiful night – no rain. I park my Heinkel outside 6 Lower Artane on the Malahide Road. I take off my cap, and up I go to Teresa's front door. While waiting for the door to open, I look over to the opposite side of the Malahide Road. To my surprise, I notice that those dreaded Artane Reformatory entrance gates are straight across from Teresa's house.

Teresa comes out. The horror of seeing those gates vanishes. She looks so gorgeous. She takes my breath away.

"Are you all right, Niall?" she asks. It is as if I've been stricken with something or other. I just stand there, wide-eyed and utterly dumbfounded with Teresa's surprisingly astonishing beauty.

Before I've time even to say hello, she gasps, grabs my arm and drags me into the hallway.

"Oh God," she exclaims. "Garret is over there sittin' in his car. Come in quick, Niall."

There's a green Vauxhall parked on the other side of the road. As Teresa's front door is closing, I glance over, and sure enough, there's the woman beater, scowling across at us.

"He was sittin' out there last night as well," she continues.

"Don't tell my mother he's there, Niall," Teresa whispers, as we stand together in the small hallway. "I've told her we broke up, but if she sees him sittin' outside like that she'll be worried."

"OK, Teresa," I answer. "But that eejit is stalkin' you. If you let me, I'll go over and tell him to cut it out."

"No, Niall. You stay well away from him. He's treacherous, so he is. We'll ignore him altogether."

"Come inside and say hello to my Ma," she continues. "She's dyin' to meet you."

"Before we go in, Teresa," says I, taking her two hands in mine. "I've got to tell you. You're lookin' gorgeous. I've been workin' with you for nearly two years, and apart from your hands, I never knew you were as beautiful as you are. I never even thought of you as a girl, and here you are, takin' my breath away."

Teresa looks at me; leaning over, she kisses me gently on the cheek.

"Thanks, Niall," she says, with a twinkle in her laughing eyes. I had learned to respect, trust and admire Teresa, and I always liked being in her company, but that was a work thing; the effect she's now having on me is immense. Her, to me newly discovered beauty, is overwhelming. It's totally unexpected.

"And Niall," she continues. "I'm feelin' the same. Look at you, all spruced-up in your monkey suit, lookin' like a film star."

"Film star me arse. I mean what I've said, Teresa; you're gorgeous, and thanks for comin' to the dance with me."

"Thank you for bringin' me, Niall," she replies. "And I meant what I said too." That bright twinkle in her eyes is accompanied with a teasing smile as she says, "Let's go in and say hello to my Ma. Her name is Rita. I think you'll like her."

****

THAT EVENING I said hello to a lot more than just Rita. I said hello to the next thirty-seven years of my life with Teresa. A whole new set of laughter, tears, and wonders began, bringing another era of memories and the makings of many more yarns.

****

Yarn #64 Footnote
[1] The Irish Postal Service.